Historicism and the Human Sciences in Victorian Britain

Historicism and the Human Sciences in Victorian Britain explores the rise and nature of historicist thinking about such varied topics as life, race, character, literature, language, economics, empire and law. The contributors show that the Victorians typically understood life and society as developing historically in a way that made history central to their intellectual inquiries and their public culture. Although their historicist ideas drew on some Enlightenment themes, they drew at least as much on organic ideas and metaphors in ways that lent them a developmental character. This developmental historicism flourished alongside evolutionary motifs and romantic ideas of the self. The human sciences were approached through narratives, and often narratives of reason and progress. Life, individuals, society, government and literature all unfolded gradually in accord with underlying principles, such as those of rationality, nationhood and liberty. This book will appeal to those interested in Victorian Britain, historiography and intellectual history.

MARK BEVIR is Professor of Political Science and Director of the Center for British Studies, University of California, Berkeley. He is the author of various books, including *A Theory of Governance* (2013), *Governance: A Very Short Introduction* (2012), *The Making of British Socialism* (2011), *Democratic Governance* (2010) and *The Logic of the History of Ideas* (1999). *Historicism and the Human Sciences in Victorian Britain* is a product of a Mellon project on Britain's Modernity. Cambridge University Press is also publishing the companion volume on *Modernism and the Social Sciences*.

Historicism and the Human Sciences in Victorian Britain

Edited by

Mark Bevir

University of California, Berkeley

CAMBRIDGE
UNIVERSITY PRESS

CAMBRIDGE
UNIVERSITY PRESS

University Printing House, Cambridge CB2 8BS, United Kingdom

One Liberty Plaza, 20th Floor, New York, NY 10006, USA

477 Williamstown Road, Port Melbourne, VIC 3207, Australia

4843/24, 2nd Floor, Ansari Road, Daryaganj, Delhi – 110002, India

79 Anson Road, #06–04/06, Singapore 079906

Cambridge University Press is part of the University of Cambridge.

It furthers the University's mission by disseminating knowledge in the pursuit of education, learning, and research at the highest international levels of excellence.

www.cambridge.org
Information on this title: www.cambridge.org/9781107166684
DOI: 10.1017/9781316711286

© Cambridge University Press 2017

First published 2017

Printed in the United States of America by Sheridan Books, Inc.

A catalogue record for this publication is available from the British Library.

Library of Congress Cataloging-in-Publication Data
Names: Bevir, Mark, editor of compilation.
Title: Historicism and the human sciences in Victorian Britain / edited by Mark Bevir (University of California, Berkeley).
Description: Cambridge, United Kingdom ; New York, NY : Cambridge University Press, 2017. | Includes bibliographical references and index.
Identifiers: LCCN 2016044607 | ISBN 9781107166684 (Hardback)
Subjects: LCSH: Great Britain–Intellectual life–19th century. | Great Britain–Historiography. | Historicism–History–19th century. | Social sciences–Great Britain–History–19th century. | Great Britain–History–Victoria, 1837–1901.
Classification: LCC DA533 .H565 2017 | DDC 941.081–dc23 LC record available at https://lccn.loc.gov/2016044607

ISBN 978-1-107-16668-4 Hardback

Contents

List of Contributors

DUNCAN BELL, Reader in Political Thought and International Relations and Fellow of Christ's College, University of Cambridge, UK.

MARK BEVIR, Professor of Political Science and Director of the Center for British Studies, University of California, Berkeley, USA.

IAN DUNCAN, Florence Green Bixby Professor of English, University of California, Berkeley, USA.

LAUREN M. E. GOODLAD, Kathryn Paul Professorial Scholar and Professor of English and Criticism & Interpretive Theory, University of Illinois, Urbana-Champaign, USA.

FREDRIK ALBRITTON JONSSON, Associate Professor of History, University of Chicago, USA.

BERNARD LIGHTMAN, Professor of Humanities and Science and Technology Studies, York University, Toronto, Canada.

JENNIFER PITTS, Associate Professor of Political Science, University of Chicago, USA.

EFRAM SERA-SHRIAR, Lecturer in Modern History, Leeds Centre for Victorian Studies, Leeds Trinity University, UK.

MARCUS TOMALIN, Lecturer in English and Fellow of Downing College, University of Cambridge, UK.

BRIAN YOUNG, University Lecturer and Student and Tutor of Christ Church, University of Oxford, UK.

1 Historicism and the Human Sciences in Victorian Britain

Mark Bevir

The Victorians themselves did not use the word "historicism." In the middle of the nineteenth century, the historian George Grote used the word "historicize" to describe the act of representing something as historic.[1] By the end of the century, the word "historicize" had also been used to describe the act of recounting events historically. It was at this time that the word "historicism" first entered the English language. "Historicism" was a translation of the Italian word "storicisimo," as used by Benedetto Croce, or the German "historismus," as used by Friedrich Meinecke and Ernst Troeltsch.[2] Although these European thinkers openly debated a crisis of historicism, the phrase "crisis of historicism" is misleading. The debate concerned worries about the philosophical and social consequences of too strong an emphasis on the historical nature of human life, but the worries affected people who were themselves historicists. It is arguably more accurate, therefore, to talk of a crisis in historicism. Historicists were worried that their worldview undercut itself, leading to destructive relativism in epistemology and in ethics.

Historicism is a philosophy that emphasizes the importance of history in understanding, explaining, or evaluating phenomena. If that definition seems question-begging, it at least serves to distinguish historicism from history. Historicism is a philosophical worldview that usually applies to human life or to life in general but not to mere matter. History is the study of the past. Historicists need not study the past; instead, they might draw out arguments for historicism from everyday concepts, or they

---

[1] For a useful guide to the changing use of related words at this time, see J. Murray, ed., *A New English Dictionary on Historical Principles: Founded Mainly on the Materials Collected by the Philological Society*, 9 vols. (Oxford: Clarendon Press, 1844–1933).

[2] C. Rand, "Two Meanings of Historicism in the Writings of Dilthey, Troeltsch, and Meinecke," *Journal of the History of Ideas* 25 (1964), 503–18. For a broader historical discussion see R. Bambach, *Heidegger, Dilthey, and the Crisis of Historicism* (Ithaca: Cornell University Press, 1995), and for an alternative discussion of one attempt to retain historicism while avoiding relativism, see J. Cho, "The Crisis of Historicism and Troeltsch's Europeanism," *History of European Ideas* 21 (1995), 195–207.

might discuss the implications that historicism has for other concepts, debates, or practices. Equally, historians need not be historicists; they might explain past events not by reference to historical contexts but by, for example, formal models, mechanisms, or correlations.

A historicist philosophy has been contrasted with reductionism. The historicist stress on the significance of historical contexts certainly distinguishes it from social theories that postulate general and often immutable laws. Historicists are suspicious of the formalism of so much social science, and arguably of the kind of economic determinism associated with Marxism. However, a historicist philosophy has also been contrasted with social theories that present historical change as either random or the product of unfettered agency or free will. Historicism certainly suggests that historical events are, in some sense, products of the circumstances in which they occur. Historicists present historical developments as explicable in terms of those circumstances. Some historicists have postulated a religious or secular logic to historical events, making those events seem not only explicable given the historical context, but also inevitable given the teleological direction of human affairs.

Victorian historicists generally relied on a more or less explicit teleology. The main argument of this book is, indeed, that the Victorian era was the heyday of what might be called "developmental historicism." The Victorians characteristically made sense of human life first by locating actions, events, practices, and institutions in their historical contexts, and second by treating history as a progressive unfolding of principles such as character, sociability, reason, and liberty.

This book traces the rise, extent, content, and decline of developmental historicism in the Victorian era. Each chapter focuses on Victorian thought about a particular topic, such as life, race, language, literature, character, history, political economy, empire, or international law. The chapters focus on topics, rather than modernist disciplines, because that is how the Victorians thought about the world. Victorian learning was not divided into disciplines – political science, economics, sociology – that focused on different empirical domains and that were held together primarily by a shared modernist concept of social science as based on the search for correlations, classifications, and formal models. Rather, Victorian learning tended to pick particular objects, explore facts about them, and then make sense of these facts by locating them in a developmental narrative that covered the whole of human life, perhaps the natural world, and sometimes even the divine.

As each chapter focuses on historicism in the study of a particular topic, I will use this introduction to highlight general themes. I will start by discussing the rise of developmental historicism alongside romanticism or, perhaps more accurately, a broad organicism. Organicism infused, to varying degrees, each of the three main strands of Victorian historicism. These three strands of historicism differed because they drew on the somewhat distinctive traditions of Whig historiography, German romanticism, and positivism. Next I will discuss some of the issues and debates that confronted Victorian historicists. These included whether or not historicism applied to the natural world; the relationship of historicism to religious faith; the place of the individual in society; how to balance progress with nostalgia; and the telos and universality of historical development. Finally, to conclude, I suggest that the decline of developmental historicism can be traced to the rise of modernist ideas in the late nineteenth century and the way in which the First World War undermined the Victorian faith in reason and progress. Ironically, therefore, the word "historicism" entered the English language at the very moment when the historicist worldview that had dominated the Victorian era was beginning to give way to the modernist sensibility that came to dominate the twentieth century.

The Rise of Historicism

For much of the early modern era up to the late eighteenth century, learning could be divided into three broad disciplines, namely, natural philosophy, natural history, and human history.[3] Natural philosophy focused on astronomy and cosmology. Natural history was the study of living organisms. Human history focused on the classical world, political history, and literature, defined broadly to cover all written texts.

   Despite its title, "natural history" was often not particularly historical, let alone historicist. Natural historians attempted to perceive an order within the living world of plants and animals. Much of their work involved collecting and identifying species. When they tried to explain these species, they appealed less to historical narrative than to classificatory systems. They tried to fit things into a larger and generally ahistorical order. Most natural historians believed that the order of things was divinely inspired. Studying nature was, for them, part of theology. They searched for evidence of God's design and purpose. Each specimen and each species was a fixed part of the divine creation.

---

[3] For historicist perspectives on early modern thought and on the shift from natural philosophy to natural science in the early nineteenth century, see respectively M. Osler, "Mixing Metaphors: Science and Religion or Natural Philosophy and Theology in Early Modern Europe," *History of Science* 36 (1997), 91–113, and S. Schaffer, "Scientific Discoveries and the End of Natural Philosophy," *Social Studies of Science* 16 (1986), 387–420.

While natural history continued throughout the eighteenth century to offer classifications within a divine order of things, the latter part of the century saw the study of human history take on what has been character-ized as a historicist slant.[4] Enlightenment historicism sought to make sense of historical events by placing them in the broader historical circum-stances in which they occurred. This focus on historical circumstances reflected a more critical attitude toward historical evidence and a belief that this evidence might reveal laws akin to those being discovered in natural philosophy by scientists such as Isaac Newton. The main British examples of Enlightenment historicism were the conjectural histories of Scottish Whigs such as Adam Ferguson and Adam Smith.[5] The term "conjectural history" described the process of appealing speculatively to natural (not divine) causes that might plausibly have resulted in the relevant events. Conjectural history soon became associated, more specif-ically, with the idea that all societies progress through the same four broad stages of development: Societies develop from a hunting stage, through a pastoral stage and an agricultural one, to reach a final commercial stage.

There was no decisive break between the Enlightenment and the Victo-rian historicism that occupies center stage in this book. Romanticism followed so fast on the Enlightenment that it can be almost impossible to disentangle the two. Most sharp distinctions between the two rely on a false dichotomy based on a caricature of the Enlightenment. Romanticism may have been a reaction against the Enlightenment, but it also absorbed much from the Enlightenment. One strand of Victorian historicism was a clear extension of the conjectural histories of the Whig tradition.

Much of the Victorian human sciences fused Enlightenment conjec-tural history with more explicitly evolutionary and developmental motifs.[6]

---

[4] On romantic historicism and its relation to what has come after and what went before see J. Chandler, *England in 1819: The Politics of Literary Culture and the Case of Romantic Historicism* (Chicago: University of Chicago Press, 1998), and A. Jarrels, "'Associations Respect[ing] the Past': Enlightenment and Romantic Historicism," in J. Klancher, ed., *A Concise Companion to the Romantic Age* (Oxford: Blackwells, 2009), pp. 57–76.

[5] For a survey of Enlightenment historicism across Europe see S. Bourgault and R. Sparling, *A Companion to Enlightenment Historiography* (Leiden: Brill, 2013). For its place in the human sciences see C. Fox, R. Porter, and R. Wokler, eds., *Inventing Human Science: Eighteenth Century Domains* (Berkeley: University of California Press, 1995). For its impact on the writing of history see M. Phillips, *Society and Sentiment: Genres of Historical Writing in Britain, 1740–1820* (Princeton: Princeton University Press, 2000). For its literary dimensions see N. Wolloch, *History and Nature in the Enlightenment* (Farnham: Ashgate, 2011). For a study of some broader vitalist moments in Enlighten-ment thought see C. Packham, *Eighteenth-Century Vitalism: Bodies, Culture, Politics* (New York: Palgrave Macmillan, 2012).

[6] M. Bevir, "The Long Nineteenth Century in Intellectual History," *Journal of Victorian Culture* 6 (2001), 313–35 and J. Burrow, *Evolution and Society: A Study in Victorian Social Theory* (Cambridge: Cambridge University Press, 1966).

The Whig tradition persisted most notably among liberal Anglican historians such as Thomas Arnold and Julius Hare.[7] These historians thought of reason as a key with which they could unlock history, conceived as the record of God's dealings with mankind. Although their historicism was rooted in the historical philosophy of the Scottish Whigs, it was also a reaction against the eighteenth century, for they drew on Samuel Coleridge's idealism to oppose Enlightenment rationalism. Coleridge himself was raised as a Unitarian by his father, but in his adult years he espoused a form of Anglican Trinitarianism. In his *On the Constitution of Church and State*, he offered a novel defense of establishment. He began by defining the state as an organic and ethical whole that promoted the common good of its citizens. In order to fulfill this role, he continued, the state required a Clerisy, organized in a national Church, and serving as both a repository of the knowledge of the nation and a guardian of spirit of the nation.[8] The liberal Anglican historians generally followed Coleridge in seeing the Church as a unifying force – required by the state but not subordinate to it – that embodied the national spirit. Consequently, they fused church history with the history of the nation.

Religious themes continued to infuse much history written later in the Victorian era. History was often a way of defending Christian faith. Histories were written as evidence of God's reality in the world. Lord Acton, William Stubbs, and others confidently narrated history, and especially British history, as progressive, and as a source of national pride, because they treated it as an expression of the validity of a Christian faith. Other Whig historicists, including Henry Maine, used more anthropological and sociological conjectures to develop comparative approaches to the historical development of the law.[9] Yet other Whig historicists, most notably Walter Bagehot, grounded their theories of historical development in conjectures about the psychological or biological bases of pre-history.[10]

While one strand of Victorian historicism can be seen in part as an extension of the Whig tradition, other strands were almost entirely

---

[7] D. Forbes, *The Liberal Anglican Historians* (Cambridge: Cambridge University Press, 1952). For later Whig historians in the Victorian era see P. Blaas, *Continuity and Anachronism: Parliamentary and Constitutional Development in Whig Historiography and in the Anti-Whig Reaction between 1890 and 1930* (The Hague: Martinus Nijhoff, 1978) and J. Burrow, *A Liberal Descent: Victorian Historians and the English Past* (Cambridge: Cambridge University Press, 1983).

[8] J. Morrow, *Coleridge's Political Thought* (Basingstoke: Palgrave Macmillan, 1990).

[9] H. Maine, *The Ancient Law: Its Connection with the Early History of Society and Its Relation to Modern Ideas* (London: John Murray, 1861).

[10] W. Bagehot, "Physics and Politics," in N. John-Stevas, ed., *The Collected Works of Walter Bagehot, Vol. 7: The Political Essays* (London: Economist, 1965–86), pp. 15–144.

derived from romantic or positivist thinkers. Even the liberal Anglican historians and their successors were indebted not only to Whiggism but, at least as importantly, to Coleridge's British translation and transformation of the ideas that he took from the German romantics.[11]

So, if we should not exaggerate the break between the Enlightenment and romanticism, we also should not ignore it.[12] The impact of romanticism becomes clearer once we approach romanticism less as a narrow literary and artistic movement and more as a broad stress on the organic. The romantics emphasized the ability of living things to create a fluid and changing order for themselves through deliberate activity infused with purpose, thought, and imagination. They treated mind as a vital and active force in the world. Change and imagination were seen as the norm. Less attention was given to stable mechanisms. This romanticism appears throughout the sciences in the first half of the nineteenth century as questions of time, dynamics, and evolution challenged those of system, statics, and balance. And this romanticism brought in its wake a new emphasis on both imaginative sympathy with the inner lives of agents and new evolutionary approaches to society.[13]

Romanticism appears as a broad organicist worldview most clearly and most prominently in the German context. In the late eighteenth century, German scholarship on the life sciences increasingly made use of a developmental concept of organic form.[14] Alexander von Humboldt emphasized the unity of nature, believing that science should reveal the harmony among things. By the early nineteenth century, German idealist philosophers were often building metaphysical systems around organicist themes. For example, F. W. J. Schelling's study of natural philosophy tried to show how the ideal emerged from the real. Schelling argued that

[11] On the importance of British Platonism as the background to Coleridge's engagement with German philosophy, see D. Hedley, *Coleridge, Philosophy and Religion: Aids to Reflection and the Mirror of the Spirit* (Cambridge: Cambridge University Press, 2000).

[12] For a fascinating attempt to present the nineteenth-century human sciences as a construction built on an organic concept of life see M. Foucault, *The Order of Things: An Archaeology of the Human Sciences* (London: Tavistock, 1970). For my own critical assessment of Foucault's achievement see M. Bevir, "A Humanist Critique of the Archaeology of the Human Sciences," *History of the Human Sciences* 15 (2002), 119–38.

[13] For a study of the romantic poets' attitudes to some of these broader trends in the study of natural and human history see M. McLane, *Romanticism and the Human Sciences: Poetry, Population, and the Discourse of the Species* (Cambridge: Cambridge University Press, 2006).

[14] See R. Richards, *The Romantic Conception of Life: Science and Philosophy in the Age of Goethe* (Chicago: University of Chicago Press, 2002), and more generally A. Cunningham and N. Jardine, eds., *Romanticism and the Sciences* (Cambridge: Cambridge University Press, 1990).

spirit was the invisible force driving all nature, so that nature was simply a visible manifestation of spirit. In his view, history was the progressive revelation of the absolute.

German romanticism inspired a strand of Victorian historicism that overlapped with the Whiggish one discussed earlier, but that relied less on historiographical arguments and more on romantic and idealist philosophies. Coleridge was, of course, a key figure here. In his youth, he believed in Necessitarianism, with its mechanistic outlook. But in the early nineteenth century he immersed himself in German idealism, with its dynamic outlook. This romantic organicism spread through much of the Victorian era, whether directly from German idealists or indirectly by way of Coleridge, and whether as a dominant outlook or as a strand entering other traditions such as the Whig one.

More specialized lines of influence also brought German romanticism to British soil. Germans such as Franz Bopp and Wilhelm von Humboldt crafted a more rigorous and historical approach to comparative linguistics. Max Müller studied in Germany, where he worked with Bopp, before moving to Britain, where he became successively Professor of Modern European Languages and Professor of Comparative Philology at the University of Oxford. By the middle of the nineteenth century, Müller's work had given ideas derived from the German romantics a dominant position in British studies of the historical development of languages and religions.[15] Elsewhere, German romanticism helped to inspire a historicist approach to economics. The German Historical School of Economics, from Bruno Hildebrand to Werner Sombart, drew on idealist philosophy and evolutionary theorizing to champion a historical and inductive alternative to the more deductive approach of classical and neoclassical economics from David Ricardo onward. In their view, economic activity arose in specific cultures, so economic knowledge could not be generalized outside such cultures. Their ideas helped to inspire the historical economics of figures such as T. E. Cliffe Leslie, W. J. Ashley, and William Cunningham.[16]

German romanticism was not the only European source of Victorian historicism. A contrast can be made between the romantic historicism just discussed and a positivist historicism associated perhaps with the legacy of Leopold von Ranke, and more definitely with the impact of Auguste Comte. Ranke's proposals for a science of history privileged the

---

[15] L. van den Bosch, *Friedrich Max Müller: A Life Devoted to the Humanities* (Leiden: Brill, 2002).

[16] G. Koot, *English Historical Economics, 1870–1926* (Cambridge: Cambridge University Press, 2008).

rigorous collection and sifting of facts. Comte's alternative proposals were embedded in his narrative of social evolution from a theological stage, through a metaphysical stage, to the final positive stage. This positive scientific stage dated, in Comte's view, from the Napoleonic era. Science was taking the place of theological fictions and metaphysical abstractions. A religion of humanity would soon fulfill the emotional role of the Churches, and although government had to depend on popular consent, policy would increasingly become the domain of scientifically informed engineers and experts.

Comtists such as Frederic Harrison had much in common with other developmental historicists. They too understood human life to be inherently historical, and history to be inherently progressive. The main difference was that many romantic historicists, and all Christian historicists, believed that progress was the record of God's will, whereas the positivists believed that metaphysics and Christianity would be replaced by science and a "religion of humanity." The positivists and their successors conceived of progress in more secular terms, as, for example, increased prosperity and social complexity, or the triumph of reason and morality.

Victorian positivists, including Harrison, adopted a republican positivism that sought to integrate the working class into a political vision of liberty, equality, and fraternity. Although these republican positivists remained small in number, Comte had a much wider influence, as exemplified, most famously, by George Eliot.[17] A wider evolutionary and ethical positivism, detached from Comte's liturgy and republican politics, was a common Victorian response to the problems of religious faith. In the latter half of the nineteenth century, Victorians such as Beatrice and Sidney Webb rejected evangelicalism and classical liberalism for an evolutionary and ethical positivism that fused Herbert Spencer's sociology with Comte's idea of a duty of service to man.[18]

By the late Victorian era, these strands of historicism – Whig, romantic, and positivist – were increasingly difficult to disentangle. Late Victorians drew on themes from each, creating diffuse discourses in which, typically, an evolutionary cosmology embedded the claim that the

---

[17] On liturgical, republican, and evolutionary positivisms, see respectively W. Simon, "August Comte's English Disciples," *Victorian Studies* 8 (1964), 161–72; R. Harrison, *Before the Socialists* (London: Routledge & Kegan Paul, 1965); B. Willey, *Nineteenth Century Studies* (Harmondsworth: Penguin, 1964), pp. 214–60. For a general study see also T. Wright, *The Religion of Humanity: The Impact of Comtean Positivism on Victorian Britain* (Cambridge: Cambridge University Press, 1986).

[18] M. Bevir, *The Making of British Socialism* (Princeton: Princeton University Press, 2012), pp. 173–94.

individual was part of a larger whole, and so an ethic of fellowship. Sometimes this discourse went with a militant hostility to religious faith; secularists often combined it with republican forms of positivism. At other times, it acted more like a substitute faith, providing a structure of meaning, as it did for William Jupp, who adopted a romantic pantheism inspired by Ralph Waldo Emerson and William Wordsworth. It helped to inspire new religious movements, particularly the occult, theosophical, and hermetic organizations that attracted people such as Annie Besant and Anna Kingsford. And it spread among Christians who adopted an immanentist theology, perhaps emphasizing the Incarnation over the Atonement, as did the *Lux Mundi* group, or perhaps emphasizing the moral example provided by the life of Jesus the man.[19]

The Height of Historicism

Readers might approach the chapters that follow in various ways. One would be to begin with the chapter on "History," perhaps thinking history the obvious home of historicism, and then moving on to the other chapters. This approach would suit someone interested in the nature of the study of history in Victorian Britain and in the ways in which history was used and appropriated in other fields of study. Historians of historiography and students of British history might find this approach particularly attractive. Clearly, however, I have adopted a different approach, reflecting the preceding arguments about the differences between Enlightenment and romantic historicism and the organicist nature of the latter. The order of the chapters reflects the claim that Victorian historicism can be understood as arising out of a broad intellectual shift from a Newtonian view rooted in physics to a romantic organicism rooted in the life sciences. The early chapters trace the rise of organicist historicism in the study of "Life" and "Race." The next chapters explore the place of organicist historicism in the study of the crucial romantic topics of "Language," "Literature," and self, or "Moral Character." The chapter on "History" then provides an opportunity to reflect on the overlaps and fates of various strands of historicism in the study of the past. The concluding chapters go on to look at the ways in which organicist historicism has had an impact on the study of social and political life, especially "Political Economy," "Empire," and "International Law."

---

[19] W. Jupp, *The Religion of Nature and of Human Experience* (London: P. Green, 1906); A. Kingsford and E. Maitland, *The Perfect Way* (London: Field & Tuer, 1887); C. Gore, ed., *Lux Mundi* (London: J. Murray, 1819); S. Brooke, *Christ in Modern Life* (London: H. King, 1872).

The central focus of the book is, in other words, how organicist themes transformed the intellectual landscape of Victorian Britain. Developmental historicism became all-pervasive. Although Victorian historicists sometimes echoed the Whig outlook of the Scottish Enlightenment or the proto-positivism that can perhaps be read into Ranke, they also broke dramatically with these earlier ways of thinking precisely because of romantic organicism's impact upon them. So, for example, although J. S. Mill was raised by his father to be an exemplar of the Enlightenment spirit, he ended up trying to balance Coleridge and Comte, not Smith and Ranke.[20]

Developmental historicism became ubiquitous, but it contained competing strands and it allowed for conflicting views on important issues. One issue was how far to extend historicism and, in particular, whether historicism and teleology governed natural history as well as human history. Some thinkers wanted to restrict historicism to the organic. Some of them began to distinguish between biology, conceived as the study of the evolution of life, and natural history, conceived to include topics such as geology. Charles Darwin added substantial intellectual clout to evolutionary theory, defined in contrast to natural history.[21] He lent further weight to the idea that historical lines of descent were of greater explanatory importance than formal classifications. However, Darwin's theory still left plenty of room for debate.[22] In particular, there was still no consensus on the processes by which natural selection took place. Many biologists accepted evolution, but not Darwin's theory of natural selection. Further, even when biologists accepted the theory of natural selection, they still discussed whether that theory meant that evolution was random or teleological. Darwin was widely believed to oppose teleology, but his public pronouncements on the matter were far from clear-cut, and anyway, whatever his views, other biologists generally continued to combine evolution with teleology.

In his contribution to this book, Bernard Lightman shows that even hardcore Darwinians struggled to disentangle evolutionary theory from developmentalism. Herbert Spencer, John Tyndall, and T. H. Huxley owed a debt to German romanticism, and its teleological outlook long

[20] For a study of Mill that usefully highlights his (sometimes deliberately hidden) debt to the German romantics, see N. Capaldi, *John Stuart Mill: A Biography* (Cambridge: Cambridge University Press, 2004).

[21] On the importance of natural history and natural theology in Darwin's early thought and his subsequent move away from them, see D. Ospovat, *The Development of Darwin's Theory* (Cambridge: Cambridge University Press, 1981).

[22] P. Bowler, *The Eclipse of Darwinism: Anti-Darwinian Evolution Theories in the Decades around 1900* (Baltimore: Johns Hopkins University Press, 1983).

continued to influence their views. Spencer argued, for example, that evolution rested on an Unknown Cause that guided it in a progressive direction. He postulated a cosmic evolutionary process from nebulae to advanced human societies, with their ever-increasing levels of functional differentiation. If Spencer and Tyndall were materialists, it was largely because they challenged the distinction between life and mere matter. They nonetheless conceived of both organic life and inorganic matter as governed by a hidden power. Even hardcore Darwinians, it seems, did not embrace the randomness of natural selection. On the contrary, teleological forms of evolutionary theory remained dominant right up to the 1930s, when genetic theory provided an authoritative account of the processes by which natural selection occurred.

Given that developmental historicism continued to dominate evolutionary theory long after Darwin, we should not be surprised at its also continuing to flourish right across the human sciences. In the human sciences, Darwin was almost always read as lending intellectual support to teleological forms of evolutionary theory. For example, Efram Sera-Shriar concludes his contribution to this volume by showing how Darwin's work, along with that of Edward Burnett Tylor, expanded the scope of those developmental approaches to race that had begun to arise far earlier in the nineteenth century. Sera-Shriar's argument suggests that although the Victorian era undoubtedly gave rise to a plethora of racializing analyses, many of these analyses were couched in historicist terms rather than naturalist ones. Racial distinctions could thus be seen, at least at times, as the temporary results of history, rather than of permanent results of different origins.

Throughout the human sciences, Darwin did not mark a significant break so much as lend additional support to the already widespread developmental historicism that had arisen alongside romantic organicism. Darwin's main impact was arguably in encouraging more naturalistic and materialist forms of developmental theorizing at the expense of theological and cultural ones: As we have seen, the hardcore Darwinians were characterized more by a downplaying of the organic than by a rejection of the idea of progress. But we should not overstate the differences between the organicism of the romantics and the science of the later nineteenth century. Even if a materialist naturalism did spread, it continued to be far less common than organicist forms of developmental historicism. For example, James Hunt defended a humanistic approach to race and anthropology, in contrast to the materialism of hardcore Darwinians such as Huxley.

Darwin's work was also important in the debate about the relation of historicism to religious faith. Naïve accounts of a Victorian crisis of faith might suggest that Darwin's theory of evolution was welcomed almost exclusively by the positivist strand of Victorian thought. The historical record of Darwin's reception is, however, far more complex and variegated than this naïve account allows.[23] Among the growing number of historicist and evolutionary approaches to life and race, Darwin's main theoretical innovation was arguably that he provided a purely naturalist theory of change and the origins of species. Darwin's theory of evolution relied exclusively on natural processes in this world. Many of his critics worried that he thereby left insufficient room for God. Many clergymen opposed Darwin's naturalism, but not evolutionary theory. They wanted their evolutionary theory to come wrapped with natural theology.

Victorian attitudes to faith were related less to the reception of evolutionary theory than to the traditions against the background of which people forged their historicisms. Generally, the more Victorian historicists drew on either Whig historiography or German romanticism, the more likely they were to entwine their historicism with religion, whereas the more they drew on positivism, the more likely they were to associate their historicism with a secular science. Brian Young's contribution to this volume focuses on exactly this distinction among historians. He contrasts, on the one hand, the romantic, liberal, and religious historicism of historians such as Acton and Stubbs, with, on the other, a positivist and sometimes republican and secular science of history that drew its inspiration from Comte.

Historicism provided a broad framing within which Victorians debated religion and morality. Ethical debates often concerned the individual's relation to society.[24] "Character" was a general word that the Victorians used to refer to the set of principles that they believed governed individual development. In her contribution to this volume, Lauren Goodlad shows how character was thus a prescriptive concept as well as a descriptive one. Character was the moral telos of the individual's development through time. This concept of character typically drew on early modern republican ideas of independence to promote autonomy, self-help, and self-reliance. Many Victorians believed that the spread of character was

[23] Compare, especially on the unhelpfulness of a sharp dichotomy between "faith" and "science," J. Moore, *The Post-Darwinian Controversies: A Study of the Protestant Struggle to Come to Terms with Darwin in Great Britain and America, 1870–1900* (Cambridge: Cambridge University Press, 1979). For a broader history that also sheds light on the rise of the sharp dichotomy later in the twentieth century, see P. Bowler, *Monkey Trials and Gorilla Sermons: Evolution and Christianity from Darwin to Intelligent Design* (Cambridge, MA: Harvard University Press, 2009).
[24] S. Collini, "The Idea of 'Character' in Victorian Political Thought," *Transactions of the Royal Historical Society* 35 (1985), 29–50.

vital to social progress: As elites and colonial powers spread the ideal of character to workers and to imperial subjects, so society would move toward its telos. Equally, many Victorians believed that social development was essential for character to flourish: A liberal education, a civil society, and a participatory citizenship provided the social setting within which individuals learnt the habits and practices of good character.

The developmental nature of "character" appeared particularly clearly in Victorian literature. As Ian Duncan argues in his contribution to this volume, the novel arose as a way of narrating the individual in relation to social and political history. The novel was an alternative genre for conjectural histories tracing the rise of character in the individual and the rise of liberty and nations in the political sphere. On the one hand, the German romantic idea of *Bildung*, especially Johann Wolfgang von Goethe's *Wilhelm Meister's Apprenticeship*, inspired fictional accounts of the personal maturation of the individual. If William Wordsworth's *Prelude* is the most famous British example of a literary account of the development of the author's mind and character, numerous Victorian novels tell similar stories of the hero or narrator's progress. On the other hand, other Victorian novels focus on the development of humanity, communities, or states. If the most famous example is Walter Scott's account in *Waverley* of the absorption of Scotland into Great Britain, Duncan shows how other, less obviously historical novels, such as George Eliot's *Middlemarch*, are also natural histories of human life and society.

Of course, Victorian fiction typically combined individual and social developments. The social and political histories of the realist novels provide contexts in which individual characters navigate or create their personal histories so as to recreate society and politics. Many literary discussions of the state of the nation focused in part on whether the rise of cities, commerce, and industry was an impediment to character, as well as on whether individual leaders could heal a divided nation.[25]

These social questions included ones about the early and final stages of the process of historical development. Here developmental historicism could seem to conflict with other romantic tropes such as nostalgia for personal and social innocence. A romantic yearning for lost simplicity led many Victorians not only to understand human life in historical terms but also to try to preserve and venerate aspects of the past. They faced a tension between developmental historicism, with its appeals to progress, and a historical sentimentality, with its appeals to an unsullied past.

---

[25] J. Guy, *The Victorian Social Problem Novel* (London: Macmillan, 1996).

One response to this tension was a prescriptive historicism. Marcus Tomalin's chapter in this book shows how linguists actively tried to preserve the Icelandic language precisely because they thought that it remained pure. Tomalin argues that Icelandic fascinated linguists because of its influence on early English and because it seemed to have stayed unchanged for hundreds of years. Following the lead of the Danish linguist Rasmus Rask, British scholars came to adopt a preservationist stance toward Icelandic. They justified active measures to keep the language intact even though they knew that they were thereby intervening in the natural process of change and development. This kind of prescriptive historicism found a wider cultural expression in, for example, the Society for the Protection of Ancient Buildings, which William Morris and Philip Webb founded to promote historically sensitive repairs to old buildings.[26]

Another response to the tension between developmental historicism and historical sentimentality was the adoption of a more cyclical concept of time. Duncan Bell's chapter in this volume shows how accounts of Empire revolved around both a linear temporality conceived solely in terms of progress and a cyclical temporality that facilitated veneration of the ancient world. A cyclical treatment of time undermined simple notions of progress, but it was, perhaps for this very reason, not commonly held. Even when Victorian thinkers believed that empires followed a cyclical trajectory, they often appealed, as did James Froude, to the possibility of constant personal and social development and progress alongside the rise and fall of empires. The most widespread arguments were, however, as Bell explains, those that exempted the British Empire from the fate of its historical predecessors. Some Victorians simply denied that the British Empire was, properly speaking, an empire. Others argued that the British Empire was uniquely progressive; it would escape the fate of previous empires because of the success of its "civilizing mission" or because of its development as a federal commonwealth.

Those Victorians who held a linear concept of time generally postulated an endpoint to history. Generally the Victorians tacitly agreed that the values and principles of their time were the telos toward which history had been moving. The heights of human development had been reached with, for example, their civil society, nation states, and popular liberty. For Whigs, the existing commercial stage of society was the final one. For positivists, the fast-approaching triumph of reason in a positive polity would be the final stage of history. Of course, Victorians did not

---

[26] A. Donovan, *William Morris and the Society for the Protection of Ancient Buildings* (London: Routledge, 2007).

necessarily conclude that the triumph of these values brought an end to all change and development. On the contrary, many Victorians believed that there was still a great deal that science, technology, and public policy might achieve. Many appear to have foreseen practical progress continuing more or less indefinitely even after a kind of moral telos had been reached.

As Fredrik Albritton Jonsson reminds us in his contribution to this volume, however, other Victorians believed that practical progress, like moral progress, would cease, giving rise to a stationary state. Albritton Jonsson focuses on the use that some economists made of natural history and geology. In their view, the natural world placed limits on economic development and so on human history. Thomas Malthus was an early exponent of such arguments. His gloomy outlook rested heavily on the idea that the finite supply of land meant that there were physical limits to populations, and if populations overshot these limits, the competition for work would drive wages down. Similar ideas appear in the work of liberal, romantic, and neoclassical economists such as J. S. Mill, John Ruskin, and W. S. Jevons. For all of them, human life was embedded in a natural world that contains finite resources of, for example, coal and energy. Humans should thus seek to live in a settled and stationary state that would not exhaust the resources available to them. If they failed to do so, progress might even turn into decline.

Finally, Victorian historicists faced questions about the universality of their accounts of human history. Exploration and Empire gave immediate practical import to these questions. Studies of races, languages, and cultures drew on the early modern discovery and cataloguing of indigenous peoples. The voyages of explorers such as James Cook and the scholarship of the East India Company and imperial officers such as William Jones generated vast amounts of new information. In the late eighteenth century, the dominant approaches to this information resembled the natural histories of the time. The new data got fed into existing classifications or helped to inspire new classifications. By the nineteenth century, however, scholars were increasingly asking questions about the historical roots of the variety they were finding among races, languages, and cultures. William Lawrence and James Prichard argued, for example, that the various races had a single ancestral root. These appeals to a shared human origin raised the problem of how to explain the extent of the latter variety that had arisen. One popular solution to this problem was to place various races, languages, and cultures on a single developmental spectrum, as found in so much Whig historiography.

Even if Victorians believed that all societies were following the same historical path, they generally placed societies at varied stages on this path.

Questions arose therefore about how to govern the interactions between highly different communities. Empire provided one possible response: The allegedly more advanced heads of empires were tutors overseeing their wards. Other possible responses could be found in international law. Where the Enlightenment had seen many thinkers basing their accounts of law on claims and conjectures about nature and natural rights, Maine and other Victorian thinkers advocated historical research into the origins of law in primitive societies. Thus, as Jennifer Pitts argues in her contribution to this book, the Victorian era witnessed the emergence of a consensus that international law was itself a product of the level of historical development reached in Europe. International lawyers thus sought, on the one hand, to assert the universal normative authority of a European-based set of laws on the grounds that these laws reflected the height of social evolution, and on the other, to define pre-requisites that were necessary for less advanced societies to be properly included in the international community.

Much of this volume concerns these kinds of intellectual debates about historicism. It is important briefly to mention, therefore, that historicism was not just an academic philosophy. On the contrary, historicism was a crucial ingredient in the glue that fused Victorian scholarship, society, and public policy.[27] The Universities of Cambridge and Oxford placed great importance on the study of history and, especially, the classics. They turned out generalists with a historicist and humanist bent. Their students then entered the professions, politics, and of course civil and imperial administrations. The actors who dominate this book were not university professors but rather members of the educated strata of society. Some, but not all, of them had been educated at the Universities. The Victorians treated the human sciences as part of a wider public debate about how to understand themselves and their society, and so about how to govern. Their ideas were guides to personal life, social action, and public policy. Historicist narratives did not merely act as post-hoc justifications for laws, policies, and imperial expansion; they actively inspired and directed them.

The Fall of Historicism

This book appeals to "the human sciences" rather than "the social sciences" in order to denaturalize contemporary categories, the

---

[27] For an extensive illustration of these kinds of networks see L. Goldman, *Science, Reform and Politics in Victorian Britain: The Social Science Association, 1857–1886* (Cambridge: Cambridge University Press, 2002). For an illustration that focuses on imperial policies see K. Mantena, *Alibis of Empire: Henry Maine and the Ends of Liberal Imperialism* (Princeton: Princeton University Press, 2010).

assumptions informing them, and the institutions to which they have given rise. As just mentioned, many of the leading actors in these pages had little or no connection to universities. They were politicians, administrators, clergymen, poets, amateur scientists, and men of letters. Even within Victorian universities, there was little use of modern disciplinary categories. The modern "social sciences" as a cluster of relatively coherent disciplines did not begin to emerge until the end of the nineteenth century. It was only during the twentieth century that many of them became housed in distinct university departments with their own appointments, bolstered by professional associations and journals, and legitimized by their own norms. The rise of the modern social sciences both reflected and contributed to the replacement of Victorian historicism by other approaches to knowledge.

Although historicism was unquestionably dominant throughout the Victorian era, there were alternatives. Some of the alternatives flowered only briefly and left little behind. Others were more important. One of these was the utilitarian tradition. Utilitarianism embodied a more rationalistic strand of Enlightenment thinking than did Whig historiography. It persisted well into the nineteenth century, especially in the study of law, where Jeremy Bentham and John Austin inspired a tradition of legal positivism.[28] Crucially, utilitarianism also helped to inspire more formal synchronic approaches to economics, giving greater scope to deductive and mathematical reasoning. Jevons extended the utilitarian analysis of rationality to economics, analyzing all costs in terms of disutility thereby making them substitutable for one another, and analyzing the price of commodities as a result of their final degree of utility.[29] His neoclassical economics, unlike the classical political economy of the Victorian era, could focus on the formal and static analysis of a system in equilibrium.

In the later nineteenth and early twentieth centuries, economists generally attempted to combine historicist narratives with formal deductive and mathematical reasoning.[30] The leading example was the famous synthesis of Alfred Marshall. If Marshall is famous for his attempt to combine neoclassical and classical economics, it should also be remembered that he aspired to locate his synthesis within a larger historicist framework. Nonetheless, although Marshall and other neoclassical economists made historicist gestures, there can be no doubting

[28] P. Schofield, "Jeremy Bentham and Nineteenth Century English Jurisprudence," *Journal of Legal History* 12 (1991), 58–88.

[29] M. Schabas, *A World Ruled by Number: William Stanley Jevons and the Rise of Mathematical Economics* (Princeton: Princeton University Press, 1990).

[30] D. Winch, *Wealth and Life: Essays on the Intellectual History of Political Economy in Britain, 1848–1914* (Cambridge: Cambridge University Press, 2009).

that they were the first wave of a modernist tide that would eventually sweep away Victorian historicism.

Modernism had roots not only in the utilitarian tradition but also in a kind of Victorian skepticism. Although the Victorian crisis of faith generally inspired immanentist theologies that reflected the impact of organicism, it also gave rise to modernist forms of skepticism that ran counter to this immanentism. This skepticism made nineteenth-century narratives of universal progress appear too optimistic and ambitious. It made nineteenth-century notions of truth and duty appear too rigid and austere, perhaps even hypocritical shams. Modernism thus came to contain more cautious, more constrained, and less self-confident ways of knowing and of being. Scientists and social thinkers shifted their focus from wholes and their evolution to atomistic and analytical studies of discrete and discontinuous elements and the assemblages these created. For example, Graham Wallas rejected both idealist historicism and utilitarian rationalism. He called for a political science based on the quantitative study of actual behavior, not deductions from assumptions about reason, character, and social evolution.[31] Similarly, artists and moralists, notably the Bloomsbury group, turned from individual and social duties to good states of mind and personal relations. E. M. Foster and especially Virginia Woolf wrote in more uncertain voices about more fragmented and private worlds than had Charlotte Bronte and Charles Dickens.[32] At the edge of such modernism, there emerged new ideas of self-reference, incompleteness, and radical subjectivity that had been almost entirely absent from earlier thinking.

If modernism had Victorian roots, it was nonetheless the experience of the First World War that decisively undermined developmental historicism. The War shattered the Victorians' confidence in progress and reason, the romantic belief in the role of spirit within organic life, and the purposive nature of social evolution.[33] History and social life could no longer be seen as expressions of the development of moral character and social reason. For Victorians, human action had been "conduct" infused with reason, morality, and purpose. In the twentieth century, human action became "behavior" to be analyzed either apart from all assumptions about mind or in relation to hidden desires and forces that were all too likely to overpower reason and morality. The collapse

[31] G. Wallas, *Human Nature in Politics* (London: Archibald Constable, 1908).
[32] C. Froula, *Virginia Woolf and the Bloomsbury Avant-Garde: War, Civilization, Modernity* (New York: Columbia University Press, 2005).
[33] S. Hynes, *A War Imagined: The First World War and English Culture* (London: Bodley Head, 1991).

of developmental historicism thus coincided with the rise of new approaches to the human sciences such as structuralism, behaviorism, and psychoanalysis.

Images and ideals of progress still appeared after the First World War, but progress was increasingly seen as a contingent victory of human activity. Progress was no longer guaranteed by an evolutionary cosmology or Whig historiography. On the contrary, the contingent victory of progress was thought to depend on the promotion of new sciences that could guide attempts to resolve social and political problems. The First World War thus encouraged calls for new sciences even as it eroded older historical narratives. The new social sciences that arose in this context were modernist–empiricist. Some, but not all, drew on the mathematical and logical innovations of the nineteenth century. Some, but not all, extended the skepticism or inductive empiricism associated with the crisis of faith.

Throughout the first half of the twentieth century, modernist empiricism replaced developmental historicism.[34] Modernist empiricism was atomistic and analytic. It broke up the continuities and gradual changes of earlier evolutionary narratives. It divided the world into discrete, discontinuous units, whether these were empirical facts or single propositions. It made sense of these units through mathematical rules and analytic schemes. And it used synchronic models, calculations, typologies, systems, and structures to explain the nature and behavior of the atomized units. For example, when political scientists pursued the study of comparative institutions in the way already made familiar by James Bryce, they increasingly treated each institution as a discrete atom to be compared and classified together with similar atoms in other systems, rather than as part of a whole political system to be understood in terms of its historical evolution. As early as 1921, Herman Finer added to his study of comparative government an analytic index of topics that enabled readers to compare similar institutions across states. By 1932, he had begun to present his studies in analytic rather than historical terms, proceeding topic by topic, discussing institutions in comparison with similar ones in other countries rather than in the context of a historical narrative.[35]

---

[34] W. Everdell, *First Moderns* (Chicago: University of Chicago Press, 1997); T. Porter, *Trust in Numbers: The Pursuit of Objectivity in Science and Public Life* (Princeton: Princeton University Press, 1995); D. Ross, *The Origins of American Social Science* (Cambridge: Cambridge University Press, 1991), chaps. 8–10.

[35] H. Finer, *Foreign Governments at Work: An Introductory Study* (New York: Oxford University Press, 1921); H. Finer, *The Theory and Practice of Modern Government*, 2 vols. (New York: The Dial Press, 1932).

Of course, Victorian historicism did not disappear overnight. Up until at least 1940, developmental historicism remained prominent in British culture.[36] Nonetheless, in the twentieth century, historicism lost its confidence in any telos. Historicist narratives began to exhibit self-doubt and nostalgia. Modernist synchronic explanations took their place.[37] The focus shifted away from wholes and their evolution toward atomistic and analytical studies of elements and their combination. Formal social science replaced historical narratives as the leading guide to corporate and public policies.

---

[36] For a study that extends the Whig tradition into the twentieth century see J. Stapleton, *Englishness and the Study of Politics: The Social and Political Thought of Ernest Barker* (Cambridge: Cambridge University Press, 1994).

[37] Compare M. Bevir, ed., *Modernism and the Social Sciences: Anglo-American Exchanges, cc. 1918–1980* (forthcoming); D. Ross, ed., *Modernist Impulses in the Human Sciences, 1870–1930* (Baltimore: Johns Hopkins University Press, 1994).

2   Life

Bernard Lightman

A gigantic historicizing of all thought took place during the nineteenth century. The unlikely driver of the historicizing of nineteenth-century thought was science – to be more precise, evolutionary science – rather than any of the human sciences, history included. The unexpected agents of this historicizing process were the evolutionary naturalists: men such as Charles Darwin, T. H. Huxley, Herbert Spencer, and John Tyndall. For they were responsible for transforming a static notion of nature into a dynamic one, where the history of living things became important for the first time. And then they argued that this notion of nature should be used to understand the development of the human world. Inspired by German romanticism, their historicism was dependent on organic and teleological modes of thought.

Natural History, Biology, and Historicizing Nature

Before the nineteenth century, living beings were studied through the discipline of natural history. Natural history involved the systematic investigation of animals, plants, and minerals with the aim of uncovering their overall order. Order was revealed through the method of describing, collecting, identifying, classifying, utilizing, and displaying nature. Natural history was one of three disciplines. The other two were natural philosophy and civil history. Natural history had a lower status than natural philosophy, which surpassed it in explanatory power. Natural history was also distinguished from civil history, the history of the voluntary actions of men in commonwealths.[1] From its revival in the sixteenth century to its decline in the nineteenth century, natural history played a key role in the understanding of the natural world. During this period, in which European powers explored exotic regions of the world, ships

---

[1] Peter Harrison, "Natural History," in Peter Harrison, Ronald L. Numbers, and Michael H. Shank, eds., *Wrestling with Nature: From Omens to Science* (Chicago and London: University of Chicago Press, 2011), p. 132.

returned with specimens that had previously been unknown. Fitting new specimens into a larger scheme of things was the job of the natural historian. For many natural historians, the order they sought to detect was unambiguously divine. Natural history was viewed in the early modern period, as Peter Harrison has asserted, as "an intrinsically theological activity."[2] Informed by natural theology – the notion that evidences of divine design could be found in nature – natural historians believed that knowledge consisted in understanding the purpose God had given to a living being in the economy of nature. Some natural historians even attempted to combine the natural history of the Earth with the sacred chronology of the Bible.[3] However, the term "natural history" appears to the modern reader to be an oxymoron. Despite its title, natural history was predominantly ahistorical. The order in nature was derived, at least in part, from the idea that species were fixed entities or distinct units in the plan of creation. Nature was therefore static.

Darwin, Huxley, and their allies sought to undermine the power of natural history, its ahistorical approach to understanding nature, and its reliance on natural theology. Those who still worked within the natural history tradition, which included the typical clergyman naturalist, opposed the Darwinians, as did those who believed that the study of nature had to be undertaken within a natural theology framework. In his essay "On the Study of Biology" (1876), Huxley characterized natural history as an outmoded term and urged those who studied living beings to embrace the term "biology." Whereas natural history included "very heterogeneous constituents," such as geology, mineralogy, botany, and zoology, discerning men had realized that the last two subjects could be united into "one whole" and dealt with "as one discipline." As a result, Huxley asserted, by the 1870s the term "natural history" had come to be seen as "old" and "confusing," and "all clear thinkers and lovers of consistent nomenclature" used "biology" to characterize the study of the totality of living phenomena.[4] In comparison to natural history, Huxley's biology was stripped of all religious content. The study of living phenomena did not involve the analysis of exquisitely designed organs of perfection, and it could be conducted without having to deal with any questions concerning the wisdom, power, and benevolence of a divine being.

Huxley had already defended Darwin's right to put forward a purely naturalistic theory when *On the Origin of Species* was first published

---

[2] Harrison, "Natural History," p. 131.   [3] Harrison, "Natural History," p. 135.
[4] Thomas H. Huxley, *Science and Education* (New York: D. Appleton and Company, 1894), pp. 263, 267–8.

in 1859. But he also agreed with Darwin that the theory of evolution provided a better scientific explanation of why there were affinities between living beings than the old theory of independent acts of creation. Darwin asserted: "the real affinities of all organic beings are due to inheritance or community of descent. The natural system is a genealogical arrangement, in which we have to discover the lines of descent by the most permanent characters, however slight their vital importance may be."[5] By pointing to lines of descent and genealogical arrangement, Darwin was emphasizing the historicism of nature embedded in evolutionary theory. Whereas natural historians vainly searched "for the undiscovered and undiscoverable essence of the term species,"[6] assuming that species were fixed, Darwin claimed that biologists could now make real progress in understanding the role of history in the development of living beings. Evolutionary biology, then, was one of the chief means by which historicist modes of thought became an integral part of the scientific study of life, undermining the static world envisioned by the natural historian.

But nature was historicized in many ways, since there was no consensus on the nature of the evolutionary process. Did evolution have a goal, or a telos? If so, what was it? Was Darwin's theory of natural selection teleological or did it imply that evolution was merely a random process? Darwin himself seemed ambivalent about this issue, though he was widely interpreted as having rejected teleology. But whatever Darwin's views were, we should not overemphasize his importance in the latter part of the nineteenth century. More than thirty years ago, in his book *The Eclipse of Darwinism*, Peter Bowler pointed to the peculiar status of evolutionary theory in the decades following the publication of *On the Origin of Species*. Although Darwin had persuaded scientists of the validity of evolution, his theory of natural selection was not widely accepted by elite scientists. Bowler acknowledged that the title of his book was somewhat misleading. There was no eclipse of Darwinism "because *Darwinism* – in the modern sense of that term – had never been very popular."[7] Evolution became associated with the unfolding of a goal-directed plan or pattern, whatever Darwin's views on teleology may have been. Within biology, the "*Origin* was hijacked by the prevailing enthusiasm for a progressive and powerful developmental trend in nature."[8]

---

[5] Charles Darwin, *The Origin of Species* (London: Penguin, 1985), p. 451.

[6] Darwin, *Origin of Species*, p. 456.

[7] Peter J. Bowler, *The Eclipse of Darwinism: Anti-Darwinian Evolution Theories in the Decades around 1900* (Baltimore and London: The Johns Hopkins University Press, 1983), p. x.

[8] Peter J. Bowler, "Revisiting the Eclipse of Darwinism," *Journal of the History of Biology* 38 (2005), 22.

In his more appropriately titled *The Non-Darwinian Revolution,* Bowler argued that the developmental view of evolution wasn't eliminated until the 1930s, "when genetics was synthesized with a revived Darwinism to give an evolutionary mechanism capable of winning support in all areas of biology."[9] It wasn't until the emergence of the modern synthesis that Darwin's theory of natural selection became widely accepted by biologists.

The uncertain scientific status of Darwin's theory provided the justification for popularizers to provide evolution with a teleological basis. At least four different teleological versions of evolution were circulating among members of the British reading audience up to the end of the nineteenth century. The influential French evolutionist of the early nineteenth century, J. B. Lamarck, proposed that living beings strived to acquire useful new modifications that were inherited by their offspring and succeeding generations. Variation was therefore not random; rather, the process was inherently progressive. Neo-Lamarckism was popularized by Samuel Butler, Alice Bodington, Grant Allen, Edward Clodd, and Richard Proctor. Alfred Russel Wallace and Arabella Buckley promulgated spiritualistic evolution while Benjamin Kidd, in his *Social Evolution* (1894), found a huge audience for his religious evolutionism. By June 1895, 10,823 copies of Kidd's book had been sold in England and it later became an international best-seller. Finally, a large group of Christian evolutionists, such as Henry Drummond, Charles Kingsley, and George Henslow, argued that the best way to make sense of the meaning of evolution was to put it into a traditional Christian context. Drummond's *Ascent of Man* (1894) had sold 30,000 copies by 1902. Books written by these popularizers allowed their readers to imagine alternative interpretations of evolution before a scientific consensus had formed around a specific mechanism for the evolutionary process. British readers who could not accept the Darwinian version of evolution could turn to Proctor, Wallace, Kidd, or Drummond and find in their works an evolutionary vision that satisfied their yearning for meaning.[10]

If many elite biologists and popularizers of evolution rejected Darwin's theory of natural selection and embraced a teleological version of evolution, then surely the Darwinians – the men who defended Darwin – rejected teleology completely. The Darwinians have in the past been seen as forerunners of the modern, dysteleological evolutionary view.

---

[9] Peter J. Bowler, *The Non-Darwinian Revolution: Reinterpreting a Historical Myth* (Baltimore and London: The Johns Hopkins University Press, 1988), p. 105.

[10] Bernard Lightman, "Darwin and the Popularization of Evolution," *Notes and Records of the Royal Society* 64 (2010), 5–24.

But even they were not the mechanistic, materialistic evolutionists that their opponents made them out to be. If we analyze the evolutionary theory of three of the leading Darwinians – Spencer, Tyndall, and Huxley – it will become clear that they were attracted to organic and teleological modes of thought, partly as a result of their encounter with German Romanticism. The more dynamic view of nature emerging in Germany in the early part of the nineteenth century was another important conceptual stream contributing to the development of historicist modes of thought.[11] The organic, teleological turn in the thought of German figures such as Goethe and Oken was to have a significant impact on Spencer, Tyndall, and Huxley. Darwinian thought is likely the last place in which one would expect to find a progressive evolutionary narrative framed by developmental and organic principles implying progress. But the Darwinians' attraction to teleology and organicism is a startling verification of how deeply the Victorians were indebted to the developmental way of thinking.

Herbert Spencer and Cosmic Evolution

First published in 1850, nine years before the appearance of Darwin's *On the Origin of Species*, Spencer's *Social Statics* described an evolutionary process that automatically moved toward the elimination of all evil. "Evil," he writes, "perpetually tends to disappear." This tendency is built into the entire evolutionary process. Spencer asserted, "in virtue of an essential principle of life, this non-adaptation of an organism to its conditions is ever being rectified; and modification of one or both, continues until the adaptation is complete." For Spencer, the disappearance of evil was identical to the gradual appearance of progress. He stressed, "progress, therefore, is not an accident, but a necessity."[12] The evolutionary process governed everything that existed, from the inorganic to the organic world, including the development of human thought. Spencer concluded that progress was inevitable – dictated by a law of nature:

Instead of civilization being artificial it is a part of nature; all of a piece with the development of an embryo or the unfolding of a flower. The modifications mankind has undergone, and are still undergoing, result from a law underlying the whole organic creation...[13]

---

[11] Bowler, *Non-Darwinian Revolution*, pp. 53–4.
[12] Herbert Spencer, *Social Statics, Abridged and Revised; Together with the Man versus the State* (New York: D. Appleton and Company, 1896), pp. 28, 32.
[13] Spencer, *Social Statics*, p. 32.

Since human society was organic, it was subject to a larger progressive process that governed the entire natural world. Spencer was unambiguous about the progressive direction of both nature and human society. His conception of evolution had more in common with Lamarck and his emphasis on the inheritance of acquired characteristics than with Darwin and his theory of natural selection. Scholars often treat Spencer as a neo-Lamarckian.[14]

Spencer's importance as an evolutionary thinker in the latter half of the nineteenth century cannot be overstated. As Mark Francis has pointed out, Spencer became "the world philosopher of the late-nineteenth century."[15] Michael Taylor has referred to Spencer as "the first international public intellectual" who was read by a large global audience.[16] In Britain, disciples celebrated him as the foremost evolutionist of the day. Even Darwin was overshadowed by Spencer's brilliance, according to his followers. Grant Allen, novelist and popularizer of science, ranked Spencer higher than Darwin when evaluating their contributions to evolutionary science. It was to Spencer that we owed "the word evolution itself, and the general concept of evolution as a single all-pervading natural process." It was "in Spencer," and not Darwin, that "evolutionism finds it personal avatar: he has been at once its prophet, its priest, its architect, and its builder."[17] Albert Simmons, part of a circle of dissident secularists who adopted Spencer's agnosticism as their creed, described Spencer as "the greatest philosopher that the world has ever seen." According to Simmons, Spencer towered over Darwin intellectually. "By the side of Spencer," Simmons declared, "Darwin is a dwarf."[18] Of course, Spencer's Darwinian allies were not as enthusiastic as his disciples in their estimation of his importance. They had a higher opinion of Darwin. But they respected Spencer's abilities and believed that his work was important. Huxley read and criticized the proof of Spencer's *First Principles*. Almost everything that Spencer wrote was sent to Tyndall prior to publication.[19]

---

[14] Bowler, *The Eclipse of Darwinism*, p. 69.

[15] Mark Francis, *Herbert Spencer and the Invention of Modern Life* (Ithaca, NY: Cornell University Press, 2007), p. 8.

[16] Michael Taylor, *The Philosophy of Herbert Spencer* (London: Continuum, 2007), p. 2.

[17] Grant Allen, "The Progress of Science from 1836 to 1886," *Fortnightly Review* 47 (1887), 875–6.

[18] Albert Simmons, *Agnostic First Principles* (London: Watts & Co., 1885), pp. 1, 4. For more on dissident secularism see Bernard Lightman, "Ideology, Evolution and Late-Victorian Agnostic Popularizers," in James R. Moore, ed., *History, Humanity and Evolution: Essays for John C. Greene* (Cambridge: Cambridge University Press, 1989), pp. 285–309.

[19] Bernard Lightman, *The Origins of Agnosticism: Victorian Unbelief and the Limits of Knowledge* (Baltimore: Johns Hopkins University Press, 1987), pp. 105–6.

The optimistic spirit of Spencer's philosophy is sadly at odds with the story of his life. Born in 1820 in Derby, Spencer was the only surviving child of William George Spencer, a schoolmaster of progressive educational views and a property owner. Spencer had a lonely and joyless childhood. Surrounded by the austere atmosphere of English middle-class dissent, with its emphasis on individualism and moralism, he grew introverted and intensely reflective. Later he became a railway engineer (1837–46), then a subeditor at *The Economist* (1848–53), and finally, in 1853, a freelance journalist. Overwork, financial insecurity, and a feeling of indecision took their toll in 1854 when he suffered a nervous breakdown. For the rest of his life, Spencer could only work in short spurts and frequently complained of both physical and mental illness. In 1858, while correcting essays for republication, Spencer suddenly realized that they all shared the same underlying assumption. The laws of development, according to which everything evolved from the homogeneous to the heterogeneous, were at work throughout the entire universe. For Spencer, it was a revelation. He decided to devote the remainder of his life to the systematic dissemination of his grand insight into the workings of the universe. Over the next thirty-six years, Spencer wrote the multi-volumed *System of Synthetic Philosophy* (1862–96). It included volumes on sociology, psychology, biology, and ethics. A grand synthesis of knowledge, the key lay in interpreting all phenomena according to the law of evolution. Never marrying, Spencer embraced a hermit-like existence and adhered to a life of asceticism in order to complete his task.

The first volume of Spencer's Synthetic Philosophy, titled *First Principles of a New System of Philosophy* (1862), outlined his evolutionary synthesis. In Part 1 of the book, titled "The Unknowable," Spencer sought a complete reconciliation between science and religion. He began by dividing them into two separate spheres, but found, after examining each, that they both pointed to "the consciousness of an Inscrutable Power manifested to us through all phenomena."[20] Spencer affirmed the consciousness of a God, though he also maintained that nothing could be known of this being. Spencer's name for this elusive deity was the "Unknowable." While religion was placed firmly in the sphere of the unknowable, in Part 2 of the book, "The Knowable," he searched for truths that would allow him to synthesize scientific knowledge into one system. He rejected the idea that the Newtonian universe, composed of matter, force, and motion, could provide the unifying truth that he sought. Instead, he concluded that "the universal law of distribution of

---

[20] Herbert Spencer, *First Principles of a New System of Philosophy*, 4th edn. (New York: D. Appleton, 1882), p. 108.

matter and motion" is "evolution," which meant that evolutionary law was more fundamental than Newton's law of gravity.[21] This philosophical deduction was then empirically verified by empirical proof drawn from astronomy, geology, biology, psychology, and sociology. Spencer concluded that all phenomena were subject to the evolutionary process. "Alike during the evolution of the Solar System," he declared, "of a planet, of an organism or a nation, there is progressive aggregation of the entire mass."[22] This insight led Spencer to articulate his final definition of evolution. The "formula" read: *"Evolution is an integration of matter and concomitant dissipation of motion; during which the matter passes from an indefinite, incoherent homogeneity to a definite, coherent heterogeneity; and during which the retained motion undergoes a parallel transformation."*[23]

Spencer insisted on the unity of the evolutionary process. There were not "several kinds of Evolution having certain traits in common"; there was "but one Evolution going on everywhere after the same manner."[24] If "the phenomena going on everywhere are parts of the general process of Evolution," then "all phenomena receive their complete interpretation, only when recognized as parts of these processes."[25] Evolution was the key to understanding all things. When, at the conclusion of the book, Spencer deals with the "Philosophico-Religious doctrine" of his book, he denies that it tends toward materialism. To the contrary, Spencer argues, he has asserted the existence of an "Unknown Cause," or "Unknowable," that lies behind the natural world.[26] It is therefore the Unknowable that guides evolution in a progressive direction. In *Social Statics*, Spencer spelled out the goal of the process. He envisioned evolution as eventually leading to the creation of the perfectly adapted human in a utopian society. "The development of the higher creation is a progress towards a form of being," Spencer declared, "capable of a happiness undiminished by these drawbacks." It was in "the human race that the consummation is to accomplished," and "the ideal man is the man in whom all the conditions to that accomplishment are fulfilled."[27] For Spencer, the progressive evolutionary process would lead to a perfect equilibrium.

Tracing the intellectual roots of Spencer's theory of goal-directed cosmic evolution is not easy. He was reticent to acknowledge his debts, in part because he was eager to be seen as an original thinker. His general debts to British empiricism are clear. So is his acceptance of

---

[21] Spencer, *First Principles*, p. 285.   [22] Spencer, *First Principles*, p. 327.
[23] Spencer, *First Principles*, p. 396.   [24] Spencer, *First Principles*, pp. 545–6.
[25] Spencer, *First Principles*, p. 554.   [26] Spencer, *First Principles*, p. 557.
[27] Spencer, *Social Statics*, p. 150.

the Lamarckian principle of inheritance of acquired characteristics in his evolutionary theory. However, evolutionary deism and German transcendental biology or *Naturphilosophie* also played an integral role in the formation of Spencer's evolutionism.[28] Like Erasmus Darwin and Robert Chambers, both evolutionary deists, Spencer put forward a vision of cosmic evolution that presented a story of progress from the nebulae to human society. Spencer's links to German transcendental biology are surprising and I will concentrate on them here. As we shall see, he shares with Tyndall and Huxley an interest in German Romanticism, though the figures that attracted him were different. Lorenz Oken, Karl Ernst von Baer, and Samuel Taylor Coleridge, a British figure deeply influenced by German Romanticism, shaped Spencer's thinking on evolution.

Oken provided a model for cosmic evolution that resembled Spencer's more closely than the one he would have found in the *Vestiges*. In his *Autobiography*, Spencer acknowledged the parallels between his system and Oken's cosmogony.[29] Oken's goal was to interpret nature as a self-development toward high levels of organization. Spencer found out about von Baer through his reading of William Carpenter's *Principles of General and Comparative Physiology* (1838), which he examined carefully in 1852. Spencer was struck by Carpenter's account of von Baer's analysis of embryonic development. Von Baer emphasized that a heterogeneous structure grew out of a more homogeneous structure, and that this process was indicative of the purposiveness of organic development.[30] Since Spencer later defined evolution as the move from homogeneity to heterogeneity, von Baer's impact is clear. Finally, Spencer mentioned Coleridge's essay *The Theory of Life* (1848) in his *Autobiography*.[31] Inspired by Schelling's *Naturphilosophie*, Coleridge conceived of life as the principle of individuation, or the power that united the whole to its parts. Coleridge provided Spencer with a number of ideas that he incorporated into his concept of evolution. As Michael Taylor has asserted, they included "the idea of a whole being formed from mutually dependent parts; the idea that progressively more advanced forms of life

---

[28] For what follows on Spencer and German Romanticism I am heavily indebted to Michael Taylor's "Herbert Spencer and the Metaphysical Roots of Evolutionary Naturalism," in Bernard Lightman and Michael S. Reidy, eds., *The Age of Scientific Naturalism: Tyndall and His Contemporaries* (London: Pickering and Chatoo, 2014), pp. 71–88.

[29] Herbert Spencer, *Autobiography* (London: Williams and Norgate, 1904), II, p. 489.

[30] Robert Richards, *Darwin and the Development of Evolutionary Theories of Mind and Behavior* (Chicago: Chicago University Press, 1987), p. 269.

[31] Spencer, *Autobiography*, I, p. 351.

exhibited more advanced forms of organization; and the idea that the outcome of the developmental process would combine highly individuated component parts of a whole in a way in which their individuality was nonetheless preserved."[32] In sum, German *Naturphilosophen* and a British figure heavily influenced by German Romanticism played a key role in the shaping of Spencer's conception of evolution. They pushed Spencer in the direction of adopting a version of evolution that moved toward a rational end, unfolding continuously in accord with underlying principles.

They also led Spencer to reject a materialist conception of life. In the concluding chapter of *First Principles*, Spencer explained how the reader should understand his conception of how the "detailed phenomena of Life, and Mind, and Society" were to be interpreted "in terms of Matter, Motion, and Force." Spencer objected to the charge of materialism being leveled against "those who ascribed the more involved phenomena to agencies like those which produce the simplest phenomena." He protested that he, like other men of science, showed that the "more involved phenomena" were "marvelous in their attributes the more they are investigated, and are also proved to be in their ultimate natures absolutely incomprehensible." Spencer claimed that, rather than degrading the "so-called higher," he was elevating the "so-called lower."[33]

John Tyndall and the Evolution of Organic Being

At an address delivered to students at University College, London, in the late 1860s, Tyndall discussed how he came to be a scientist. Three men, none of them scientists, had inspired him. Tyndall recalled how when he was a Ph.D. student at the University of Marburg in Germany, he had endured taking baths in freezing water at five o'clock each morning. He credited Thomas Carlyle and Ralph Waldo Emerson with having given him the determination to rise early, bathe in these conditions, and get through analytical geometry and calculus lessons. "To Carlyle and Emerson I ought to add Fichte," Tyndall asserted, "the greatest representative of pure idealism. These three unscientific men made me a practical scientific worker."[34] In contrast to Spencer, Tyndall was not reticent about revealing his intellectual obligations. But like Spencer, he was indebted to Romanticism, and this had an impact on how he

---

[32] Taylor, "Herbert Spencer," p. 83.   [33] Spencer, *First Principles*, p. 556.

[34] John Tyndall, *Fragments of Science*, 8th edn., 2 vols. (London: Longmans, Green, and Co., 1892), II, p. 96. Tyndall also acknowledges his debts to Carlyle, Fichte, and Emerson elsewhere. See Tyndall, *Fragments of Science*, II, pp. 382–3.

conceived of evolution. A physicist, Tyndall was not as familiar with the previous history of biology as was Spencer. Romanticism shaped his thinking about evolution much more at a metaphysical level. Scholars have recognized Tyndall's debt to Romanticism. John Holmes has argued that Tyndall's thought is markedly Romantic in his view of science and in the role he accords to the scientist himself.[35] Here I will emphasize the connection between Tyndall's Romanticism and his concept of evolution. It led him to conceive of all nature as a living, organic being, and evolution as full of purpose.

John Tyndall (1820–93) was born at Leighlinbridge, County Carlow, in southern Ireland. The Tyndall family struggled to make ends meet. His father, unsuccessful as a shoemaker and leather dealer, joined the Irish Constabulary. He was an ardent Orangeman who insisted on a strong Protestant household and educated his son in the art of theological debate. At the age of eighteen, Tyndall joined the Irish Ordnance Survey as a civil assistant. In 1842, he was transferred to the English Survey in Preston. In his position as surveyor, Tyndall experienced firsthand the hard times of the forties when riots broke out among the starving weavers in Preston. Social problems, Chartist unrest, and Thomas Carlyle's writings moved him toward a more radical political position. Unhappy with the inefficiency of the survey's administration and their unfairness to the Irish assistants, Tyndall formally protested and was dismissed in November 1843. In July 1844, he found a position in a private surveyor's office in Preston, and for the next three years Tyndall found himself in the middle of the railway mania. By 1847, the railway boom was coming to an end, and Tyndall accepted an appointment as teacher of mathematics at Queenwood College in Hampshire. He became fascinated by natural philosophy and went to Germany in 1848 to attend Marburg University, where he earned his doctoral degree. Returning in 1851 to England, where scientific posts were scarce, he was forced to take up his old position at Queenwood. Over the next few years, Tyndall applied unsuccessfully for several university positions. Despite having worked with some of the most eminent German scientists of the time, he was passed over for seemingly less qualified men. His Irish, lower-class background made it difficult for him to win the trust of the London scientific elite. Finally, in 1853, he was elected Professor of

[35] John Holmes, "The X Club: Romanticism and Victorian Science," in Amanda Mordavsky Caleb, ed., *(Re)Creating Science in Nineteenth-Century Britain* (Newcastle: Cambridge Scholars Publishing, 2007), p. 14. See also N. D. McMillan and J. Meehan, *John Tyndall: 'X'emplar of Scientific and Technological Education* (Dublin: NCEA, n.d.), pp. 75–7.

Natural Philosophy at the Royal Institution, a plum position. He remained at the Royal Institution for the rest of his career, establishing himself as a leading natural philosopher, a well-respected public lecturer, and Michael Faraday's successor as the director of the Institution.

A close friend of Spencer's, Tyndall was known to his contemporaries as one of the Darwinians. But he could be cautious about voicing his support of evolutionary theory. In 1870 he stated, "those who hold the doctrine of Evolution are by no means ignorant of the uncertainty of their data, and they only yield to it a provisional assent."[36] But in 1874, when he delivered his notorious "Belfast Address" as President of the British Association for the Advancement of Science, he was more forceful when he reviewed the accomplishments of Darwin and Spencer. He presented their theories as answers to the question of how progress had taken place in nature. The geological strata showed that "as we climb higher among the superimposed strata, more perfect forms appear." By what law of growth had these forms, which showed "unmistakeable general advance," been developed? Tyndall argued that religious beliefs had blinded previous scientists to the existence of a law of growth and led them to accept "the anthropomorphism which regarded each successive stratum as a kind of mechanic's bench for the manufacture of new species out of relation to the old."[37] He discussed *On the Origin of Species*, the theory of natural selection, and Darwin's opposition to the notion of creative power acting in human fashion. Darwin, he told his audience, had been right to reject the teleology that sought to refer the exquisite adaptations to be found in nature to a supernatural Artificer. Instead, Darwin attributed their existence to natural causes. "They illustrate, according to him," Tyndall declared, "the method of nature, not the 'technic' of a manlike Artificer."[38] Tyndall found the notion of a supernatural Artificer of natural theology to be too mechanistic.

Tyndall also discussed Spencer's contributions to science, especially in his *Principles of Psychology*. Whereas Darwin answered the question of how "gradations" in physical life had come about through natural law, Spencer dealt with "similar gradations" in psychical life. Spencer had answered the question: "What is the principle of growth of that mysterious power which on our planet culminates in Reason?" In his discussion of Spencer's theory of evolution of mind, Tyndall did not mention Darwin's theory of natural selection. For Tyndall, and rightly so, Spencer's approach laid heavy emphasis on Lamarckian factors.

---

[36] Tyndall, *Fragments of Science*, II, p. 133.   [37] Tyndall, *Fragments of Science*, II, p. 171.
[38] Tyndall, *Fragments of Science*, II, pp. 176–7.

When Tyndall sums up the operation of human evolution, he again stresses Lamarckian elements. "The doctrine of Evolution derives man, in his totality," Tyndall stated, "from the interaction of organism and environment through countless ages past."[39] Like Spencer, Tyndall linked evolution with the action of a mysterious deity. "In fact," he insisted, "the whole process of evolution is the manifestation of a Power absolutely inscrutable to the intellect of man."[40]

Tyndall believed that the chief obstacle to the acceptance of evolution was the mistaken belief that it necessarily entailed a crude materialism. The idea that all philosophy, poetry, art, and even science "are potential in the fires of the sun" seemed, Tyndall admitted, absurd and "too monstrous to be entertained by any sane mind." But why? They were thought of in this way only because of "the ideas concerning matter which were drilled into us when young." Spirit was presented as noble and matter as completely vile. But, Tyndall asked, supposing that spirit and matter are "equally wonderful" and "two opposite faces of the self-same mystery"? Supposing that as a youth you were "impregnated with the notion of the poet Goethe ... and taught to look upon matter, not as 'brute matter,' but as the 'living garment of God'"?[41] Tyndall's acceptance of Goethe's notion of matter takes us to his encounter with German Romanticism, which made it possible for him to accept evolutionary theory. In his many essays and books he attempted to show his readers an alternative conception of matter that owed a great deal to his attraction to German Romanticism.

Tyndall first came into contact with German Romanticism through his reading of Thomas Carlyle in the early 1840s, before he went to Germany. Tyndall saw some extracts from Carlyle's *Past and Present* in the Preston newspapers in 1843. Working as a surveyor in Preston, he was an eyewitness to the misery that had moved Carlyle. He was attracted to Carlyle's "reasonable, and humane" radicalism.[42] But he was also interested in Carlyle's organicism, which he later contrasted with Robert Boyle's mechanistic thinking. He agreed with Carlyle's conception of the universe as a tree, as "an organism with life and direction within." This led Tyndall to a rejection of William Paley's mechanistic natural theology and to a quasi-pantheism. "The order and energy of the universe I hold to be inherent," he believed, "and not imposed from without, the

---

[39] Tyndall, *Fragments of Science*, II, pp. 182–3, 195.

[40] Tyndall, *Fragments of Science*, II, p. 193.

[41] Tyndall, *Fragments of Science*, II, pp. 131–2. Tyndall explores the same theme in the "Belfast Address." See Tyndall, *Fragments of Science*, II, pp. 191–2.

[42] John Tyndall, *New Fragments* (New York: D. Appleton & Company, 1898), pp. 348–9.

expression of fixed law and not of arbitrary will, exercised by what Carlyle would call an Almighty Clockmaker."[43]

Tyndall's time in Germany left a deep impression on him that lasted for the rest of his life. He learned German while listening to Robert Bunsen's chemistry lectures at Marburg.[44] Unlike Spencer, who could only read the German Romantics in translation, Tyndall's grasp of the language gave him more extensive access to their work. While he worked on chemistry, physics, and mathematics, Tyndall also read the German Romantics. His journal and correspondence is filled with his reactions to reading them. When he compared the German Romantics to the British empiricists, he found the latter wanting. He wrote in his journal for December 30, 1848, that it was possible to read Locke and "rise no better from your work. This is impossible with Fichte, the life within him is contagious."[45] Though he became fascinated with German philosophy, he retained his respect for Carlyle. Both Carlyle and Emerson "still continue to exercise a great influence upon me," he wrote on April 7, 1850.[46] Several months later Tyndall wrote to his close friend Thomas Archer Hirst that Carlyle's concept of God was far superior to William Paley's clock-making deity. Paley's God was "an omnipotent mechanic detached from his work," basically "the same as the atheist." But with Carlyle "the universe is the blood and bones of Jehovah—he climbs in the sap of trees and falls in cateracts."[47] After Tyndall returned from Germany, he was still engrossed by the German Romantics and their counterparts in Britain, such as Carlyle. While working at the Royal Institution after he returned from Germany, he discussed "matters of religion" with Michael Faraday. Tyndall noted in his journal on March 2, 1855 that Faraday had told his wife he feared Tyndall was "tinctured by the Germans on religious matters."[48]

It is unclear when Tyndall first encountered Goethe, but he discovered him through Carlyle. He recollected in 1880 that his reverence for Goethe "had been awakened by the writings of Carlyle, and it was afterwards confirmed and consolidated by the writings of Goethe himself."[49] In his "Belfast Address," Tyndall declared that Goethe was not only a great poet, but also an important contributor to natural history.[50] Tyndall quoted from Goethe on several occasions and penned an entire

---

[43] Tyndall, *Fragments of Science*, II, p. 337.   [44] Tyndall, *New Fragments*, p. 238.
[45] Journals of John Tyndall, Tyndall Papers, Royal Institution of Great Britain, Vol. 2, 409.
[46] Journals of John Tyndall, Vol. 2, 484.
[47] Tyndall Papers, Correspondence between Thomas Archer Hirst and John Tyndall, Royal Institution, London, RI MSS T, 31/B7, p. 32.
[48] Journals of John Tyndall, Vol. 3, p. 731.   [49] Tyndall, *New Fragments*, p. 47.
[50] Tyndall, *Fragments of Science*, II, p. 148.

essay on his *Farbenlehre*.[51] For Tyndall, Goethe summed up in his poetry the mystery underlying nature. "To many of us who feel that there are more things in heaven and earth than are dreamt of in the present philosophy of science," Tyndall declared, "but who have been also taught, by baffled efforts, how vain is the attempt to grapple with the Inscrutable, the ultimate frame of mind is that of Goethe."[52]

Tyndall's mind was not just tinctured by the Germans on religious matters. German Romanticism profoundly affected his scientific thinking. It was through science that humanity could draw closer to the transcendental mystery behind nature. He constantly drew on Romantic concepts of creativity, imagination, and organicism to conceive of how nature operated and how the scientist should try to understand the natural world. When trying to decide between the hypothesis of creation and natural evolution, Tyndall asked his readers to think about which of the two accorded best with notions of a "creative energy."[53] Tyndall raised this question in his essay on "Scientific Use of the Imagination," where he argued that imagination was indispensable to scientific discovery. The Romantic emphasis on organicism was so important to Tyndall that he conceived of science itself as organic. "Science is an organic growth," he asserted, "and accurate measurements give coherence to the scientific organism."[54]

Tyndall's conception of life was also shaped by his debt to Romanticism. In his essay on "Vitality" (1864) he discussed the differences between organic and inorganic matter.[55] Tyndall declared that "the philosophy of the present day" undermined the distinction between life and dead matter. "The tendency, indeed, of modern science," Tyndall asserted, "is to break down the wall of partition between organic and inorganic, and to reduce both to the operation of forces which are the same in kind, but which are differently compounded." These statements, and many more like them spread throughout his writings, are what led to the suspicion that Tyndall was a materialist. But Tyndall steadfastly maintained throughout his life that he wasn't a materialist, at least not in the common understanding of the term. Instead of reducing the organic to the inorganic, Tyndall tended to conceive of the inorganic as being alive. On the following page of "Vitality" he explored a very unmaterialistic concept of what constituted life. "Life," he insisted, "is a *wave* which in no two consecutive moments of its existence is composed

[51] Tyndall, *Fragments of Science*, II, pp. 52, 101; Tyndall, *New Fragments*, pp. 47–77.
[52] Tyndall, *Fragments of Science*, II, p. 52.   [53] Tyndall, *Fragments of Science*, II, p. 130.
[54] Tyndall, *New Fragments*, p. 201.
[55] John Tyndall, "Science. Vitality", *The Reader* 4 (October 29, 1864), pp. 545–6.

of the same particles." The development of organic forms could arise through the "possible play of molecules in a cooling planet" because matter was "essentially mystical and transcendental."[56] Tyndall's conception of life as the result of the development of mystical matter seems unusual for a Darwinian. His contemporaries routinely saw him as a materialist and hardheaded empiricist who supported a mechanistic version of evolution. But adopting this picture amounts to reading Tyndall through the eyes of his opponents. He offered a vision of life, and the evolution of life, that was at odds with dysteleological, mechanistic materialism.

Like Spencer, Tyndall conceived of evolution as the manifestation of an unknown power behind, and in, nature. This mysterious power ensured that the process was generally one of advancement or progress. Both men were indebted to German Romantics for their views on the evolution of life. But whereas Coleridge and Oken shaped Spencer's thinking, Tyndall learned from Carlyle, Fichte, and Goethe to view nature as a living being rather than a dead mechanism. While the cerebral Spencer was far more restrained, Tyndall's writing is filled with poetic expressions of the transcendental meaning to be found in nature. Tyndall was an avid mountain-climber. On the slopes of the Alps, Tyndall was often struck by a sense of awe. At the summit of the Weisshorn he experienced a "delight and exultation" that was not "of Reason or of Knowledge, but of BEING:–I was part of it and it of me, and in the transcendent glory of Nature I entirely forgot myself as man."[57]

T. H. Huxley and a Wider Teleology

When Huxley was asked by his friend Norman Lockyer to write the opening article for the first issue of *Nature*, a poem by Goethe came into his mind. This "wonderful rhapsody on 'Nature'" had "been a delight to me from my youth up." To Huxley, "no more fitting preface could be put before a Journal, which aims to mirror the progress of that fashioning by Nature of a picture of herself, in the mind of man, which we call the progress of Science." After this endorsement of the German Romantics' idealism, Huxley offered his translation of Goethe's poem, and then remarked on the eternal character of art. For "long after the theories of the philosophers whose achievements are recorded in these pages, are obsolete," Huxley predicted, "the vision of the poet will remain as a

---

[56] Tyndall, *Fragments of Science*, II, pp. 50–1.

[57] John Tyndall, *The Glaciers of the Alps and Mountaineering in 1861* (London: J. M. Dent & Co., 1906), p. 239.

truthful and efficient symbol of the wonder and the mystery of nature."[58] In preferring Goethe's poem to the transitory theories of his scientific colleagues, Huxley reveals his debt to German Romanticism. As in the cases of Spencer and Tyndall, German Romanticism significantly shaped Huxley's formulation of evolution, giving it a teleological quality.

Thomas Henry Huxley was born into an impoverished lower-middle-class family. He studied medicine and then entered the Royal Navy medical service in 1846. Just as Darwin had received important scientific training while aboard the *Beagle*, Huxley was assistant surgeon and naturalist of the HMS *Rattlesnake* from 1846 to 1850. Moving into the area of biological research, Huxley was appointed lecturer at the Royal School of Mines in 1854, and then later moved up to professor. He enjoyed a long and distinguished career as one of Victorian England's greatest scientists and popularizers of science due to his unwearying efforts in public lecture halls, in the pages of fashionable journals, and in important government committees. Huxley was also notorious for his vigorous defense of evolutionary theory, which won him the title "Darwin's bulldog."

In 1885, Huxley argued that Darwin's *On the Origin of Species* had had an enormous impact. It had led to "a great renewal ... of the zoological and botanical sciences" and it had "stirred" psychology, ethics, and cosmology "to their foundations."[59] But, ironically, Huxley was never a convinced supporter of the theory of natural selection – the core of *On the Origin of Species* and Darwin's chief contribution to the debate over evolution. Huxley liked the theory because it was naturalistic, and he defended Darwin's right to put forward such a theory. However, he called for more research to verify whether or not Darwin's theory constituted the primary mechanism for evolution. In "The Darwinian Hypothesis" (1859), Huxley declared: "the combined investigations of another twenty years may, perhaps, enable naturalists to say whether the modifying causes and the selective power, which Darwin has satisfactorily shown to exist in nature, are competent to produce all the effects he ascribes to them." Strikingly, Huxley recommended Goethe's "Thätige Skepsis," or active doubt, as the most appropriate state of mind with respect to Darwin's theory.[60] A year later, in "The Origin of Species" (1860), Huxley wrote that Darwin's position might have been stronger if he had not adopted the notion that nature does not make jumps.

---

[58] T. H. Huxley, "Nature: Aphorisms by Goethe," *Nature* I (November 1869–April 1870), 10–11.
[59] T. H. Huxley, *Darwiniana* (London: Macmillan & Co., 1894), p. 249.
[60] Huxley, *Darwiniana*, p. 20.

"We believe," Huxley announced, "that Nature does make jumps now and then, and a recognition of the fact is of no small importance in disposing of many minor objections to the doctrine of transmutation."[61] Huxley saw an important role for mutations in the evolutionary process. Almost twenty years later, Huxley was still unsure about the importance of natural selection. In "Evolution in Biology" (1878) he stated that it remained to be seen how far natural selection "suffices for the production of species."[62] In "The Coming of Age of 'The Origin of Species'" (1880), Huxley characterized the "fundamental doctrine" of Darwin's book as being the idea that species have descended from common parents and have been modified in the course of descent.[63] When Darwin read the essay he was alarmed that Huxley might be giving up natural selection.[64]

Despite his reluctance to fully endorse natural selection, Huxley was an evolutionist, at least in theory.[65] Although he believed that Darwin's *Origin* had had a wide impact on the social and natural sciences, he thought it was too early to construct an evolutionary system *à la* Herbert Spencer. In 1892 he remarked, "I have nothing to say to any 'Philosophy of Evolution.' Attempts to construct such a philosophy may be as useful, nay, even as admirable, as was the attempt of Descartes to get at a theory of the universe by the same *a priori* road; but, in my judgment, they are premature."[66] If Huxley was not a Spencerian, neither was he a Lamarckian.[67] The inheritance of acquired characteristics played no role in Huxley's conception of evolution. But Huxley's notion of evolution had a developmental aspect to it. In 1878, he argued that biologists used the terms "development" and "evolution" indiscriminately. "Evolution, or development, is, in fact, at present employed in biology as a general name for the history of the steps by which any living being has acquired the morphological and the physiological characters which distinguish it," he declared.[68] This is hard to square with some of Huxley's statements on teleology.

---

[61] Huxley, *Darwiniana*, p. 77.   [62] Huxley, *Darwiniana*, p. 223.
[63] Huxley, *Darwiniana*, p. 232.
[64] Lightman, *Origins of Agnosticism*, p. 157; Michael Bartholomew, "Huxley's Defence of Darwin," *Annals of Science* 32 (1975), 525–35.
[65] Huxley was not an evolutionist in practice immediately after the publication of the *Origin of Species*. It was only from 1868 that he began to apply evolutionary concepts to his own work. See Mario A. Di Gregorio, *T. H. Huxley's Place in Natural Science* (New Haven and London: Yale University Press, 1984), p. xviii.
[66] T. H. Huxley, *Science and Christian Tradition* (London: Macmillan & Co., 1909), p. 41.
[67] T. H. Huxley to Charles Lyell, August 17, 1862, vol. 30, Scientific and General Correspondence, Huxley Papers, Imperial College, London.
[68] Huxley, *Darwiniana*, p. 196.

Initially, in 1864, Huxley argued that Darwin was not a teleologist. Instead of picturing each organism as having been created for a purpose, Darwin substituted a "method of trial and error." Darwinian evolution was profoundly opposed, Huxley insisted, to the "ordinary" teleological conception. Gradual progress toward perfection was not a "necessary part of the Darwinian creed," which was consistent "with indefinite persistence in one state, or with a gradual retrogression."[69] But in 1869 Huxley made a provocative statement that must have puzzled his contemporaries. He insisted, "there is a wider Teleology, which is not touched by the doctrine of Evolution, but is actually based upon the fundamental proposition of Evolution."[70] The term "teleology" was associated in Huxley's time with the study of ends or final causes, especially as related to the evidences of design or purpose in nature.[71] Huxley's endorsement of a "wider Teleology" would have seemed strange to his readers because the search for design in nature was identified with what was known as natural theology.

However, Huxley conceived of nature as subject to deterministic laws. His wider teleology was built upon this notion. Huxley realized that Darwin had re-invented teleology. Natural selection was a mechanism for selection among a random set of alternatives – it preserved traits in virtue of their advantageous consequences. It allowed for teleology without a designing divine being. Huxley tried to explain this several times. It was difficult for his audiences to comprehend because evolutionary teleology did not fit any model of teleological explanation existing in the nineteenth century. Before Darwin, teleologists had to choose between goal-directed vital forces or a divinely designed adaptation. But when Darwin proposed a selection-based teleology, he provided the doctrine of final causes with a new theoretical base.[72]

Huxley's new teleology is outlined primarily in his essay "The Genealogy of Animals" (1869) and his chapter in the *Life and Letters of Charles Darwin* (1888), edited by Darwin's son Francis. The earlier essay was a review of German evolutionist Ernst Haeckel's *The Natural History of Creation* (1868). Huxley rejected Haeckel's assertion that *On the Origin of Species* opposed the causal or mechanical view of living nature to the teleological one. Huxley agreed with Haeckel that the theory of evolution was "the most formidable opponent of all the commoner and coarser

---

[69] Huxley, *Darwiniana*, pp. 84–6, 90.   [70] Huxley, *Darwiniana*, p. 110.

[71] "Teleology," in James A. H. Murray, Henry Bradley, W. A. Craigie, and C. T. Onions, eds., *A New English Dictionary on Historical Principles* (Oxford: Oxford Clarendon Press, 1919), Vol. IX, Part II, p. 149.

[72] James G. Lennox, "Darwin Was a Teleologist", *Biology and Philosophy* 8 (1993), 410, 416–17.

forms of Teleology." Darwin had delivered the "death-blow" to "the Teleology which supposes that the eye, such as we see it in man or one of the higher *Vertebrata*, was made with the precise structure which it exhibits, for the purpose of enabling the animal which possesses it to see." Darwin had destroyed Paley's form of teleology, with its emphasis on organs of perfection such as the eye. Nevertheless, Huxley insisted, a wider teleology can be established that is based upon the fundamental proposition of evolution. "That proposition," Huxley wrote, "is that the whole world, living and not living, in [sic] the result of the mutual interaction, according to definite laws, of the forces possessed by the molecules by which the primitive nebulosity of the universe was composed." A "sufficient intelligence" in existence when the universe was formed could have predicted the state of living things in Britain in 1869 with as much certainty as anyone living in 1869 could predict what will happen "to the vapour of the breath in a cold winter's day."[73] The laws of nature never vary, and they determine what will unfold from the beginning of time. Since evolution is one of the laws of nature, it is evidence of the determinism that Huxley is defending.

Huxley hinted in several essays what the implications of his teleological emphasis on natural law might mean for the workings of the evolutionary process, particularly in reference to the issue of variation. In "Mr. Darwin's Critics" (1871) he denied that the theory of natural selection dictated that variation was indefinite or fortuitous. Variation might appear to be accidental, but it was an expression of the operation of molecular forces within the organism. "And," Huxley argued, "as these forces certainly operate according to definite laws, their general result is, doubtless, in accordance with some general law which subsumes them all." Huxley had no objection to calling this "an 'evolutionary law,'" though he acknowledged that the law itself remained unknown.[74] Seven years later he developed a similar line of thought in "Evolution in Biology" (1878). The importance of the theory of natural selection would not be undermined if further research revealed that variability was "definite" and "determined in certain directions rather than in others, by conditions inherent in that which varies."[75]

Huxley's acceptance of the notion of a wider teleology is just one indication of his debt to German Romanticism. We have already seen his interest in Goethe. Di Gregorio claims that Goethe was Huxley's favorite author.[76] By likening nature to a poem, Huxley was rejecting

---

[73] Huxley, *Darwiniana*, pp. 109–110.   [74] Huxley, *Darwiniana*, pp. 181–2.
[75] Huxley, *Darwiniana*, p. 223. I am indebted to Peter Bowler for this reference and the previous one.
[76] Di Gregorio, *T. H. Huxley's Place in Natural Science*, p. xvii.

materialistic mechanism. In his "On Natural History, as Knowledge, Discipline, and Power" (1856), Huxley explained how he reconciled mechanical with organic pictures of nature. "Thus in traveling from one end to the other of the scale of life," Huxley declared, "we are taught one lesson, that living nature is not a mechanism but a poem; not a mere rough engine-house for the due keeping of pleasure and pain machines, but a palace whose foundations, indeed, are laid on the strictest and safest mechanical principles, but whose superstructure is a manifestation of the highest and noblest act."[77] While Huxley believed it was important to adopt a mechanistic methodology to study the "foundations" of nature, he nevertheless conceived of the "superstructure" in organic terms. Though Huxley later discussed his attraction to the notion of animals as machines in his "On the Hypothesis that Animals are Automata, and Its History" in an 1874 issue of *Nature*, it is not clear that he had moved away from his earlier adherence to methodological materialism. His endorsement of Goethe's conception of nature as a poem had just been published five years earlier in the same journal.[78]

Like Tyndall, Huxley was also attracted to Carlyle.[79] In his appreciation of Tyndall, written shortly after Tyndall's death, Huxley recalled that they were both students of Carlyle when they first met in 1851. But, Huxley wrote, the grounds of their appreciation for Carlyle were different. Whereas Tyndall saw Carlyle as a great teacher, Huxley was "rather inclined to take him as a great tonic, as a source of intellectual invigoration and moral stimulus and refreshment, rather than of theoretical or practical guidance."[80] Huxley's statement notwithstanding, he shared Tyndall's attraction to Carlyle's natural supernaturalism – the idea that at the bottom of nature was a profound mystery that could never be fully fathomed.[81] Huxley was more restrained than Tyndall when he discussed this theme. Huxley articulated the notion of a transcendent meaning in nature in his 1860 anonymous review of *On the Origin of Species* in the *Westminster Review*. Science, Huxley believed, drew a picture of the world of "harmonious order governing eternally continuous progress —the web and woof of matter and force interweaving by

[77] Professor Michael Foster and Professor E. Ray Lankester, eds., *The Scientific Memoirs of Thomas Henry Huxley*, 4 vols. (London: Macmillan & Co., Limited, 1898–1902), I, p. 311.
[78] Paradis argues that Huxley abandoned his early Romanticism, and tendency towards vitalism, in the mid-sixties. I would maintain that the rejection of the latter did not entail a repudiation of the former. See James G. Paradis, *T. H. Huxley: Man's Place in Nature* (Lincoln and London: University of Nebraska Press, 1978), p. 73.
[79] Frank Turner, "Victorian Scientific Naturalism and Thomas Carlyle," *Victorian Studies* 18 (1975), 325–76.
[80] T. H. Huxley, "Professor Tyndall," *Nineteenth Century* 35 (1894), 3.
[81] Holmes, "The X Club," p. 24.

slow degrees, without a broken thread, that veil which lies between us and the Infinite—that universe which alone we know or can know."[82] The image of the veil, a Romantic image of a hidden world of transcendental truth just out of reach, is here connected to Huxley's deterministic evolutionary process.[83]

Though his enemies labeled him a materialist, Huxley's concept of life, like Tyndall's, was shaped by his debt to Romanticism. In his lecture "On the Physical Basis of Life" (1868) Huxley attempted to "prove the existence of a general uniformity in the character of the protoplasm, or physical basis, of life, in whatever group of living beings it may be studied."[84] In a letter dated June 14, 1870, Huxley complained to Tyndall that his essay had been totally misunderstood. "The paper upon the Physical Basis of Life," he told Tyndall, "was intended by me to contain a simple statement of one of the greatest tendencies of modern biological thought, accompanied by a protest from the philosophical side against what is commonly called materialism. The result of my well-meant efforts I find to be, that I am generally credited with having invented 'protoplasm' in the interests of materialism."[85] All this despite Huxley's declaration in the essay that "I, individually, am no materialist, but, on the contrary, believe materialism to involve grave philosophical error."[86] Tyndall understood that Huxley had rejected materialism in this essay on protoplasm and had hinted at a transcendental understanding of what constituted life. After reading the final page of Huxley's essay, where Huxley discussed how "the errors of systematic materialism may paralyze the energies and destroy the beauty of a life," on June 16, 1870 Tyndall wrote to express his agreement. "I hope some day to see you develop the last page," Tyndall declared, "and particularly the last paragraph of 'Physical Basis of Life.' I probably am the only living man who sees the meaning shadowed forth in that page and paragraph!!"[87]

In his famous essay on "Agnosticism" in 1889, Huxley was critical of Samuel Laing for endorsing a creed of agnosticism, complete with articles. In article eight, Laing had listed the concept of "polarity" as one of the key beliefs of the devout agnostic. Huxley remarked that he had heard a lot about polarity "in my youth, when 'Naturphilosophie' was in fashion, and greatly did I suffer from it."[88] This seemingly outright

[82] Huxley, *Darwiniana*, p. 59.   [83] Holmes, "The X Club," p. 25.
[84] T. H. Huxley, *Method and Results* (London: Macmillan & Co., 1894), p. 144.
[85] Huxley Papers, Imperial College, London, 8:80.
[86] Huxley, *Method and Results*, p. 155.
[87] Royal Institution, Tyndall Papers, Tyndall Correspondence, 2933 (RI MSS T, 14/C3, 41).
[88] Huxley, *Science and Christian Tradition*, p. 247.

rejection of *Naturphilosophie* in 1889 must be weighed against Huxley's article on "Past and Present" in *Nature* in 1894, shortly before his death. Written twenty-five years after his piece for the first issue of *Nature*, Huxley returned again to Goethe's "wonderful rhapsody *Die Natur*." He recalled that many readers of the journal had thought that Huxley had written the poem rather than translated it. Huxley realized that he could not expect scientists deeply immersed in their own fields of specialization to understand Goethe and the Romantic insight that nature was like a poem. But by bringing *Nature*'s audience back to Goethe, Huxley implied that the insight continued to be valid. Then Huxley moved on to evaluate the evidence for evolution, asserting that it was a fact, not a hypothesis, even though the physiological factors in the evolutionary process, such as Darwin's theory of natural selection, were still open to discussion.[89] Though the link between Goethe and evolution was not made explicit here, it was evident throughout Huxley's writings when he discussed his teleological interpretation of evolution, the importance of organicism, and the glimmers of transcendent meaning in nature.

Darwinian Historicism and the Human Sciences

The Darwinian historicizing of biology inevitably led to a historicizing of the social sciences. In his essay "On the Study of Biology," Huxley claimed that evolutionary biology covered "all the phenomena which are exhibited by living things," including the higher forms. This meant that humans and all their ways were within the scope of biology. Huxley gave an evolutionary justification for subsuming psychology, politics, political economy, and civil history within the domain of the biologist. The "rudiments and outlines of our own mental phenomena are traceable among the lower animals" who have "their economy and their polity." If the "polity of bees and the commonwealth of wolves fall within the purview of the biologist proper," Huxley declared, "it becomes hard to say why we should not include therein human affairs." But biologists had, at great sacrifice, given up civil history to a different branch of science, which, following Auguste Comte, Huxley called "sociology," though he warned that it should not seem surprising if a biologist dealt with philosophy, politics, or social issues "because, after all, that is a part of his kingdom which he has only voluntarily forsaken."[90] Huxley's biological imperialism not only justified the use of biological theories to

[89] T. H. Huxley, "Past and Present," *Nature* 51 (November 1894), 1–3.
[90] Huxley, *Science and Education*, pp. 270–1.

solve social problems, but also led to the widespread application of evolutionary theory to the human sciences, including anthropology, history, psychology, and sociology. But Spencer pushed even more for the application of evolutionary theory outside of natural science.

For Spencer, to understand how the world had come to be in its present state required a grasp of the dynamic processes operating since the creation of the earth. Evolution was at work in every stage, from the formation of the solar system by the condensation of white-hot nebular matter into planets (the nebular hypothesis); to the geological forces that determined the nature of the earth's crust; to the development of life, from monad to man. Even the intellectual and cultural achievements of humanity, including science, were a part of the cosmic evolutionary process. Spencer laid out this vision of cosmic evolution in his multi-volumed *System of Synthetic Philosophy*, his synthesis of all knowledge connected through the concept of evolution. He applied evolutionary theory to understand the human mind, to analyse the nature of society, and to outline a system of ethics. Spencer was not the first to develop this notion of cosmic evolution, but he was among the most influential proponents of it.

As we have seen, in Huxley's opinion, attempts to construct a philosophy of evolution in the second half of the nineteenth century were premature. Instead of opting for cosmic evolution, Huxley was content to promote a new naturalistic discipline that focused on the study of life in all its forms. Late in life he pulled back from even this idea, as he was appalled by Spencer's attempts to find a principle for ethics in the evolutionary process. His "Evolution and Ethics" (1893) and his "Evolution and Ethics–Prolegomena" (1894) were public expressions of his opposition to Spencer, though he never mentioned his friend by name. Huxley begins by explaining what evolution tells us about the natural world. First, nature is subject to deterministic laws that allow for no contingency. He asserts, "As a natural process, of the same character as the development of a tree from its seed, or of a fowl from its egg, evolution excludes creation and all other kinds of supernatural intervention. As the expression of a fixed order, every stage of which is the effect of causes operating according to definite rules, the conception of evolution no less excludes that of chance."[91] Second, evolution operates on all phenomena. Scientific knowledge, "that limited revelation of the nature of things," had led to the belief that all living things, the fabric of the

[91] Thomas H. Huxley, *Evolution and Ethics and Other Essays* (London: Macmillan & Co., 1911), p. 6.

earth, the solar system, and millions of similar bodies "are all working out their predestined courses of evolution."[92]

So far, Huxley sounds very much like a deterministic, cosmic evolutionist of Spencer's ilk. But he had referred to scientific knowledge as a "limited revelation of the nature of things" because something other than nature also existed: the human world, which Huxley designates as a "garden." A "work of art, or artifice," since it was brought into existence due to the "operation of human energy and intelligence," Huxley considers whether or not the "garden" is a part of the cosmic evolutionary process. He reminds his readers that in the past thirty years he has tried to show that humans are "as much a part of nature, as purely a product of the cosmic process, as the humblest weed."[93] However, the cosmic process, he insists, is in opposition to what he calls the "horticultural process."[94] Huxley acknowledges that it seems absurd to point to the existence of both the cosmic and horticultural process since they are antagonistic, but "the fact is so."[95] He concludes the essay by discussing the challenges that lie ahead for the human race in its "constant struggle to maintain and improve, in opposition to the State of Nature, the State of Art of an organized polity; in which, and by which, man may develop a worthy civilization."[96] In effect, Huxley was denying that evolutionary theory offered a full explanation for human ethics, politics, or society. Spencer's cosmic evolutionism, which extended evolutionary historicism into all aspects of human life, wasn't just premature. It was a tragic mistake. This profound disagreement between two evolutionists came after Spencer's fame and influence had peaked in the 1870s and 1880s, and may have contributed to the rather rapid decline of his reputation thereafter.

Conclusion: Darwin, the Darwinians, and Romanticism

In a Friday-evening discourse at the Royal Institution in 1880, Tyndall recalled the thrill he received two years earlier when Thomas Carlyle presented him with a farewell gift. Carlyle, then eighty-three, had decided to give some of his books away to his friends before the final end. He gave a copy of Goethe's *Farbenlehre* to Tyndall. This same copy must have been highly valued by Carlyle, as Goethe himself had sent it to him.[97] Tyndall would have appreciated the symbolic meaning of Carlyle's gift. Just as Goethe had passed on to Carlyle his insights into the

[92] Huxley, *Evolution and Ethics*, pp. 6–7.   [93] Huxley, *Evolution and Ethics*, p. 11.
[94] Huxley, *Evolution and Ethics*, p. 12.   [95] Huxley, *Evolution and Ethics*, p. 12.
[96] Huxley, *Evolution and Ethics*, pp. 44–5.   [97] Tyndall, *New Fragments*, p. 48.

workings of nature so that Carlyle could continue to disseminate the Romantic perspective to a British audience, so Carlyle was entrusting Tyndall with the same role after he was gone. Tyndall's lecture at the Royal Institution fulfilled Tyndall's promise to Carlyle to examine the book "with a view of setting forth what it really contained."[98] In the lecture Tyndall analyzed Goethe's theory of colors, comparing it to Newton's, while evaluating both in the light of modern science. Judged by contemporary standards, Tyndall admitted, Newton's theory was more accurate, and it was the result of using strict scientific method. Nevertheless, Tyndall pointed to errors made by Newton, who had adopted "a wrong mechanical conception in his theory of light." In the conclusion of the lecture, Tyndall asserted that Goethe's poetic approach to nature was just as important as Newton's exclusively mechanical method. "The feelings and aims with which Newton and Goethe respectively approached Nature were radically different," Tyndall declared, "but they had an equal warrant in the constitution of man."[99] Here Tyndall elevated Goethe, the representative of German Romanticism, to the same status as Newton, the British hero of scientific empiricism.

Despite the expressions of admiration for Goethe and other German Romantics in Tyndall's works, their contemporaries often saw him, as well as Spencer and Huxley, as mechanistic materialists who defended a theory – the theory of evolution – which destroyed the idea of finding transcendental meaning in nature. However, Tyndall and his friends were deeply indebted to German Romanticism. As young men, they learned about the German Romantics through British intermediaries such as Carlyle or Coleridge. Though they were attracted to different German Romantics – Spencer to Oken, Tyndall to Fichte and Goethe, and Huxley to Goethe – from them they all learned the value of organic and teleological modes of thought. They also learned that the quest to find transcendental meaning in nature, sometimes best expressed in poetic terms, was not necessarily in opposition to adopting empiricist and materialistic methods in science. Their commitment to the ideals of German Romanticism may explain, at least in part, why none of them emphasized randomness in their formulation of evolution. Their concept of evolution was teleological, even though highly secular in nature compared to Christian evolutionists of their period. As aggressive proponents of this view of evolution, they played a major role in pushing the science of their age towards historicist modes of thought.

---

[98] Tyndall, *New Fragments*, p. 48.   [99] Tyndall, *New Fragments*, pp. 76–7.

A greater appreciation of the links between German Romanticism and leading Darwinians has broader implications for three important issues for Victorianists. First, the Darwinians can now be seen as being more in line with other groups who accepted evolutionary theory. Christian evolutionists, for example, such as liberal Anglicans Charles Kingsley and Frederick Temple, also embraced a teleological interpretation of the evolutionary process. The periodic alliance between these two groups is more explicable. Second, this study sheds light on where Darwin himself fits into the story. Darwin's conception of nature has often been seen, as Robert Richards has asserted, as mechanistic and therefore the antithesis of the Romantic. But if some of Darwin's closest colleagues were profoundly indebted to Romanticism, then Richards' contention that "in important respects Darwin was a Romantic biologist" deserves serious consideration. Richards argues that for Darwin nature was "organic," not mechanistic, and that the link connecting Darwin to Romanticism was Alexander von Humboldt.[100] While Richards argues that instead of eliminating all values from nature, Darwin aimed to recover them for a secularized notion of nature, a similar point has been made about Darwin's teleology. Lennox has asserted that Darwin proposed a selection-based, secular teleology rather than completely destroying the concept of purpose in nature.[101]

Finally, for those scholars who emphasize the continuing power of Romanticism in Britain in the second half of the nineteenth century, it becomes possible to point to the Darwinians to support the validity of this approach. It is more difficult to sustain the position that the Romantic period is superseded by a radically different age, the age of the worship of science, if some of the leading scientists are indebted to the Romantics. The continuity between the first and second halves of the nineteenth century begins to stand out far more. Organic, romantic, developmental historicisms were influential in the natural, as well as the human, sciences throughout the nineteenth century.

---

[100] Robert Richards, *The Romantic Conception of Life: Science and Philosophy in the Age of Goethe* (Chicago and London: University of Chicago Press, 2002), pp. 513, 515–6, 518. David Kohn also traced Darwin's Romanticism to Humboldt in an earlier article. See David Kohn, "The Aesthetic Construction of Darwin's Theory," in Alfred Tauber, ed., *Aesthetics and Science: The Elusive Synthesis* (Dordrecht: Kluwer, 1996), pp. 13–48.

[101] Richards, *Romantic Conception of Life*, p. 516; Lennox, "Darwin Was a Teleologist," p. 410.

3   Race

Efram Sera-Shriar

> It may have struck some readers as an omission, that in a work on civilisation insisting so strenuously on a theory of development or evolution, mention should scarcely have been made of Mr. Darwin ... whose influence on the whole course of modern thought on such subjects should not be left without formal recognition. This absence of particular reference is accounted for by the present work, arranged on its own lines, coming scarcely into contact of detail with the previous works of [this] eminent philosopher.[1]

The year 1871 was an important one for British anthropology. Some scholars have canonised it as the beginning of a new era for the young discipline. For much of the 1860s, two competing groups interested in human diversity fought for control of the science. On the one hand, there were the ethnologists, led by the anatomist and biologist Thomas Huxley (1825–95), who promoted the significance of Darwinian evolutionary theory for explicating the causes that produced variation among the races. On the other, there were the anthropologists, led by the physician and speech therapist James Hunt (1833–69), who argued against all forms of developmental theories – including evolution – and wanted to place more emphasis on the current state of human varieties. At the centre of their disciplinary debates was the issue of human origin. Did the various races living throughout the world develop from a single location, or were their physical and social differences evidence for their separate genesis? Was it even possible to trace the development of humans, or had too much time passed since the dawn of their emergence?

These were some of the many questions that British ethnologists and anthropologists disputed during the middle of the nineteenth century. However, after the sudden death of Hunt in 1869, British anthropology lost its figurehead, and Huxley and some of the other leading members of the ethnological community, including John Lubbock (1834–1913) and

---

[1] E. B. Tylor, *Primitive Culture: Researches into the Development of Mythology, Philosophy, Religion, Art and Custom*, 2nd edn., 2 vols. (London: John Murray, 1889), vol. 1, pp. vii–viii.

George Busk (1807–86), were able to broker a deal between the two sides. In 1871, British ethnologists and anthropologists amalgamated and formed the Anthropological Institute of Great Britain and Ireland (RAI). Both sides were forced to make compromises and the ethnologists agreed in principle to accept the designation of 'anthropologist' as their new name, so long as Lubbock was the president of the Anthropological Institute. The hope was that under the leadership of one of the leading scientific naturalists of the mid-Victorian period, human variation studies would continue to move forward on sound empirical principles. As part of this disciplinary shift, traditional ethnological theories of human development were redefined along Darwinian and Tylorian evolutionary lines.[2]

There were two important books published on human diversity topics in 1871, which, taken together, helped to further strengthen the significance of new forms of developmental theories within the recently amalgamated discipline of anthropology. The first book was Charles Darwin's *The Descent of Man, and Selection in Relation to Sex*, which he claimed was his first major contribution to discussions on human variation. The other significant text was by Edward Burnett Tylor and was entitled *Primitive Culture: Researches into the Development of Mythology, Philosophy, Religion, Language, Art and Custom*. It was his second major contribution to the sciences relating to human diversity and his aim was to formulate a system that plotted the non-physical pronouncements of different societies – such as their religions, customs and languages – onto a developmental framework. It built upon older Prichardian ethnological techniques which attempted to link the different tribes and nations of the world to a single ancestral origin.[3]

[2] For more on the anthropological debates of the 1860s see J. W. Burrow, 'Evolution and Anthropology in the 1860's: The Anthropological Society of London, 1863–71', *Victorian Studies* 7 (1963), 137–49; G. W. Stocking, 'What's in a Name? The Origins of the Royal Anthropological Institute (1837–71)', *Man* 6 (1971), 369–90; R. Kenny, 'From the Curse of Ham to the Curse of Nature: The Influence of Natural Selection on the Debate on Human Unity before the Publication of *The Descent of Man*', *British Journal for the History of Science* 40 (2007), 363–88; H. Kuklick, 'The British Tradition', in H. Kuklick, ed., *A New History of Anthropology* (Oxford: Blackwell Publishing, 2008), pp. 52–6; E. Sera-Shriar, 'Observing Human Difference: James Hunt, Thomas Huxley and Competing Disciplinary Strategies in the 1860s', *Annals of Science* 70 (2013), 461–91. For more on Tylorian cultural development, see J. Leopold, *Culture in Comparative and Evolutionary Perspective: E.B. Tylor and the Making of Primitive Culture* (Berlin: Dietrich Reimer Verlag, 1980).
[3] C. Darwin, *The Descent of Man, and Selection in Relation to Sex*, 2 vols. (London: John Murray, 1871); E. B. Tylor, *Primitive Culture: Researches into the Development of Mythology, Philosophy, Religion, Art and Custom*, 2 vols. (London: John Murray, 1871). For more on the anthropology of Darwin and Tylor see chapter 5 of E. Sera-Shriar, *The Making of British Anthropology, 1813–1871* (London: Pickering and Chatto, 2013), pp. 147–76.

This chapter seeks to enlarge our understanding of the history of British anthropology by looking at the relationship between developmental theories and human diversity studies during the decades leading up to 1871. Traditionally, scholars have described the 1870s as the beginning of the 'evolutionist era', framing the decade as a decisive moment in the history of British anthropology. There has been a penchant to separate the 1870s from the earlier period and position it as the starting point of the modern discipline. According to the standard historiographical narrative, the formation of the RAI, in combination with the publication of Darwin's *The Descent of Man* and Tylor's *Primitive Culture*, helped to affirm the importance of evolutionary theories within British human diversity studies. George Stocking, for example, wrote: 'For several generations of anthropologists, and many still today, the work of E.B. Tylor marked a disjunctive founding moment in the history of anglophone [sic] anthropological thought.'[4] The application of evolutionary mechanisms within the discipline was presented as a novel methodological approach to studying races, and older techniques for tracing human origins were pushed to the margins of the research field.

In making this point – that evolution became a new preoccupation for anthropologists in the 1870s – scholars interested in the disciplinary history of anthropology have underemphasised the significance of other developmental processes in the works of earlier writers, including James Cowles Prichard (1786–1848), William Lawrence (1783–1867), Ernest Dieffenbach (1811–55), Robert Knox (1791–1862), James Hunt, Thomas Huxley, and Francis Galton (1822–1911). Whether they were supporting the hypothesis that humans descended from a single origin, or were rejecting evolution and other developmental theories by arguing that the races of the world were separate species, developmental frameworks were at the centre of their discussions. By comparing both the physical and cultural attributes of races, these figures wanted to extrapolate the reasons for their similitude or divergence, and the historicisation of race was an essential part of this dialectic.[5] What follows is a reconsideration of the period before 1871 that demonstrates the significance of developmental processes in the works of these nineteenth-century practitioners. What will emerge is a much more fluid picture of British anthropology that traces the application of developmental theories from

---

[4] G. W. Stocking, *Delimiting Anthropology: Occasional Essays and Reflections* (Madison, WI: University of Wisconsin Press, 2001), p. 105.

[5] Before Edward Burnett Tylor defined the word 'culture' in 1871, practitioners interested in the non-physical study of human variations referred to these qualities as moral or historical pronouncements of races. For more see Tylor, *Primitive Culture*, vol. 1, pp. 26–30.

Prichard in the 1810s to Francis Galton in the 1860s. The emergence of evolutionary thinking within the human sciences was not a sudden break from the theories of earlier developmental writers, but a reconfiguration and expansion of those ideas.[6]

The New Science of Ethnology

The growth of the British Empire from the eighteenth century onward had a huge impact on scientific race studies. As newly formed colonies settled throughout the world, the British government became increasingly interested in cataloguing the indigenous peoples inhabiting these territories. Within this cultural climate, the scientific study of races transformed in the early nineteenth century. Naturalists began honing their skills and developing sophisticated techniques for investigating human variation. Before the disciplinary formation of anthropology, researchers interested in racial diversity used an array of terminologies to describe their research programmes. These terms included the natural history of man, the scientific study of man or race, ethnology, anthropology, and ethnography. Each of these terms had varying definitions and this highlights the fractured and transitional state of the science. Practitioners interested in human variation studies recognised the problems associated with their theories and practices, and throughout the century there was growth in specialised literature relating to racial varieties. This literature was designed with the intention of stimulating discussions about humans and strengthening their investigations.

In the opening decades of the nineteenth century there was also growth in the amount of natural history data and social descriptions of races returning to Britain. Voyages of exploration led by figures such as James Cook (1728–79) and Phillip Parker King (1791–1856) generated an abundance of new information on the peoples that populated the world. This new evidence made it possible for researchers interested in human diversity to greatly expand their understandings of races. Practitioners interested in studying human variation were interested in both the physical and cultural pronouncements of different populations, and the

---

[6] For a general overview of the historiography on the history of British anthropology see G. W. Stocking, *Victorian Anthropology* (New York, NY: The Free Press, 1987), pp. 238–73; G. W. Stocking, *After Tylor: British Social Anthropology 1888–1951* (Madison, WI: University of Wisconsin Press, 1995); Stocking, *Delimiting Anthropology*, pp. 103–12; F. Barth, 'Britain and the Commonwealth', in F. Barth et al., eds., *One Discipline Four Ways: British, German, French and American Anthropology* (Chicago, IL: University of Chicago Press, 2005), pp. 3–10; Kuklick, 'The British Tradition', pp. 52–5; Sera-Shriar, *The Making of British Anthropology*, pp. 1–20.

distinction between these two modes of inquiry was not clearly demarcated in this period. Whether researchers were gleaning historical documents and travelogues for information about the habits and customs of different tribes and nations, or comparing and contrasting the anatomy and physiology of different racial groups, the primary aim of their studies was to locate any kind of evidence that would allow practitioners to trace the origins of humans. The scope of the discipline was wide-ranging in other ways. Practitioners did not necessarily prioritise the study of isolated communities on remote islands in their research. There was a wealth of material on the ethnographies of Europe.[7]

Before evolution was adopted as the focal point of racial studies in the middle of the nineteenth century, there was a long tradition of developmental theorising within the human sciences. Under the rubric of 'origin theories' that traced human lineages to different ancestral roots, early practitioners attempted to explicate the causes that created variation among the races.[8] One of the earliest British scholars to produce a comprehensive study of human diversity was James Cowles Prichard. Although he was an Anglican convert, in the early part of his life Prichard was a member of the Society of Friends. His research on human diversity was indebted to his Quaker upbringing and he was committed to the notion of racial parity. For Prichard, all humans shared a single ancestral origin, and therefore the various extra-European races had the potential to achieve the same level of civilisation as Europeans. In 1813, he published a book based on his MD dissertation, entitled *Researches into the Physical History of Man*. It was his first major contribution to human variation studies and it influenced many future texts on topics relating to racial diversity. For instance, Darwin referred to Prichard's writings in his notebook on the transmutation of species from 1838, while Tylor named his second book *Researches into the Early History of Mankind and the Development of Civilisation* (1865) after Prichard's seminal study.[9]

From the opening pages of Prichard's book, monogenetic developmental theory was at the forefront of his discussions. He attempted to

[7] Stocking, *Victorian Anthropology*, pp. 48–51; Sera-Shriar, *The Making of British Anthropology*, pp. 100–2.

[8] D. Livingstone, *Adam's Ancestors: Race, Religion and the Politics of Human Origins* (Baltimore, MD: Johns Hopkins University Press, 2008), pp. 109–36.

[9] For example see C. Darwin, 'Transmutation of Species (1838.02–1838.07)', Notebook C, MS Cambridge, University Library, p. 204; E. B. Tylor, *Researches into the Early History of Mankind and the Development of Civilisation* (London: John Murray, 1865). See also A. Desmond and J. Moore, *Darwin's Sacred Cause: Race, Slavery and the Quest for Human Origins* (London: Penguin Books, 2009), pp. 157–8; Leopold, *Culture in Comparative and Evolutionary Perspective*.

trace the history of humans and link the various tribes and nations of the world to a single ancestral origin.[10] He wrote:

In the following pages I shall endeavour to state as clearly as possible the principal facts whether physiological or historical ... whether it is probable that all mankind are the offspring of one family, and shall afterwards proceed to trace the affinities of different nations, as far as an inquiry of this nature may tend to throw any light on the physical history of man. I shall in the course of this investigation endeavour to obtain some idea of the efficacy of those causes, which have been supposed capable of producing the divestitures of the human kind [sic].[11]

For Prichard, the differences perceived among the various races of the world were of variety and not of species, and, using his training in natural history, medicine, and linguistics, he attempted to show the unity of humans and trace their developmental histories.[12] This form of monogenism was a precursor to evolution, albeit with some distinct differences. For instance, it did not include mechanisms such as the transmutation of species or natural selection. Instead, Prichard compared the physical features of different races, studied and contrasted the etymological roots of various languages, examined and brought together numerous historical accounts and classified humans according to the principles of natural history taxonomies. Because he lacked first-hand experience engaging directly with extra-European peoples *in situ*, he substantiated the credibility of his work by using the eye-witnessed reports of explorers and travellers.[13]

Over the course of the next thirty years, he reworked and broadened his study of human races and published two more editions of his *Researches*.[14] As more information on human varieties returned to Britain, Prichard was able to stockpile additional evidence and enlarge his descriptions of different races. He could also deepen his analysis of

[10] For more on Prichard see Stocking, 'What's in a Name?', 369–90; G. W. Stocking, 'From Chronology to Ethnology: James Cowles Prichard and British Anthropology 1800–1850', in J. C. Prichard, *Researches into the Physical History of Man*, ed. G. W. Stocking (Chicago, IL: University of Chicago Press, 1973), pp. ix–cx; J. Efron, *Defenders of Race: Jewish Doctors and Race Science in Fin-de-Siècle Europe* (New Haven, CT: Yale University Press, 1994), pp. 44–5; H. F. Augstein, *James Cowles Prichard's Anthropology: Remaking the Science of Man in Early Nineteenth-Century Britain* (Amsterdam: Rodopi BV, 1999); Kenny, 'From the Curse of Ham to the Curse of Nature', 363–88; Sera-Shriar, *The Making of British Anthropology*, pp. 21–52.

[11] J. C. Prichard, *Researches into the Physical History of Man* (London: John and Arthur Arch, 1813), p. 3.

[12] Prichard, *Researches* (1813), pp. 2–10.

[13] Prichard, *Researches* (1813), pp. 56–8, 213–6, 243–7.

[14] J. C. Prichard, *Researches into the Physical History of Mankind*, 2nd edn., 2 vols. (London: John and Arthur Arch, 1826); J. C. Prichard, *Researches into the Physical History of Mankind*, 3rd edn., 5 vols. (London: Sherwood, Gilbert and Piper, 1836–47).

their developmental histories. This helped him strengthen his argument for their unity. In the third edition of his *Researches*, which was published in five volumes, Prichard was able to devote an entire volume to each of the main regions of the world, with detailed accounts of the people who inhabited them. He has also been credited as the first researcher in Britain to use the term 'ethnology' to describe the scientific study of human diversity. It was mentioned in his 1843 book *The Natural History of Man*.[15]

Another British writer to discuss human diversity in the 1810s was the physician and lecturer William Lawrence. Historians have undervalued his contributions to the disciplinary history of anthropology. For the most part he has been remembered for his medical work and his dispute with his former teacher John Abernethy (1764–1831), which led to him being branded as a materialist. Despite this controversy, in the first half of the nineteenth century many of his contemporaries identified him as a progenitor of human diversity studies in Britain.[16] In his lectures *On the Natural History of Man* (1819), Lawrence examined the history of races and argued in favour of a monogenetic developmental theory for their single ancestral origin. This was similar to the arguments articulated in Prichard's *Researches*. One of the reasons for this overlap was that both of these figures based their racial classifications on the principles outlined in Johann Friedrich Blumenbach's famous work, *De Generis Humani Varietate Nativa* (1775).[17] Lawrence believed that the differences perceived between humans were of varieties and not of distinct species, and he wrote: 'we may suppose that one kind of human beings only was formed in the first instance; and account for the diversity, which is now observable, by the agency of the various physical and moral causes to which they have been subsequently exposed; in which case they will only be for

[15] T. Barfield, ed., *The Dictionary of Anthropology* (Oxford: Blackwell Publishing, 1997), p. 157; J. C. Prichard, *The Natural History of Man: Comprising Inquiries into the Modifying Influence of Physical and Moral Agencies on the Different Tribes of the Human Family*, 1st edn. (London: H. Baillière, 1843), p. 132; Sera-Shriar, *The Making of British Anthropology*, pp. 19–20.

[16] For accounts of Lawrence see J. Goodfield-Toulmin, 'Some Aspects of English Physiology: 1780–1840', *Journal of the History of Biology* 2 (1969), 283–320; L. S. Jacyna, 'Immanence or Transcendence: Theories of Life and Organisation in Britain, 1790–1835', *Isis* 74 (1983), 311–29; Stocking, *Victorian Anthropology*, pp. 43, 66, 97; A. Desmond, *The Politics of Evolution: Morphology, Medicine, and Reform* (Chicago, IL: University of Chicago Press, 1989), pp. 117–21; Efron, *Defenders of Race*, pp. 44–5; Sera-Shriar, *The Making of British Anthropology*, pp. 21–52.

[17] J. F. Blumenbach, *De Generis Humani Varietate Nativa* (Göttingen: University of Göttingen, 1775). For more on the influence of Blumenbach's work on the writings of Lawrence and Prichard see Sera-Shriar, *The Making of British Anthropology*, pp. 21–52.

different *varieties* of the same species.'[18] Under this model, the physical appearances of races, and their habits and customs, were shaped over long periods of time by different external influences.

A central problem for many early nineteenth-century writers arguing in favour of common descent was how to account for the extreme differences perceived in races. If all humans developed from a single ancestral origin, why did Africans and Europeans possess strikingly different external features and social conditions? In an attempt to solve this problem, Lawrence believed that human races should be placed on a developmental scale and brought together through their gradual variations. By comparing physical and social similarities and dissimilarities, he argued that it was possible to show how these deviations came together in a spectrum. He wrote: 'It is necessary to examine, not only the more marked differences, but also the numerous gradations by which opposite extremes are in all cases connected and gradually brought together.'[19]

This method for linking the races together through their gradual variation could be applied to any aspect of their physical conformation. If, for example, the researcher was interested in looking at skin tone, Lawrence stated that 'it is necessary to fix on the most strongly-marked tints, between which there is very conceivable intermediate shades of colour. The opposite extremes run into each other by the nicest and most delicate gradations; and it is the same in every other particular, in which the various tribes of human species differ.'[20] Researchers could also assign the same principles to the cultural pronouncements of different racial groups by examining the subtle and extreme deviations that existed among the languages, customs and habits of diverse tribes and nations. By analysing in detail the gradations that existed between the different races of the world, Lawrence believed it was possible to trace the history of humans and demonstrate their common ancestry. Along with Prichard's work outlined in the *Researches*, Lawrence's lectures on the *Natural History of Man* aimed to understand human diversity and explain racial difference through developmental processes.

There were other significant transformations occurring within British human variation studies during the first half of the nineteenth century. Before there was a society strictly devoted to the scientific study of races, the examination of human diversity was discussed by several different learned bodies. The most notable group was the Aborigines Protection

---

[18] William Lawrence, *Lectures on Physiology, Zoology, and the Natural History of Man, Delivered at the Royal College of Surgeons* (Salem, MA: Foote and Brown, 1828), p. 213.
[19] Lawrence, *Lectures*, pp. 215–16.   [20] Lawrence, *Lectures*, p. 252.

Society (APS), which was founded in 1837. The primary leaders within the APS were the Quaker abolitionists Thomas Hodgkin (1798–1866) and Thomas Buxton (1786–1845). The APS was dedicated to the preservation and protection of indigenous populations throughout the empire. Its motto was the Latin phrase *ab uno sanguine*, which translates into 'of one blood', relating to the idea of a common human ancestral origin. Politically, the APS was an important agency for vocalising the mistreatment of indigenous populations throughout the British Empire. The APS had two primary goals. The first was to establish civil freedom for extra-Europeans and recognise their rights to land and a legal status within the empire. The second was to improve them morally, physically, socially and intellectually. The rhetoric within this society was embedded in the evangelical mission, which aimed to civilise the races of the world and place them on an equal footing with Europeans. However, as Robert Kenny has noted, 'the APS, with its philanthropic and political priorities, was limited as a scientific society'.[21]

Responding to these scientific limitations at the APS, in 1843 Hodgkin and the Arctic explorer and surgeon Richard King (1811–76) organised a new group named the Ethnological Society of London (ESL). The ESL's primary aim was to create a forum in which gentlemen of science could discuss the anatomy and physiology of different races, examine historical records, trace the form and meaning of various languages, investigate the customs and habits of different cultures, present papers and debate issues such as whether all humans shared a single ancestral origin.[22] Although it was separate from the APS, the strong Quaker presence at the ESL had a significant impact on the emerging science's theories and practices. As Michael Bravo has stated, 'The driving force behind ethnology was a group of Quaker philanthropists (predominantly middle-class manufacturers and industrialists), whose commitment to religious tolerance (in contrast with the orthodox Anglicans of the day) inclined them to be relativistic and sympathetic to peoples holding religious beliefs other than

---

[21] Kenny, 'From the Curse of Ham to the Curse of Nature', 369. For more on the APS see Stocking, 'What's in a Name?', 369–70; D. Lorimer, 'Science and the Secularisation of Victorian Images of Race,' in B. Lightman, ed., *Victorian Science in Context* (Chicago, IL: University of Chicago Press, 1997), pp. 214–7; Sera-Shriar, *The Making of British Anthropology*, p. 56.

[22] For more on the Ethnological Society of London see Stocking, *Victorian Anthropology*, pp. 244–57; G. Cantor, *Quakers, Jews and Science: Religious Responses to Modernity and the Sciences in Britain 1650–1900* (Oxford: Oxford University Press, 2005), pp. 133–8; Kenny, 'From the Curse of Ham to the Curse of Nature', 363–88; S. Qureshi, *Peoples on Parade: Exhibitions, Empire and Anthropology in Nineteenth-Century Britain* (Chicago, IL: University of Chicago Press, 2011), pp. 186–7; Sera-Shriar, *The Making of British Anthropology*, pp. 53–79.

their own.'[23] These sympathies were extended to different races. Mono-genism, according to Bravo, supplied these Quaker philanthropists and abolitionists with a scientifically grounded argument against the exploit-ation of extra-Europeans and encouraged arguments in favour of racial equality through moral, physical, intellectual and social improvement.[24] Thus, set against the backdrop of the ESL's scientific activities was an underlying campaign for the civilising mission led by key members of the society such as Hodgkin, Prichard and the philanthropist and banker Henry Christy (1810–65).

From the earliest stages of its formation, members of the society were committed to expanding the discipline's theories and practices, and they initiated several schemes to encourage the collection of information on different racial types. Once collected, these materials were used to support ethnological developmental theories. The first volume of the *Journal of the Ethnological Society of London* (*JESL*) (1848) included several articles that explicated methods for collecting, analysing and representing ethnological data. This was significant because members of the ethnological community were trying to establish the research scope of their emerging discipline. Human origin theories were a major theme within this literature and these theoretical models were synonymous with developmental ideas.

In 1847, Prichard was elected to the post of President of the ESL. In his opening address, published in the first volume of the society's journal, he outlined the research boundaries of the nascent discipline. He stated, 'Ethnology is the history of human races, or of the various tribes of men who constitute the population of the world. It comprehends all that can be learned as to their origin and relations to each other.'[25] According to Prichard, ethnologists were to focus on the past to see if ethnology could reveal information about the present. He argued, 'Ethnology refers to the past. It traces the history of human families from the most remote times that are within the reach of investigation, inquires into their mutual relations, and endeavours to arrive at conclusions, either prob-able or certain, as to the question of their affinity or diversity of origin.'[26]

---

[23] M. Bravo, 'Ethnological Encounters', in Nicholas Jardine, James Secord, and Emma Spary, eds., *Cultures of Natural History* (Cambridge: Cambridge University Press, 1996), pp. 339–40.

[24] For more on the civilising mission in nineteenth-century Britain see C. Hall, *Civilising Subjects: Metropole and Colony in the English Imagination, 1830–1867* (Chicago, IL: University of Chicago Press, 2002).

[25] J. C. Prichard, 'On the Relations of Ethnology to Other Branches of Knowledge', *Journal of the Ethnological Society of London* 1 (1848), 302.

[26] Prichard, 'On the Relations of Ethnology', 302.

By studying the history of human development, ethnologists could determine the causes and influences that shaped the physical and cultural attributes of contemporary races.

Prichard continued his discussion by trying to establish the scientific credibility of ethnology through comparing its methods and theories to those of geology. This was part of his disciplinary strategy for strengthening ethnology's place within the larger scientific community. British geology was thriving during the 1840s, and many practitioners in other fields viewed its disciplinary structure as the benchmark for other sciences to emulate.[27] He wrote:

> Geology, as every one knows, is not an account of what Nature produces in the present day, but of what it has long ago produced. It is an investigation of the changes which the surface of our planet has undergone in ages long since past ... Both of these sciences [geology and ethnology] derive the data on which they found conclusions from the different departments of natural history. But ethnology likewise obtains resources for pursuing the investigation of the history of nations and of mankind from many other quarters. It derives information from the works of ancient historians, and still more extensively from the history of languages and their affiliations.[28]

Geology and ethnology both based their analysis on the principles of natural history. Moreover, Prichard also argued that geological and ethnological investigations were similar because they both examined the effect different influences had on the developmental structure of things. Whether geologists were trying to understand how the movement of tectonic plates shaped the formation of rocks, or ethnologists were analysing the impact new food resources had on human populations, they were both looking at how these changes 'in ages long since past' stimulated and altered their specimens over time.

Aside from geology, other disciplines also offered ethnologists useful techniques for understanding human varieties and their development. Prichard, for instance, borrowed methods from natural history, anatomy and physiology, historical studies and linguistics. He had acquired an extensive knowledge of each of these modes of investigation from his time at Edinburgh between 1804 and 1808, and in his later studies at both Cambridge and Oxford between 1808 and 1809.[29] For Prichard, all

---

[27] For more on the disciplinary history of geology in nineteenth-century Britain see M. Rudwick, *The Great Devonian Controversy: The Shaping of Scientific Knowledge among Gentlemanly Specialists* (Chicago, IL: University of Chicago Press, 1985); R. O'Connor, *The Earth on Show: Fossils and the Poetics of Popular Science, 1802–1856* (Chicago, IL: University of Chicago Press, 2007).

[28] Prichard, 'On the Relations of Ethnology', 303–4.

[29] Prichard, 'On the Relations of Ethnology', 304. For more on Prichard's training at Edinburgh and Oxbridge, and its influence on his ethnological methods, see Stocking,

of these fields of inquiry provided ethnologists with specialised skills for identifying, classifying, analysing and representing different kinds of data relating to humans. This was useful for explicating the reasons why different races possessed specific attributes. In his address he also described the various writers who he believed had contributed important theories and practices to ethnological investigations. In the case of anatomical and physiological observations, he included brief sketches of the German anatomist Johann Friedrich Blumenbach (1752–1840), the Dutch anatomist Petrus Camper (1722–89) and the Swedish anatomist Anders Retzius (1796–1860).[30] Each of these figures, Prichard argued, had formulated important systems for examining and comparing human crania. Prichard also explained why it was important for ethnologists to use the observations of historical actors to expand their understanding of human history. He stated:

Historical researches that may be applicable to ethnology, must occupy a wide field. They must collect all the different lights that can be brought to bear on the history of nations, whether from the testimony of ancient writers, or from manners, customs, and institutions – from old popular traditions, poetry, mythology – from the remains of ancient art, such as architecture, sculpture inscriptions – and from sepulchral relics discovered in many countries, consisting of embalmed bodies, or more often the mere skulls and skeletons of the ancient inhabitants, which furnish the most authentic testimony, where it can be procured, as to the physical characters of various races of people.[31]

Prichard's presidential address at the 1847 meeting of the ESL articulated a comprehensive method for collecting ethnological data, analysing the material and representing its results. Using a combination of physical descriptions of races and documentation of their customs, habits, languages and histories, he believed ethnologists could postulate a theory that explained the origin of humans and the causes that created their physical and social deviations.

In the same volume of the *JESL* the German physician Ernest Dieffenbach, who had been living in London for several years, published a paper entitled 'On the Study of Ethnology'. In his paper he wanted to show the reciprocal relationship between the British Empire and ethnology. He believed that Britain, above all other European nations, was

'From Chronology to Ethnology', pp. ix–cx; Augstein, *James Cowles Prichard's Anthropology*, pp. 3–5; Sera-Shriar, *The Making of British Anthropology*, pp. 21–52. For more on the medical programme at the university of Edinburgh see L. S. Jacyna, *Philosophical Whigs: Medicine, Science and Citizenship in Edinburgh, 1789–1848* (London: Routledge, 1994); L. Rosner, *Medical Education in the Age of Improvement: Edinburgh Students and Apprentices, 1760–1826* (Edinburgh: Edinburgh University Press, 1991).
[30] Prichard, 'On the Relations of Ethnology', 304–7.
[31] Prichard, 'On the Relations of Ethnology', 310–1.

able to expand ethnological studies, because its territorial settlements stretched across the globe. The progress of the discipline, according to Dieffenbach, was tied to the growth of British imperialism. He wrote:

England encircles the globe in glorious enterprise: her sons come in contact with the Esquimaux [sic] of the Arctic Seas, with the red hunter of Northern America, with the cunning Chinese, with the mild Hindoo [sic], and with the mountaineer of Affghanistan [sic]. The same is the case in the Southern Hemisphere. New empires are springing up in New Zealand, New South-Wales, Van Diemen's Land, and at the Cape of Good Hope, where the Englishman has intercourse with man in the most opposite stages of development.[32]

Under Dieffenbach's model, the British Empire provided ethnology with a massive network of informants who collected data on different populations living throughout the world. The makeup of this network was fairly diverse and included travellers, naturalists, colonial officers, missionaries and any other kind of European resident living abroad. Central to this process of acquiring data was identifying and recording the developmental stage of each race. Once these informants collected their data for ethnologists, they were to send the material back to Britain for members of the ESL to examine in their studies. Dieffenbach stated that the ESL was to be 'a focus for Travellers of all nations, where information regarding the human race may be received and given – a Society which will not reject the minutest [sic] detail that may elucidate the history of the human race, and spread an interest in the subject among the different classes of the community'.[33]

As was the case in Prichard's work, Dieffenbach argued that ethnologists were to incorporate data from many different fields of inquiry. This included historical accounts, linguistic records, geographical surveys and anatomical and physiological descriptions. Using these different sources, Dieffenbach argued that ethnologists could look at human variation in two ways. He stated: '1st, we may glance at them as they present themselves at the present moment, contemporaneously; and 2dly, we may not only trace back the nations to their sources, and from actual remains and

---

[32] E. Dieffenbach, 'The Study of Ethnology', *Journal of the Ethnological Society of London* 1 (1848), 16.

[33] Dieffenbach, 'The Study of Ethnology', 16. For more on nineteenth-century colonial networks of exchange see Z. Laidlaw, *Colonial Connections 1815–1845: Patronage, the Information Revolution and Colonial Government* (Manchester: Manchester University Press, 2005); A. Secord, 'Corresponding Interests: Artisans and Gentlemen in Nineteenth-Century Natural History', *British Journal for the History of Science* 27 (1994), 383–408; A. Secord, Artisan Naturalists: Science as Popular Culture in Nineteenth-Century England (PhD diss., University of London, 2002); J. Endersby, *Imperial Nature: Joseph Hooker and the Practice of Victorian Science* (Chicago, IL: University of Chicago Press, 2008).

historical survey, give a true picture of the changes which their physical nature has undergone in the vicissitudes of time, but we may bring to light the nations which have disappeared.'[34]

Linguistics, metagraphy and philology were key components of this methodological approach to studying humans. For Dieffenbach, comparative language studies helped the researcher trace the history of different racial populations and demonstrate their cognitive and social development. He stated:

Language distinguishes man from the inferior animals ... From his language we can perceive the structure and disposition of his mind, his prevailing passions and tendencies: in language the changes and revolutions which the mind of a nation has undergone have left indelible traces: its structure alone allows us to search into the character of a people, and throw a light into the dark labyrinth of their history, if no written or monumental record and not even a tradition, has been preserved.[35]

Language was a valuable source for ethnologists to utilise in their studies. By comparing and contrasting the grammar and vocabulary of different racial groups, figures such as Dieffenbach and others believed it was possible to show links between various peoples and their development over time. Moreover, according to Dieffenbach, language was a window into the minds of different races because it provided ethnologists with a mechanism for understanding how different groups understood and interacted with the world. In short, Dieffenbach's paper 'On the Study of Ethnology' built upon the ethnological frameworks of earlier scholars, such as Prichard and Lawrence, from the first half of the nineteenth century, and outlined a scheme that placed different racial varieties on a developmental scale. Using different kinds of data such as anatomical and physiological descriptions of tribes, documentation of languages, customs and habits and historical records, these early ethnologists believed it was possible to trace the history of humans.

Not all researchers interested in human diversity, however, argued in favour of their common origin. During the 1850s and 1860s British ethnology witnessed the emergence of several competing analytical models. There were some figures that argued against monogenism. They believed that the differences perceived in humans were evidence for their separate origins, and that the races inhabiting the globe were all distinct species. Others took a different view and stated that too much time had passed since the dawn of humanity; therefore, accurately tracing the deep

[34] Dieffenbach, 'The Study of Ethnology', 17.
[35] Dieffenbach, 'The Study of Ethnology', 21. See also Bravo, 'Ethnological Encounters', p. 339.

history of human development was improbable. These figures believed that more emphasis was to be placed on the contemporary state of races. Robert Knox and James Hunt were two of the main instigators of the promotion of alternative research models in Britain. Both of them challenged the monogenism of figures such as Prichard, Lawrence and Dieffenbach from the earlier part of the century.

The Emergence of British Anthropology

Knox was one of the most controversial and outspoken British figures to engage in ethnological debates during the middle of the nineteenth century. He began his career during the 1820s as a leading anatomical instructor in Edinburgh. However, after his involvement in the West Port murders between 1827 and 1828, his reputation as a respected gentleman of science steadily declined.[36] Nevertheless, during the 1840s and 1850s Knox had a small group of loyal followers such as Hunt, Charles Carter Blake (1840–87) and Henry Lonsdale (1816–76). All of them were vocal supporters of his work, and they praised his abilities as a scientific and medical practitioner.[37]

Knox's most famous contribution to human diversity studies was his book *The Races of Men* (1850). His theoretical framework differed extensively from the work of other figures such as Prichard and Lawrence, and for him an individual's race was everything. It shaped not only a person's physical structure but also their social behaviour.[38] In the preface to

[36] The William Burke and William Hare murders occurred in a neighbourhood of Edinburgh known as West Port. For details of the Burke and Hare murders see Anon., *An Account of the Life of William Burke, Who Was Executed on Wednesday the 28th Day of January, 1829, For Murder: With the Confession He Made While under Sentence of Death* (Dunfermline: John Miller, 1829); Anon., 'A Sketch of the Life and Writings of Robert Knox, the Anatomist', *Examiner* 3279 (1870), 773–4; Isobel Rae, *Knox the Anatomist* (Edinburgh: Oliver and Boyd, 1964), pp. 122–54; Henry Lonsdale, *A Sketch of the Life and Writings of Robert Knox, the Anatomist* (London: Macmillan, 1870), pp. 73–89.

[37] Knox's followers regularly promoted his importance to science and medicine. For examples see C. C. Blake, 'The Life of Robert Knox, the Anatomist. A Sketch of His Life and Writings by Henry Lonsdale', *Journal of Anthropology* 1 (1871), 332–8; J. Hunt, 'On the Origin of the Anthropological Review and Its Connection with the Anthropological Society', *Anthropological Review* 6 (1868), 431–42.

[38] For more on Knox's ethnology and its significance to the history of British anthropology see E. Sera-Shriar, 'Ethnology in the Metropole: Robert Knox, Robert Gordon Latham and Local Sites of Observational Training', *Studies in History and Philosophy of Biological and Biomedical Sciences* 42 (2011), 486–96. See also Stocking, *Victorian Anthropology*, pp. 65–9, 245–7; E. Richards, 'The "Moral Anatomy" of Robert Knox: The Interplay between Biological and Social Thought in Victorian Scientific Naturalism', *Journal of the History of Biology* 22 (1989), 373–436; Efron, *Defenders of Race*, pp. 45–57; Desmond and Moore, *Darwin's Sacred Cause*, pp. 38–45, 103–4, 188–91, 304–6, 335–41, 381–3;

The Races of Men, he positioned himself in opposition to the monogenetic developmental narratives of figures such as Prichard and Lawrence. He stated: 'The "Fragment" I here present to the world has cost me much thought and anxiety; the views it contains being so wholly at variance with long received doctrines, stereotyped prejudices, national delusions, and a physiology and philosophy ... as old at least as the Hebrew record.'[39] He continued by arguing:

The human character, individual and national, is traceable solely to the nature of that race to which the individual or nation belongs, is a statement which I know must meet with the severest opposition. It runs counter to nearly all the chronicles of events, called histories; it shocks the theories of statesmen, theologians, [and] philanthropists of all shades.[40]

Knox was ruthless in his attack on traditional British ethnological theories and practices. He referred to researchers such as Prichard and Lawrence as 'hack compilers' because they based their examinations on the reports of travellers. He also argued that these ethnologists were committed to 'false doctrines' such as monogenism and the civilising mission, and he believed that his opponents would omit his divergent theories and discussions from their work because it would discredit their research.[41]

Knox presented a vastly different approach to the study of human variation by forwarding a polygenetic view, which described each race as a separate species. Unlike other ethnological models, which examined racial histories through developmental frameworks such as monogenism, Knox did not attempt to trace human origins because he believed there was insufficient evidence available to accurately show their genesis. He wrote: 'Of man's origin we know nothing correctly; we know not when he first appeared in space; [and] his place in time, then, is unknown.'[42] He continued by criticising the chronologies of other researchers who had attempted to trace the histories of different races, and he stated: 'how worthless are these chronologies! How replete with error human history has been proved to be.'[43] For Knox, human origin theories were a secondary concern for any scientific study of races. Instead, the primary aim was to observe and describe the current state of different peoples. French naturalism was central to Knox's analytical approach, and his work was heavily influenced by comparative anatomy and transcendentalism.

A. W. Bates, *The Anatomy of Robert Knox: Murder, Mad Science and Medical Regulation in Nineteenth-Century Edinburgh* (Eastbourne: Sussex Academic Press, 2010).
[39] R. Knox, *The Races of Man: A Fragment* (London: Henry Renshaw, 1850), p. 7.
[40] Knox, *The Races of Man*, p. 7.   [41] Knox, *The Races of Man*, p. 8.
[42] Knox, *The Races of Man*, p. 9.   [43] Knox, *The Races of Man*, p. 9.

In 1821, Knox had visited Paris, and during his time in the French capital he had studied comparative anatomy and transcendentalism with the naturalists Georges Cuvier (1769–1832) and Étienne Geoffroy Saint-Hilaire (1772–1844). For Knox, comparative anatomy provided researchers with a practical method for organising humans into groupings based on their similarities and differences, while transcendentalism furnished them with a basis for all of their theories on races. He argued that 'transcendental anatomy ... affords us a glimpse and a hope of a true "theory of nature"'[44] and continued by asserting that the physical structure of different humans was the cornerstone of his ethnology. He stated:

> The basis of the view I take of man is his Physical structure; if I may so say his Zoological history. To know this must be the first step in all inquiries into man's history: all abstractions, neglecting or despising this great element, the physical character and constitution of man, his mental and corporeal attributes must, of necessity be at the least Utopian if not erroneous.[45]

Knox promoted a racial theory that argued that all humans were biologically determined. Under this model, all non-physical attributes were dependent upon physical conditions. He argued that if an African were educated in Britain and enculturated into European society, their intellectual abilities and social position would never exceed the 'natural capabilities' of their race. Moreover, even if their immersion into a culture influenced their behaviour, he still believed they would ultimately remain biologically distinct. He wrote: 'If any one insists that a Negro or Tasmanian accidentally born in England becomes thereby an Englishman, I yield the point; but should he further insist, that he, the said Negro or Tasmanian, may become also a Saxon or Scandinavian, I must contend against so ludicrous an error.'[46]

Knox's analytical framework was markedly different from the monogenism of Prichard and Lawrence. He viewed all humans as distinct from one another and stated: 'With me, race, or hereditary descent, is everything; it stamps the man. Setting aside all theories, I have endeavoured to view mankind as they now exist, divided as they are, and seem always to have been, into distinct races.'[47] Instead of tracing the developmental history of races by demonstrating the causes that shaped their physical and non-physical features, Knox wanted to place more emphasis on their contemporary appearances and social behaviours. It was a highly controversial approach to studying human variation and it clashed with the religious and social ideologies of some of the leading figures within the

[44] Knox, *The Races of Man*, p. 20.   [45] Knox, *The Races of Man*, p. 9.
[46] Knox, *The Races of Man*, p. 12.   [47] Knox, *The Races of Man*, p. 13.

community, including Hodgkin, Christy and Prichard. All three of these figures were staunch abolitionists and monogenists who were committed to the civilising mission that aimed to improve the moral, physical, intellectual and social conditions of extra-Europeans. By the start of the 1860s, other researchers had built upon and further expanded Knox's approach to studying races. The most notable figure was James Hunt.

Debates about disciplinary theories and practices came to a head in 1863 when Hunt and the explorer, colonial agent and writer Richard Francis Burton (1821–90) organised a new group called the Anthropological Society of London (ASL). Hunt, who became the leader of the new society, wanted anthropologists to distinguish themselves from ethnologists by prioritising research that focused on the physical conformation of races. By contrast, he positioned ethnology as a humanistic pursuit that was influenced by Christian morality and sentimentality. Instead of anatomical and physiological studies, ethnologists focused on the philology, material culture, customs and habits and social organisation of human varieties. Hunt was also anti-evolution and, under his research model, anthropologists were to prioritise the current state of humans. This is significant because it was during the 1860s that the Darwinian evolutionary model began replacing older forms of developmental theories regarding humans.[48]

To substantiate the scientific criteria on which researchers based their analyses, Hunt argued for the application of the Baconian method of induction. He asserted that Baconianism, with its emphasis on facts, was the most reliable way to do scientific research. He wrote:

It has been solely the application of this [Baconian] method which has given such weight to our deliberations and our deductions. Loyalty to facts with regard to ... anthropology brought us face to face with popular assumptions, and the contest has resulted in victory to those who used the right method. Having then seen the advantage of conducting our investigations ... according to the inductive method.[49]

[48] For more on Hunt and the Anthropological Society of London see Burrow, 'Evolution and Anthropology in the 1860's', 137–49; Stocking, 'What's in a Name?', 369–90; Stocking, *Victorian Anthropology*, pp. 247–55; F. Spencer, 'Hunt, James (1833–1869)', in F. Spencer, ed., *History of Physical Anthropology*, 2 vols. (London: Garland Publishing, Inc., 1997), vol. 1, pp. 506–8; Qureshi, *Peoples on Parade*, pp. 211–20; Kenny, 'From the Curse of Ham to the Curse of Nature', 363–88; Kuklick, 'The British Tradition', pp. 52–5; Sera-Shriar, 'Observing Human Difference', 461–91.
[49] J. Hunt, 'On Physio-Anthropology, Its Aim and Method', *Journal of the Anthropological Society of London* 5 (1867), ccxii. For more on Baconianism and disciplinary formation in nineteenth-century Britain see Rudwick, *The Great Devonian Controversy*, pp. 24–5; R. Porter, *The Making of Geology: Earth Science in Britain 1660–1815* (Cambridge: Cambridge University Press, 1977), pp. 66–70; R. Yeo, 'Scientific Method and the

For Hunt, the scientific study of races had to be based on directly observable evidence, and he criticised research which attempted to explain the origin of humans because he believed there was insufficient data available to substantiate any origin theory. He wrote: 'What time has not been wasted in idle speculations, assumptions and theories respecting the history of Man!'[50]

Hunt was particularly resistant to the application of Darwinian principles within anthropological research. Challenging Darwinian evolution became a key preoccupation for him in the late 1860s. In his 1867 article 'On the Doctrine of Continuity Applied to Anthropology', he wrote: 'All science must be based on facts or on philosophical deductive reasoning.' He continued by stating that he was 'willing to admit that the mutability of species is a fair and philosophical hypothesis', but that it was 'neither warranted by scientific facts, by logical reasoning, nor by philosophical assumption'.[51] According to Hunt, Darwinian evolutionary theory, and specifically the mutability of species, was an interesting hypothesis but required more extensive observable data to substantiate its claims.

The application of Darwinism to human diversity studies was further problematic because Hunt argued that Huxley and the naturalist Alfred Russel Wallace (1823–1913), who was the co-discoverer of the theory of natural selection, misrepresented Darwin's work within their own research. He stated, 'There are no facts at present which throw any light on the origin of mankind. Mr. Darwin is only to be blamed because he has not curbed the restless impatience of his disciples. The mischief is being done by Professor Huxley a[n]d Mr. Wallace; but Mr. Darwin has hitherto refrained from coming forward to protest against the abuse which is being made of his theory.'[52] Accordingly, for Hunt, the mutability of species 'may be true when applied to botany or zoology', but there was not enough evidence to support its application in anthropology.[53]

Hunt was equally critical of natural selection, and argued that Darwin's commitment to slow change over vast periods of time was problematic

Rhetoric of Science in Britain 1830–1917', in J. Schuster and R. Yeo, eds., *The Politics and Rhetoric of Scientific Method* (Dordrecht: D. Reidel Publishing Company, 1986), pp. 259–97.

[50] J. Hunt, 'Introductory Address on the Study of Anthropology', *Anthropological Review* 1 (1863), 2.

[51] J. Hunt, 'On the Doctrine of Continuity Applied to Anthropology', *Anthropological Review* 5 (1867), 111–2.

[52] Hunt, 'On the Doctrine of Continuity', 113. Darwin did not openly discuss human evolution until the publication of *The Descent of Man* in 1871. In it he responded to some of the criticisms levelled at him by the anthropologicals. See Darwin, *The Descent of Man*, vol. 1, p. 228. See also Sera-Shriar, *The Making of British Anthropology*, pp. 147–8.

[53] Hunt, 'On the Doctrine of Continuity', 113.

because it lacked sufficient observable evidence.[54] Moreover, he asserted that believing in natural selection was no different to believing in 'divine intervention'. He wrote that there was 'no difference between natural selection with unlimited power, and [what] the other calls in a Deity provided in the same manner'. Hunt stated:

> Mr. Darwin is most successful in his sneers at those who resort to the hypothesis of independent creation to explain the existing species of plants and animals, apparently entirely oblivious to the fact that he lays himself open to exactly the same charge. Men that sneer at special creation must expect in their turn to be treated in a similar manner. Spontaneous generation forms no part of Darwinism. When spontaneous generation is proved to be true, Darwinism will necessarily, by implication, be found to be false ... Future generations will be able to decide on the respective merits of the two systems better than we can do at this time.[55]

Hunt prioritised physical descriptions of contemporary races over studies that attempted to trace the developmental histories of humans. Under this model, the Baconian method of induction was strategically used as the cornerstone of his anthropological framework. Observable facts such as anatomical and physiological data lay at the foundation of any good study of races, and non-physical examinations of humans, such as linguistic and philological comparisons or analyses of customs and habits, were positioned as a secondary concern. Any theory attempting to explain human origins unsubstantiated by what Hunt believed to be sufficient visible evidence was framed as erroneous. There were many who argued against Hunt's anti-developmental methods for studying races, and during the 1860s figures such as Huxley and Galton continued to champion the importance of evolutionary theories within human diversity studies.

Ethnology Reconsidered

Although early developmental models by figures such as Prichard and Lawrence varied substantially from later Darwinian theories, they still resonated with the growing community of scientific naturalists such as Lubbock, Busk, Tylor and Huxley, who were becoming increasingly active within British ethnological circles during the middle of the nineteenth century. By the 1860s, the leadership of the discipline was also

---

[54] Hunt attacked the theory of natural selection in his response to Huxley's article 'On the Methods and Results of Ethnology'. See J. Hunt, 'On the Application of the Principle of Natural Selection to Anthropology, in Reply to the Views Advocated by Some of Mr Darwin's Disciples', *Anthropological Review* 4 (1866), 320–40; T. H. Huxley, 'On the Methods and Results of Ethnology', *Fortnightly Review* 1 (1865), 257–77.

[55] Hunt, 'On the Doctrine of Continuity', 117–8.

transforming, as members of the older generation such as Hodgkin, Christy and the explorer, philologist and surgeon John Crawfurd (1783–1868) were slowly passing away. Their deaths created new opportunities for the younger generation to reform the theories and practices of the research field. What this meant was that it became gradually more possible to redefine ethnological developmental theories along evolutionary and secular lines. The fundamental difference between the earlier monogenetic writings of figures such as Prichard and the later evolutionary ideas of figures such as Darwin was that these newer theories articulated comprehensive mechanisms for explaining the causes that produced deviation in nature. As Adrian Desmond and James Moore wrote in their book *Darwin's Sacred Cause*, 'Prichard stockpiled evidence to prove the races were one; Darwin went beyond that to plot hypothetical mechanisms that splinter them, push them apart – in short, point out how they could have originated naturally'.[56]

During the 1860s, Huxley in particular was actively engaged in reforming the theories and practices of a broad range of disciplines, including botany, zoology, anatomy, physiology and ethnology. His strategy for reforming most natural sciences followed a similar process. First, he would introduce Darwinian evolutionary principles, such as the mutability of species, into the discipline. This was fairly straightforward for ethnology because many of its practitioners already argued in favour of common descent, and issues such as whether the races of the world were varieties of the same species or distinct species of separate origins were at the forefront of ethnological discussions.[57] The next step for Huxley was to make the science ideologically neutral and separate it from both religious and political debates. It was a highly effective strategy for achieving an influential social status because Huxley and other scientific naturalists such as Lubbock and the physicist John Tyndall (1820–93) could emphasise the important and impartial perspective the sciences had on a broad range of issues.[58] The third step for Huxley was

---

[56] Desmond and Moore, *Darwin's Sacred Cause*, p. 158.

[57] Huxley's drive to place all scientific disciplines onto an evolutionary framework is far too big a subject for discussion here. For more on Huxley and evolutionary theory see M. Di Gregorio, *T.H. Huxley's Place in Natural Science* (New Haven, CT: Yale University Press, 1984), pp. 53–67. For more on the relationship between ethnology and Darwinism and the debates between monogenists and polygenists see chapter 8 of Desmond and Moore, *Darwin's Sacred Cause*, pp. 199–227.

[58] For more on the debates relating to politics, religion and human origins in the nineteenth century see Livingstone, *Adam's Ancestors*, pp. 109–36; M. Fichman, 'Biology and Politics: Defining the Boundaries', in B. Lightman, ed., *Victorian Science in Context* (Chicago, IL: University of Chicago Press, 1997), pp. 94–101.

to villainise researchers in the discipline who did not adopt an evolutionary stance and scientific neutrality.[59]

Building upon the earlier research programmes of figures such as Prichard, Lawrence and others, Huxley promoted a monogenetic argument for the common origin of humans, which he based on the principles of Darwinian evolution and natural history classificatory practices. In his 1865 article 'On the Methods and Results of Ethnology', published in the *Fortnightly Review*, Huxley outlined various techniques for understanding human difference and tracing the history of races. He departed from earlier ethnological developmental theories in two ways. First, he insisted that human evolution be linked to the larger biological picture of the world. Humans did not possess a privileged position within Huxley's ethnological system and they followed the same natural laws as all other organic beings. Second, he argued that the research field should be separated from ideologically driven campaigns such as the civilising mission, which was wrapped up in both political and religious dogmatism. One of Huxley's key concerns for British ethnology was changing the terminologies that researchers utilised in their studies. He argued that terms such as 'varieties', 'races' and 'species' were often associated with the vocational and socio-political agendas of different key figures within human diversity studies.

Huxley wanted to distance British ethnology from all political and religious discourses and keep it ideologically neutral. Ethnologists therefore were to replace their older terminologies, which he viewed as politically motivated, with a new lexicon. He wrote:

I speak of 'persistent modifications' or 'stocks' rather than of 'varieties,' or 'races,' or 'species,' because each of these last well-known terms implies, on the part of its employer, a preconceived opinion touching one of those problems, the solution of which is the ultimate object of the science; and in regard to which, therefore, ethnologists are especially bound to keep their minds open and their judgments freely balanced.[60]

Huxley's argument for replacing the older disciplinary language with newer terms was part of his strategy for linking ethnology's vocabulary

---

[59] For more on Huxley's vocational strategy see E. Caudill, 'The Bishop-Eaters: The Publicity Campaign for Darwin and on the Origin of Species', *Journal of the History of Ideas* 55 (1994), 441–60; Paul White, *Thomas Huxley: Making the "Man of Science"* (Cambridge: Cambridge University Press, 2003), pp. 51–8; J. Elwick, *Styles of Reasoning in the British Life Sciences: Shared Assumptions, 1820–1858* (London: Pickering and Chatto, 2007), pp. 131–59; B. Lightman, *Victorian Popularizers of Science: Designing Nature for New Audiences* (Chicago, IL: University of Chicago Press, 2007), pp. 359–61.

[60] Huxley, 'On the Methods and Results of Ethnology', 257.

to Darwinism. Despite his claims that he was distancing the science from the political and religious orientations of its practitioners, Huxley was trying to assert his own agenda in ethnology. Hunt, who was Huxley's most vocal opponent within human diversity studies, argued that the new terminologies were not ideologically neutral, and that their meanings were shaped by personal biases. He argued that the inclusion of Darwinian language within human diversity studies was part of Huxley's career-building tactics in pursuit of a leading role within the discipline. In 1866 Hunt openly voiced his criticisms of Huxley and Darwinism in his article 'On the Application of the Principle of Natural Selection to Anthropology', writing: 'the term "persistent modification" equally involves a theory on the part of those who use it.'[61] As such, the application to ethnology of this new terminology was part of Huxley's larger motivating ambitions to transform the life sciences along evolutionary principles.

Huxley also tried to reform the discipline in other ways. For many ethnologists during the first half of the nineteenth century, philology and linguistics were important tools for tracing the history of races and linking them to a single origin. Huxley saw the value of these kinds of studies, but argued that researchers had to be more critically aware of its limitations. For example, was it possible that the languages of different races were altered in certain cases through their contact with neighbouring populations? If this was the case, the commonalities between their languages were not because the two populations derived from a single origin. Their similarities were developed through cultural contact with each other. Huxley wrote:

it seems to me obvious that, though, in the absence of any evidence to the contrary, unity of languages may afford a certain presumption in favour of the unity of stock of the people speaking those languages, it cannot be held to prove that unity of stock, unless philologers are prepared to demonstrate, that no nation can lose its language and acquire that of a distinct nation, without a change of blood corresponding with the change of language.[62]

Huxley was even prepared to critique Prichard's use of linguistic data, because he believed that it lacked an introspective analysis of philological techniques. In addition, he claimed that Prichardian ethnology placed more weight on language than it did on anatomy and physiology. Accordingly, Huxley argued that ethnologists were to prioritise the physical study of humans because it was a more empirically grounded

[61] Hunt, 'On the Application of the Principle of Natural Selection', 322–3.
[62] Huxley, 'On the Methods and Results of Ethnology', 260.

approach to examining races. He wrote: 'it is plain that the zoological court of appeal is the highest for the ethnologist, and that no evidence can be set against that derived from physical character'.[63] Although Huxley was critical of Prichard's language studies, he did approve of his classificatory practices when organising humans into groupings based on their anatomy and physiology. Huxley based his racial taxonomy on the system outlined by Prichard in the various editions of the *Researches*, and it formed the bulk of his analysis in his 1865 article.[64]

Although Huxley was steadfast about applying Darwinian principles to ethnology, he did have some reservations about the theory of natural selection. First, he argued that Darwin's hypothesis was excellent because it was naturalistic, but it required further evidence. Second, Huxley remained unconvinced by Darwin's commitment to the principle that 'Nature makes no leaps', and he argued that the smallest change at the molecular level could create sudden and major transformations in an organism. Therefore, Huxley did not staunchly support natural selection, as he did other Darwinian theories such as transmutationism.[65] In summary, Huxley built upon and transformed the theories and methods of earlier nineteenth-century British ethnologists. One of Huxley's central concerns was raising the scientific criteria on which researchers based their arguments. As was the case with his predecessors, he argued in favour of a common origin for all races. To demonstrate their unity, he adapted evolutionary language and principles to the discipline's theories and practices and neutralised ethnology's political and religious stance. Moreover, Huxley did not prioritise human development over the rest of the animal kingdom, and every race was shaped by the same evolutionary mechanisms as the rest of the organic world.

There were other mid-nineteenth-century practitioners, who were applying evolutionary principles to human variation studies. The Victorian polymath Francis Galton utilised Darwin's theories in his writings on human races, and in his book *Hereditary Genius* (1869) he attempted to trace the developmental history of human intelligence. He believed that the cognitive abilities of individuals were passed down generationally. They were transmitted through the mechanism of acquired

---

[63] Huxley, 'On the Methods and Results of Ethnology', 263.
[64] Huxley, 'On the Methods and Results of Ethnology', 263–70.
[65] T. H. Huxley, 'Time and Life: Mr. Darwin's "Origin of Species"', *Macmillan's Magazine* 2 (1859), 148. See also M. Bartholomew, 'Huxley's Defense of Darwin', *Annals of Science* 32 (1975), 525–35; B. Lightman, *The Origins of Agnosticism: Victorian Unbelief and the Limits of Knowledge* (Baltimore, MD: Johns Hopkins University Press, 1987), pp. 156–7; G. Radick, *The Simian Tongue: The Long Debate about Animal Language* (Chicago, IL: University of Chicago Press, 2007), pp. 32–3.

characteristics. In his 'Preface' he stated: 'The idea of investigating the subject of hereditary genius occurred to me during the course of a purely ethnological inquiry, into the mental peculiarities of races.'[66] Using his training in mathematics, which he studied at Cambridge during the 1840s, Galton statistically analysed individuals and groups, and determined the average intelligence of humans. Once this was calculated, he attempted to show the causes that strengthened or weakened the cognitive abilities of people. He also plotted individuals and groups onto a developmental scheme to see whether they were above or below the average intelligence of humans.[67]

In his chapter entitled 'The Comparative Worth of Different Races', Galton began by stating that each human group was conditioned by natural laws. As a survival mechanism, they all had to adapt to their own environments or perish. The result, he argued, was that 'Every long-established race has necessarily its peculiar fitness for the conditions under which it has lived, owing to the sure operation of Darwin's law of natural selection'.[68] He continued by comparing the aptitudes and skills of different races and ranking them based on their abilities. This system, according to Galton, allowed him to show the developmental stage of each race. Galton believed that the greatest civilisations had developed in Europe. At the core of his argument was the idea that Europeans would take over the world unless other populations learned to adapt to their superior qualities and compete with them. He stated, 'the most intelligent variety is sure to prevail in the battle of life'.[69] Galton's civilising rhetoric differed from the earlier discussions articulated by figures such as Hodgkin, Prichard and Christy at the ESL. He was not promoting the moral, physical, intellectual and social improvement of extra-Europeans. Instead, Galton naturalised racial inequality. Races achieved higher levels of civilisation by altering their behaviour, or risked being weeded out by nature. The success of a people was completely dependent on inherent abilities that were biologically determined.

Galton's examination was highly Eurocentric and placed more value on European skills. Thus, for example, races were seen as intellectually

[66] F. Galton, *Hereditary Genius: An Inquiry into Its Laws and Consequences* (London: Macmillan and Co., 1869), p. v.
[67] Galton, *Hereditary Genius*, p. vi, pp. 1–6. For more information on Francis Galton's *Hereditary Genius* and his larger anthropological and ethnological work see K. Pearson, *The Life, Letters and Labours of Francis Galton*, 3 vols. (Cambridge: Cambridge University Press, 1914–30), vol. 2, pp. 70–130; D. W. Forrest, *Francis Galton: The Life and Work of a Victorian Genius* (London: Paul Elek, 1974), pp. 133–8; N. W. Gillham, *A Life of Sir Francis Galton: From African Exploration to the Birth of Eugenics* (Oxford: Oxford University Press, 2001), p. 195.
[68] Galton, *Hereditary Genius*, p. 336.   [69] Galton, *Hereditary Genius*, p. 336.

superior if they had produced lots of judges and physicians. Using his statistical methods for determining the intelligence of humans, Galton compared the races of the world and counted the number of eminent and influential figures they had produced. He wrote: 'Let us, then, compare the negro race with the Anglo-Saxon, with respect to those qualities alone which are capable of producing judges, statesmen, commanders, men of literature and science, poets, artists and divines.'[70] He argued that overall Africans had produced far less men of standing, and he calculated that 'the average intellectual standard of the negro race is some two grades below our own'.[71] Thus, according to Galton, they had not developed to the same intellectual stage as the British. However, he did not consider how the social conditions of Africans differed from those of Europeans. In his analysis there was no mention of the limited (if any) educational opportunities for Africans to acquire the skills necessary for achieving eminent possessions in medicine, law or the military. Europeans' success in these fields was interpreted as a mark of their racial ascendency, not cultural affluence.

Galton had an even lesser estimation of Australian aborigines. He believed that they were three grades lower than Europeans. Interestingly, he went on to say that he did not have enough data to elaborate further on his reasons for giving them this low ranking. He wrote, 'The Australian Type is at least one grade below the African negro. I possess a few serviceable data about the natural capacity of the Australian, but not sufficient to induce me to invite the reader to consider them.'[72] In addition to comparing Europeans with extra-European races, Galton also examined groups that lived within the same regions. He argued, for instance, that 'The average standard of the Lowland Scotch and the English North-country men is decidedly a fraction of a grade superior to that of the ordinary English, because the number of the former who attain to eminence is far greater than the proportionate number of their race would have led us to expect'.[73] According to Galton, there were more intelligent people living in the North of Britain.

Galton also compared the cognitive abilities of contemporary races with those of historical civilisations. He claimed that the greatest race in human history was the ancient Greeks. He wrote: 'The ablest race of whom history bears record is unquestionably the ancient Greek, partly because their master-pieces in the principal departments of intellectual activity are still unsurpassed, and in many respects unequalled, and partly because the population that gave birth to the creators of those

[70] Galton, *Hereditary Genius*, p. 338.   [71] Galton, *Hereditary Genius*, pp. 337–8.
[72] Galton, *Hereditary Genius*, pp. 339–40.   [73] Galton, *Hereditary Genius*, p. 357.

master-pieces was very small.'[74] Of all the ancient Greek nations, it was the Attica who Galton believed were the most intelligent. He explained the reasons why this small population was able to produce so many eminent and influential figures:

Of the various Greek sub-races, that of the Attica was the ablest and she was no doubt largely indebted to the following cause, for her superiority. Athens opened her arms to immigrants, but not indiscriminately, for her social life was such that none but the very able men could take any pleasure in it; on the other hand, she offered attractions such as men of the highest ability and culture could find in no other city.[75]

This was an important passage in Galton's text because it demonstrated an example of how social conditions could influence the intellectual abilities of humans over time. In Athens' case, the brightest minds moved to the city to take advantage of its unique resources. No other place in ancient Greece had comparable assets. However, this illustrious age eventually came to an end, and Galton argued that 2,000 years of human diaspora destroyed Athenian culture. The intermixture of Athenian blood with that of races of lesser abilities weakened their intelligence over generations. To illustrate this denigration, Galton estimated that the Athenian race was two grades higher on his developmental scale than the British of the nineteenth century.[76] Galton's portrayal of ancient Greece was strikingly different to his representation of Africa, and he was trying to establish the superiority of Athenian society. It was a clear indication that he was biased toward Europeans and their ancestry.

Both Huxley and Galton applied evolutionary theory to the study of races in the years prior to 1871. As was the case with earlier figures such as Prichard and Lawrence, they attempted to trace the history of humans and explain the causes that produced differences among the races. In the case of Huxley, he also firmly linked human evolution to the rest of the natural world. This was a significant divergence from the earlier developmental models of British ethnologists. By the time that Darwin and Tylor published their works in the early 1870s, arguments about human evolution were firmly part of the discipline's discourse. What therefore emerged in the 1870s was a reconfiguration and expansion of earlier developmental theories along secular and politically neutral lines. It was not the beginning of a new era that was separate from the research activities of the decades before 1871, but a realignment of the discipline's ideological, theoretical and methodological core.

---

[74] Galton, *Hereditary Genius*, p. 340.   [75] Galton, *Hereditary Genius*, pp. 340–1.
[76] Galton, *Hereditary Genius*, p. 342.

Conclusion

As the 1860s came to a close, significant changes were occurring within the disciplinary makeups of British ethnology and anthropology. With the sudden death of Hunt in 1869, the ASL was left without a figurehead. There was no guiding voice to direct anthropological research practices, and therefore many of its members started to gravitate towards the ESL. This made it possible for Huxley and other leading ethnological figures such as Lubbock to broker a deal between the two sides. In 1871, the ESL and ASL amalgamated and formed the RAI. In an effort to push out the remnants of Hunt's research programme, and older ethnological developmental theories such as those forwarded by Prichard, it was essential for Huxley and the other scientific naturalists to reaffirm the significance of evolutionary theories within the newly formed Institute. The promotion of Darwinian evolution was brought to the fore of disciplinary discussions, and this was part of the scientific naturalists' strategy for gaining a controlling influence within the science. Under the banner of disciplinary reform, evolution was reconstructed as the new core of the discipline's theories. The publication of Darwin's *The Descent of Man* and Tylor's *Primitive Culture* further strengthened this disciplinary shift within British anthropology.[77]

This chapter has examined the research programmes of early British ethnologists and anthropologists in the first half of the nineteenth century. Traditionally, the secondary literature has positioned the year 1871 as marking the beginning of the evolutionist era. It allegedly represented a sudden shift in the disciplinary preoccupations of researchers interested in human variation. However, as this chapter has shown, developmental theories formed an important part of human diversity studies throughout the first half of the nineteenth century. Figures such as Prichard, Lawrence, Huxley and Galton all attempted to trace the history of races and identify the causes that shaped their physical and social differences. Even in cases where scholars argued against the application of developmental theories when studying humans, the historicisation of races was still a major discussion point within their treatises. Both Knox and Hunt examined at length the potential value of using developmental processes and human histories before rejecting them.

A secondary aim of this chapter was to shift away from disciplinary narratives that divide the history of British anthropology into distinct

---

[77] Sera-Shriar, *The Making of British Anthropology*, pp. 147–76.

theoretical and methodological epochs.[78] In the case of this study, we reconsidered the significance of the year 1871 as marking the beginning of the modern discipline of anthropology and the emergence of the evolutionist era. By challenging this disciplinary myth, we gained a much more extensive understanding of the significance of developmental theories within human diversity studies during the first half of the nineteenth century. It is highly instructive to trace the continuities that exist throughout the discipline's history. Understanding how ideas transformed and how practitioners readapted and appropriated these theories and methods in their research programmes gives us a much richer contextual picture of anthropology's past. It allows us to ask new questions about the histories of human sciences. What other assumptions do scholars make about the history of anthropology, psychology or sociology? What can we gain by revisiting some of the foundational questions of social-scientific inquiries? Should we be scrutinising the taken-for-granted assumptions that researchers utilise in their daily work?

These critical re-evaluations of the histories of human sciences and their theories and practices can also be applied to the natural and physical sciences. They begin by being more conscious of the activities, categories, vocational strategies and theoretical and methodological frameworks of historical actors. Whenever scholars canonise a particular moment in history, such as 1871, we should consider the reason why it has been given a privileged status. As Tylor remarked in his anthropological textbook from 1881, 'Reason and logic is itself a science, but like other sciences, it began as an art which man practiced without stopping to ask himself why or how'.[79] This astute observation still has a bearing on our understanding of the past today.

---

[78] For more on the disciplinary epochs of British anthropology see B. Tedlock, 'From Participant Observation to Observation of Participation: The Emergence of Narrative Ethnography', *Journal of Anthropological Research* 41 (1991), 69; J. Urry, 'Notes and Queries on Anthropology and the Development of Field Methods in British Anthropology, 1870–1920', *Proceedings of the Royal Anthropological Institute of Great Britain and Ireland* (1972), 45; Sera-Shriar, *The Making of British Anthropology, 1813–1871*, pp. 1–20.

[79] E. B. Tylor, *Anthropology: An Introduction to the Study of Man and Civilisation* (London: Macmillan, 1881), pp. 336–7.

4   Language

Marcus Tomalin

The language sciences in Victorian Britain constitute a daunting topic for academic enquiry, and only a small number of well-known preoccupations and projects have received considerable scholarly attention over the years.[1] These include the influence of diachronic Teutonic comparative and historical linguistics (*à la* Franz Bopp and Jacob Grimm), the increasingly sophisticated analysis of 'Anglo-Saxon', the search for universal linguistic laws, the prescriptive grammar textbook tradition, the remarkable lexicographical labours that resulted in the *Oxford English Dictionary* (*OED*), the gradual institutionalisation of language study and the development of theories concerning linguistic evolution. Such topics undeniably characterised the period 1837–1901, as attested in Anna Morpurgo Davies' authoritative overview:

---

[1] There are various terminological intricacies that require elucidation from the outset. The words 'philology' and 'philologist' had been current since at least the seventeenth century, and they could refer either to a general concern with learning and literature, or to a more specific kind of linguistic expertise. As the nineteenth century progressed, 'philology' began to denote more particularly an interest in the historical development of language. By contrast, the noun 'linguist' had conventionally been used since the sixteenth century to refer to a person who was adept at learning languages. While the word had, from time to time, been used as a rough synonym for philologist, and although the word 'linguistics' started to be used from the 1840s onwards in contradistinction to 'philology', it was not until the twentieth century that it came to denote a person who studies linguistics specifically (as a free-standing academic discipline). Given these complexities, I will in this paper risk minor anachronisms by referring to those Victorians who were fascinated by the theoretical study of languages as 'linguists'. Unfortunately, the thorny words 'science' and 'scientist' are equally problematical during this period. The latter was coined by William Whewell in 1833, but not widely adopted until later in the century, as summarised by Richard Yeo in *Defining Science: William Whewell, Natural Knowledge, and Public Debate in Early Victorian Britain* (Cambridge: Cambridge University Press, 1993), 5. Consequently, it is somewhat anachronistic to speak of the 'language sciences' or 'linguistics' in relation to the Victorian era, yet this need not cause any great problems. For further terminological discussion in the context of European linguistics, see Anna Morpurgo Davies, *Nineteenth-century Linguistics* [History of Linguistics Vol. 4] (London: Longmans, 1998), chapter 1. In preparing this chapter, I would like to acknowledge the inspiration and assistance I received from Anja Thorsteinsdóttir and Orri Tomasson.

the main concern of the century is with linguistic history and linguistic comparison. The main achievements are, on the one hand, the establishment of a set of discovery procedures which are used to classify languages from a genetic point of view in language families ... on the other hand, the collection and classification ... of an immense amount of linguistic data and philosophical material.[2]

Scholars such as Christine Ferguson have bolstered this kind of assessment by observing that '[t]he period continues to be viewed as a predominantly historical, empirical, and often nationalistic interlude between the whimsical speculations of the eighteenth-century philosophical tradition and the revolutionary semiotics of Ferdinand de Saussure and the Neogrammarians'.[3] Many of these tendencies can, of course, be traced back to the influence of German linguists in the early nineteenth century, and especially Franz Bopp and Jacob Grimm. Bopp's interest in comparative linguistics had been piqued by Friedrich Schlegel's *Über die Sprache und Weisheit der Indier* (*On the Language and Wisdom of the Indians*, 1808). He studied Sanskrit in Paris and his first publication, *Über das Conjugationssystem der Sanskritsprache* (*On the Sanskrit Conjunction System*, 1816), attempted to demonstrate that certain verbal forms in Greek, Latin, Persian and Sanskrit shared a common ancestor. In subsequent work he extended this analysis to the whole language system, and published his monumental *Vergleichende Grammatik* (*Comparative Grammar*, 6 parts, 1833–52). His analyses frequently juxtaposed linguistic forms so as to reveal genealogical similarities:[4]

	Singular Present-Tense Verb Forms			
	Sanskrit	**Greek**	**Latin**	**Gothic**
1ˢᵗ Person.	Pà mi	φα μί	Do	Haba
2ⁿᵈ Person.	Pà si	φη ς	Da s	Habai s
3ʳᵈ Person.	Pà ti	φα τί	Da t	Habai th

Comparative paradigms such as this suggested that certain languages could be grouped into families based on the presence of similar lexical, phonological or syntactic structures. As far as British linguists were concerned, Bopp demonstrated that comparative language study could be approached in a systematic and more 'scientific' manner than eighteenth-century studies had implied. In a similar way, Jacob Grimm effectively

---

[2] Davies, *Nineteenth-century Linguistics*, 1–2.

[3] Christine Ferguson, *Language, Science, and Popular Fiction in the Victorian Fin-de-Siècle: The Brutal Tongue* (Aldershot: Ashgate, 2006), 13.

[4] The following example is based on Franz Bopp, 'Analytical Comparison of Sanskrit, Greek, Latin, and Teutonic Languages', *Annals of Oriental Literature* (London: Longman, Hurst, Rees, Orne, and Brown., 1820), 17. The verb Pà in Sanskrit means 'to reign'.

established the framework for historical linguistics in the nineteenth century in his epochal *Deutsche Grammatik* (*German Grammar*, 4 vols., 1819–37).[5] He focused attention on the ways in which the various sub-systems of natural language (e.g., syntax, morphology, phonology, semantics) changed over time in rule-governed ways. Such research helped to illuminate the pre-history of the Indo-European languages, revealing the existence of proto-languages which could be hypothetically reconstructed. In particular, he identified phonological changes by comparing the systems of Greek, Latin and Sanskrit with those of modern members of the Germanic language family, and the laws he identified included the following:[6]

Unvoiced Plosives become Unvoiced Fricatives:

/p/ → /f/
/t/ → /θ/
/k/ → /x/

Voiced Plosives become Unvoiced Plosives

/b/ → /p/
/d/ → /t/
/g/ → /k/

Such patterns suggested that historical linguistic change could be analysed in a principled and scientific manner: seemingly arbitrary irregularities could be accounted for in terms of underlying regularities. In many cases, the routes by which these ideas entered into British linguistics can be traced quite easily. The linguist Friedrich Max Müller, for example, was born in Germany and studied in Leipzig, Berlin and Paris, where he specialised in philology (especially Greek, Latin, Arabic, Persian and Sanskrit). He worked closely with Franz Bopp, and therefore became familiar with the analytical frameworks favoured by the rising generation of comparative linguists. He was appointed Professor of Modern European Languages at Oxford in 1850, and Professor of Comparative Philology in 1868.[7] In his popular and influential *Lectures on the*

---

[5] Joep Leerssen, *National Thought in Europe: A Cultural History* (Amsterdam: Amsterdam University Press, 2006), 123–5.

[6] Based on Jacob Grimm, *Deutsche Grammatik* (Göttingen: Dieterich, 1822), 583–92. For an insightful discussion of 'Grimm's Law', see Frans van Coetsem, 'Grimm's Law: A Reappraisal of Grimm's Formulation from a Present-day Perspective', in Elmer H. Antonsen, James W. Marchand and Ladislav Zgusta, eds., *The Grimm Brothers and the Germanic Past* [Studies in the History of the Language Sciences 54] (Amsterdam: John Benjamins, 1990), 43–60.

[7] For a recent biography, see Lourens P. van den Bosch, *Friedrich Max Müller: A Life Devoted to the Humanities* (Leiden: E.J. Brill, 2002).

Science of Language (1864), he argued that a recognisably scientific approach to linguistic study was 'of very modern date' and had arisen due to developments since 1810 in England, France and Germany which had unearthed discoveries in a 'newly-opened mine of scientific inquiry'.[8] For Müller, a 'scientific' discipline was one which progressed through three phases – 'the *Empirical*, the *Classificatory*, and the *Theoretical*' – and he was convinced that the work of Bopp, as well as Wilhelm von Humboldt, Jacob Grimm and others, had ensured that the study of language had become truly scientific, thereby acquiring a rigour and respectability comparable to that of geology, anatomy, physics, biology and chemistry.[9] The painstaking comparative and historical research that traced the development of lexical items and specific grammatical forms profoundly influenced British linguists from the 1820s onwards, creating the historicist scholarly environment out of which the *OED* eventually emerged.

The *OED* began in 1857 as a relatively small enterprise proposed by the Philological Society. Founded in 1842, the Society was directed by enthusiastic members such as Richard Trench (Dean of Westminster Abbey and amateur linguist), Herbert Coleridge (grandson of Samuel Taylor Coleridge, barrister and amateur linguist) and Frederick Furnivall (lawyer and amateur linguist). Two of Trench's papers, published together as *On Some Deficiencies in our English Dictionaries* (1857), helped to determine the focus of the lexicographical research that eventually culminated in the *OED*. Materials were accumulated for *A New English Dictionary on Historical Principles*, as it was then called, and after a succession of editors, James Murray (bank clerk, schoolmaster and amateur linguist) took over this onerous responsibility in 1879. The dictionary was eventually published in ten parts (or 'fascicles') from 1884 to 1928, and supplements began to appear soon afterwards. The title pages of the separate volumes solemnly declared that the entries had been prepared 'with assistance of many scholars and men of science', thereby emphasising the systematic, evidence-based approach adopted.[10] As this suggests, there are many good reasons why the *OED* has become an archetypal manifestation of the most characteristic tendencies of Victorian linguistics. It reveals the predominant fascination with the historical development of English, it prioritises etymological analysis, it implements a

---

[8] Friedrich Max Müller, *Lectures on the Science of Language*, 4th ed. (London: Longman, 1864), 3, 1.
[9] Müller, *Lectures*, 5.
[10] James Murray, ed., *A New English Dictionary on Historical Principles*, Vol. 1 (Oxford: The Clarendon Press, 1884), title page.

strongly diachronic methodology, it reveals the importance of classificatory rigour, it demonstrates the increasing professionalism of the language sciences in Britain and its ambitious exhaustiveness makes it a
viable linguistic counterpart to other imposing Victorian undertakings
such as the creation of the railway network.

Seemingly, then, the particular historicism of the *OED* neatly encap-
sulates some of the most popular and dominant narratives that are
understood to have characterised (certain kinds of) linguistic research
in nineteenth-century Britain – and similar tendencies can be perceived
in the labours of noted contemporaneous linguists such as Robert
Gordon Latham and John Mitchell Kemble. Having studied at King's
College, Cambridge, Latham was elected a Fellow there in 1832 and
concentrated on philological research. He spent time in Germany and
Denmark, where he encountered the influential linguist Rasmus Rask
(about whom more later), and was elected Professor of English Language
and Literature at University College London in 1839. Academic positions of this kind were unusual in Victorian Britain, though they had
been common in Germany since the early nineteenth century: Glasgow
did not introduce a similar professorship until 1861, King's College
London waited until 1877, Oxford followed suit in 1885 and (true to
form) Cambridge delayed until 1911.[11] The distinctive historical tendency of Latham's work is manifest in *Elements of English Grammar*
(1849). Although essentially a synchronic self-study textbook in the
eighteenth-century tradition of Robert Lowth's *A Short Introduction to
English Grammar* (1762) and Lindley Murray's *English Grammar* (1795),
it begins with a detailed twenty-one-page history of the language (Part I)
which discusses the 'Anglo-Saxon' dialects and the influence of Norman
French. The inclusion of such material in a pedagogical text of this kind
reveals the dominant historicism that is frequently claimed to be so
characteristic of the Victorian language sciences – and a similar propen-
sity is manifest in Kemble's work. Having come under the influence of
Jacob Grimm (with whom he studied at Göttingen in the early 1830s),
Kemble lectured at Cambridge on the history of the English language
and published a literal translation of *Beowulf* in 1837.[12] Via analogy with
the methodology of the physical sciences, he repeatedly stressed the need
to reveal hidden linguistic laws. In his essay 'On English Praeterites'
(1833), he remarked that

---

[11] Georg Friedrich Benecke was appointed to the first post in German philology at the
University of Göttingen in 1805.

[12] Raymond A. Wiley, *John Mitchell Kemble and Jakob Grimm* (Leiden: E.J. Brill, 1971).

I am not without hope, that the thought may occur to some readers, that much which they have looked upon as arbitrary and irregular, appeared so to them, only because they had not learnt to cast their eyes over a sufficiently extensive circle of facts; and that they may feel, that in exact proportion to the number of elements which we introduce into the calculation, is our chance of perceiving the deep-laid and ever-ruling laws on which as a foundation, Teutonic etymology is raised. In the following pages it will be shewn that a strict system prevails throughout our verbal forms; that it is complete within itself and incapable of alterations; that as such it has subsisted in the written Teutonic languages for upwards of fourteen centuries, and may, before the languages were written down have subsisted for as many more.[13]

The phrase 'Teutonic etymology' is telling. The kinds of hidden regularities, or 'deep-laid and ever-ruling laws', that Kemble has in mind here are similar to those that Grimm had presented in his *Deutsche Grammatik*. The strongly comparative and diachronic emphasis of Kemble's work has as much to do with national identity as with philology, since linguistic origins are necessarily intertwined with the development of human societies and/or cultures. As Tuska Benes has recently observed of German linguistics in the nineteenth century, '[l]anguage provided a semblance of historical continuity that gave credence to the new cultural memories and narratives of national origins that defined the national elite'.[14] Grimm's language-based research suggested that the various Teutonic cultures stemmed from the same origin, and this conclusion had broad socio-cultural implications.[15] It is this 'semblance of historical continuity' that was often so important, since the partly synthetic historical reconstructions ensured that the linguistic studies published by Victorian linguists manifested different historicisms which created a range of 'new cultural memories'.[16] It is worth noting, though, that this strongly historicist tendency existed in parallel with more prescriptive pedagogical practices which were the legacy of the eighteenth-century grammar textbook tradition. Even in texts which evinced a knowledge of, and interest in, the historical evolution of language, there were frequently evaluative classifications which distinguished the grammatical from the ungrammatical. To take just one example, William Cramp presented a series of rules in his *The Philosophy of Language* (1833), and his 'Rule IV' concerning adjectives was expressed as follows:

[13] John Mitchell Kemble, 'On English Praeterites', *The Philosophical Museum* 2 (1833), 373.

[14] Tuska Benes, *In Babel's Shadow: Language, Philology, and Nation in Nineteenth Century Germany* (Detroit, MI: Wayne State University Press, 2008), 115–16.

[15] Benes, *Babel's Shadow*, 123.

[16] For a brief discussion of different historicisms, see Paul Hamilton, *Historicism: The New Critical Idiom*, 2nd ed. (London: Routledge, 2003), 1–44.

Double comparatives, or double superlatives, are improper; and although they were formerly admitted and sanctioned by reputable writers, they were nevertheless as UNGRAMMATICAL *then* as they are justly pronounced to be so *now*.[17]

The message is clear: although the historical development of English may suggest that, at certain times in the past, particular structures were deemed to be grammatical (or at least acceptable) by 'reputable writers', this conclusion is in fact fallacious. The rather bizarre contrary assertion is that, despite appearances, grammaticality has remained constant throughout the convoluted development of the English language. It has often been claimed that nineteenth-century prescriptivism was a remnant from the eighteenth century, and that the descriptive and historicist movements within linguistics that emerged in the 1810s and 1820s arose partly from 'a specific revolt against the mechanical nature of rote learning' and partly from 'the development of national consciousness'.[18] Nonetheless, as the example from Cramp indicates, prescriptivism still flourished in Britain in the 1830s, and well beyond. While historicism and prescriptivism may not be inherently incompatible, they naturally tend in opposing directions (the former seeking to describe and explain, the latter seeking to intervene and alter), and yet some Victorian linguists sought to reconcile these two conflicting forces. This important topic will provide a central focus later in this chapter.

The developmental historicisms summarised so far all relate to the analysis of natural languages (and mainly those within the Indo-European family) since about 4000 BC. However, an increasing number of linguists, philosophers, biologists and ethnologists were equally intrigued by the development of human language over a much longer chronological period. In particular, musings about the earliest origins of language featured prominently in the debates about evolution, especially from the 1850s onwards. It is well known that Alfred Russel Wallace, one of the co-originators of the theory of evolution by means of natural selection, argued in 1869 that human language was a puzzle from an evolutionary perspective: 'natural selection could only have endowed the savage with a brain a little superior to that of an ape, whereas he actually possesses one but very little inferior to that of the average members of our learned societies.'[19] Wallace therefore concluded, somewhat opaquely,

---

[17] William Cramp, *The Philosophy of Language: Containing Practical Rules for Acquiring a Knowledge of English Grammar* (London: Relfe and Fletcher, 1833), 72.

[18] Glendon F. Drake, *The Role of Prescriptivism in American Linguistics: 1820–1970* [Studies in the History of the Languages Sciences 13] (Amsterdam: John Benjamins, 1977), 6.

[19] Alfred Russel Wallace, 'Sir Charles Lyell on Geological Climates and the Origin of Species', *Quarterly Review* 76 (April 1869), 362.

that a 'Higher Intelligence' must have guided human evolution.[20] As he saw it, this was the only way to account for the existence of natural language. Charles Darwin was, of course, horrified by what he perceived to be Wallace's defection, and in *The Decent of Man, and Selection in Relation to Sex* (1871) he argued that 'there is no fundamental difference between man and the higher mammals in their mental faculties'.[21] He attempted to substantiate this claim by considering animal communication systems, and he concluded that '[a]rticulate language is ... peculiar to man; but he uses in common with the lower animals inarticulate cries to express his meaning, aided by gestures and the movements of the muscles of the face'.[22] In adopting his contrary view, Wallace necessarily aligned his own thinking about this topic with that of Friedrich Max Müller. Müller was convinced that humans and animals were separated by a profound cognitive divide:

no one can doubt that certain animals possess all the physical requirements for articulate speech. There is no letter of the alphabet which a parrot will not learn to pronounce. The fact, therefore, that the parrot is without a language of its own, must be explained by a difference between the mental, not between the physical, faculties of the animal and man.[23]

During the early 1870s, Müller and Darwin exchanged several letters in which they debated the origins of natural language. It is clear that Darwin had considerable respect for Müller, admitting that he himself lacked a sufficiently detailed knowledge of language to be able to rebut the latter's linguistic arguments. Similarly, Müller greatly admired Darwin, describing himself as 'a thorough Darwinian' but choosing to demur when it came to human language:

I take my stand against Darwin on language, because language is the necessary condition of every other mental activity, religion not excluded, and I am able to prove that this indispensible condition of all mental growth is entirely absent in animals.[24]

These important debates pervaded certain sub-domains of Victorian linguistics. However, it would be misleading to conclude that such concerns dominated to the exclusion of all others. Indeed, they are only

---

[20] Wallace, 'Sir Charles Lyell', 394.
[21] Charles Darwin, *The Decent of Man, and Selection in Relation to Sex*, Vol. 1 (London: John Murray, 1871), 34.
[22] Darwin, *Descent of Man*, 52.
[23] Friedrich Max Müller, *Lectures on the Science of Language*, 4th ed. (London: Longman, 1864), 362.
[24] 'Letter to the Duke of Argyll, January 29th 1875', in Georgina Adelaide Müller, ed., *The Life and Letters of the Right Honourable Friedrich Max Müller*, Vol. 1 (London: Longmans, Green, 1902), 508.

part of a much richer story, and, when assessed in its totality, Victorian linguistics constitutes a far more forbiddingly heterogeneous field than most cursory overviews acknowledge. This is partly because natural language was discussed by researchers in many disciplines, including ethnology, theology, philosophy, sociology, biology and nascent psychology. Unfortunately, this heterogeneity has been neglected in recent academic studies, and this disregard is surprising given the many attempts to evaluate and re-evaluate linguistic theorising from the sixteenth, seventeenth, eighteenth and twentieth centuries.[25] The persistent focus given to the *OED*, for instance, has caused that particular project to be viewed as *the* prototypical embodiment of the Victorian language sciences, effectively becoming 'a kind of national monument', and many other undertakings, which deployed different classificatory schemes and/ or contrasting analytical methodologies, have been cast into the shade.[26] The truth is that the language sciences in Victorian Britain comprised such a bafflingly assorted collection of different conventions, methodologies, preoccupations and approaches that the sheer complexity and diversity of the topic tends to prohibit brief lucid précis. Consequently, although it is often acknowledged that 'Victorian philology is a tremendously vital and vibrant nineteenth-century discourse that is imbricated with larger questions concerning history, class, national identity and culture', it is also recognised that there is currently a 'dearth of scholarship on Victorian philology'.[27]

It is intriguing that such a vital and vibrant subject should be treated with such scant regard by linguistic historiographers and cultural historians. The situation has been exacerbated by the fact that many of the most influential discussions have been glaringly selective. Hans Aarslef's omnipresent *From Locke to Saussure: Essays on the Study of Language and Intellectual History* (1982) continues to be cited with startling frequency, yet, after more than thirty years, the discussion offered there has

---

[25] For instance, topics such as seventeenth-century language planning and the development of Generative Grammar have received particular attention. See David Cram and Jaap Maat, *George Dalgarno on Universal Language: 'The Art of Signs' (1661), 'The Deaf and Dumb Man's Tutor' (1680), and the Unpublished Papers* (Oxford: Oxford University Press, 2001); Jaap Maat, *Philosophical Languages in the Seventeenth Century: Dalgarno, Wilkins, Leibniz* (Dordrecht: Kluwer Academic Publishers, 2004); Peter H. Matthews, *Grammatical Theory in the United States from Bloomfield to Chomsky* (Cambridge: Cambridge University Press, 1993); Marcus Tomalin, *Linguistics and the Formal Sciences: The Origins of Generative Grammar* (Cambridge: Cambridge University Press, 2006).

[26] Charlotte Brewer, *Treasure-house of the Language: The Living OED* (New Haven, CT: Yale University Press, 2007), 214.

[27] Daniel S. Kline, Educated Speech: Victorian Philology and the Literary Languages of Matthew Arnold and Arthur Hugh Clough, PhD Thesis (Ohio State University, 2007), 7; Ferguson, *Language*, 4.

inevitably started to show signs of age. Subsequent studies, such as Tony Crowley's *Standard English and the Politics of Language* (1989) and Anna Morpurgo Davies' *Nineteenth Century Linguistics* (1998), have emphasised the relationship between linguistics and national identity and the increasingly scientific classificatory methodologies adopted. Other texts have focused mainly on literature rather than linguistics, and James C. McKusick's *Coleridge's Philosophy of Language* (1986), Linda Dowling's *Language and Decadence in the Victorian Fin-De-Siècle* (1986), Cary Plotkin's *The Tenth Muse: Victorian Philology and the Genesis of the Poetic Language of Gerard Manley Hopkins* (1989) and Dennis Taylor's *Hardy's Literary Language and Victorian Philology* (1994) are all representative examples of this type. It is impossible, though, fully to understand the pervasive developmental historicisms if contemporaneous counter-currents remain unexplored.

In order to demonstrate that these counter-currents are worthy of serious scholarly attention, this chapter will now focus on Victorian analyses of Icelandic. This topic is of especial relevance since it complicates the view that developmental historicisms dominated Victorian linguistics in a simplistic manner. Icelandic is a member of the North Germanic, or Nordic, branch of the Germanic language family, and therefore it fascinated those early nineteenth-century linguists who were exploring the connections between the various Germanic tongues. The most significant of these people was undoubtedly Rasmus Rask. Born on the Danish island of Funen in 1787, Rask studied at the University of Copenhagen, where he was appointed assistant keeper of the university library in 1808; he subsequently published his *Lexicon Islandico-Latino-Danicum* (1814; with Björn Haldorsen), which was swiftly followed by his *Undersøgelse om det gamle Nordiske eller Islandske Sprogs Oprindelse* (*Essay on the Origin of the Ancient Norse or Icelandic Tongue*; wrt. 1814, pub. 1818) and *Anvisning till Isländskan eller Nordiska Fornspråket* (*A Manual of Icelandic or the Old Norse Tongue*; 1818; from henceforth *Anvisning*). In addition, he was pivotal in the founding of *Hið íslenska bókmenntafélagið* (the Icelandic Literary Society) in 1816, and these combined endeavours ensured that the Icelandic language and its literature gradually became more accessible – at least to anyone fluent in Danish or Swedish. The impact of this work in Britain is manifest in texts such as Joseph Bosworth's *The Origin of the Germanic and Scandinavian Languages and Nations* (1836), which cites Rask's work several times and refers to 'the unwearied toil of Rask and Grimm'.[28] Most

---

[28] Joseph Bosworth, *The Origin of the Germanic and Scandinavian Languages and Nations* (London: Longman, Rees, Orme, Brown, and Green, 1836), 61.

importantly, though, George Webbe Dasent published *A Grammar of the Icelandic or Old Norse Tongue* in 1843. This was the first English-language grammar of either Old Norse or Modern Icelandic to be printed in Britain.[29] The text was essentially a translation of Rasmus Rask's *Anvisning*, and it made Icelandic accessible to a British audience for the first time, thereby encouraging the steadily growing interest in Scandinaviana.[30] During the eighteenth century, medieval Icelandic literature (especially the Eddas and the Sagas) had come to the attention of the British public rather sporadically. In the 1760s, Thomas Percy's *Five Pieces of Runic Poetry* (1763) and Thomas Gray's 'Norse Odes' (wrt. 1761; pub. 1768) cultivated a taste for Nordic culture, and this nascent curiosity was further piqued by the appearance of Thomas Percy's *Northern Antiquities* (1770), essentially a translation of Paul Henri Mallett's *Monuments de la mythologie et de la poesie des Celtes, et particuliere-ment des anciens Scandinaves* (1756). Mallett's discussion of Icelandic texts relied heavily on Latin translations, and subsequent works such as Amos Simon Cottle and Robert Southey's *Icelandic Poetry or The Edda of Sæmund* (1797) and William Herbert's *Select Icelandic Poetry* (1804) also used existing translations as a crutch. However, despite the pervasive ignorance of Old Norse, there was a prevailing conviction in Europe that the language of the 'Vikings' had survived untouched and unmodified for centuries, and therefore possessed a startling linguistic purity unrivalled by any other European language.[31] Thomas Percy remarked in 1763 that, in Iceland, '[Icelandic] was supposed to be spoken with the greatest purity, and where it is to this day in use'.[32] The renowned naturalist Joseph Banks, famed for accompanying Captain Cook on his first voyage of discovery (1768–71), visited Iceland in July 1772, and Uno von Troil, the Archbishop of Uppsala, who was part of Banks' retinue, wrote about the trip in *Letters on Iceland* (1780). Although von Troil mainly describes natural geographical phenomena (such as the geysers) and social customs, the language of the country is also subjected to scrutiny. At one point he notes that Icelandic 'has preserved itself so pure, that any Icelander understands the most ancient traditional history, as easily as we

---

[29] The first English-language grammar of Icelandic was George Perkins Marsh's *A Compendious Grammar of the Old Northern or Icelandic Language, Compiled and Translated from the Grammars of Rask* (Burlington, IA: H. Johnson & Co., 1838).

[30] Andrew Wawn, *The Vikings and the Victorians: Inventing the Old North in Nineteenth-century Britain* (Cambridge: D.S. Brewer, 2000).

[31] The word 'Viking' is a problematical one with an ambiguous etymology. For specifics, see Wawn, *Vikings*, 4.

[32] Thomas Percy, *Five Pieces of Runic Poetry* (London: R. and J. Dodsley, 1763), Preface.

do letters written in the time of Charles IX'.[33] Similarly, in his *Journal of a Tour in Iceland in the Summer of 1809* (1811), William Jackson Hooker remarked that Icelandic had retained 'its original purity'.[34] Such pronouncements were commonplace in the late eighteenth and early nineteenth centuries and they inculcated the belief that Icelandic had remained unaltered for centuries, seemingly impervious to the passing of time.

This preoccupation with Icelandic's unchanged, pristine state persisted into the Victorian period. It had become a dominant notion that language change inevitably results in corruption and decay; therefore, the 'purest' linguistic forms were considered to be the oldest ones. In many respects, this view was compatible with the trope of decline deployed by some imperialists when arguing that all living things, including socio-political entities such as commonwealths, passed through three successive stages: growth, transformation and decay.[35] Indeed, the linguists were often even more pessimistic than the political theorists, since they did not always find much to celebrate in the growth and transformation stages. In his *Lectures on the Science of Language*, for instance, Müller observed somewhat ruefully that '[o]n the whole, the history of all the Aryan languages is nothing but a gradual process of decay', and for some this phenomenon was not confined merely to Germanic phylogenies. William Chauncey Fowler expressed it pithily as a universal truth: '[a]s languages grow, so they decay.'[36] In particular, hybrid languages (such as English), formed from the conflux of several tongues, were often deemed to be irreparably tarnished. John Keats' appreciation of Thomas Chatterton, for instance, was largely predicated upon such assumptions: '[h]e is the purest writer in the English Language. He has no french idiom or particles, like Chaucer – 'tis genuine English Idiom in English words.'[37] The underlying conviction here is that 'genuine English' had ceased to exist at some point during the Middle Ages. Similarly Teutonistic attitudes can be detected in the lexically selective English prose of the historian Edward Freeman, in the Icelandic translations of William Morris and even in Henry Fowler's and Francis Fowler's post-Victorian

---

[33] Uno von Troil, *Letters on Iceland*, 2nd ed. (London: J. Robson, 1780), 174.

[34] William Jackson Hooker, *Journal of a Tour in Iceland in the Summer of 1809* (Yarmouth: J. Keymer, 1811), lxv.

[35] Duncan Bell, 'Empire', this volume.

[36] Müller, *Science of Language*, 244; William Chauncey Fowler, *The English Language in Its Elements and Forms*, rev. ed. (New York: Harper and Brothers, 1855), 41.

[37] 'Letter to J. H. Reynolds, 21st September 1819', in Robert Gittings, ed., *The Letters of John Keats: A Selection Edited by Robert Gittings* (Oxford: Oxford University Press, 1990), 292.

The King's English (1906), which advised readers to '[p]refer the Saxon word to the Romance'.[38] Given these persistent concerns, Icelandic provided a fascinating case-study for Victorian linguists, and one which tested their commitment to developmental historicism as a viable framework for linguistic research. Müller may have been convinced that the 'Aryan languages' were undergoing a process of continual and inevitable decay, yet he was still able to reiterate the prevailing belief that the language which had once been common to Sweden, Norway and Denmark 'was preserved almost intact in Iceland'.[39] This seems paradoxical. It implies that Icelandic is strikingly anomalous, that it magically resisted the otherwise inevitable forces of linguistic change which caused all the other Germanic languages to fall (allegedly) into a state of disrepair. Two great themes of the Victorian language sciences collide here. The desire to understand historical development encounters the conviction that linguistic change inevitably leads to decay, and Icelandic mesmerised Victorian linguists because it appeared to have remained immune to both these natural processes: by not changing, it had avoided deterioration.

It is both intriguing and ironic, then, that by the time British linguists were marvelling at Icelandic's blemish-free state, several generations of Icelanders had bewailed what they perceived to be its flawed and corrupted nature. As early as 1609, Arngrímur Jónsson had noted in his Latin poem *Crymogoea* that the language had been weakened by the influence of German and Danish syntax and vocabulary, and later texts such as Eggert Ólafsson's poem *Sótt og dauði íslenskunnar* (*Sickness and Death of the Icelandic Language*; wrt. 1752–7) helped to inspire the linguistic purism movement that became such a characteristic feature of Icelandic nationalism during the nineteenth century.[40] The poem describes Icelandic as an old woman who has become mortally ill due to the contagion caused by the influx of Danish and German loanwords. In response to such concerns, the nascent purism movement advocated replacing all borrowed lexemes with Old Norse words (either directly or by creating compounds). This stance was overtly enshrined in the 1780 statutes of *Hið íslenska lærdómslistafélag* (The Icelandic Society for Learned Arts):

5. ... the Society shall treasure and preserve the Norse tongue as a beautiful, noble language, which has been spoken in the Nordic countries for a long time, and seek to cleanse [*að hreinsa*] the same from foreign words [*útlendum orðum*]

---

[38] Henry Watson Fowler and Francis George Fowler, *The King's English* (Oxford: Clarendon Press, 1906), 11.
[39] Müller, *Science of Language*, 195.
[40] Halldór Halldórsson, 'Icelandic Purism and Its History', *Word* 30 (1979), 76–86.

and expressions which have now begun to corrupt it [*nú taka henni að spilla*]. Therefore, in the Society's publications, foreign words shall not be used about sports, tools or anything else, insofar as one may find other old or Mediaeval Norse terms.

6. Therefore, instead of such foreign words [*útlendra orða*] one may coin new words [*ný orð*], compounded of other Nordic ones, which explain well the nature of the object that they are to denote; in so doing, one should examine well the rules [*reglur*] pertaining to and employed in this language as to the structure of good, old words [*í smíði góðra, gamallra orða*]; such words should be given a clear explanation and translation in order that they become easily comprehensible for the public.[41]

These guidelines had a significant impact on the Icelandic literature produced during the nineteenth century, and especially translations of foreign texts. Rather than importing loanwords, Icelandic authors devised *ex interno* neologisms based on Old Norse lexical roots. This culture of creative linguistic recycling (re)introduced such words as *sími* (*telephone*; a neo-archaism, introduced by Pálmi Pálsson in 1896). Originally an Old Norse word meaning *thread* or *rope*, its (re)introduction to Modern Icelandic broadened and complicated its semantic denotation. Consequently, far from being a static, fixed and unchangingly pure language, since the thirteenth century and the fall of the commonwealth Modern Icelandic had been strongly influenced by Danish, Latin, Norwegian and German, and was undergoing an extensive process of pseudo-archaising *ex interno* expansion and reformation throughout the late eighteenth and nineteenth centuries. In many respects, these linguistic concerns can be related to broader socio-political developments. The national parliament of Iceland, the Althing, had been founded in 930 at Þingvellir and although its function changed after the union with Norway in 1262, it continued to hold sessions until it was disbanded in 1799 and replaced by a High Court. During the first decades of the nineteenth century there was increasing demand for more extensive internal rule in Iceland. A new Althing was established by means of a royal decree in 1843 and the first assembly met in 1845.[42] This important development was part of a broader nationalistic socio-political tendency to modernise and restructure Icelandic culture by returning to elements associated with its medieval past – and the linguistic purism movement was part of this reforming endeavour.[43] Significantly, it was during this period of

---

[41] Based on Halldórsson, 'Icelandic Purism', 223.

[42] Gunnar Karlsson, *Iceland's 1100 Years: The History of a Marginal Society* (London: Hurst & Company, 2000), 200–208.

[43] This kind of mythologising of cultural continuity has featured repeatedly in assessments of Iceland's past. For a discussion of this issue in relation to Icelandic literature, see

linguistic and socio-cultural reconfiguration that Dasent prepared his
translation of Rask's *Anvisning*.

Having been born in the West Indies and educated at Westminster
School, King's College London and Oxford University, Dasent was
appointed to a diplomatic post in Stockholm in 1840. He rapidly
acquired a mastery of Swedish and Danish, and his interest specifically
in Scandinavian literature was largely inspired by his friendship with
Jacob Grimm. In many respects, therefore, Dasent is a representative
example of a certain kind of early Victorian linguist. Although not a
professional academic (that is, he did not earn a salary from his linguistic
research; there were few opportunities to do so at the time), he was fluent
in several languages and he produced analytical linguistic studies and
translations. He was, in effect, a skilled amateur, but one whose knowledge of Scandinavian languages and literatures was far greater than
that of the few professional academic linguistics working in Britain at
the time. His translation of *The Prose or Younger Edda* appeared in
1843 and his celebrated rendering of *The Story of Burnt Njal* (a translation
of *Brennu-Njáls Saga*) followed in 1861. Given the comparative dearth
of academic positions for professional linguists in Victorian Britain,
figures such as Dasent were central to the development of linguistics as
a discipline.[44] They functioned partly as conduits, providing access to
research undertaken in other countries, and making otherwise arcane
and esoteric studies available to the British general public and specialists
alike. Always a savvy businessman with a good eye for his target market,
Dasent recognised that the study of Icelandic would appeal to his contemporaries for both linguistic and nationalistic reasons, and he emphasised that, although Icelandic had been 'hitherto little understood or
valued in England', it was nonetheless of considerable national importance to anyone interested in the English language.[45] He rebuked those
who were largely oblivious of the past – 'we are so eagerly bent on going
forwards that we cannot spare a glance behind'[46] – and argued forcibly
that this indifference was characteristic of early Victorian society in
general, but particularly the study of language: 'we have mutilated, and
in some respects wellnigh forgotten, the speech of our ancestors, and
have got instead a monstrous mosaic, a patchwork of various tongues

Daisy Neijmann, 'In Search of an Icelandic Literature: The History and Practice of Early
 Icelandic Literary Historiography', *Scandinavica* 45:1 (May 2006), 43–73.
[44] For a discussion of the increasing professionalization of linguistics in nineteenth-century
 Europe, see Davies, *Nineteenth-century Linguistics*, 1–13.
[45] George Webbe Dasent, *A Grammar of the Icelandic or Old Norse Tongue* (London:
 William Pickering, 1843), iii.
[46] Dasent, *Grammar*, iii.

which we have picked up and pieced together as we went along.'[47] The accusation of hybridity had of course already become a traditional criticism of the English language, the mongrel nature of which had disturbed British linguists for centuries, and the same preoccupations have recently resurfaced in debates concerning whether or not Middle English was a creole.[48] What is distinctive here, though, is Dasent's emphasis on the importance of a deep understanding of the origins and historical development of English – a task (he claims) which requires a secure knowledge of Icelandic. He presents this as being contrary to the prevailing forward-looking obsession with the future. The Victorian age may have been preoccupied with social reform, scientific advances, modernisation and the like, but, following the lead of Bopp, Rask, Jacob Grimm and others, many of its most influential linguists were starting to argue that the nature of the present, and the future, could best be revealed by an exploration of the past. As Philippa Levine has astutely observed, '[p]aradox lay at the heart of Victorian culture and nowhere was it more apparent than in their simultaneous adulation of their own age and their reverent fascination for the past'.[49] In this context, Dasent's rhetoric borders on extremism, at times hinting at a radical reforming agenda: 'the present Age is responsible for the sins of those that preceded it if it can atone for them and will not.'[50] It is unclear whether he is here advocating mild spelling reforms or more extreme kinds of linguistic purism, such as the eradication of all loanwords. Nonetheless, his observation reveals an obvious tension between historicism and prescriptivism, two dominant approaches to linguistics in Britain during the nineteenth century. These contrasting perspectives potentially oppose each other, since historical linguistics seeks merely to offer a diachronic description of the development of a language system, while prescriptive linguistics attempts to intervene, alter and develop what it analyses. Dasent, therefore, advocates a form of what David Simpson has called 'prescriptive historicism' – that is, a type of historicism which encourages the conscious 'improvement' of the language system being described – and (as shown below) this strongly influenced his analysis of Icelandic.[51]

[47] Dasent, *Grammar*, iv.
[48] Richard J. Watts, *Language Myths and the History of English* (Oxford: Oxford University Press, 2011), chapter 4.
[49] Philippa J. A. Levine, *The Amateur and the Professional: Antiquarians, Historians, and Archaeologists in Victorian England 1838–1886* (Cambridge: Cambridge University Press, 1986), 1.
[50] Dasent, *Grammar*, iv.
[51] David Simpson introduces the phrase in his article 'Literary Criticism and the Return to History', *Critical Inquiry* 14:4 (Summer 1988), 721–47. He distinguishes 'analytical' historicism from 'prescriptive' historicism, and describes the latter as embodying 'an

Indeed, the nostalgic and synthetic Teutonism of Dasent and some of his contemporaries and successors was often overtly manifest. The *OED* itself contained a patriotic indigenous 'Foreword', rather than a foreign Latinate 'Preface', and the tensions and inconsistencies of these stances illuminate the underlying theoretical commitments. The English language borrowed many words from Icelandic from the eighth to the eleventh centuries, yet Dasent seems to consider these comparatively ancient borrowings to be purer and more acceptable than more recent loanwords, implying that linguistic impurities somehow become mysteriously decontaminated as time passes. These chronological difficulties often emerge when languages are assessed subjectively in terms of their respective cleanliness.

Dasent's views about such matters were no doubt influenced by Rask's own purism, and certainly the latter's studies of Icelandic were, at times, both archaising and prescriptively descriptive. Rask was keen to salvage and foster what he considered to be best practice, rather than merely describe the natural development of Old Norse into Modern Icelandic. The *Anvisning* contains a section (chapter 26) which describes 'Nyare Språket' (The Modern Language). Dasent translates this, somewhat misleadingly, as 'The Modern Dialect', presumably because he was reluctant to imply that Old Norse and Modern Icelandic were different languages.[52] When considering 'Nyare Språket', Rask's initial focus was on orthographical corruptions. He traces the problem back to the medieval period – 'ortografin var i medeltiden mycket förskämd' ('the orthography was very corrupt in the Middle Ages') – and exemplifies this by discussing phenomena such as vowel doubling (e.g., <foor> rather than <för>).[53] In his translation of this section, Dasent interlards the claim that these corruptions are due to 'many Danicisms' infiltrating the language.[54] At times, though, Dasent's championing of linguistic reform manifests itself even more vividly. Rask mentions, in passing, that many of the corrupt forms have now been 'mera lyckligtvis åter bortlagde' ('more happily done away with'), but Dasent embellishes this remark considerably, observing that the language 'has been in a good degree restored to its pristine simplicity and purity, by the extirpation of these barbarisms, within the last half century'.[55] He evidently approves of such interventionist prescriptivism. Rask had mentioned specific linguistic

---

attitude to the present and the future, a directive about we are behaving or should behave in the world' (p. 727).

[52] Dasent, *Grammar*, 157.

[53] Rasmus Rask, *Anvisning till Isländskan eller Nordiska Fornspråket* (Copenhagen: Olof Grahn, 1818), 293.

[54] Dasent, *Grammar*, 157.   [55] Dasent, *Grammar*, 157.

reforms elsewhere in the *Averning*. For instance, two declension patterns are given for *–ir* nouns such as *læknir* (doctor):[56]

		Modern Icelandic	Old Norse
Sing.	Nom	læknir	læknir
	Acc	læknir	lækni
	Dat	læknir	lækni
	Gen	læknirs	læknis
Pl.	Nom	læknirar	læknar
	Acc	læknira	lækna
	Dat	læknirum	læknum
	Gen	læknira	lækna

This suggests that in spoken Icelandic of the early nineteenth century, *laeknir–* had become the regular root for all grammatical cases in this paradigm, and that this simplified declension was the norm. Nonetheless, Rask makes it clear that the Old Norse paradigm is the correct one that ought to be used. As usual, Dasent follows his source closely, and in subsequent English-language grammars of Icelandic, the Old Norse paradigm is the only one presented. Rask's prescriptivism proved to be potent, since the Old Norse paradigm has been reinstated as the conventional one for Modern Icelandic.[57] There is further evidence for this kind of prescriptivism in relation to other aspects of the language system. Following Rask, Dasent observes that '[a]ll good writers now endeavour to substitute genuine old words, or words newly formed according to the genius of the language, for the Danicisms and other innovations which the moderns have introduced' and suggests that *endrbætn* (reform) should be used instead of the Latinate loanword *reformera*, and *lagamaðr* instead of *juristi* (lawyer).[58] Once again the tendency here is primarily prescriptive, and practices deemed to be detrimental are actively discouraged. While it is possible, as in this instance, to discourage by overtly prohibiting, it is also possible to influence by means of silence – and Rask (and therefore Dasent) adopted that approach too, at times. For instance, the progressive aspect is most commonly expressed in Modern Icelandic by means of phrases that involve an infinitival complement: *ég er að lesa* (*I am reading*; literally, *I am to read*).[59] These structures were far from common in Old Norse, and nor are they mentioned by either Rask or Dasent. Presumably this omission insinuates disapproval rather than ignorance.

[56] Based on Rask, *Anvisning*, 76 and 295.
[57] Stefán Einarsson, *Icelandic: Grammar, Texts, Glossary*, 11th impression (Baltimore, MD: Johns Hopkins, 1994), 33.
[58] Dasent, *Grammar*, 452; compare Rask, *Anvisning*, 297.
[59] See Höskuldur Thráinsson, *The Syntax of Icelandic* (Cambridge: Cambridge University Press, 2007), 13–15.

When viewed from a strictly historicist perspective, the prescriptivist agenda favoured by Rask and Dasent necessarily blurred the distinction between Old Norse and Modern Icelandic. The grammatical analyses modified and reconfigured that which they purported merely to describe, and, as a result, Icelandic was altered so that it regained many words and grammatical forms from Old Norse which had been gradually lost during the intervening centuries. It is not clear whether the majority of British Icelandophiles were aware of these complexities, but words and phrases such as 'Icelandic', 'Old Northern' and 'Old Norse' were used interchangeably, and sometimes 'Modern Icelandic' was deployed when recent (perceived) solecisms or deviant grammatical forms were being highlighted. This terminological obfuscation certainly gave the misleading impression that the language spoken in 874 and the language spoken in 1874 were essentially identical, bolstering presuppositions concerning purity and continuity. This contrasts curiously with the strongly historicist Victorian exploration of the differences between, say, 'Anglo-Saxon' and 'Modern English'. As mentioned earlier, the diachronic scholarly endeavours of linguists such as John Mitchell Kemble, Benjamin Thorpe and Robert Gordon Latham were unremittingly historical in nature, seeking to delineate the way in which Old English had gradually developed into Modern English. There were no meaningful attempts to reform Modern English so that it resembled Old English again, though (as mentioned earlier) some writers favoured a Germanic rather than Romance vocabulary, while others offered archaising precriptivist guidance concerning grammar. Sometimes the underlying tendencies seem to have been more apparent to external observers than to those most actively involved in the research. In his *Lectures on the English Language* (1860), the American George Perkins Marsh commented on 'the spirit of nationality and linguistic purism' which he considered to be so typical of nineteenth-century Europe, adding that

[it] has revived so many dying, and purged and renovated so many decayed and corrupted European languages within the last century. In almost every Continental country, foreign words and phrases have been expelled, and their places supplied by native derivatives, compounds and constructions; obsolete words have been restored, vague and anomalous orthography conformed to etymology or to ortheopy, and thus the whole dress and the essential spirit of each made more national and idiomatic, and, therefore, more diverse from all others, and less capable of being adequately rendered into any of them.[60]

---

[60] George Perkins Marsh, *Lectures on the English Language*, 4th ed. (New York and London: John Murray, 1863), 598. 'Ortheopy' is the study of 'correct' pronunciation.

Reading this strikingly pertinent summary, it is important to remember that Marsh had produced the first English translation of Rask's *Averning* in 1838, so he understood fully how linguistic purism had moulded and shaped Icelandic since the late eighteenth century. As he saw it, linguistic reforms of this kind were prompted in part by nationalist sentiments which inculcated a need for a distinct cultural identity.

So, like his mentor Rask and many of his British contemporaries, Dasent longed for Old Norse and Modern Icelandic to be indistinguishable, and his own variety of prescriptive historicism was intended to ameliorate the language while appearing merely to describe its features. Unsurprisingly, this agenda proved to be unsustainable. From the 1840s onwards, Britons visited Iceland in increasing numbers as tourists, and this brought them into close contact with Modern Icelandic. The tourism boom was partly the result of the popularity of English translations of the sagas: English-speaking readers were keen to visit Bergþórshvoll, Hlíðarendi, Laxárdalur, Hítardalur, Vestfirðir and so on – the very places where Unnr The Deep-Minded, Guðrun Ósvífrsdóttir, Kjartan Ólafsson, Bolli Bollason, Njáll Þorgeirsson, Grettir Ásmundarson, Egill Skallagrímsson, Gísli Súrsson and other legendary figures from the settlement period had lived, loved and fought. Publications such as Frederick Metcalfe's *An Oxonian in Iceland* (1861) and William Gershom Collingwood and Jón Stefánsson's *A Pilgrimage to the Sagasteads of Iceland* (1899) encouraged this kind of literary sightseeing. Metcalfe frequently associates the Icelandic landscape with details from specific sagas, and this was typical of the genre. Arriving in Undirfell, he remarks that '[t]he whole scene hereabout is described with such minuteness by the [Vasdal] saga . . . that the actual localities can be easily identified'.[61] However, most Britons who arrived in Iceland clutching their translations of Old Norse texts and perhaps a copy of Dasent's *Grammar* soon found they could not communicate easily with the natives. Consequently, they gradually came to realise that the much-vaunted linguistic continuity of Icelandic was, in fact, a myth. A few enterprising publishers sought to rectify the situation. In 1866 Franz Thimm published *A Short Practical and Easy Method of Learning the Old Norsk Tongue or Icelandic Language*. The text had been written by a certain 'H. Lund' (about whom little is known) and it mainly offers an English translation of various parts of Rask's grammars, though at times it recalls Dasent's Introduction to his *Grammar*. Lund describes Old Norse and 'Anglo-Saxon' as being 'the parents of the English Language', and he claims that a knowledge of them is 'absolutely necessary

---

[61] Frederick Metcalfe, *An Oxonian in Iceland* (London: Longman, Green, Longman, and Roberts, 1860), 215.

to every educated Englishman who looks upon his language with the
eye of a historian and philosopher'.[62] What distinguishes Lund's book,
though, is the inclusion of a section devoted to 'Modern Icelandic for
Travellers'. This is effectively a free-standing phrasebook, which is not
derived from Rask, and which is neither prescriptivist nor archaising. It
was designed to familiarise Victorian travellers with colloquial Modern
Icelandic. It includes vocabulary such as *járnbrautin* (railway; an *ex interno*
neologism which literally means 'iron path') and *skrúfugufuskip* (screw
steamer; another *ex interno* neologism). Although Lund never discusses
and analyses these neologisms, they embody the linguistic purism that
had become so characteristic of Icelandic culture by the 1860s. New
objects and ideas were expressed using existing vocabulary, usually by
means of compounding and lexical recycling – but Lund does not discuss
these processes. He does, though, include practical sentences which
indirectly cast light on the British views of Iceland:[63]

The Icelanders think little of time	Íslendingar hugsa eigi mikið un tímann
What is that called in Danish?	Hvað er það kallad á dönsku?
Society here [i.e., Reykjavik] is purely Danish	Samkvoemin eru hér með alveg dönsku sniði

These sorts of examples convey crude caricatured, sometimes xeno-
phobic, stereotypes, but the second and third sentences at least provide
context for recent claims that the language spoken during the mid-
nineteenth century in the ports and harbours such as Reykjavík was
actually a mixed Dano–Icelandic hybrid which had emerged to facilitate
trade.[64] And Danish was not the only source of influence at this time.
During his travels around Iceland in 1871 and 1876, William Morris was
addressed in French and even Latin, in addition to English and
Icelandic.[65] Given these socio-linguistic complexities, it soon becomes
apparent that even a person with a comprehensive knowledge of Old
Norse would struggle to communicate in such a mixed linguistic environment, hence the need for supplementary phrasebooks. This meant
that, by the 1860s, there was a growing realisation in Britain that
Old Norse and Modern Icelandic were noticeably distinct (though

---

[62] H. Lund, *A Short Practical and Easy Method of Learning the Old Norsk Tongue or Icelandic
Language* (London: Franz Thimm, 1866), Preface.
[63] Lund, *Easy Method*, 105, 120.
[64] Judith Rosenhouse and Rotem Kowner, eds., *Globally Speaking: Motives for Adopting
English Vocabulary in Other Languages* (Clevedon: Multilingual Matters, 2008), 23;
Kjartan G. Ottósson, *Íslensk málhreinsun: Sögulegt yfirlit* [Purism in Icelandic: An
Historical Perspective] (Reykjavík: Íslensk málnefnd, 1990), 29–52.
[65] William Morris, *Journals of Travel in Iceland, 1871, 1873: The Collected Works of William
Morris*, Vol. 8 (Cambridge: Cambridge University Press, 2012), 27, 63.

historically related) linguistic systems which, despite systematic purism, were increasingly separated by the rapid proliferation of *ex interno* neologisms as well as natural processes of language change (e.g., the emergence of the grammatical forms which convey the progressive aspect). Consequently, English–Icelandic phrasebooks began to appear during the second half of the Victorian period, and this development continued well beyond 1901.[66]

This growing appreciation of the difference between Old Norse and Modern Icelandic caused difficulties for Victorian linguists interested in Icelandic grammar. George Bayldon's *An Elementary Grammar of the Old Norse or Icelandic Language* (1870) and Henry Sweet's *An Icelandic Primer* (1886) provide an informative contrast. Neither Bayldon nor Sweet held tenured university positions during their careers, yet both produced important linguistic studies. Bayldon was a polyglot clergyman who taught himself Icelandic. His obituary in *The Yorkshire Post* claimed he knew 'no fewer than seventeen languages'. It also stated that his Icelandic *Grammar* was 'the only thing of the kind in English which has not been translated from confusing foreign works', adding that '[i]t was the fruit of original research, made at a time when Oxford cared nothing about the origins of English, and our indebtedness to Old Norse was suspected by very few'.[67] This overstates the case considerably, since Bayldon was surely at least familiar with Rask's, Dasent's and possibly even Lund's grammars. He does not name any of these authors directly in his *Grammar*, though he does refer to 'the standard authorities'.[68] By contrast, Henry Sweet studied languages at Heidelberg and Oxford; he specialised in German and Nordic linguistics (especially Old English and Old Norse) as well as phonetics, and he eventually became president of the Philological Society. However, despite these similarities, Bayldon's *Grammar* and Sweet's *Primer* differ significantly in their handling of the relationship between Old Norse and Modern Icelandic. Since Bayldon's *Grammar* self-professedly seeks to provide an introduction to the language with 'the utmost brevity', he presents many conjugation and declension tables without much accompanying discussion, and although the emphasis is primarily on Old Norse, he identifies differences between it and Modern Icelandic.[69] For instance, he gives

---

[66] For instance, see Anon., *The Englishman on Iceland: How to Make Yourself Understood* (Bonn, 1909).

[67] W. Paley Baildon, *Baildon and the Baildons: A History of a Yorkshire Manor and Family*, Vol. 1 (London: St. Catherine Press, 1912), 413.

[68] George Bayldon, *An Elementary Grammar of the Old Norse or Icelandic Language* (London: Edinburgh, Williams and Norgate, 1870), iii.

[69] Bayldon, *Grammar*, iii.

the declension for *orð* (*word*; a neuter noun) in the singular with the suffixed definite article as follows:

Nom.	orð-it
Acc,	orð-it
Dat.	orði-nu
Gen.	orðs-ins

He adds that '[t]he neuter *it* occurs in some books in the form *ið*, especially after the radical *t*; and in all cases of Modern Icelandic'.[70] This small detail is not mentioned by Rask, Dasent or Lund, which suggests that Bayldon is not merely following pre-existing sources slavishly. He goes on to say that in 'modern Icelandic' the words *sá, sú,* and *þat* are 'used instead of *hinn* as an article', another point that had not been mentioned by his predecessors.[71] It is worth pausing to wonder why Bayldon chose to include this kind of information. If his text was designed to enable readers to acquire a good working knowledge of Old Norse, so they could read the Sagas and the Eddas in the original, then there was no need to mention modern usage at all. Seemingly he was struggling to reconcile the tension between a synchronic presentation of Old Norse and a diachronic account of the development of Icelandic, and, in trying to accomplish both tasks, he accomplished neither satisfactorily. By contrast, Sweet handles all of this far more decisively. In so doing he acknowledges his profound debt to Alfred Noreen's *Altisländische und altnorwegische Grammatik* (*A Grammar of Old Icelandic and Old Norse*; 1884), describing it as 'by far the best Icelandic grammar that has yet appeared'.[72] Accordingly, his own *Primer* opens with a pithy declarative: '[t]his book deals with Old Icelandic in its classical period, between 1200 and 1350.'[73] There is no ambiguity here: the dates are unarguable, and there is no attempt to perpetuate the myth of continuity in the main sections of his *Primer*. His emphasis is consistently descriptive and synchronic: he is simply trying to delineate the language system as it existed during the period 1200–1350. He is not seeking to offer a detailed diachronic overview of the historical development of Icelandic through the centuries. Therefore, although the *Primer* is, in effect, an historical grammar (since it analyses a language system that is no longer extant), the main purpose of the text is not strictly historicist since it is not concerned with developmental processes.

---

[70] Bayldon, *Grammar*, 28, 35.   [71] Bayldon, *Grammar*, 93.
[72] Henry Sweet, *An Icelandic Primer*, 2nd ed. (Oxford: Clarendon Press, 1895), iv.
[73] Sweet, *Primer*, 1.

The same methodological difficulties also affected lexicographers, of course. The initial inspiration for an Icelandic–English dictionary came from the amateur linguist Richard Cleasby, who outlined his plan for *A General Dictionary of the Old Scandinavian Language* in 1840. Cleasby died in 1847 after collating material with the help of collaborators such as Konrad Gislason and Sveinbjörn Egilsson.[74] After a period of uncertainty and misfortune during which some of Cleasby's papers were lost, the surviving documents found their way to Dasent in 1855, and he negotiated with the Oxford Clarendon Press. He urged them to publish the dictionary, which they agreed to do after realising that the work would be of considerable interest to students of 'Old English'.[75] Dasent enlisted the assistance of the Icelandic scholar Guðbrandur Vigfússon (who subsequently became Reader in Scandinavian Studies at Oxford University) in 1864, and the latter eventually took over the long-delayed project. The completed work was finally published in 1873 as *An Icelandic–English Dictionary*, thirty-three years after Cleasby had originally mooted the idea. The Introduction was written by Henry Liddell, the Vice-Chancellor of Oxford University and a lexicographer, who, along with Robert Scott, had compiled *A Greek–English Lexicon* (1843). Liddell invokes the myth of continuity overtly in his text, observing that '[t]he history of the preservation of this language in its ancient form is remarkable'.[76] He offers a brief historical overview of the settlement of Iceland, and comments that 'while new dialects formed themselves throughout Scandinavia, in Iceland the old tongue rose to the dignity of a literary language, and thereby retained its original form. It has thus been preserved to our days.'[77] Curiously, however, when emphasising the scope of the dictionary itself, he undermines this alluring vision of uniformity: 'though the Dictionary is mainly intended for the old authors, both in prose and poetry, it endeavours to embrace an account of the whole language, old and new.'[78] By contrast, Guðbrandur is consistently unambiguous about the nature of his task: '[n]o Icelandic dictionary can be said to be complete that does not pay attention to the present language: the old literature, however rich, does not give the whole language, but must be supplemented and illustrated by the living tongue.'[79] Consequently, the dictionary includes information about

[74] Richard Cleasby and Guðbrandur Vigfússon, *An Icelandic–English Dictionary* (Oxford: Clarendon Press, 1874), Introduction.
[75] Cleasby and Vigfússon, *Dictionary*, Introduction.
[76] Cleasby and Vigfússon, *Dictionary*, Introduction.
[77] Cleasby and Vigfússon, *Dictionary*, Introduction.
[78] Cleasby and Vigfússon, *Dictionary*, Introduction.
[79] Cleasby and Vigfússon, *Dictionary*, xii.

Old Norse *and* Modern Icelandic. To select just one example, the entry for *tungl* (moon) notes that 'the modern phrase "new moon" (nýtt tungl), = the young moon, is derived from the Latin'.[80] These sorts of analogical forms are not suppressed or stigmatised. They are recognised as constituting a valid part of the Modern Icelandic lexicon.

During the last decades of the Victorian era, grammatical studies such as Sweet's *Primer* and lexicographical projects such as Guðbrandur's *An Icelandic–English Dictionary* bifurcated the study of Icelandic into two parallel channels, both of which were descriptive, rather than prescriptive, and synchronic, rather than diachronic. It became obvious that the scholarly historical study of Old Norse needed to be approached separately from the analysis of Modern Icelandic, and the myth of continuity waned rapidly as a result. Specialist dictionaries such as Geir T. Zoëga's *A Concise Dictionary of Old Icelandic* (1910) served a very specific academic purpose, as did updated primers such as E. V. Gordon's *A Introduction to Old Norse* (1938). By contrast, texts such as Snæbjörn Jónsson's *A Primer of Modern Icelandic* (1927) assisted those who sought a working knowledge of the modern language specifically. The emergence of these separate scholarly domains created a divide which still exists today, and it undermined both the historicist and prescriptivist tendencies of nineteenth-century linguistic research. There was no place in an Old Norse grammar or dictionary for the sort of prescriptivism that Dasent had championed, since the language of the Sagas and the Eddas did not need to be reformed. Conversely, the grammars and dictionaries of Modern Icelandic did not need to focus on the historical development of the language since that is not a prerequisite for understanding the language in its current manifestation. Consequently, the two separate traditions that emerged simply analysed Icelandic at two different stages in its development – namely, 1200–1350 (Old Norse) and 1850–present (Modern Icelandic). Crucially, the Second World War helped to reinforce this division, since it created a greater urgency for reliable linguistic analyses of colloquial Modern Icelandic. Iceland was invaded by British troops on 10 May 1940 and US Marines were stationed there from 1941 onwards. Stefán Einarsson's monumental textbook *Icelandic: Grammar, Texts, Glossary*, which was eventually published in 1945, was written primarily to assist military personnel, and it remains an authoritative, if dated, resource to this day. Revealingly, though, a detailed diachronic study of the development of the language from the ninth century to the present has yet to be written, either in English or in Icelandic.

[80] Cleasby and Vigfússon, *Dictionary*, 644, *tungl*.

Conclusion

It is a curious fact that recent research into Victorian linguistics has been simultaneously both selectively exhaustive and eclectically parsimonious. A small number of important topics have received disproportionate attention, while other fascinating and significant endeavours have barely been discussed at all. Anna Morpurgo Davies has identified this problem acutely: 'our historiography has blotted away not only "minor" authors, but also unpalatable work by "major" authors', and although these reductive approaches have occasionally enabled some kind of coherent characterisation of the age to emerge, such depictions are unavoidably distorted caricatures.[81] Ironically, this tendency towards 'blotting out' is manifest in Davies' own work. Her monograph boldly claims to consider the vast domain of nineteenth-century linguistics, and yet *Victorian* linguists are rarely considered. Even the *OED* is only name-checked briefly, in passing, three times.[82] Predictably (and understandably), when the Victorians have been discussed in academic studies, the main focus has fallen upon the way in which they responded to Germanic historicism and organicism, as embodied in the work of Friedrich Schlegel, Franz Bopp, Jacob Grimm and, later, the Neogrammarians. This interest in the methodology and emphasis of comparative and historical approaches inevitably fostered an indigenous preoccupation with the origins and development of the English language – a trend that resulted both in a deeper academic understanding of Old English and in the creation of the *OED*. However, this broadly historicist tendency was not confined only to the chronological period associated with the emergence of the Indo-European language family. Indeed, the vibrant interdisciplinary discussions concerning evolution, which increased in intensity from the late 1850s onwards, encouraged linguists to reflect upon the origins of human language more generally. These debates played a crucial role, since, as mentioned earlier, influential figures such as Müller and Wallace considered the emergence of natural language to be unexplained by natural selection, though Darwin strongly disagreed.

So, the conventional picture, as sketched above, is that historicism was the dominant ideology that guided linguistic research in the Victorian period. However, a simple statement of this kind disguises many of the complexities that arose as subtly different kinds of historicism were adopted, adapted and, sometimes, rejected by a wide range of linguists. This chapter has sought to initiate a more detailed discussion of these

---

[81] Davies, *Nineteenth-century Linguistics*, 2.
[82] Davies, *Nineteenth-century Linguistics*, 85, 154, 160.

intricacies by probing the Victorian fascination with Icelandic, a linguistic system which appeared to confute conventional theorising about the development of natural language. The pervasive conviction that languages inevitably decay was problematised by the fact that Icelandic seemed to have existed in a pure and unaltered state for more than a thousand years. The language appeared to be an inexplicable anomaly, at once ossified and yet alive. This appearance was deceptive, though, since the attractive closeness between Modern Icelandic and Old Norse was largely synthetic, the result of decades of sustained linguistic purism by Icelandic and Dutch intellectuals from the eighteenth century onwards, which had been influentially bolstered by the prescriptive historicism favoured by Rask.

In Britain specifically, the grammatical studies produced by Dasent and his immediate successors during the 1840s and 1850s reveal the extent to which Victorian linguists attempted to reconcile the potentially opposing ideologies of prescriptivism and historicism. They wanted objectively to analyse the historical development of Icelandic in comparison to genealogically related languages, but they also wanted to modify and alter the language so as to improve and/or restore it. In many respects, this undertaking is similar in spirit to contemporaneous developments such as the nascent interest in ecological conservation and the increasingly vocal calls to preserve and restore Britain's ancient cultural heritage.[83] Accordingly, the linguists sought to unite passively descriptive and actively interventionist analytical methodologies, a task that required considerable ingenuity. The attempted merging of these potentially antithetical approaches temporarily sustained the myth of Icelandic's continuity, but, as the nineteenth century advanced, this fabrication became increasingly untenable. By the 1870s and 1880s, Victorian linguists, such as Sweet and Guðbrandur, had begun routinely to treat Modern Icelandic and Old Norse as two historically related but distinct linguistic systems, and the emphasis of the analyses was generally descriptive and synchronic rather than prescriptive and diachronic. Without understanding in some detail these complex developments, it is impossible to appreciate the ways in which historicism (broadly conceived) informed the language sciences in Victorian Britain. In assessing this topic, one might be tempted to frame the discussion in strongly theoretical terms,

---

[83] Victorian environmentalism is discussed at length in James Winters, *Secure From Rash Assault: Sustaining the Victorian Environment* (Berkeley: University of California Press, 1999). In Britain, notable figures such as John Lubbock helped to initiate the heritage movement which resulted in the Ancient Monuments Protection Act of 1882. For details, see Horace G. Hutchinson, *Life of Sir John Lubbock, Lord Avebury* (London: Macmillan, 1914).

seeking to identify a Kuhnian paradigm shift or a succession of Foucauldian *épistémès*. However, such an endeavour would be risibly premature at this stage since so little is known about the vast majority of trends and sub-movements which prevailed during the period. Indeed, even if this knowledge were readily available, the domain of enquiry would be so vastly heterogeneous that any attempt to identify a small set of fundamental common principles, conventions or rules would produce an account that was flimsy and ephemeral. Consequently, this chapter has adopted a more cautious approach by concentrating instead on one particular, but particularly problematical, case-study. It is only by reflecting upon such specific instances at length that we will be able, eventually, to obtain an appropriately detailed understanding of the many ways in which historicism influenced the language sciences in Victorian Britain.

5   Literature

Ian Duncan

Literature in the Human Age

At the opening of *Middlemarch*, George Eliot aligns her work of fiction with the mid-Victorian human sciences. "Who that cares much to know the history of man, and how the mysterious mixture behaves under the varying experiments of Time," she writes, "has not dwelt, at least briefly, on the life of Saint Theresa": The type or specimen of a woman who aspires to realize "a national idea" but is excluded from the masculine fields of endeavor in which national ideas are realized.[1] Where the sixteenth-century saint could "[find] her epos in the reform of a religious order," *Middlemarch* calls our attention to innumerable "later-born Theresas" (3) destined to lead lives composed of "unhistoric acts" (838) through the lack of an institutional medium in which to accomplish their ambition. The novel assumes the task of producing scientific knowledge of those unhistoric lives, absent from official reckonings of "the history of man," in the form of a conjectural case history: that of a "new Theresa" (838), Dorothea Brooke.

George Eliot's invocation of the history of man recalls Henry Fielding's manifesto for the novel in the introduction to *Tom Jones* (1749):

The provision, then, which we have here made, is no other than *Human Nature*. ... [N]or can the learned reader be ignorant, that in human nature, though here collected under one general name, is such prodigious variety, that a cook will have sooner gone through all the several species of animal and vegetable food in the world, than an author will be able to exhaust so extensive a subject.[2]

More comprehensively than other, ostensibly philosophical discourses, the novel can represent the prodigious variety of human nature while

---

[1] George Eliot, *Middlemarch*, ed. Rosemary Ashton (Harmondsworth: Penguin, 1994), p. 3. Future references to this edition will be cited in the text.
[2] Henry Fielding, *The History of Tom Jones, a Foundling*, ed. Simon Stern and John Bender (Oxford: Oxford University Press, 1996), p. 30.

maintaining its essential unity. Fielding annexes his "new province of writing" to the experimental science of man invoked by David Hume, ten years earlier, as the basis for all secular knowledge – as the totalizing, systematizing project of Enlightenment:

There is no question of importance, whose decision is not compriz'd in the science of man; and there is none, which can be decided with any certainty, before we become acquainted with that science. In pretending therefore to explain the principles of human nature, we in effect propose a compleat system of the sciences, built on a foundation almost entirely new, and the only one upon which they can stand with any security.[3]

The novel too, an upstart genre in search of legitimacy, stakes its claim on that new foundation.

The claim, it seemed, paid off. A long-standing critical consensus holds that the appearance of *Middlemarch* (1871–2) confirmed the pre-eminence of the novel over other genres in the nineteenth-century literary field. Meanwhile, a few months before *Middlemarch* began serial publication, Charles Darwin formally subsumed the constituent disciplines of the science of man, from anthropology to aesthetics, into the explanatory authority of the new natural history he had proposed a dozen years earlier in *On the Origin of Species*. *The Descent of Man* completed a historicization of human nature that had radically transformed its object in the 130 years since Hume's *Treatise*. Both these developments – the literary ascendancy of the novel and the scientific historicization of human nature – participated in a larger structural shift in the western knowledge system. "Literature" in the age of Hume and Fielding designated the general domain of the Enlightenment republic of letters, covering every kind of written discourse: treatises of natural and moral philosophy as well as history, memoirs, travelogues, sermons, conduct manuals, and *belles lettres*. The disaggregation of the republic of letters into the nineteenth-century "arts and sciences" brought the realignment of literature around the genres of poetry, drama, and prose fiction, split off from the knowledge-bearing discourses as these underwent reorganization into professional disciplines.[4] Human nature could no longer be the theme of a universal discourse, a science of man, as an emergent

---

[3] David Hume, *A Treatise of Human Nature*, ed. Ernest C. Mossner (Harmondsworth: Penguin, 1984), p. 43.

[4] See, e.g., Alan Bewell, *Wordsworth and the Enlightenment: Nature, Man and Society in the Experimental Poetry* (New Haven: Yale University Press, 1998), p. 13; Paul Keen, *The Crisis of Literature in the 1790s: Print Culture and the Public Sphere* (Cambridge: Cambridge University Press, 1999); Maureen McLane, *Romanticism and the Human Sciences: Poetry, Population, and the Discourse of the Species* (Cambridge: Cambridge University Press, 2000), pp. 10–13; Jon Klancher, *Transfiguring the Arts and Sciences: Knowledge and*

range of disciplines and ideologies laid rival claims on it. Instead it was literature that took over the role of a general writing that could be read by everyone, mediated not by specialist knowledge or technical language, but by the shared sensibilities and affections that constitute "our common nature."[5]

Maureen McLane has remarked on the emergence circa 1800 of "the structure of a literary anthropology – a conscious conjunction of the literary and the human," in which poetry arises as literature's ideal, "absolute" mode: "Poetry models itself as a totality for man, a synthesis of his faculties and powers, a return of human language to the human body."[6] Writing in 1802, William Wordsworth compared the poet, who "converses with general nature," with the man of science, who "[converses] with those particular parts of nature which are the objects of his studies":

The Man of Science seeks truth as a remote and unknown benefactor; he cherishes and loves it in his solitude: the Poet, singing a song in which all human beings join with him, rejoices in the presence of truth as our visible friend and hourly companion. Poetry is the breath and finer spirit of all knowledge; it is the impassioned expression which is in the countenance of all Science.[7]

Investing scientific knowledge with a human spirit and form, the poet reclaims a universal humanity that the rising scientific disciplines are dividing and dispersing among themselves.

A developmental model of organic form, originating in the late-Enlightenment German life sciences, systematized in Kant's *Critique of Judgment* and F. W. J. Schelling's *Naturphilosophie* and variously absorbed into the aesthetic theory of British Romanticism, supplied a physiological basis for this conjunction of the literary and the human.[8] Wordsworth's great "poem on the growth of my own mind," first drafted

Cultural Institutions in the Romantic Age (Cambridge: Cambridge University Press, 2013). On the formation of scientific disciplines see, e.g., Jan Golinski, *Making Natural Knowledge: Constructivism and the History of Science* (Cambridge: Cambridge University Press, 1998). For a critical view of the "rise of disciplinarity" see Luisa Calè and Adriana Craciun, "The Disorder of Things," *Eighteenth-Century Studies*, 45: 1 (2011), 1–13.

[5] Klancher, *Transfiguring the Arts and Sciences*, pp. 154–61. The phrase is Walter Scott's: *Ivanhoe*, ed. Ian Duncan (Oxford: Oxford University Press, 1998), p. 18.

[6] McLane, *Romanticism and the Human Sciences*, pp. 11, 19.

[7] William Wordsworth and S. T. Coleridge, *Lyrical Ballads 1798 and 1800*, ed. Michael Gamer and Dahlia Porter (Peterborough: Broadview, 2008): Wordsworth, 'Preface' (1802), pp. 422–3.

[8] See Robert J. Richards, *The Romantic Conception of Life: Science and Philosophy in the Age of Goethe* (Chicago: University of Chicago Press, 2000), pp. 6–14; Denise Gigante, *Life: Organic Form and Romanticism* (New Haven: Yale University Press, 2009), pp. 23–35; Jennifer Mensch, *Kant's Organicism* (Chicago: University of Chicago Press, 2014).

in 1798–9 and published posthumously in 1850 as *The Prelude*, undertook the most original and ambitious reclamation of human faculties
and powers through a literary performance of organic development in
nineteenth-century English poetry. A work not so much *written* as perpetually *in writing*, emergent throughout its author's long career, *The
Prelude* realizes a developmental poetics that eschews history in the
sense – codified by Enlightenment philosophical historicism – of an
objective, universal chronology of successive events and discrete social
stages. Modeling, instead, a generative oscillation among interior temporal states, an involution of the memory and imagination gestating
potential futures, Wordsworth's poem subsumes narrative to lyric on
an unprecedentedly grand scale.[9] In its investment in a developmental
organicism, a complex historicism at the level of individual sensation and
thought, *The Prelude* exemplifies a resistance to the authority of collective
models of history as national or human progress, since the French
Revolution, betraying its transformative promise, has failed the poetic
imagination. Modern criticism has taken this resistance to be constitutive
of Romantic poetry as such. Jerome Christensen, for example, sets
Romanticism's "rejection of the inevitability of history" via "the willful
commission of anachronism, the assertion of the historical as that which
could not be over because it has not yet really happened," against the
post-revolutionary, liberal model of universal history as "normal change"
(Immanuel Wallerstein's phrase) that would be naturalized in the
Victorian era.[10]

The present essay considers the tactically different assumption of an
anthropological project, a history of man, by the nineteenth-century
realist novel, which also absorbed the developmental model of organic
form via the Romantic Bildungsroman and (later) Auguste Comte's
social physics. "With the (modern) novel, literary form becomes a matter
no longer of poetical forms but of the form of life," writes Rüdiger
Campe, referring to Goethe's *Wilhelm Meister's Apprenticeship* and drawing the analogy with "instances of forming life in other fields (politics,
ethics, biology etc.)."[11] The German *Bildungsroman*, in this light, kept
faith with the Romantic ideology of an emergent, transhistorical organic
power or life force (*Lebenskraft*) that exceeded traditional historicist
accountings. In the British tradition, however, the novel remained a form

[9] See Monique R. Morgan, "Narrative Means to Lyric Ends in Wordsworth's Prelude," *Narrative* 16: 3 (2008), 298–330.
[10] Jerome Christensen, *Romanticism at the End of History* (Baltimore: The Johns Hopkins University Press, 2000), pp. 2, 7, 25.
[11] Rüdiger Campe, "Form and Life in the Theory of the Novel," *Constellations* 18: 1 (2011), 53.

of history as well as a form of life. The task of the novel became the reconciliation of organicist and historicist principles of development, bearing rival imperatives for the formation of human nature, which Romantic ideology had split apart. The most influential novels of the first half of the century – Walter Scott's – harnessed the developmental plot of *Bildung* to the progressive, stadial scheme of conjectural history devised in Scottish Enlightenment moral philosophy, bringing scientific rigour to the category – history – that had been routinely invoked on the title pages of eighteenth-century English novels, including Fielding's and Richardson's. National history would provide a framework for containing and stabilizing human nature amid the transformative surges of organic life.

George Eliot, whose mid-Victorian literary career coincided with the modern revolutions in the natural and human sciences, from sociology and cultural anthropology to evolutionary biology, understood her fiction as extending the tasks both of the historical novel and of the *Bildungsroman* in a complex synthesis of the developmental imperatives modeled by Enlightenment historicism (the medium of human progress) and Romantic organicism (the medium of life). Early in Book Two of *Middlemarch*, the narrator looks back to Fielding, by now a classical forebear, to compare their projects:

> A great historian, as he insisted on calling himself, who had the happiness to be dead a hundred and twenty years ago, and so to take his place among the colossi whose huge legs our living pettiness is observed to walk under, glories in his copious remarks and digressions as the least imitable part of his work, and especially in those initial chapters to the successive books of his history, where he seems to bring his arm-chair to the proscenium and chat with us in all the lusty ease of his fine English. But Fielding lived when the days were longer (for time, like money, is measured by our needs), when summer afternoons were spacious, and the clock ticked slowly in the winter evenings. We belated historians must not linger after his example ... I at least have so much to do in unravelling certain human lots, and seeing how they were woven and interwoven, that all the light I can command must be concentrated on this particular web, and not dispersed over that tempting range of relevancies called the universe. (141)

Fielding is "a great historian," the author of *Middlemarch* a "belated" one. Fielding called his work a history, meaning the history of an individual life (*The History of Tom Jones, A Foundling*), while affirming the unity and consistency of his multifarious theme, human nature. Eliot, with stylized anxiety (peering and picking at an illimitable text by candle-light), has designated her topic as "the history of man" – a history that makes man a "mysterious mixture," no longer uniform or stable, subject to "the varying experiments of Time." Time makes the difference.

Fielding is greater than us because he had more time. The diminished state of the human present is measured by a temporal acceleration (and a concomitant intensification of "our needs") even as the universe, the potential totality of "human lots," has expanded beyond our field of view. Fielding could enjoy longer days, more spacious summer afternoons, in a universe less than 6,000 years old. The scientific revolution that issued in Charles Lyell's *Principles of Geology* in the early 1830s (the period in which *Middlemarch* is set) dilated the history of the world, considered as a physical object or system, to an unimaginable magnitude. In 1869, the year Eliot began writing *Middlemarch*, T. H. Huxley locked horns with William Thomson (the future Lord Kelvin) in a public debate over the age of the earth, in which Huxley refuted Thomson's estimate (based on his thermodynamic theory) of a range of between 20 and 400 million years, with an outer limit of 100 million years for the accommodation of life: A reckoning insufficient to accommodate the operations of random individual variation and natural selection prescribed in Darwin's theory of the transmutation of species.[12]

The "belated historian" is writing, in short, when her theme, the history of man, is undergoing a seismic change: Preceded by sublime stretches of geological time, untenanted by human life, and followed, hypothetically, by a no less immense (potentially infinite) duration – in which the human, just as it has developed out of some other biological form, may continue to mutate into forms scarcely if at all conceivable to us now. "Life in its plenitude – in the sheer gusto of its living power – threatens to overwhelm formal containment" and generate "a new mode of monstrosity," writes Denise Gigante of Romantic vitalism.[13] Evolutionary time all but guaranteed the monstrous reshaping of human form by "living power." The prospect of a dispersal of interwoven human lots across the universe daunts the author of *Middlemarch* as a temporal more than a spatial contingency.

[12] See Martin Meisel, "On the Age of the Universe," *BRANCH: Britain, Representation and Nineteenth-Century History*, ed. Dino Franco Felluga (extension of *Romanticism and Victorianism on the Net*; www.branchcollective.org/?ps_articles=martin-meisel-on-the-age-of-the-universe, accessed 11/17/2013). On the rise of geology, "the first truly *historical* natural science," see Martin Rudwick, *Bursting the Limits of Time: The Reconstruction of Geohistory in the Age of Revolution* (Chicago: University of Chicago Press, 2005) and *Worlds Before Adam: The Reconstruction of Geohistory in the Age of Reform* (Chicago: University of Chicago Press, 2008), p. 2. On Romantic-period cultural analogues of "deep time" see Noah Heringman, *Sciences of Antiquity: Romantic Antiquarianism, Natural History and Knowledge Work* (Oxford: Oxford University Press, 2013).
[13] Gigante, *Life*, p. 48.

In the famous peroration to *On the Origin of Species*, Darwin sought to reconcile his readers to "this view of life" by invoking an aesthetic register of the beautiful and sublime:

There is grandeur in this view of life, with its several powers, having been originally breathed into a few forms or into one; and that, whilst this planet has gone cycling on according to the fixed law of gravity, from so simple a beginning endless forms most beautiful and most wonderful have been, and are being, evolved.[14]

But as the new branches of natural history delivered the human wholly to nature, they made it strange. Darwin jolts his readers affectively as well as cognitively out of the comfort of species-being in the conclusion to *The Descent of Man*, where he juxtaposes the autobiographical memory of his revulsion from the natives of Tierra del Fuego – bloody, superstitious, indecent, yet indubitably types of "our ancestors" – with anecdotes of the heroic bravery (morally speaking, the *humanity*) of monkeys and baboons: "He who has seen a savage in his native land will not feel much shame, if forced to acknowledge that the blood of some more humble creature flows in his veins."[15] Darwin has already drawn on the doctrine of embryological recapitulation, early in *The Descent*, to show how our physiology is haunted by pre-human ancestral forms, manifest in the stages of fetal development. Against these uncanny possibilities, nineteenth-century literary realism assumes its task as one of re-centering and re-familiarizing the human in the reader's field of view: returning us to an anthropomorphic scale of everyday life and feeling.

George Eliot came to understand the novelist's task as a shoring up of human nature, a defense of its coherence and integrity, against the flux of cosmic time. The radical historicization of "man" and "nature" and (at the same time) the invocation of a transhistorical, transhuman principle of "life" supply the philosophical conditions for the celebrated humanism of *Middlemarch* and of Victorian realism more generally. Eliot pursues that historicization all the way down, to the organic stuff of life, as well as upward, to the macroscopic register of the world (strategically circumscribed, in the subtitle of *Middlemarch*, in the form of "provincial life"). In what follows I consider how the changing conceptual conditions of human nature informed the reorganization of the novel as a genre in the Romantic period, before attending to Eliot's

[14] Charles Darwin, *On the Origin of Species*, ed. William Bynum (London: Penguin, 2009), p. 427.
[15] Charles Darwin, *The Descent of Man, and Selection in Relation to Sex*, ed. James Moore and Adrian Desmond (London: Penguin, 2004), p. 689.

fiction and its tracking of a turn from national history to natural history as the novel's grand temporal frame.

The Natural History of Man

History became the chief discourse for articulating human nature in the half-century after Hume and Fielding, in the proto-anthropological conjectural histories of the late Enlightenment. In his *Natural History, General and Particular* (successive editions, 1749–88), Buffon redefined the concept of species from a fixed essence, positioned on a taxonomic grid, to "an entity distributed in time and space," realized through its physical reproduction from generation to generation. The "Buffonian revolution" (in Philip Sloan's summary) entailed "a radical historicizing and naturalizing of the human species": Mankind, belonging to the earth, was dynamically formed by geography and history.[16] Providing a philosophical habitat for that quintessentially modern, secular genre, the novel, the new natural history brought to bear a set of urgent critical problems. Major Enlightenment thinkers, beginning with Buffon, sought to redraw the boundary of human distinctiveness even as they embedded man more deeply in the natural order. In the most influential attempt at a solution, given radical expression by Rousseau and variously developed by Scottish and German exponents of the new conjectural anthropology, two causally linked characteristics set man apart from other species. Both would provide key conditions for the "novelistic revolution" of European Romanticism, in which experimental new forms, most decisively the *Bildungsroman* and historical novel, re-equipped the novel for its nineteenth-century ascendancy.[17] In blunt summary: Man is distinguished from other creatures in that he has no form; what he has, instead, is history.[18] The human form, that is, is not given, prescribed, but unfolds itself historically, through time. The novel and its protagonist become distinguished, accordingly, by their commitment to formal principles of openness, heterogeneity, and plasticity, and to a developmental historicism.

---

[16] Phillip Sloan, "The Gaze of Natural History," in *Inventing Human Science: Eighteenth Century Domains*, ed. C. Fox, R. Porter, and R. Wokler (Berkeley: University of California Press, 1995), pp. 123, 126–7. On the taxonomic grid see Michel Foucault, *The Order of Things: An Archeology of the Human Sciences* (New York: Vintage Books, 1994), pp. 71–6, 128–57.

[17] On the novelistic revolution see Franco Moretti, "Modern European Literature: A Geographical Sketch," in *Distant Reading* (London: Verso, 2013), pp. 19–21.

[18] I shall be reproducing the period usage "man" in this essay; its gender problematic will come into focus at the end of the discussion.

More precisely, and problematically, man has a double history. In Rousseau's summary, in the *Discourse on the Origins of Inequality*, the "very specific property that distinguishes" man from other animals is "the faculty of perfecting oneself" (*la faculté de se perfectionner*):

[This faculty], with the aid of circumstances, successively develops all the others, and resides in us, in the species as well as in the individual, whereas an animal is at the end of several months what it will be for the rest of its life, and its species is after a thousand years what it was in the first year of those thousand.[19]

While animals have a single, stunted history, that of their ontogenetic development from infancy to maturity, not only does each human life have a history but so also does the human race or species. In more optimistic accounts, the two histories occupy a recursive relation – Herder's "chain of culture" (*Kette der Bildung, Kette der Kultur*) – in which each developmental track boosts the other, and in which the immanent, universal character of species-history precipitates the emergent singularity of the individual life. For Rousseau, however, perfectibility unmakes the human nature that it should secure. The (contingent but irreversible) entry into history is a fall out of nature: "the Mankind of one age is not the Mankind of another age"; "the human soul and passions, by imperceptible adulterations, so to speak change in Nature"; "as original man gradually vanishes, Society no longer offers to the eyes of the wise man anything but an assemblage of artificial men and factitious passions which are the product of all these relationships, and have no true foundation in Nature."[20]

In his early *Treatise on the Origin of Language*, Herder set out to answer the challenge posed by Rousseau: to account for the properties of human distinctiveness (language, history, culture) without severing man from nature. Herder develops (via H. S. Reimarus) Rousseau's observation "that each species has but its own instinct, while man perhaps having none that belongs to him, appropriates them all."[21] Man appropriates the instinctual skills of other creatures by observation and imitation. "His forces of soul are distributed over the world"; unfettered by instinct to a specialized task, "he has free space to practice in many things, and hence to improve himself constantly."[22] The human being's lack of natural predetermination, his lack of a given form, affords the freedom, the plasticity, through which he is able to develop – to take on all forms,

[19] Jean-Jacques Rousseau, *The Discourses and Other Political Writings*, ed. Victor Gourevich (Cambridge: Cambridge University Press, 1997), p. 141.
[20] Rousseau, *The Discourses*, p. 186.   [21] Rousseau, *The Discourses*, p. 135.
[22] Johann Gottfried Herder, *Philosophical Writings*, ed. Michael N. Forster (Cambridge: Cambridge University Press, 2002), p. 79.

to occupy all spaces and functions, to engage the world as a totality. Thus far, Herder recapitulates an enlightened idea of human exceptionalism that goes back (at least) to Pico della Mirandola's 1486 oration *De hominis dignitate*. The modern conception of secular, open-ended historical time makes the difference:

> [A man is] never the *whole human being*; always in development, in progression, in process of perfection ... We are always growing out of a childhood, however old we may be, are ever in motion, restless, unsatisfied. The essential feature of our life is never enjoyment but always progression, and we have never been human beings until we – have lived out our lives. By contrast, the bee was a bee when it built its first cell.[23]

Herder reinserts the disjunction between the life of the individual and the life of the species that preoccupied Rousseau, but he redirects its horizon of unity from a hypothetical (and inaccessible) past to an optative future. Nature does not reside in an original condition from which we have fallen but in a potential that realizes itself historically, in a continuous, never-ending process of emergence – human becoming rather than human being. An individual life cannot coincide with the life of the species since it is always developing, unfinished: "we have never been human beings until we have lived out our lives."

Herder amplifies this naturalistic conception of development, enfolding the species as well as the individual, and linking all living beings in a continuous organic series, in his magnum opus *Ideas for a Philosophy of the History of Mankind* (1784–91). There he draws on the hypotheses of an organic life-force (*Lebenskraft*) and formative drive (*Bildungstrieb*) articulated by German natural philosophers, notably Johann Friedrich Blumenbach, who drew in turn on the "epigenetic" embryology of Caspar Friedrich Wolff.[24] Herder acknowledges a division between "mankind" (*Menschheit*), or empirical species being, and "humanity" (*Humanität*), the fullness of moral and spiritual development. Any particular life history is a rehearsal of, a stage toward, a grand *Bildung der Humanität* – which nevertheless resides, Herder insists, within the faculties of human nature, and thus within human history, rather than at some unreachable, transcendental horizon.

Kant, Herder's former teacher, criticized Herder's invocation of the life-force for being mystical and poetic rather than truly scientific or philosophical, reliant on analogy rather than on a verifiable causal principle, and for unwittingly opening the door to the scandalous

---

[23] Herder, *Philosophical Writings*, pp. 130–1.
[24] See Richards, *Romantic Conception of Life*, pp. 211–22; Gigante, *Life*, pp. 16–22.

hypothesis of the transmutation of species.[25] Kant was not wrong to glimpse the prospect of a dissolution of species boundaries in Herder's vision of an organic developmental force flowing through the order of nature and culminating in the ascent of man, even as Herder sought to preserve human exceptionalism with the contention that man could command his own development by virtue of his emancipation from the bonds of instinct. It would not be long before radical thinkers, notably Jean Baptiste Lamarck, mobilized organic development to undo that exceptionalism. Lamarck's *Zoological Philosophy* (1809) fully immerses man in the complex tides of life – comprising the interaction of an organic developmental drive with geographical constraints and opportunities – such that the human form, like all natural forms, is open, plastic, mutable, shaped by environmental pressure on wants and habits.

The Novelistic Revolution

Formlessness or unformedness as the condition of the human, and of a freedom realized in development; and a doubled history, of the individual life and the life of the race or species. These are the "uniquely human" conditions or attributes around which the novel reorganizes itself in the Romantic period. The revolutions of the age were not, of course, only intellectual. "In the traumatic, fast-moving years between 1789 and 1815, human actions seem to have become indecipherable and threatening; to have – quite literally – lost their meaning," writes Franco Moretti: "Restoring a 'sense of history' becomes one of the great symbolic tasks of the age ... a task uniquely suited for novelists." New narrative technologies – a regulated diversity of languages and ideologies, omniscient narration, an intensified focus on "individual biography" – seek to recover "the anthropomorphism that modern history seems to have lost."[26] The novel attempts to capture a dialectic whereby the unformed protagonist, acquiring a form through history, gives history back a human form.

That protagonist finds a correlative in the formless form of the novel itself, in the work now universally designated as the original *Bildungsroman* or novel of development, Goethe's *Wilhelm Meister's Apprenticeship* (1795–6). *Wilhelm Meister* introduces a new protagonist – the subject of the new anthropology – into European fiction: sensitive, unsettled, drifting with circumstance, open to the world. Wilhelm is remarkable

---

[25] See John H. Zammito, *The Genesis of Kant's Critique of Judgment* (Chicago: University of Chicago Press, 1992), pp. 178–88; Richards, *Romantic Conception of Life*, pp. 222–7.
[26] Moretti, "Modern European Literature," p. 20.

for his "many-sided receptivity," according to Friedrich Schlegel, while his protean malleability and restlessness make him the representative creature of modernity, according to Moretti.[27] The form of Goethe's novel is likewise fluid, miscellaneous (accommodating other genres and discourses, from lyric poetry to treatises on the drama), as well as unfinished, open-ended (the story does not conclude but breaks off, with Wilhelm about to set out on another journey). "Not only is literary history in demand of novels, but the novel is always in demand of its own form," writes Campe: "Novels don't have form, they are in quest of it."[28]

Schlegel, the contemporary critic best attuned to this quality in *Wilhelm Meister* and to the emergent form of the Romantic novel, illuminates the difference between the German *Bildungsroman* and the other major new genre of Romantic fiction, the Scottish historical novel. "A novel is a romantic book" (*Ein Roman ist ein romantisches Buch*), in Schlegel's famous formulation, equivalent to what he elsewhere calls "a universal, progressive poetry":[29] The literary work as medium of a recombinatory developmental energy that reconstitutes all genres and discourses in its drive toward a yet-unrealized horizon of universality. It is a work homologous, in other words, with the new, Romantic conception of life and with the Herderian conception of human nature.[30] The heterogeneous, fragmentary, open-ended fictions – in Schlegel's phrase, mixtures of "storytelling, song, and other forms" – written in Germany, exemplified by *Wilhelm Meister*, are conspicuously at odds with the ascendant norms of novelistic practice in early nineteenth-century Great Britain, where Walter Scott, Jane Austen, and others consolidate the techniques of realism around the *topoi* of national history and domestic manners. In Germany, lacking a unified national state, a main tradition of the realist novel does not take hold until later in the century. The absence of a central state, far from impeding *Bildung*, keeps open its horizon of universal potentiality. Accordingly, in a taxonomic scandal much discussed in recent criticism, the *Bildungsroman* is not a clear-cut, stable genre, categorically commensurate with other genres like the historical

[27] F. Schlegel, "On Goethe's *Meister*," in *Classic and Romantic German Aesthetics*, ed. J. M. Bernstein (Cambridge: Cambridge University Press, 2003), p. 271; Franco Moretti, *The Way of the World: The Bildungsroman in European Culture* (London: Verso, 1987), pp. 5–6, 11.

[28] Campe, "Form and Life in the Theory of the Novel," p. 55.

[29] Schlegel, "Letter on the Novel" and "*Athenaeum* Fragment No. 118," in Bernstein, ed., *Classic and Romantic German Aesthetics*, pp. 293, 249.

[30] See Tobias Boes, "Apprenticeship of the Novel: The Bildungsroman and the Invention of History, ca. 1770–1820," *Comparative Literature Studies* 45: 3 (2008), 269–88 (esp. 273–5).

novel, so much as it is a principle that pervades the modern novel – the formative drive or life-force of the novel as such.[31]

In contrast to the German *Bildungsroman*, the Scottish historical novel is the flower of a strong modern state, which it makes its theme, at least to begin with. In Scott's *Waverley* (1814), the defeat of the 1745 Jacobite Rising completes the political absorption of Scotland into the United Kingdom. The plot of national formation, structured by the stadial social history developed in the Scottish Enlightenment, contains the energy of *Bildung* and gives form to the novel's protagonist: or rather, to put the case more accurately, it stabilizes his internal formlessness. Scott rewrites young Waverley's notoriously unfixed ("wavering") character as a weakness that conceals a secret strength, since Waverley's passive, receptive nature and adaptability to circumstances, the looseness of his commitment to any cause or interest, ensure his survival. Floating on the aesthetic surfaces of life, he drifts as lightly out of rebellion as he has drifted into it, to emerge as the prototypical liberal subject of modern civil society.[32]

Scott offers national history as a provisional solution to the predicament broached in Enlightenment anthropology: the disjunction between the contingent life of the individual and the open, universal life of species-being. Recasting the disjunction as a lack of fit between temporal scales, Scott binds the intimate lifespan of the individual to the destiny of the state. *Waverley* and its successors install "historical time," in Paul Ricoeur's formulation, as the interface between lived time (the "time of the soul") and cosmological time (the "time of the world").[33] The regional geography of a small nation (Scotland) and the lifespan of human memory define a gravitational field within which the forces of custom and sympathy can hold together a habitable domain of common life. Scott's formula "sixty years since" curbs what might otherwise be a dislocating historical distance by shaping the difference between then and now with a human form, human proportions. In his Scottish novels, at least, Scott stays close to a familiar terrain, one where the collective mnemonics of oral tradition and custom maintain a vital human measure

---

[31] On the taxonomic scandal see, e.g., Marc Redfield, *Phantom Formations: Aesthetic Ideology and the Bildungsroman* (Ithaca: Cornell University Press, 1996), pp. 40–3. Redfield quotes Robert Musil: "with every true experiment a cultured man educates himself [*bildet sich ein geistiger Mensch*]. This is the organic plasticity of man. In this sense every novel worthy of the name is a *Bildungsroman*" (pp. 42–3).

[32] See Ian Duncan, *Modern Romance and Transformations of the Novel: The Gothic, Scott, Dickens* (Cambridge: Cambridge University Press, 1992), pp. 79–92.

[33] Paul Ricoeur, *Memory, History, Forgetting* (Chicago: University of Chicago Press, 2009), p. 101.

between past and present and where the human, accordingly, is still knowable and readable, even when figured – in the person of the Waverley-hero – as chronically malleable and mutable, provisionally rather than absolutely fixed by a local domestic settlement.

In the introductory chapter to *Waverley*, Scott reassures his readers of his commitment to an unchanging core of human nature, counterbalancing the vertiginous intuition of historical process as wholesale, interminable transformation. The author has anchored his story in "those passions common to men in all stages of society, and which have alike agitated the human heart, whether it throbbed under the steel corslet of the fifteenth century, the brocaded coat of the eighteenth, or the blue frock and white dimity waistcoat of the present day." Scott adds: "It is from the great book of Nature, the same through a thousand editions, whether of black letter or wire-wove and hot-pressed, that I have venturously essayed to read a chapter to the public."[34] The Enlightenment wager proclaimed here – that, even though the human race may have a history, an enduring human nature transcends it – begins to falter in Scott's later fiction, as it moves its settings to more remote times and places, and we glimpse the drift of cultural difference into racial difference, of racial difference into species difference.[35]

György Lukács argued, famously, that the historical novel lost its critical edge, forged in the "classical form" established by Scott, with the European bourgeoisie's abdication of its progressive role after the 1848 revolutions.[36] I am sketching a different (although perhaps complementary) scenario, whereby the stabilizing, liberal–conservative schema of a regulated national history, founded on the Enlightenment idea of a universal human nature, buckles under the impact of radical hypotheses of developmental organic form and species transmutation – themselves associated with revolutionary political movements and events.[37] National history, as it loses its explanatory authority, dissolves into the larger, turbulent forcefield of natural history. By the late 1820s a more radical historicization of nature was overtaking human nature too, with polygenetic and transformist morphologies, once associated with revolutionary

---

[34] Walter Scott, *Waverley*, ed. P. D. Garside (London: Penguin Classics, 2011), pp. 6–7.

[35] See Ian Duncan, "The Trouble with Man: Scott, Romance, and World History in the Age of Lamarck," *Romantic Frictions*, ed. Theresa Kelley. *Romantic Circles: Praxis Series* (Sept. 2011). Web: http://romantic.arhu.umd.edu/praxis/frictions/HTML/praxis.2011 .duncan.html

[36] Georg Lukács, *The Historical Novel*, trans. Hannah Mitchell and Stanley Mitchell (Lincoln: University of Nebraska Press, 1983), pp. 239–45.

[37] On this see Adrian Desmond, *The Politics of Evolution: Morphology, Medicine and Reform in Radical London* (Chicago: University of Chicago Press, 1989).

materialism and atheism, gaining public ground. The plasticity, the developmental potential, that had set man apart from other creatures now compromised the boundary between them, as radical thinkers invested all life and the very category of species with the capacity to evolve – to change form. The surge in Lamarck's reputation in the decade leading up to the 1830 Revolution in France, and the embrace of transformist theory by radical and republican intellectuals on both sides of the English Channel, provoked vigorous rebuttals from powerful establishment scientists, notably Georges Cuvier and Charles Lyell. Lyell's summary of Lamarck's hypothesis in the second volume (1832) of *Principles of Geology* served to broadcast it to a wider British public, since no English translation would appear until 1914.

The Social Organism

George Eliot learned the application of organic developmentalism to human history from the science of society founded by Auguste Comte in the late 1830s and promoted in the early 1850s by her close associates at *The Westminster Review*, Herbert Spencer and George Henry Lewes.[38] Comte based his "social physics" on the natural sciences, and stressed the analogy with organic laws of development: "the succession of social states exactly corresponds, in a scientific sense, with the gradation of organisms in biology."[39] The principle was derived from Lamarck, whom Comte hailed (although rejecting the theory of species transmutation) as having "by far the clearer and profounder conception of the organic hierarchy" than Lamarck's great opponent, Cuvier.[40] With Spencer, the hypothesis of a biological infrastructure for social forms hardened into dogma. Popularizing Comte's term *"organisme social,"* he argued for a homological – no longer just analogical – relation between societies and organic bodies, subject alike to a progressive law of development from simple to more complex forms with increasingly individuated but interdependent parts.

[38] On Eliot's readings in Victorian social sciences and organic form see Sally Shuttleworth, *George Eliot and Nineteenth-Century Science: The Make Believe of a Beginning* (Cambridge: Cambridge University Press, 1984), pp. 4–23. See also (on Eliot's early work with Strauss and Feuerbach) Hina Nazar, "The Continental Eliot," in *A Companion to George Eliot*, ed. Amanda Anderson and Harry E. Shaw (Oxford: Wiley-Blackwell, 2013), pp. 417–18.

[39] Auguste Comte, *The Positive Philosophy*, "freely translated" by Harriet Martineau (New York: Blanchard, 1858), p. 91.

[40] Comte, *The Positive Philosophy*, p. 346.

Eliot summarizes the Comtean–Spencerian thesis in "The Natural History of German Life" (a review of the first two volumes of Wilhelm Heinrich Riehl's *Naturgeschichte des deutschen Volkes*), published in *The Westminster Review* in 1856, shortly before she turned to writing fiction:

The external conditions which society has inherited from the past are but the manifestation of inherited internal conditions in the human beings who compose it; the internal conditions and the external are related to each other as the organism and its medium, and development can take place only by the gradual consentaneous development of both ... Social Science, while it has departments which in their fundamental generality correspond to mathematics and physics, namely, those grand and simple generalizations which trace out the inevitable march of the human race as a whole, and, as a ramification of these, the laws of economical science, has also, in the departments of government and jurisprudence, which embrace the conditions of social life in all their complexity, what may be called its Biology, carrying us on to innumerable special phenomena which outlie the sphere of science, and belong to Natural History.[41]

Eliot's essay raises a key question for her novelistic practice and, more largely, for the novel's assumption of the anthropological history formulated in the late Enlightenment. She poses the question in two, complementary ways: that of the relation between the individual and the race, and that of the relation between the developmental drives of natural history and human history.

Eliot emphasizes the pre-modern character of Riehl's subject, the German *Volk*, bound by an organic temporality of the race that is anterior to – and resistant to – individual development:

In Germany, perhaps more than in any other country, it is among the peasantry that we must look for the historical type of the national physique. In the towns this type has become so modified to express the personality of the individual, that even "family likeness" is often but faintly marked. But the peasants may still be distinguished into groups by their physical peculiarities. In one part of the country we find a longer-legged, in another a broader-shouldered race, which has inherited these peculiarities for centuries ... [T]he cultured man acts more as an individual; the peasant, more as one of a group. Hans drives the plough, lives, and thinks just as Kunz does; and it is this fact, that many thousands of men are as like each other in thoughts and habits as so many sheep or oysters, which constitutes the weight of the peasantry in the social and political scale.[42]

Riehl's natural history consigns the peasantry to a prehistoric timescale regulated by biological laws of inheritance, the cycle of seasons, and the inertial force of custom. The antithetical temporality of culture, which

---

[41] Thomas Pinney, ed., *The Essays of George Eliot* (New York: Columbia University Press, 1963), pp. 286, 289–90.
[42] Pinney, *The Essays of George Eliot*, pp. 274–5.

belongs to urban life, comprises both national historical progress and individual development. Here we glimpse the schema of the nineteenth-century (post-Goethean) *Bildungsroman*, from Balzac through Hardy, in which characters escape from rural stagnation to enter the accelerated time of modernity – the time of the city and its institutions, of human history as change rather than continuity, of individual experience as growth and choice. A central paradox, with its roots in Enlightenment conjectural anthropology, takes shape. Human nature resides with the organic, communal life of the people; yet one becomes fully human only by quitting that life, struggling into individuation, into historical and ethical identity.

The project of a natural history of human life governs the fictions Eliot wrote after her review of Riehl: *Scenes of Clerical Life* (1857), *Adam Bede* (1859), and *The Mill on the Floss* (1860). As Sally Shuttleworth notes, the sequence of tales admits an increasing tension between the imperatives of organic continuity at the level of collective being and of developmental differentiation at the level of the individual.[43] Idyllic set-pieces of every-day life at the Hall Farm instantiate the social organism in *Adam Bede*, which opens in 1799 (the canonical "sixty years since" of *Waverley*) and closes with a present-tense glimpse of Adam's and Dinah's ongoing domestic felicity, synchronized grammatically with the time of reading. Individual and communal destinies may harmoniously merge once the self-destructive egotists Hetty Sorrel and Arthur Donnithorne have been expelled from the novel's world.

In contrast, the dragging, thwarting force of the social organism pre-dominates in *The Mill on the Floss*. That novel tracks the painful growth of the Tulliver children ("still very much like young animals"[44]) into the sexual, social, and ethical differentiations of adulthood. In its notorious conclusion, the cyclical time of natural catastrophe, materialized in the great flood that drowns Maggie and Tom, overwhelms the progressive temporality of *Bildung*. Eliot amplifies the rhetoric of natural history in her evocation of the story's provincial setting:

It is one of those old, old towns which impress one as a continuation and outgrowth of nature, as much as the nests of the bower-birds or the winding

---

[43] Shuttleworth, *George Eliot and Nineteenth-Century Science*, pp. 24–5, 48–50, 64–8, 76–7.

[44] George Eliot, *The Mill on the Floss*, ed. Gordon S. Haight (Oxford: Oxford University Press, 1981), p. 31. The narrator goes on to note the children's "resemblance to two friendly ponies." Elsewhere, Maggie is likened to "a small Shetland pony" (p. 13) and "a Skye terrier" (pp. 16, 28); Tom is "one of those lads that grow everywhere in England, and at twelve or thirteen years of age look as much alike as goslings" (p. 33); Maggie and Lucy are compared to "a rough, dark, overgrown puppy and a white kitten" (p. 61). Future references to this edition will be given in the text.

galleries of the white ants; a town which carries the traces of its long growth and history like a millennial tree, and has sprung up and developed in the same spot between the river and the low hill from the time when the Roman legions turned their backs on it from the camp on the hillside, and the long-haired sea-kings came up the river and looked with fierce, eager eyes at the fatness of the land. (115–6)

The town's population inhabits a collective mentality that is closed to its own deep past: "The mind of St. Ogg's did not look extensively before or after. It inherited a long past without thinking of it, and had no eyes for the spirits that walk the streets." To live in organic time is to live outside historical consciousness.

Halfway through *The Mill on the Floss*, the narrator pauses to reflect upon "the mental condition of these emmet-like Dodsons and Tullivers," with their custom-bound, unreflective, "semi-pagan" lives:

I share with you this sense of oppressive narrowness; but it is necessary that we should feel it, if we care to understand how it acted on the lives of Tom and Maggie, – how it has acted on young natures in many generations, that in the onward tendency of human things have risen above the mental level of the generation before them, to which they have been nevertheless tied by the strongest fibres of their hearts. The suffering, whether of martyr or victim, which belongs to every historical advance of mankind, is represented in this way in every town, and by hundreds of obscure hearths; and we need not shrink from this comparison of small things with great; for does not science tell us that its highest striving is after the ascertainment of a unity which shall bind the smallest things with the greatest? In natural science, I have understood, there is nothing petty to the mind that has a large vision of relations, and to which every single object suggests a vast sum of conditions. It is surely the same with the observation of human life. (272–3)

Suffering attends human progress, which the novel reckons in the scale of individual development. Thus Eliot derives a tragic ethos from the "large vision of relations" proper to "natural science." Early on she has awarded her heroine "that superior power of misery which distinguishes the human being, and places him at a proud distance from the most melancholy chimpanzee" (46–7). The irony saddens into truth as Maggie grows older and takes her place among "the dark unhappy ones" (332), tragic heroines of nineteenth-century fiction. To suffer – the authentic, inward stigma of development – is to be human. Still more, following the female *Bildungsroman* of Germaine de Staël and Charlotte Brontë, it is to be a woman, entangled more inextricably than men are in the meshes of custom.[45] By virtue of their suffering, their relegation to the sacrificial

---

[45] On *The Mill on the Floss* as a critique of the (gendered) protocols of the Goethean *Bildungsroman* see Susan Fraiman, *Unbecoming Women: British Women Writers and the Novel of Development* (New York: Columbia University Press, 1993), pp. 124–35.

role of "martyr or victim," women earn their status as the most fully human beings in Victorian fiction.

"Involuntary, Palpitating Life"

Middlemarch revisits the scenario of the heroine barred from the plot of *Bildung* by the ineluctable force of the social organism. The novel is generally regarded as the crowning achievement, at least in English fiction, of a nineteenth-century realism that represents the complex, evolving totality of individual lives that constitute a "social medium." "The highest Form," as George Eliot herself put it in an unpublished essay, "Notes on Form in Art" (1868), "is the highest organism, that is to say, the most varied group of relations bound together in a wholeness which again has the most varied relations with all other phenomena."[46] *Middlemarch* admits – via thematic and allusive networks extending across the text – the new sciences that were bringing organic developmentalism to bear on human life more rigorously than Comtean social physics, notably evolutionary and cell biology. At the same time, *Middlemarch* reclaims the traditional ground of the historical novel: a reclamation for which *Romola* (1863), Eliot's romance of quattrocento Florence, had constituted the antiquarian preparation. *Middlemarch* is set not only in the recent past, a generation since, but also around an epochal national event, the 1832 Reform Act, designating Reform (like Union in *Waverley*) as the public, historical correlative of the organic project of *Bildung*. With a precision and complexity unmatched in British fiction, Eliot's narrative calibrates the relations between historical change effected through human agency, both at the national level and within the ethical domain of character, and the organic tempos of individual and social life. In a striking turn from the earlier novels, *Middlemarch* compensates for the heroine's exclusion from historical agency by representing her ethical commitment – rather than involuntary submission – to the larger domain of organic life.

In 1868 (the year before Eliot began work on *Middlemarch*), G. H. Lewes published a four-part assessment of the new natural history, "Mr. Darwin's Hypotheses," in *The Fortnightly Review*; Gillian Beer calls this "a watershed in George Eliot's understanding of the implications of Darwin's thought."[47] Lewes opens the essay with a retrospect on the

---

[46] Pinney, ed., *Essays of George Eliot*, p. 433.
[47] Gillian Beer, *Darwin's Plots: Evolutionary Narrative in Darwin, George Eliot and Nineteenth-Century Fiction* (3rd ed., Cambridge: Cambridge University Press, 2009), p. 275, n. 12.

century-long rise of "the Development Hypothesis," from "the 'Theoria
Generationis' of Wolff (1759), which by the doctrine of Epigenesis laid
the foundation-stone of the theory of Development, [to] the 'Origin of
Species' (1859), which supplied the coping-stone."[48] Lewes hails the
Victorian apotheosis of "Development" as a totalizing principle that
construes all phenomena as historical, from the stars all the way down
to the organic building blocks of life. He and Eliot had read *On the Origin
of Species* together when it was first published. "It is an elaborate expos-
ition of the evidence in favour of the Development Theory, and so makes
an epoch," Eliot wrote, assimilating Darwin's argument to the more
diffuse evolutionism propounded by Comte and Spencer, and not yet
appreciating the full force of the theory of natural selection.[49] Evolutionary biology would make it possible for her, more than for any of her
literary predecessors or contemporaries, to extend historicism radically
throughout the entire domain of life, beyond the human scale.

Michel Foucault has accustomed us to the dictum that the Enlightenment figure of "man" gave way to the figure of "life" as the horizon of the
human sciences after 1800.[50] The Victorian sciences of life redistributed
meaning outward, from the scale of the human body and lifespan – no
longer now, as it was for a neoclassical (Vitruvian) aesthetics, the measure of the cosmos – to the macroscopic scale of populations and species,
in Malthusian political economy and Darwinian natural history.[51] At the
same time, the new cell biology coming out of Germany (Matthias
Schleiden and Theodor Schwann in the 1830s; Rudolf Virchow in the
1850s) redistributed life inward, downward, to the microscopic scale.
A human body was no longer a self-enclosed, integral being but an
aggregate of living units at the level of the cell.

Eliot lists Schwann and Schleiden in her "Quarry" for *Middlemarch*,
along with Huxley's 1853 essay "The Cell-Theory"; she and Lewes also
knew Virchow's work, and owned several of his books.[52] The advent of
the new histology is thematized in *Middlemarch* through Lydgate's quest

[48] G. H. Lewes, "Mr. Darwin's Hypotheses," *Fortnightly Review* (New Series) 3 (1868), 357.
[49] George Eliot, *The George Eliot Letters*, ed. Gordon Haight (9 vols.; New Haven: Yale University Press, 1954–83), vol. 3: p. 214; see Beer, *Darwin's Plots*, p. 146.
[50] Foucault, *The Order of Things*, pp. 160–2, 263–79. Foucault makes Cuvier the revolutionary figure, eliding Buffon, perhaps to maintain his *c*. 1800 periodization.
[51] See Catherine Gallagher, *The Body Economic: Life, Death, and Sensation in Political Economy and the Victorian Novel* (Princeton: Princeton University Press, 2006).
[52] George Eliot, *Quarry for Middlemarch*, ed. Anna Theresa Kitchel (Berkeley: University of California Press, 1950), p. 131; Kirstie Blair, "Contagious Sympathies: George Eliot and Rudolf Virchow," in *Unmapped Countries: Biological Visions in Nineteenth-Century Literature and Culture*, ed. Anne-Julia Zwierlein (London: Anthem Press, 2005), pp. 151–2.

for "the primitive tissue," rendered critically if sympathetically by Eliot's narrator. Most commentators have assumed that Lydgate's formulation of his research question "not quite in the way required by the waiting answer" (*Middlemarch*, 148) reflects his adherence to Xavier Bichat's tissue biology, on the cusp of its supersession by the new cell theory.[53] It is likely, however, that Eliot is also taking on Huxley's pointed critique of Schleiden and Schwann in the name of Wolffian epigenesis in his influential (if controversial) review of the field in "The Cell-Theory." The German cell theory, according to Huxley, forgets the fundamental principle of organic form, that of epigenetic development: "For Huxley, cells were not separate and independent entities – they were interconnected elements within the integrated organism, seamlessly interfacing with specialized body parts, such as tissues and organs."[54] As Laura Otis has argued, *Middlemarch* unfolds a "network" rather than a "membrane" model of the social organism.[55] Lydgate's desire "to demonstrate the more intimate relations of living structure" (148) harmonizes after all with the larger narrative emphasis, throughout *Middlemarch*, on the dynamic interaction between the distributed parts of social life within a complex totality.

Lydgate's failure to realize his scientific and reforming ambitions, due to his inability to resist the capillary pressure of the social organism, marks one extreme in the novel's uneven array of plots of *Bildung*. The character who conforms most closely to the figure of the romantic *Bildungsheld*, Will Ladislaw, expresses the archetypal traits of adaptive plasticity, sympathetic susceptibility, and openness to experience, charged with the vocabulary of organic development. Things go fortunately for him, as they did for Wilhelm Meister. Married to Dorothea, Will becomes "an ardent public man" in the early years of Reform

[53] See, e.g., W. J. Harvey, "The Intellectual Background of the Novel: Casaubon and Lydgate," in *Middlemarch: Critical Approaches to the Novel*, ed. Barbara Hardy (London: Athlone Press, 1967), p. 36; Patrick J. McCarthy, "Lydgate, 'The New, Young Surgeon' of *Middlemarch*," *SEL: Studies in English Literature* 10: 4 (1970), 805–16; Lawrence Rothfield, *Vital Signs: Medical Realism in Nineteenth-Century Literature* (Princeton: Princeton University Press, 1992), pp. 92–9; Blair, "Contagious Sympathies," p. 147.
[54] Marsha L. Richmond, "Thomas Huxley's Developmental View of the Cell," *Nature Reviews* 3 (2002), 61–5 (p. 64). See Richmond's more detailed statement of her argument, "T. H. Huxley's Criticism of German Cell Theory: An Epigenetic and Physiological Interpretation of Cell Structure," *Journal of the History of Biology* 33: 2 (2000), 247–89. See also L. S. Jacyna, "The Romantic Programme and the Reception of Cell Theory in Britain," *Journal of the History of Biology* 17: 1 (1984), 13–48 (pp. 19–20, 15).
[55] Laura Otis, *Networking: Communicating with Bodies and Machines in the Nineteenth Century* (Ann Arbor: University of Michigan Press, 2001), pp. 81–119.

legislation (836): Personal and national histories converge. But the true protagonist of *Middlemarch* is Dorothea, whose destiny charts the novel's most complicated relation between history, the public chronology of events and acts, and life, an organic totality rendered through symbolic patterning. The novel's closing paragraph definitively resolves the heroine's progress into the "unhistoric" mode of private influence rather than public action:

Her finely-touched spirit had still its fine issues, though they were not widely visible. Her full nature, like that river of which Cyrus broke the strength, spent itself in channels which had no great name on the earth. But the effect of her being on those around her was incalculably diffusive: for the growing good of the world is partly dependent on unhistoric acts ... (838)

The simile of the river, "broken" for purposes of military conquest (according to Eliot's source, Herodotus' *Histories* I: 189) but thence useful for agricultural irrigation, powerfully rewrites the great flood at the end of *The Mill on the Floss*. It converts tragic-heroic catastrophe into a tonally ambivalent – comic yet melancholic – evocation of ongoing domestic life. Event (the unit of historical reckoning) is subsumed into metaphor, with the "diffusive" maze of fertile channels reiterating, for the last time, the novel's master figure for organic form, the web.[56]

The ethical preparation for this resolution comes a few chapters earlier, in the spectacular epiphany of organic form vouchsafed to Dorothea after her night of spiritual trial:

She opened her curtains, and looked out towards the bit of road that lay in view, with fields beyond outside the entrance-gates. On the road there was a man with a bundle on his back and a woman carrying her baby; in the field she could see figures moving – perhaps the shepherd with his dog. Far off in the bending sky was the pearly light; and she felt the largeness of the world and the manifold wakings of men to labor and endurance. She was a part of that involuntary, palpitating life, and could neither look out on it from her luxurious shelter as a mere spectator, nor hide her eyes in selfish complaining. (788)

This bravura passage reaches beyond the human realm, economic and biological, of work and the family that it makes visible. It affirms Dorothea's membership in something larger than any geographically and historically located society: "involuntary, palpitating life," an entity at once superhuman and subhuman, enfolding every individual body and internal to each. It is all life, the totality of living beings, and it is also the substance that Lydgate was looking for, "the primitive tissue": in Lewes's phrase, "a microscopic lump of jelly-like substance,

---

[56] On the figure of the web see Beer, *Darwin's Plots*, pp. 156–61.

or protoplasm," evincing "the cardinal phenomena of life: Nutrition, Reproduction, and Contractility."[57]

We can see how this visionary appeal to the far reaches of organic form may strengthen and stabilize, rather than disperse, the integrity of human nature: Hence the language of an ethical reengagement on Dorothea's part. Eliot's figure balances the "family of man" between the scales of the biotic and the cellular in a moral as well as a formal equipoise. The scene of provincial life opens onto a sublime destiny that awaits the heroine's (and our) attention. Yet the figure also suggests something at least faintly monstrous – even if we do not go so far as to read it in the light of Lewes's startling conjecture that "the earth at the dawn of life was like a vast germinal membrane, every slightly diversified point providing its own vital form."[58] Manifest as a presence or power that exceeds the human, "involuntary, palpitating life" cancels (as it absorbs) what the novel – what "literature" – has been teaching us to value: any particular, individual life, with its sustaining, sympathetic properties of consciousness and freedom. For the new Theresa, as for women in general, if not humankind, biology subsumes history: And it is by no means clear what difference, what reclamation of freedom and consciousness, the ethical embrace of that destiny might afford. Organic form discloses the horizon of nineteenth-century literary realism – and its limit.

---

[57] Lewes, "Mr. Darwin's Hypotheses," 4 (1868), 61. On the figure of protoplasm in this passage see Ian Duncan, "George Eliot's Science Fiction," *Representations* 125 (2014), 26–7.

[58] Lewes, "Mr. Darwin's Hypotheses," 4 (1868), 494.

6   Moral Character

Lauren Goodlad

In his influential study, *After Virtue* (1981), the philosopher Alasdair MacIntyre portrays modernity as a scene of fragmented selfhood in which the remnants of Aristotelian virtue provide a mere simulacrum of moral backbone. What is left to modernity, according to MacIntyre, is *emotivism*: "the doctrine that all evaluative judgments and ... all moral judgments are *nothing but* expressions of preference, expressions of attitude or feeling, insofar as they are moral or evaluative in character."[1] Thus, whereas Aristotle's virtuous subject emerged from a morality embedded in "larger totalities of theory and practice," the modern emotivist rehearses a moral vocabulary deprived of living substrate.[2] Bereft of an active vision of the good, modern selfhood founders in a wilderness dominated by instrumental rationalities and Nietzschean will-to-power. In this way, MacIntyre's communitarian outlook complements Michel Foucault's genealogy of discipline and subsequent turn to an ethics of the self. That is to say, despite MacIntyre's depreciation of Nietzsche, and Foucault's embrace, both thinkers emphasize the Enlightenment's failings and both prescribe micropolitical practices of the self.[3]

Crucially for this chapter on nineteenth-century moral discourse, MacIntyre's fallen condition includes the Victorian-era virtues that conservative eulogists such as Gertrude Himmelfarb have opposed to modernity.[4] For according to MacIntyre, the Enlightenment's shortcomings were as fateful for the nineteenth century as for the present day – the Victorians as prone to idealizing the mere semblance of virtue as any generation since. On this view, modernity gives plausible form to moral

---

[1] A. MacIntyre, *After Virtue* (Notre Dame: University of Notre Dame Press, 1984), pp. 11–12.

[2] MacIntyre, *After Virtue*, p. 10.

[3] See, e.g., M. Foucault, "The Ethics of the Concern for Self as a Practice of Freedom," in R. Rabinow, ed., *Foucault: Ethics, Subjectivity and Truth: The Essential Works of Michel Foucault, 1954–84*, vol. 1 (London: Penguin), pp. 281–301.

[4] G. Himmelfarb, *The De-Moralization of Society: From Victorian Virtues to Modern Values* (London: IEA Health and Welfare Unit, 1995).

ideas through the staging of representative types that MacIntyre calls *characters*. By fusing institutional "role" with individual "personality," MacIntyre's characters "morally legitimate a mode of social existence" which would otherwise stand forth as virtueless. The "characters" he identifies for the 1980s include the Therapist and the Manager, but their Victorian precursors were "the Public School Headmaster, the Explorer and the Engineer."[5] Thus, whereas the Victorians regarded "character" as a measure of individual and national fiber, for MacIntyre, "*characters*" are but "the masks worn by moral philosophies."[6]

To be sure, MacIntyre's description of Victorian culture and society is relatively scant. *After Virtue* tells us little about the shift from a producing to a consumer economy, or the eventual transition away from a language of character and toward one of *personality*.[7] The book takes hardly any notice of historical contexts such as the globalization of capital, the rise and institutionalization of a territorial empire, and the tensions between these border-crossing practices of sovereign expansion and the ideal of a bounded national culture borne of shared history. MacIntyre does not, therefore, pause to describe the emergence of racializing pseudo-sciences in the wake of imperial crises such as the Indian "mutiny." Although he writes at length on utilitarianism, his analysis lacks an adequate appreciation of John Stuart Mill's influential renovation of that thought, which – as we shall see – anticipates MacIntyre's own commitment to republican ethics. And while *After Virtue* memorably puts forward Jane Austen as "the last great" exponent of Aristotelian ethics,[8] its silence on potential Victorian successors such as George Eliot is not explained.

Nevertheless, to consider Victorian character from MacIntyre's perspective is to set aside the cliché of "Victorian virtue" in favor of a refreshingly unfamiliar set of questions. What if Victorian modernity was *not* the moral bedrock hallowed by neoconservatives today? What if iconic texts such as Thomas Carlyle's *On Heroes and Hero Worship* (1841) and Samuel Smiles's *Self-Help* (1859) were but the masks of a moral discourse that, in actuality, had been snuffed out a generation before? In this chapter I propose to keep such questions in mind as I discuss the

[5] MacIntyre, *After Virtue*, pp. 28–9.   [6] MacIntyre, *After Virtue*, p. 28.
[7] As the Americanist historian Warren Susman notes, the "Puritan-republican, producer-capitalist" culture of the nineteenth-century "demanded something it called 'character'" which stressed moral qualities" while "the newer culture" that developed in the twentieth century, "insisted on 'personality' which emphasized being liked and admired": *Culture as History* (New York: Pantheon, 1984), pp. 23–4. On the mid-Victorian-era change to a consumer economy, see R. Gagnier, *The Insatiability of Human Wants: Economics and Aesthetics in Market* (Chicago: University of Chicago Press, 2000).
[8] MacIntyre, *After Virtue*, p. 240.

historical determinants of "character" during the transition from the early Victorian period (focused on rising industrialism, trade, and social reform) to the more reactionary mid- and late Victorian decades (invested in the formalization and expansion of empire and the containment of democracy and socialism).

In the early decades of Victoria's reign, character was prominent among a wide variety of consciously progressive thinkers who perceived it as a major force for social, cultural, and material improvement in Britain and across the globe. According to Stefan Collini, the Victorian "ideal of character ... enjoyed a prominence in the political thought of the Victorian period that it had certainly not known before and that it has, arguably, not experienced since."[9] Collini goes on to distinguish between various contemporary meanings of the term. In what he calls the *evaluative* usage, "character" is as an affirmed moral attainment: what the *Oxford English Dictionary* defines as "moral qualities strongly developed or strikingly displayed." J. S. Mill exemplifies this usage in *On Liberty* (1859) when he writes: "One whose desires and impulses are not his own, has no character, no more than a steam-engine has a character."[10] As the historian J. W. Burrow notes, *character* in this affirmative sense was a modern adaptation of "independence" – an older ideal that, from Aristotle's time through the eighteenth century, had functioned to preserve civic participation for the socially privileged. In contrast to an "independence" thus premised on inherited wealth and position, "character" stood for republican virtues that could apply "to a wider, less exclusive, more mobile, more competitive, and certainly no longer necessarily landed society."[11] For example, an 1853 essay in the *Edinburgh Review* assures its readers that perceived social impediments such as illegitimate birth need not "impair that freedom and independence of bearing which are essential to the character."[12]

Prescriptive Character

In a second prominent nineteenth-century usage, *character* is open-ended. Rather than confirmed moral attainment, character in this neutral

---

[9] S. Collini, "The Idea of 'Character' in Victorian Political Thought," 35 *Transactions of the Royal Historical Society* (1985), pp. 29–50.

[10] J. S. Mill, *On Liberty*, 1859, edited by Edward Alexander (Peterborough, ON: Broadview Press, 1999), p. 106.

[11] J. Burrow, *Whigs and Liberals: Continuity and Change in English Political Thought* (Oxford: Clarendon, 1988), p. 89.

[12] [A. Hayward], "Mr. Disraeli: His Character and Career," *Edinburgh Review* (April 1853), p. 423.

sense indexes faculties that might be virtuous *or* corrupt, free *or* overdetermined, cultivated *or* uncultivated, desirable or not. Hence, the title of an 1849 article, "Four Years' Experience of the Catholic Religion; with Observations on its Effects upon the Character, Intellectual, Moral, and Spiritual," leaves open the question of what precisely those effects might be.[13] In my own writing on this topic, I explore two distinct variations *within* this open-ended usage of character which correspond to the early and later decades of Victoria's reign.[14] In what I have called the *prescriptive* sense that descends from the Enlightenment, character stands for the plasticity of human moral, mental, and spiritual capacities regardless of *descriptive* features such as class, nationality, race, or environmental condition. Thus, as Robert Owen wrote in his *Essays on the Formation of Human Character* (1817), "Any general character, from the best to the worst, from the most ignorant to the most enlightened, may be given to any community, even to the world at large, by the application of proper means."[15] Such a view of character was important to early Victorian imperial administrators such as Charles Trevelyan, whose book *On the Education of the People of India* (1838) prophesied that the "institution of caste" would disappear under British rule: "All we have to do," he wrote, is assemble Indian youths of many ranks "to impress the same character upon them, and to leave the yielding and affectionate mind of youth to its natural impulse."[16]

In this infinitely malleable, normatively charged, but highly contingent sense, the idea of character could help to reinforce the politico-economic doctrines that were slowly eroding the fixed social hierarchies of the past. Whereas the lenient poor laws of the Elizabethan era had naturalized economic aid for the propertyless, Thomas Malthus argued that such charitable practices caused the very impoverishment they were created to palliate. In his "An Essay on the Principle of Population" (1803), Malthus argued that once the lower classes were rescued from degrading dependence, "the great mass" of them would reduce family size and

---

[13] Anonymous, "Four Years' Experience of the Catholic Religion; with Observations on Its Effects upon the Character, Intellectual, Moral, and Spiritual," 4.20 *The Rambler* (August 1849), pp. 221–33.

[14] L. Goodlad, *Victorian Literature and the Victorian State: Character and Governance in a Liberal Society* (Baltimore: Johns Hopkins, 2003).

[15] R. Owen, *Essays on the Formation of Character*, 3rd Edition (London: Longman, 1817), n.p.

[16] C. E. Trevelyan, *Education of the People of India* (London: Longman, 1838), p. 20. The same prescriptive logic underlay Thomas Babington Macaulay's influential 1835 "Minute" on Indian education which anticipated a "class of persons Indian in colour and blood, but English in tastes, in opinions, in morals, and intellect": "Minute of the 2nd of February, 1835: Indian Education," in G. M. Young, ed., *Macaulay, Prose and Poetry* (Cambridge: Harvard University Press, 1967), p. 729.

acquire those "conveniences and comforts, which ... tend unquestion-ably to improve the mind and elevate the character."[17] The rural rate-payers who welcomed this case for poor law reform were motivated largely by desire to reduce public expenditures. But for urban radicals such as J. A. Roebuck, MP for Sheffield, the project of building working-class character offered a means of affirming one's own moral mettle. Roebuck told his constituents that his life's goal had been to make the British "working-man as exalted and civilized a creature as I could make him. ... I wanted to make the working-man like me ... a civilized human being, cultivating my mind, thinking only of whatever would elevate me and make me that which I ought to be, a representative of my race."[18]

Prescriptive character discourse thus entailed a strong emphasis on moral outcomes as well as an arduous and even anxious commitment on the part of would-be mentors and exemplars. For even as the presumed elasticity of character gave rise to ambitious schemes of moral perfect-ibility, the success of such endeavors was hardly guaranteed. To the contrary, Enlightenment prescriptions, as the French Revolution had shown, could be difficult to translate from theory to practice. Hence, in the conservative political climate that followed the First Reform Act's enfranchisement of middle-class men in 1832, even self-styled radicals such as Harriet Martineau began to conceive social progress in gradual and individualistic terms. In *Society in America* (1837–8), Martineau advocated a program of "exalt[ing] the aims, and strengthen[ing] the self-discipline of the whole of society, by each one being as good as he can make himself, and relying on his own efforts after self-perfection."[19]

Character-building on this individual scale invited middle-class exem-plars to perform a tutelary role even as they admitted the precarity of their

---

[17] T. Malthus, *An Essay on the Principle of Population*, edited by Donald Winch (Cambridge: Cambridge University Press, 1992 [1803]), p. 190. As F. Block and M. Somers note, Malthus broke through centuries of tradition when he converted "poverty from a structural status in society to a behavioral choice." This redefinition made poverty "a moral condition based on personal behavior and lack of biological restraint": *The Power of Market Fundamentalism* (Cambridge, MA: Harvard University Press, 2014), p. 175.

[18] J. A. Roebuck, *The Life and Letters of John Arthur Roebuck* (London: Edward Arnold, 1897), p. 325. See also A. J. Kidd, who has argued that the Victorian "obsession" with character was a means to simulating mutual exchange between socially and economically unequal actors. Through the combined efforts of the New Poor Law and middle-class charity work, impoverished recipients of such aid were expected to "reciprocate" by exhibiting moral probity in an exchange that enhanced the status of their benefactors: "Philanthropy and the 'Social History Paradigm'," 21.2 *Social History* (May 1996), pp. 183 and 186–87. On the interrelation between charity and poor law reform during this period see Goodlad, *Victorian Literature*, ch. 2.

[19] H. Martineau, *Society in America*, vol. 2 (London: Saunders and Otley, 1837), p. 244.

good works. According to Rufus Clark's *Lectures on the Formation of Character, Temptations and Mission of Young Men* (1853), a popular US guide to child-rearing, "it is a lamentable fact that" many youths "fall victim to the power of vice," despite the scrupulous efforts made to promote their "moral culture" and "guard them against the perils to which they are exposed." Precisely because character was so pliant, "evil habits" could be formed just as readily as virtuous ones.[20] "The primary meaning of the word *character*," Clark reminded his readers, "is a mark made by cutting or engraving on any substance." It follows that "[e]very thought that enters the mind, every purpose that is formed, as well as every external action, leaves its mark."[21] Character defined in such terms required the endless vigilance Roebuck set forth when he upheld himself as a model of self-improvement, "thinking *only* of whatever would elevate" him to representative status.

   In a recent study of mid-Victorian culture, Elaine Hadley argues that discourses of "character and progress" helped a relatively abstract and deracinated subject to succeed a social order that had hitherto favored "common cultural embedment in rituals and customs."[22] Hadley's point – that what had been imagined as a holistic social world became ever more palpably atomized during the course of the nineteenth century – is indisputable. But it is important to recognize that while character talk invariably emphasized the individual as the bearer of moral qualities, as a republican discourse, rooted in Aristotelian ethics and buttressed by German Romantic notions of *Bildung*, character provided a potential means of *resisting* the abstracting, commodifying, and atomizing tendencies of bourgeois modernity. In *The Political Theory of Possessive Individualism* (1962), C. B. Macpherson describes the emergence of a bourgeois liberal subject who, as "the proprietor of his own person or capacities," owes "nothing to society for them." Such an individual "was seen neither as a moral whole, nor as a part of a larger social whole, but," rather, "as an owner of himself" whose ostensible freedom consisted in an atomized sphere of self-interested exchange between proprietors. With such a subject at its center, Macpherson wrote, "[p]olitical society becomes a calculated device for the protection of this property and for the maintenance of an orderly relation of exchange."[23] Yet, as Macpherson makes

---

[20] R. W. Clark, *Lectures on the Formation of Character, Temptations and Mission of Young Men* (Boston: Jewett, 1853), p. 1.

[21] Clark, *Lectures on the Formation of Character*, p. 28.

[22] E. Hadley, *Living Liberalism: Practical Citizenship in Mid-Victorian Britain* (Chicago: University of Chicago Press, 2010), p. 5.

[23] C. B. Macpherson, *The Political Theory of Possessive Individualism: Hobbes and Locke* (Oxford: Clarendon, 1962), p. 3.

clear, influential nineteenth-century political thinkers such as J. S. Mill and T. H. Green sought to counter this embourgeoisement with a civic subject whose "worth" was inextricable from "the moral value of community."[24] Understanding character in its prescriptive sense thus requires us to consider the political valences specific to each usage.

As the mid-nineteenth century's most philosophically ambitious radical, Mill believed that the flourishing of democracy and the gradual transition from market capitalism to cooperative socialism required "an equivalent change of character" in both capitalists and workers.[25] In the 1840s, as he became increasingly alienated from the Benthamite stress on legislative tutelage and discouraged by the failure of parliamentary politics to realize the public good, Mill explored "ethology" or the "science of character" as a means to developing *homo civicus*.[26] Ethology, he hoped, could provide a bridge between individual morality and collective good – spurring that "improving state of the human mind" which "tend[s] to generate in each individual a feeling of unity with all the rest."[27] But since Mill was both chary of state power and skeptical of positivist arguments grounded in biology or statistics, he eventually abandoned ethology. As a radical or "advanced liberal," Mill could hardly suppose a modernity that had become irretrievably virtueless, but neither could he imagine any certain *telos* or philosophical foundation for the moral progress he hoped for. Mill's *homo civicus* was, thus, the contingent product of equalitarian social relations, liberal education, and participatory citizenship— character-building practices that were difficult to actualize and impossible to assure. Much as Aristotle had written that "moral virtue arises from habit,"[28] so Mill insisted that that the "mental and moral, like the muscular powers, are, improved only by being used."[29] A merely passive adherence to prevailing social norms was, therefore, inimical to virtuous citizenship – all too likely to produce human steam-engines "whose desires and impulses are not [their] own."[30] In this way, Mill's influential ethics combined a Romantic focus on individuality and diversity with a republican emphasis on citizenship.

[24] Macpherson, *Political Theory of Possessive Individualism*, pp. 2–3.

[25] J. S. Mill, *Autobiography of John Stuart Mill*, 1873, edited by Jack Stillinger (Boston: Riverside, 1969), p. 138.

[26] J. S. Mill, "System of Logic," 1843, in J. Robson, ed., *Collected Works of John Stuart Mill*, vol. 8 (Toronto: University of Toronto Press, 1974), p. 4.

[27] J. S. Mill, "Utilitarianism," 1861, in A. Ryan, ed., *Utilitarianism and Other Essays* (Harmondsworth: Penguin, 1987), p. 305.

[28] Aristotle, *The Nicomachean Ethics*, edited by Lesley Brown and translated by David Ross (Oxford: Oxford University Press, 2009), p. 23.

[29] Mill, *On Liberty*, p. 104.   [30] Mill, *On Liberty*, p. 106.

Mill's legacy provides an interesting comparison for the contemporaneous prescriptions of Samuel Smiles, whose iconic book *Self-Help: with Illustrations of Character and Conduct* (1859) appeared in the same year as *On Liberty*.[31] Whereas the thriving of Mill's *homo civicus* required social conditions that might fail to materialize, Smiles' more autonomous subject emerged through the radical transcendence of history and environment. This turn to transcendentalism, like Mill's to ethology, was motivated partly by the failure of political radicalism after 1832. Almost fifty years old when the success of his book won him renown, the author of *Self-Help* had spent decades struggling to achieve a secure middle-class foothold. Thus, as R. J. Morris writes, so far from "an expression of mid-Victorian optimism," *Self-Help* was the "sublimated" product of Smiles' frustrated lower-middle-class political and professional aspirations.[32] Critical to this new outlook was the influence of American transcendentalists such as William Ellery Channing and Ralph Waldo Emerson. In "Man the Reformer," a lecture Emerson delivered to Boston workers in 1841, Smiles found an alternative to legislative politics framed by a catalyzing question: "Can we not learn the lesson of self-help?"[33] As Smiles began delivering similar lectures to workingmen's groups in the 1840s, he created the underpinnings of *Self-Help*. When the book appeared in 1859, its paean to the immeasurable powers of "individual character" provided the ideal mantra for a mid-Victorian interval that combined growing economic prosperity with continuing resistance to radical political change.[34] In a follow-up book titled *Character* (1871), Smiles reiterated the point that "the soul of every great character" was a question of "energy of will" and "self-originating force."[35]

One finds a similar blend of radical aspiration, transcendental philosophy, political disaffection, and incipient conservatism in Thomas Carlyle, whose collected oeuvre was described in 1870 by the editor of *The Fortnightly Review* as a "monument of the industry, originality, conscientiousness, and genius of a noble character ... that has exercised the profoundest sort of influence upon English feeling."[36] Penned by John Morley, a disciple of J. S. Mill, the review essay provides strong

---

[31] S. Smiles, *Self-Help: With Illustrations of Character and Conduct*, 1859 (Boston: Ticknor, 1861).

[32] R. J. Morris, "Samuel Smiles and the Genesis of *Self-Help*; The Retreat to Petit Bourgeois Utopia," 24.1 *The Historical Journal* (1981), p. 91.

[33] R. W. Emerson, "Man the Reformer," 1849, in Kenneth Sacks, ed., *Political Writings* (Cambridge: Cambridge University Press, 2008), p. 109.

[34] Smiles, *Self-Help*, p. 18.

[35] S. Smiles, *Character*, 1871 (reprinted by Burt, n.d.), pp. 27–8.

[36] J. Morley, "Carlyle," 14 *Fortnightly Review* (July 1870), p. 1.

testimony to Carlyle's influence on early Victorian moral discourse. Yet, while groundbreaking essays such as "Signs of the Times" (1829) and "Characteristics" (1831) diagnosed the ailings of a mechanical age, Carlyle's writings, we should note, did not affirm character talk in its prescriptive form. Instead, as befits an author fond of root meanings, Carlyle often uses "character" to stand for a glaring signifier of moral failure, as when the narrator of *Past and Present* (1843) observes the "fire-characters" burned into the "hearts that witnessed" the massacre of unarmed workers at Peterloo.[37] To be sure, Carlyle repeatedly champions heroic characters – those of Robert Burns, Oliver Cromwell, and Frederick the Great, for example – as well as heroic *types* of character, such as the "character of Poet" he put forward in his lectures on Dante and Shakespeare in 1840.[38] Yet, with his proto-Nietzschean contempt for average humanity and his idealization of social hierarchy, Carlyle simultaneously rejected the Enlightenment presumption of moral perfectibility for all. Writing of modern "progress," he takes care to insist that "we can know nothing, or almost nothing" about "the grand Course of Providence."[39] On the topic of human character more generally, he is less prone to imagine a confirmed "habit of willing" wrested from the determining power of external conditions[40] than to evoke the altogether more elusive moral freedom put forward in *Sartor Resartus* (1832). There Carlyle depicts a "Life-Philosophy" of "Clothes" which culminates in "Natural Supernaturalism"[41] – a transcendental philosophy that paradoxically "originates ... in the Character," but cannot "attain its significance till the Character itself is known and seen."[42] Described by M. H. Abrams as the effort to sustain "a New Jerusalem," not "by changing the world, but by changing our world view,"[43] Natural Supernaturalism inspired the American transcendentalists whose self-reliant vision made such an impact on Smiles. But from Morley's more equalitarian, rational, and democratic outlook, the flipside of Carlyle's "mystic and transcendental" elements was a "cold-hearted" fatalism ready to doom the greatest part of humanity to "destiny." "Devotion to the heroic," wrote Morley, does not prevent Carlyle's "assumption of a tone towards the

---

[37] T. Carlyle, *Past and Present*, 1843 (New York: New York University Press, 1965), p. 17.
[38] T. Carlyle, *On Heroes and Hero Worship*, 1840 (Berkeley: University of California Press, 1993), p. 67.
[39] [T. Carlyle], "Characteristics," *Edinburgh Review* (December 1831), p. 379.
[40] Mill, "System of Logic," pp. 120–1.
[41] T. Carlyle, *Sartor Resartus*, 1832, edited by Peter Sabor and Kerry McSweeney (Oxford: Oxford University Press, 1987), p. 58 and p. 208.
[42] Carlyle, *Sartor Resartus*, p. 58.
[43] M. H. Abrams, *Natural Supernaturalism: Tradition and Revolution in Romantic Literature* (New York: Norton, 1973), p. 347.

great mass of the unheroic, which implies that they are no more than two-legged mill horses, ever treading a fixed, unalterable round."[44]

It is worth noting, then, that comparable anxieties about character and its limits permeate the classic fictional literature of the early and mid-Victorian decades. Even authors who clearly prized moral force – including Charles Dickens, George Eliot, and Anthony Trollope – wrote books in which character-building fails to proffer a reliable foundation for social progress, whether collective (through movements for socio-political change) or individual (through heroic feats of self-improvement or tran-scendence). To be sure, Martineau's popular didactic fiction, including *Illustrations of Political Economy* (1832–4) and *Poor Laws and Paupers Illustrated* (1833–4), illuminates the tenets of an emerging bourgeois social order that the author by and large affirms. Such works demonstrate what Eleanor Courtemanche has described as the shared "intellectual project" of political economy and realist fictional narrative – both of which articulate the relation "between micro and macro levels" of the social world.[45] As Martineau herself put it in an 1833 essay on the future of literature after Walter Scott, modern authors should craft a "serious" fiction trained on depicting "the birth of political principle" in a scene of major "transition." "Where are nobler heroes to be found," she asked, "than those who sustain ... the struggle" to replace "bad institutions" with the "issues of a process of renovation"?[46] Yet, whereas Martineau perceived a harmonious confluence of individual betterment and provi-dentialistic design, the most renowned authors of the period were decidedly skeptical on both counts. Such novels portray the increasing sway of commercial and industrial culture as a drain on or threat to moral character, both individual and collective. Thus, even Trollope, whose fiction is sometimes described as resigned to bourgeois norms, could write at the outset of *Doctor Thorne* (1858) that though England "may excel other nations in commerce," "it is not that in which she most prides herself," or "in which she most excels." For while "[b]uying and selling is good and necessary," "it cannot be the noblest work of man; and let us hope that it may not in our time be esteemed the noblest work of an Englishman."[47]

[44] Morley, "Carlyle," p. 16.
[45] E. Courtemanche, *The "Invisible Hand" and British Fiction, 1818–1860: Adam Smith, Political Economy, and the Genre of Realism* (New York and London: Palgrave, 2011), p. 390.
[46] H. Martineau, "The Achievements of the Genius of Scott," *Tait's Edinburgh Magazine* (January 1833), p. 459.
[47] A. Trollope, *Doctor Thorne*, 1858, edited by David Skilton (Oxford: Oxford University Press, 2000), pp. 12–13.

Dickens's oeuvre manifests an even more pronounced reluctance to put forward character-building as the answer to modern social ills. In *Oliver Twist* (1837–8), a formal blend of romance, "Newgate" novel, and "condition of England" narrative, the morality of particular characters is envisioned as simultaneously innate and acquired. Hence, while the virtues of Oliver and his friend Dick suggest a resilient state of grace (fortified in Oliver's case by hidden middle-class parentage), working-class character elsewhere in the book is the sad casualty of inheritance, environment, and the pernicious effects of atomization and embourgeoisement. To be sure, individual self-development is valued for its own sake in *Bildungsromane* such as *David Copperfield* (1849–50) and *Great Expectations* (1860–3). But though Dickens's works valorize honest enterprise – Mrs. Bagnet's industrious homemaking in *Bleak House* (1852–3) or Daniel Doyce's inventions in *Little Dorrit* (1855–7), for example – they are fervent in unmasking fraudulent self-making like that of Josiah Bounderby in *Hard Times* (1854). In the latter novel, it is not industry, moral probity, or citizenship that offers enlivening alternatives to utilitarian strictures but, rather, the imaginative and life-affirming world of the circus. And while Dickens repeatedly portrays avuncular benefactors like Mr. Brownlow and John Jarndyce, such characters lack any basis on which to generalize the crucial blend of paternalism and meritocracy they offer. In his last completed novel, *Our Mutual Friend* (1865–7), Dickens' profound skepticism toward the cult of self-improvement is expressed through the fatally upward mobility of Bradley Headstone, who rises from pauper lad to highly trained schoolmaster. Such disastrous *Bildung* tells against the ambitious tutelary projects of early Victorian educationists such as Sir James Kay-Shuttleworth, who had sought to establish a state-subsidized engine for elevating the character and social status of working-class children.[48]

One finds a more affirmative stance on prescriptive character in Eliot's *Romola* (1862–3), a historical romance set in the time of Savonarola's Florence which puts forward an ideal of republican citizenship comparable to Mill's. By inventing a female variation on the kind of everyman heroes Walter Scott envisioned in *Waverley* (1814) and *Ivanhoe* (1820), Eliot shows how civic character is corrupted by inequality between the sexes. According to Daniel S. Malachuk, *Romola* was part of a Victorian "conversation about the role of virtue in polities otherwise dedicated to the fullest realization of individual autonomy" – a "liberty problem" that extends back to the thought of Machiavelli.[49] For Eliot, writing at a time

---

[48] See Goodlad, *Victorian Literature*, ch. 5.

[49] D. Malachuk, "*Romola* and Victorian Liberalism," 36.1 *Victorian Literature and Culture* (March 2008), p. 42.

when women and working men did not stand on equal footing with the
male ruling class, the question was how to expand popular sovereignty
without exacerbating those deracinating tendencies already militating
against collectivity.[50] Informed by intensive study of the Florentine past,
Romola explores the problem of *Bildung* as an epic clash between private
desire and the public good. Savonarola, as J. G. A. Pocock writes,
envisioned Florence as the epicenter of a "divine mission" of "spiritual
renewal" through "restoration of republican citizenship"; he combined
"Aristotelian, civic, and apocalyptic language in a single synthesis."[51]
Thus, Romola's encounter with Savonarola is a species of Machiavellian
moment, albeit one shaped by the goal of accommodating female experience. While Romola herself rises to this occasion, her instantiation of a
virtuous *femina civica* points to a utopian space of possibility in contrast
to the kinds of character-building attainable in the here-and-now.[52]

In *Felix Holt: the Radical* (1866), published just a year before the
Second Reform Act doubled the adult male franchise, Eliot revisits the
kind of political novel that Benjamin Disraeli made famous. In doing so,
she substitutes an artisan protagonist for a Coningsbyesque aristocrat or
a middle-class party man like Trollope's Phineas Finn. Yet, *Felix Holt* is
arguably the most politically conservative of Eliot's novels. Depicting a
hero whose radicalism consists in "want[ing] to go to some roots a good
deal lower down than the franchise,"[53] the novel's goal is full-scale
renovation of the British populace – a long-term approach to qualifying
the people for civic virtue like that glimpsed in *Romola*. As Felix warns
a crowd of workers, "Ignorant power comes in the end to the same thing
as wicked power."[54] Thus, much like Walter Bagehot's *The English Constitution* (1867) and Matthew Arnold's *Culture and Anarchy* (1866–7),

[50] For a fuller discussion see L. Goodlad, *Victorian Geopolitical Aesthetic: Realism, Sovereignty and Transnational Experience* (Oxford: Oxford University Press, 2015), ch. 6.
[51] J. G. A. Pocock, *The Machiavellian Moment: Florentine Political Thought and the Atlantic
Republican Tradition,* Revised Edition (Princeton: Princeton University Press, 2003),
pp. 105–6.
[52] Poetry also provided a space for *feminae civicae*: for a reading of Pompilia's virtuous
public ethics tied to a discussion of character in Robert Browning's *The Ring and the
Book,* see K. A. Gilbert, who writes that "character appears" in Victorian literature "at
moments in which an individual must make decisions in the face of social or institutional
constraints, decisions that require individual agency and action in the face of conflict":
"The Politics of Character: The Lawyers and Pompilia in Robert Browning's *The Ring
and the Book* (1868–69)," 49.3 *Victorian Poetry* (2011), p. 322. On civic republican
discourses of character in a variety of Victorian poets see also S. K. Weiner, *Republic
Politics and English Poetry, 1789–1874* (London: Palgrave, 2005) and J. Saville, "'Soul-
Talk': Networks of Political Poetry in a Trans-Channel Literary Triangle," 55.2
Victorian Studies (2013), pp. 299–308.
[53] G. Eliot, *Felix Holt: The Radical,* 1866, edited by Lynda Mugglestone (London: Penguin,
1995), p. 264.
[54] Eliot, *Felix Holt,* p. 292.

Eliot's hero insists that Britain's working classes are not yet ripe for the enlarged democracy that Disraeli's Tory party would soon usher in.

Still, if *Felix Holt* amplifies the kind of middle-class conservatism that led Arnold to associate working-class character with "anarchy," it also marks a new interest in the relation between ordinary citizens and democratic structures. The point of Eliot's novel is not that a Carlylean hero such as Coningsby must arise from the upper classes to lead Britain's masses but, rather, that the British people must develop the moral qualities to govern themselves through representative institutions. Then too, the focus on Felix's future wife, Esther Lyon, like that on Dorothea Brooke in *Middlemarch* (1876) – another novel that takes the First Reform bill era for its *mise-en-scène* – affirms the commitment in *Romola* to urging citizen potential across lines of gender as well as class. Thus, while Eliot's explicit views on the female or working-class franchise were more conservative than Mill's, her fiction affirms character, female as well as male, as a malleable fiber for human striving.[55]

This republican strain of prescriptive character talk reached its apotheosis in the 1880s in the political philosophy of T. H. Green, whose Hegel-influenced social ontology concretized the shift from individualism to holism which Mill's thought had long foreshadowed. Green's insistence on freedom – not the negative liberty to be left alone but the positive power to "do or enjoy" "something worth doing or enjoying" which, moreover, "we do or enjoy in common with others"[56] – offered civic man as the basis on which to reconcile private liberty and the public good. Green thus embraced the adult male democracy that had become all but inevitable in the years leading up to the Third Reform Act (which enfranchised rural workingmen in 1884). Freedom as he defined it could not be "enjoyed by ... one set of men at the cost of a loss of freedom to others" because only a situation of relative equality could enable the mutual empowerment that underlay an ontology in which "citizens as a body ... make the most and best of themselves."[57] Civic equality so conceived required not only the right to vote but also educational and economic opportunities sufficient to enable character-building

[55] In this way, her works, while lacking a providentialistic optimism like Martineau's, exemplify what Raymond Williams has described as the "subjunctive" dimensions that enable some realist novels to "introduce a perspective which is not socially or politically available" and, thus, "connect [to] things that lay far ahead": "Forms of English Fiction in 1848," in *Writing in Society* (London: Verso, 1983), p. 161.
[56] T. H. Green, "Lecture on 'Liberal Legislation and Freedom of Contract'," in Paul Harris and John Marrow, eds., *Lectures on the Principles of Political Obligations and Other Writings* (Cambridge: Cambridge University Press, 1986), p. 199.
[57] Green, "Lecture," p. 199.

on a collective scale. Green's political philosophy thus became a defining moment in the transition from the atomistic ontology of classical liberalism and political economy to the holistic community of social democracy.[58]

To be sure, Green (who died in 1882 at the age of forty-five) never specified the means by which an enlarged male franchise transforms a market society predicated on private ownership of property into a body of substantively equal citizens, each of whom enjoys the "positive power or capacity of doing or enjoying something worth doing or enjoying." Nor does he explain how this citizenry determines which practices and pursuits are "worth doing or enjoying" without trampling on diversity and individual liberty. Still less does Green's philosophy address the unfreedom of non-citizens such as women or the colonized subjects of Britain's expanding empire. In the 1890s, these questions were taken up by a variety of New Liberals, trade unionists, and socialists who were alike in sharing a philosophical commitment to positive freedom underwritten by a holist social ontology. Yet, from the standpoint of a history of moral discourse, what is crucial to recognize is that by the end of the nineteenth century, the infinitely plastic notion of character which underwrote such visions had been under siege for some decades. In its place, new and more conservative *descriptive* notions of character were becoming ever more prevalent.

Descriptive Character

When Morley's "Carlyle" essay appeared on the heels of the Second Reform Act, as well as imperial crises including the Morant Bay rebellion in Jamaica and the subsequent controversy over Governor Eyre's imposition of martial law, it addressed a British nation on its way to becoming a mass democracy and formal empire. Fueled by the globalization of capital, the quest for dominion over world markets, and the growing competition among European powers for far-flung empires, these social and geopolitical factors were integral to the increasing rejection of an Enlightenment discourse that held human character to be fundamentally

---

[58] Green's positive freedom derived from Hegel's idea of *Sittlichkeit* (ethical life), which holds that the condition of citizenship should reconcile individual liberty with participation in and, thus, development through the community – ensuring what Green describes as the "power which each man exercises through the help or security given him by his fellow-men, and which he in turn helps to secure for them": "Lecture," p. 199. On Green's Hegelianism see B. Wempe, *T.H. Green's Theory of Positive Freedom* (Exeter: Imprint Academic, 2004). On Hegel's idea of *Sittlichkeit* see his *Elements of the Philosophy of Right* (1821).

equal and perfectible across geographic, racial, and cultural boundaries. On the one hand, the growing scale and anonymity of an increasingly urban and industrial society encouraged the modern bourgeois tendency to judge individuals, first and foremost, in terms of socio-economic status. Thus, while many supporters of poor law reform in the 1830s had hoped to strengthen paternalistic character-building bonds between rich and poor, the law's bureaucratic logic dictated that *any* able-bodied worker who required support must receive it in the punitive confines of the workhouse, regardless of "character."[59] At the same time, modern populations were increasingly evaluated through the aggregating and objectifying lens of the new human sciences. The claims to authority of burgeoning fields such as medicine, phrenology, psychology, anthropology, and sociology encouraged a *descriptive* language of character which militated against the ideal of boundless change across classes, regions, cultures, and "races." Whether conceived to address biology, environment, or a blend of the two, descriptive character implied a comparatively limited view of transformative possibility and, thus, a naturalization of relatively fixed social and geopolitical hierarchies.

Historians of "race" have argued that the full flowering of racial pseudo-science began in the 1880s, spurred by the heightened competition for territorial empires.[60] Such supposed knowledge filled the void when the so-called scramble for Africa drew rival powers into regions as unfamiliar to the English as the "far side of the moon," in the words of one of the principal architects of the New Imperialism.[61] But it is important to recognize that the turn from open-ended Enlightenment universalism to descriptive hierarchies premised on unalterable categories such as "race" was decades in the making. One therefore discerns the growing authority of "race" in the 1840s after the abolition of slavery in the British West Indies resulted in economic decline. When emancipated slaves in the Caribbean defied abolitionist assumptions by rejecting

---

[59] Character and material prosperity were, moreover, mutually intertwined in ways that inevitably conduced toward the greater determinative power of the latter. As M. C. Finn writes, "character" functioned "at once as the basis upon which lenders extended credit ... and as a broader social and cultural measure of personal worth. Perceptions of personal worth, in turn, registered the successful use of goods and services obtained on credit to construct creditworthy characters. Credit thus reflected character, but also constituted it": *The Character of Credit: Personal Debt in English Culture, 1740–1914* (Cambridge: Cambridge University Press, 2007), p. 19. On the impact of the New Poor Law on character, see also Goodlad, *Victorian Literature*, ch. 2.

[60] See, for example, D. A. Lorimer, "Theoretical Racism in Late-Victorian Anthropology, 1870–1900," 31.3 *Victorian Studies* (Spring 1988), pp. 405–430.

[61] Salisbury quoted in J. Darwin, *The Empire Project: The Rise and Fall of the British World-System, 1830–1970* (Cambridge: Cambridge University Press, 2009), p. 79.

grueling subsistence labor on sugar plantations, their "apparent opposition to market forces" constituted them as "a different kind of human
being."[62] In the 1850s and 1860s, the appeal of racial explanations was
amplified by a number of circumstances including violence between
settlers and indigenous people in Australia and New Zealand, the Indian
"mutiny" of 1857–8, identification with the South in the years leading up
to the US Civil War, the Morant Bay uprising in Jamaica, Fenian resistance among the Irish, and the political agitation of working-class Britons.
In this reactionary climate, Mill's continuing commitment to human
universality took shape in his urgent case for the American North,
defense of Irish political prisoners, and impassioned efforts to prosecute
Eyre through the Jamaica Committee.[63] The eventual failure of the latter
endeavor in 1868–9 provided a telling sign of a British public that had
become accustomed to racial discourse and weary of what Leslie
Stephen – the scion of a famous abolitionist family – did not hesitate to
describe as the cause of "niggerworshippers." "We who wished honestly
to see the nigger free," he wrote in an anonymous 1866 article in the
Cornhill, "hated him as the cause of [our Jamaica] troubles, as our
English or 'Anglo-Saxon' breed always hates an inferior race."[64]

One of the earliest pseudo-scientific publications of note, Robert
Knox's *The Races of Men* (1850; 1862), promulgated the polygenetic
theory that humanity was divided into "permanent Varieties," "races,"
or "Species."[65] Knox called upon "Saxon men of all countries" to
verify his assertion that "Celtic character" – to take just one example –
consisted in "fanaticism," "love of war and disorder," "hatred for
order and patient industry," and lack of "accumulative habits."[66] On
the cusp of the Civil War, American books such as John H. Van
Evrie's *Negroes and Negro "Slavery"; The First an Inferior Race; the Latter
Its Normal Condition* (1861) argued that British "philanthropy" had
propagated a "'negro' movement" predicated on a fallacious "theory of

[62] T. C. Holt, *The Problem of Freedom: Race, Labor, and Politics in Jamaica and Britain, 1832–1938* (Baltimore: Johns Hopkins University Press, 1992), p. 279 and p. 309.
[63] On Mill's defense of the North, see "The Contest in America," 1862, in J. Robson, ed., *Collected Works of John Stuart Mill*, vol. 21 (Toronto: University of Toronto Press, 1984), pp. 127–42. On his defense of Irish political prisoners and the effort to prosecute Eyre see, for example, B. Kinzer and J. Robson, *A Moralist in and out of Parliament: John Stuart Mill at Westminster, 1867–1868* (Toronto: University of Toronto Press, 1992). For a more detailed account of the latter effort, see B. Semmel, *Jamaican Blood and Victorian Conscience: The Governor Eyre Controversy* (Boston: Houghton Mifflin, 1963).
[64] [L. Stephen], "American Humour," 73 *Cornhill Magazine* (1866), p. 37.
[65] R. Knox, *The Races of Men: A Philosophical Enquiry into the Influence of Race over the Destinies of Nations* (London: Renshaw, 1862), pp. 9–10.
[66] Knox, *The Races of Men*, pp. 26–7.

a single race."[67] Van Evrie's writings found an avid British disciple in James Hunt, who, in 1863, founded the Anthropological Society of London, an organization committed to propagating racial pseudo-science. Mill soon became a target of their attacks, described as a figure who illustrated the "absurdities" to which "the greatest minds may be driven" when "afflicted" by the pernicious doctrine of "[h]uman equality."[68] Although still considered extreme in the 1860s, anthropological discourses of race increasingly became an established feature of "the British scientific community."[69]

From Trevelyan in the 1830s on through Mill and Morley in the 1860s, liberal imperialists had justified Britain's dominion in India as a benign civilizing mission that would culminate in Indian self-governance. But in 1883, when Liberals introduced a bill to allow Indian judges to preside over British defendants in their jurisdiction, this modest measure of equality was rejected. Decades later, as Liberal Secretary of State for India in 1909, a much older Morley assured the House of Lords that the government had no "intention to prepare India for Parliamentary government."[70] So-called liberal imperialism thus came implicitly to underwrite the quasi-permanent rule of peoples alleged to be culturally and/or racially unready for self-governance – an imperial ideology that, in practice, differed little from the Tory romanticization of empire as a lasting feudal relation. The notions of "race" which helped to underwrite this imperialism blended polygenesis and monogenesis, nature and nurture, Lamarckian and Darwinian theories of evolution, physical and cultural anthropology, new "sciences" such as forensic anthropometry, and older fields such as archeology. The result was a "richly connotative nineteenth-century sense of 'race' as accumulated cultural differences carried somehow in the blood."[71] At the same time, the vast elongation of an evolutionary timeframe led even those who believed in a single human species "to see the differences between races as so deeply rooted in time as to be almost primordial."[72]

---

[67] J. H. Van Evrie, *Negroes and Negro "Slavery"; the First an Inferior Race; the Latter Its Normal Condition* (New York: Van Evrie, Horton, & Co., 1861), p. 11.

[68] Hunt quoted in T. Ellingson, *The Myth of the Noble Savage* (Berkeley: University of California Press, 2001), p. 250.

[69] Lorimer, "Theoretical," p. 408.

[70] R. J. Moore, "Imperial India, 1858–1914," in A. Porter, ed., *The Oxford History of the British Empire, Vol. 3: The Nineteenth Century* (Oxford: Oxford University Press, 1999), p. 439.

[71] G. Stocking, "The Turn-of-the-Century Concept of Race," 1.1 *Modernism/Modernity* (1994), p. 6. See also Lorimer, "Theoretical," p. 417.

[72] Stocking, "Turn-of-the-Century," p. 12. As Stocking argues at length in his *Victorian Anthropology* (New York: Free Press, 1987), the polygenetic belief in the multiplicity of

At the biological end of this spectrum was Francis Galton, one the most influential figures in marking the transition from prescriptive to descriptive character discourse. In 1865, Galton published a two-part article, "Hereditary Talent and Character," which, as Stocking notes, anticipated his contributions to emerging disciplines such as anthropometry, experimental psychology, statistical theory, the biometric study of heredity, and "eugenics."[73] Using a dictionary of notable persons as his database, Galton found that about 10 percent were "either fathers and sons, or brothers"; exceptional traits, he reasoned, must therefore be as hereditary in people as they are "in brutes."[74] Moreover, the potential for breeding great leaders was by no means precluded by lack of physical prowess among "men of great intellectual eminence" since such men were typically "vigorous animals, with exuberant powers."[75] Galton thus envisioned a eugenic "Utopia" predicated on the reproduction of thoroughbred elites. He imagined pairing male paragons selected for superlative "talent, character, and bodily vigour" with females chosen for their "grace, beauty, health, good temper, accomplished housewifery, and disengaged affections, in addition to noble qualities of heart and brain."[76] When the article first appeared in *Macmillan's Magazine*, the idea that the breeders of "domestic animals" might provide a template for improving "our race" was largely alien to readers accustomed to the habituated virtues, self-reliant energies, and exceptional heroism put forward by Mill, Martineau, Smiles, and Carlyle.[77] But by the 1880s, Galton began to attract a receptive audience. As well as being the first writer to use the term "eugenics,"[78] he became an effective "publicist" for and long-serving president of the Anthropological Institute of Great Britain and Ireland, founded in 1871.[79]

the human species did not disappear with the publication of Darwin's contrary arguments. Moreover, the continuing authority of Lamarckianism "made it extremely difficult to distinguish between physical and cultural heredity. What was cultural at any one point in time could *become* physical; what was physical might well *have been* cultural": Stocking, "Turn-of-the-Century," p. 10. See also C. Bolt, *Victorian Attitudes to Race* (London: Routledge, 1971) and N. Stepan, *The Idea of Race in Science: Great Britain, 1800–1960* (London: Macmillan, 1982).

[73] F. Galton, "Hereditary Talent and Character [Part 1]," 12 *Macmillan's Magazine* (1865), pp. 157–66; Stocking, *Victorian Anthropology*, p. 94.

[74] Galton, "Hereditary Talent [Part 1]," p. 160 and p. 158.

[75] Galton, "Hereditary Talent [Part 1]," p. 164.

[76] Galton, "Hereditary Talent [Part 1]," p. 165.

[77] Galton, "Hereditary Talent [Part 1]," p. 157.

[78] F. Galton, *Inquiries into Human Faculty and Its Development* (New York: Macmillan, 1883), p. 25 and passim.

[79] Lorimer, "Theoretical," p. 423.

Character itself remained a central category of such analyses even as the reigning discourse became ever more skeptical about human equality (both within and between particular populations) and prone to describing essential divisions of one kind or another. Hence, in a speech urging restricted immigration to the United States in 1896, Henry Cabot Lodge explained that when "we speak of a race," we do not mean its expression in "art," "language," or "knowledge," but, rather, the "moral and intellectual characters that in their association make the soul of a race." The "men of each race possess an indestructible stock of ideas, traditions, sentiments, modes of thought, an unconscious inheritance from their ancestors, upon which argument has no effect"; these "mental" and "moral characteristics" are "the slow growth and accumulation of centuries of toil and conflict."[80] Such resolutely descriptive notions of character (premised on a Lamarckian logic of acquired characteristics passed from generation to generation) conduced toward xenophobia inside the borders of Europe and the United States as well as imperial aggression beyond them.

The most explicit racial hierarchies thus focused on regions outside of England and Europe where "race" could justify the domination of non-European peoples. At the extreme of this geopolitically varied assessment was an implicitly genocidal perspective on the indigenous peoples of the temperate regions in North America and Australia which continued to attract British settlement. Such indigenes, it was believed, were vanishing races, destined to "melt away" upon contact with a "higher race."[81] By contrast, British emigration was never a major goal on the Indian subcontinent, a densely populated land mass where expatriate Britons were "plunged into bad air" in a climate prone to "zymotic diseases."[82] Thus, in Asia as well as Africa, colonized people were conceived at best to be lagging in a temporal cultural trajectory that would eventually resemble England's, and at worst to differ incorrigibly from the normative qualities of Anglo-Saxon character.

For example, in Augustus Henry Keane's authoritative-looking *Man Past and Present* (1899), one finds an encyclopedic account of humanity divided by race and geography through chapters that detail the "mental characters" of the African Negro, the Oceanic Mongols, the American Aborigines, and the Caucasic Peoples, among others. The latter group

[80] Lodge quoted in Stocking, "Turn-of-the-Century," p. 5.
[81] A. Trollope, *Australia and New Zealand*, vol. 2 (London: Chapman and Hall, 1873), pp. 123–4. See also P. Brantlinger, *Dark Vanishings: Discourse on the Extinction of Primitive Race, 1800–1930* (Ithaca: Cornell University Press, 2003).
[82] H. Martineau, "Death or Life in India," 8 *Macmillan's* (August 1863), p. 333.

is subdivided into *"Homo Europaeus* (North European or Teutonic),"
"Homo Alpinus (Central and European, Iranic, Oceanic)," and *"Homo
Mediterranensis* (Afro-European)." Though Keane was an ethnologist
and philologist committed to a single human species, his evolutionary perspective nonetheless resisted "those sentimental philanthropists
who go about preaching the doctrine of the inherent equality of all
mankind."[83] His composite "temperament" for Caucasians described
them as "earnest, energetic," "enterprising," "steadfast," "thoughtful,"
"deeply religious," "firm, but not wantonly cruel," "brilliant, quick-witted,
excitable and impulsive," "social and courteous, but fickle, untrustworthy,
and even treacherous (Iberian, South Italian)," and "often atrociously
cruel (many Slavs, Persians, Semites, Indonesians and even South Europeans)."[84] Lest one miss the built-in distinctions between Northern and
Southern, Western and Eastern, lighter and darker phenotypes, Keane
eventually singles out Saxons (despite the acknowledged degree of racial
intermixture) as natural "ruler[s] of men" whose preference for "duty"
over "glory" and "spirit of daring enterprise" endowed them with the ideal
"qualities which make for empire." A less auspicious case of resilient
"racial temperament" was that of the "Kelt," whom Keane (though himself
an Irish Catholic) described as "mercurial, passionate, vehement, impulsive, more courteous than sincere," "quick-witted and brilliant rather than
profound," and "lacking [in] steadfastness."[85]

By contrast, Matthew Arnold's earlier ethnological work, *On the Study
of Celtic Literature* (1867), had been deeply interested in the evidence
for Britain's racial hybridity. Arnold conceived a kind of survival of the
fittest through which subaltern nationalities including the Hungarians,
Irish, and Poles would be subsumed into "great" nationalities but, in
doing so, would leave their mark.[86] Thus, the English "race" combined
the blood of Saxons with that of Celts. In the "new people" thus composed, he wrote, "the stock of the conquerors counts for most, but the
stock of the conquered, too, counts for something."[87] Racial hybridity
also dominated the more anthropometric approach of *The Races of
Britain: A Contribution to the Anthropology of Western Europe* (1885) by

[83] A. H. Keane quoted in D. Lorimer, "Science and the Secularization of Victorian Images
of Race," in B. Lightman, ed., *Victorian Science in Context* (Chicago: University of
Chicago Press, 2008), p. 227.
[84] A. H. Keane, *Man Past and Present* (Cambridge: Cambridge University Press, 1899),
p. 442.
[85] Keane, *Man Past and Present*, p. 532.
[86] M. Arnold, *England the Italian Question*, 1859 (Durham: Duke University Press, 1953),
p. 17.
[87] M. Arnold, "The Study of Celtic Literature (Part 3)," 12–13 *The Cornhill Magazine*
(1866), p. 539.

John Beddoe, who succeeded Galton as president of the Anthropological Institute.[88] Indicative of a greater attention to physical anthropology than any Arnold undertook, Beddoe's work was replete with racializing detail: for example, "The East of England heads are short, but not narrow; they seem to be higher than the Welsh ones ... whereas the Yorkshire heads are more inclined to be oblong."[89] The "Index of Nigrescence" which Beddoe began formulating in the 1860s measured the ratio of fair-skinned to darker phenotypes throughout the British Isles. Through this device, the fair skin and straight jaws of eastern Britons were held to index superiority over the darker skin and "prognathous" jaws of the Celtic west.[90] Beddoe's postulation of the "Africanoid" Celt thus gave pseudo-scientific form to a notion of Celtic inferiority already implicit in popular caricatures of the simianized Irish which were exacerbated in response to Fenian unrest.[91]

This tendency to scientifically validate existing essentializations of non-Anglo-Saxon character and "race" dovetails with contemporaneous discourses on Jewishness.[92] Anti-semitism in the Victorian era is especially interesting in its significant overlap with the political ascent of Benjamin Disraeli, a Christian convert and charismatic Tory who became the object of a harsh strain of anti-Jewish opprobrium on the part of Liberals.[93] An early example is "Mr. Disraeli: his Character and Career" (1853), an anonymous article (by Abraham Hayward) in the *Edinburgh Review* published shortly after Disraeli's high-profile stint as Chancellor of the Exchequer. Professing a high standard of objectivity, the article insists that, like illegitimate birth, "Jewish race" will not necessarily "impair" the free and independent bearing "essential to the character." Indeed, far from overtly advocating prejudice toward Jews, the article singles out Disraeli's decision to ally with the "bigoted" Tories

---

[88] An earlier version of the book was published in 1862.

[89] J. Beddoe, *The Races of Britain: A Contribution to the Anthropology of Western Europe* (Bristol: J. W. Arrowsmith and London: Bristol & Trübnermm, 1885), p. 236.

[90] Beddoe, *The Races of Britain*, p. 266.

[91] Beddoe, *The Races of Britain*, p. 11. See also L. P. Curtis, *Apes and Angels: The Irishman in Victorian Caricature*, Revised Edition (Washington, DC: Smithsonian, 1997).

[92] This is true despite the fact that the polymorphous categories that underwrote late nineteenth-century pseudo-science did not always define Jewishness as a race *per se*. For example, the American anthropologist Daniel Garrison Brinton classified Jews as a subgroup of the Chaldean group of the Semitic stock of the South Mediterranean branch of the Eurafric race"; yet, as G. Stocking points out, "it is still clear that he regarded [Jews] in racial terms, and elsewhere he indeed spoke of 'the pure current of Hebraic blood'": "Turn-of-the Century," p. 9.

[93] See, for example, A. S. Wohl, "Dizzi-Ben-Dizzi: Disraeli as Alien," 34.3 *Journal of British Studies* (July 1995), pp. 375–411.

as singular proof of his moral defects.[94] Nonetheless, the dissection that follows is larded with anti-semitic and orientalist tropes. Disraeli's performative mastery is alleged to be "clearly" traceable "to his 'eastern origin,'" while his "Protean transformations" stem from a lack of "political principles or fixed convictions" which marks him as "the lineal descendant" of Barabbas.[95] Conveying "the look, tone, and attitude of [Edmund] Kean's Shylock," he is a "rhetorician devoid of earnestness," a veritable "Paganini of the rhetorical art," and an "Oriental despot" whose "meretricious" speeches dazzle while failing to "instruct" or "improve."[96] While such "unprincipled ambition" might be suitable for a French leader such as Louis Napoleon, to admire him in Britain would be to "canker public virtue in the bud."[97]

One finds a complicated iteration of these tropes in Trollope's later novels, which, beginning with *The Eustace Diamonds* (1871–3), feature Judaized characters clearly influenced by the author's animosity toward Disraeli – a rival author as well as a statesman who led his first Tory government in 1868. As Michael Ragussis has argued, Trollope's *The Prime Minister* (1875–6), which appeared midway through Disraeli's second ministry, stages an imaginative reversal. Ferdinand Lopez, a secretive foreigner and suspected Jew who "fails to win a seat in Parliament, is the epitome" of "moral bankruptcy," while Palliser, Trollope's fictional prime minister, is "a paragon of virtue."[98] Observing this phenomenon from across the Atlantic, the editor of *Harper's Weekly* remarked on the "large class of Englishmen," including "most of what would be called genuine Englishmen, who have a feeling that Mr. Disraeli is something of a charlatan. He seems to act a part, to like melodrama in public affairs, while the English race does not like it."[99] What is remarkable in this picture is not simply the implication that Jewish character is racially overdetermined. It is also the way in which Jewish "race" anticipates precisely the language of *personality* which would displace the

---

[94] [A. Hayward], "Mr. Disraeli: His Character and Career," pp. 423–4. The issue in question was the removal of legal barriers to Jews sitting in Parliament, which, at the time of Hayward's writing, was supported by the Liberal Party but not by the Tories. As a convert to Anglicanism who was baptized by his Jewish father at the age of thirteen, Disraeli himself was not subject to this disability.

[95] [A. Hayward], "Mr. Disraeli: His Character and Career," p. 425 and p. 432.

[96] [A. Hayward], "Mr. Disraeli: His Character and Career," p. 460 and pp. 453, 454, 457.

[97] [A. Hayward], "Mr. Disraeli: His Character and Career," p. 461.

[98] M. Ragussis, *Figures of Conversion: "The Jewish Question" and English National Identity* (Durham: Duke University Press, 1995), p. 234.

[99] [Anonymous], "Editor's Easy Chair," 53 *Harper's New Monthly Magazine* (1876), p. 142. The author is probably George William Curtis, longstanding editor of *Harper's*.

Aristotelean discourse of character in the twentieth century – marking that fall from virtue which finds "moral qualities" giving way to "being liked and admired."[100] As Katherine Anne Gilbert remarks, early and mid-Victorian character concerned "public representations of the self" which "require individual agency and action in the face of conflict. Character is *not* about personality, or even ever solely the personal."[101] By contrast, Disraeli is described as a consummate *non*-character. A player of protean parts, like an actor in a melodrama if not an out-and-out charlatan, he is a "remarkable personage" whose chief quality is "aggressive personality."[102] It is as though such writers intuited MacIntyre's analysis in *After Virtue* and determined that, in the Age of Disraeli, the "masks worn by moral philosophies" belonged less to the Public School Headmaster, the Explorer, and the Engineer than to the Jewish (or Judaized) Political Impresario. Certainly that is the impression conveyed by Trollope's works after 1868. The typical hero of Disraeli's fiction, Trollope groused in *An Autobiography*, is an "audacious conjurer."[103] Yet, in the later Palliser novels, Jewish characterization of this sort pervades Trollope's own fiction, suggesting its thoroughgoing penetration of English "stock." For example, Sir Timothy Beeswax, a Tory arriviste, "invents a pseudo-patriotic conjuring phraseology which no one understood but which many admired."[104]

With Jewish (or Judaized) character thus closely aligned with a morality "after virtue," it is no wonder that the more "scientific" discourses of the late nineteenth century often placed Jews at the epicenter of modern ills. Ironically, it was Max Nordau, a Hungarian Jew, whose *Degeneration* (1895) provided the best-known account of the theory that modern life and environment were the source of "morbid states" in which "the will is vitiated and the character warped."[105] But by the 1870s, especially after the so-called Eastern Question pitted Disraeli's foreign policy against the cause of Christians in Bulgaria, Britain's Jewish-born prime minister had become a lightning rod for theories of racialized Jewishness and Judaized depravity. As the historian Goldwin Smith alleged in an anonymous three-part article in the *Fortnightly Review* (still edited by Morley), it was impossible to describe Disraeli's politics without "reference to his

---

[100] Susman, *Culture as History*, pp. 23–4.
[101] Gilbert, "The Politics of Character," p. 322, emphasis added.
[102] [A. Hayward], "Mr. Disraeli: His Character and Career," p. 459 and p. 456.
[103] A. Trollope, *An Autobiography*, 1883, edited by David Skilton (Harmondsworth: Penguin, 1996), p. 166.
[104] A. Trollope, *The Duke's Children*, 1879, edited by Hermione Lee (Oxford: Oxford University Press, 2011), p. 137.
[105] M. Nordau, *Degeneration* (New York: D. Appleton, 1895), p. 277.

Jewish blood and to the inherited qualities which are deeply stamped upon his nature, physical [as well as] moral."[106] Although his grandfather had settled in England in the mid-eighteenth century and "may, perhaps, have had Shylock or Tubal among his ancestors," "a century and a quarter of residence in England on the part of [Disraeli's] ancestors and himself has left little trace on [his] mind and character."[107] Such notions continued to circulate after Disraeli's death in 1881. Thus, in a criticism of the Boer War published in 1900, J. A. Hobson became one of the most high-minded Liberal exponents on record of the theory that "a small group of international financiers, chiefly German in origin and Jewish in race" were sufficiently powerful to manipulate the foreign policy of Europe.[108]

Conclusion

Biologistic methods like Galton's and Beddoe's were influential inside and beyond anthropological circles. Such ostensible "science" conduced toward justifications of empire-building, chauvinistic rhetorics of Anglo-Saxon exceptionalism, and discourses of racial degeneracy. All helped to foster the reactionary politics of twentieth-century Europe which Hannah

---

[106] [G. Smith], "The Political Adventures of Lord Beaconsfield, Part I," 23 *Fortnightly Review* (January–June 1878), p. 691.

[107] [G. Smith], "The Political Adventures of Lord Beaconsfield, Part I," p. 483. On the significance of the Eastern Question in exacerbating anti-Semitism and the racialization of Jewishness, see Wohl, "Dizzi-Ben-Dizzi," as well as B. Cheyette, *Between "Race" and Culture: Representations of "the Jew" in English and American Culture* (Stanford: Stanford University Press, 1996). S. Gilman describes Goldwin Smith as "the first biological anti-semite in Britain": *Smart Jews: The Construction of the Image of Jewish Superior Intelligence* (Lincoln: University of Nebraska Press, 1997), p. 71. But, as Cheyette points out, the tendency to fall back on racial explanations to articulate Jewish difference can be found in the early Victorian writings of Thomas Arnold, who opposed the admission of Jews to Parliament: *Between "Race" and Culture*, p. 16. In another 1878 article, Smith provides a racio-cultural explanation for Jewish tribalism and their allegedly weak attachment to adopted homelands such as Britain: Christianity, he argues, "was the fulfilment and the consummation of what was universal, spiritual, human, in the history and writings of the Jewish people." Those who embraced Christianity were thus "the higher part of the Jewish nation, the true heirs and representatives of David and Isaiah": G. Smith, "Can Jews Be Patriots?" 3 *The Twentieth Century* (May 1878), p. 883.

[108] J. A. Hobson, *The War in South Africa: Its Causes and Effects* (London: James Nisbet, 1900), p. 189. Hobson's most famous work, *Imperialism: A Study* (1902; Ann Arbor: University of Michigan Press, 1965), warned readers that a "cosmopolitan organization" of financiers, "situated in the very heart of the business capital of every State," was controlled by "men of a single and peculiar race, who have behind them many centuries of financial experience": p. 57 and p. 59. By the 1880s, a new spate of research devoted to identifying "a Jewish type" had illustrated the new combination of anthropometry and "historical evidence": Lorimer, "Theoretical," p. 424.

Arendt describes so vividly in *The Origins of Totalitarianism* (1951). Yet, from a late Victorian perspective, it is important to recognize that even anthropology seldom reduced character to biology alone. Nor did the republican ideal of *homo civicus* or even the transcendental view of character as a "self-originating force" entirely disappear. As I argued in *Victorian Literature and the Victorian State*, the social reform movements of the turn of the century were fought over a terrain in which sociology provided the salient disciplinary framework, materialism and idealism proffered philosophical alternatives, and Fabian ideals of state efficiency vied with the network of voluntary associations preferred by the Charity Organization Society. Both sides of the debate claimed to seek the betterment of character. As *The Encyclopedia of Social Reform* (1897) opined in an entry on "The Moral Element in Social Reform," "in economics the reason why individualist economists fear socialism is that they believe that it will deteriorate character, and the reason why socialist economists seek socialism is their belief that under individualism charac-ter is deteriorating."[109]

Looking back on the stigmatizing poor law policies of the 1830s and 1860s, the economist Alfred Marshall, testifying before Parliament in 1893, declared that "extreme poverty ought to be regarded, not indeed as a crime, but as a thing so detrimental to the State that it should not be endured."[110] Philosophical idealists such as Bernard Bosanquet recognized that capitalism required collective effort of some kind to mitigate the material forces that all too readily engulfed vulnerable popu-lations, but they held, nevertheless, that the "state compulsion" and economic redistribution sought by the Fabians lacked the moral influ-ence necessary to build character as a force "charged with mind and will."[111] Fabians such as Beatrice and Sidney Webb argued that this antiquated attitude was out of touch with "the irresistible sweep of social tendencies."[112] The challenge of twentieth-century modernity, they held, required comprehensive state action founded on social-scientific knowledge to impose "new and enlarged obligations," "unknown in a state of *laisser faire*."[113] Though H. G. Wells regarded himself as a socialist ally of the Fabians, his utopian romances demonstrated keen

---

[109] W. D. P. Bliss, ed., *The Encyclopedia of Social Reforms*, 3rd Edition (New York and London: Funk & Wagnall, 1897), p. 780.

[110] Marshall quoted in Goodlad, *Victorian Literature*, p. 209.

[111] B. Bosanquet, *Philosophical Theory of the State* (London: Macmillan, 1899), p. 198.

[112] S. Webb, "Historic," in G. B. Shaw, ed., *Fabian Essays on Socialism*, 1889 (Boston: Ball, 1911), p. 44.

[113] S. Webb and B. Webb, *English Poor Law Policy* (London: Longman, 1910), p. 270.

ambivalence toward the Webbs' normalizing agenda and a powerful pull toward Millian individuality.[114]

As we have seen, anthropological discourse tended to construe character as a category describing the slowly evolved traits particular to distinct populations. By contrast, turn-of-the-century sociology regarded character as a set of features which – though hardly as plastic as Enlightenment thinkers had imagined, or as individualistic as earlier generations had wished to believe – was amenable to social conditioning on behalf of the public good. Of course, the most racially deterministic discourses of character made it a product of selective breeding, while the most transcendental made character so "self-originating" that it risked eliding the civic dimensions that connected the ethics of Plato and Aristotle to those of Mill, Eliot, Green, and (despite their disparate viewpoints) Bosanquet and the Webbs. Yet, despite this genealogy, the notion that the nineteenth-century emphasis on character ensured a moral golden age seems just as mistaken as the MacIntyrean corrective of Victorians "after virtue." Refreshingly defamiliarizing though it is, MacIntyre's thesis on the one hand overlooks the Victorians' significant republican commitments, while on the other it underestimates Victorian literature's readiness to cast doubt on the mere semblance of virtue.

[114] See Goodlad, *Victorian Literature*, ch. 6.

7   History

*Brian Young**

> ... it is not a matter here of man's essence in general, but simply of that historical *a priori* which, since the nineteenth century, has served as an almost self-evident ground for our thought.   Michel Foucault[1]

> She pointed out a red-haired woman at another table and asked me if I liked women with red hair. When I said that I preferred Buckle's *History of Civilization*, she laughed as though I had something quite absurdly paradoxical.   Aldous Huxley[2]

To seek to demonstrate that 'Historicism' was the dominant mode in nineteenth-century British historical thought and writing might look like an exercise in justifying a pleonasm. To a degree it is; but it is also a surprisingly contentious claim. History may well have been professionalised through the universities as it established itself as a formal subject of undergraduate study, but this was only from the 1870s onwards; before then, even immediately before then, it was a subject to which there was a wide variety of approaches. Historicism was by no means the only philosophy of history available to nineteenth-century British historians or commentators on history.[3] Indeed, German historicism, '*Historismus*', had many Victorian critics. And this chapter will be attentive to such critics as it details the contest over history and its meanings that took place as History was institutionalised as a discipline. Historicism became

* I am deeply indebted to Cosima Stewart, the late Rory Allan, Joshua Bennett, William Kelley, Timothy Pleydell-Bouverie and Chandler Sterling, for reading and commenting on this essay; Ksenia Levina eloquently alerted me to the importance of Aldous, as much as of T. H. Huxley.

[1] Michel Foucault, *The Order of Things: an archaeology of the human sciences*, English translation (London: Tavistock Publications Limited, 1970), p. 344.

[2] Aldous Huxley, *Those Barren Leaves* (London: Chatto and Windus, 1925), p. 123.

[3] For a concentrated study complementary to, but far from being identical, to the arguments of this essay, see Eckhardt Fuchs, 'Contemporary Alternatives to German Historicism in the Nineteenth Century' in Stuart Macintyre, Juan Maiguashca and Attila Pók eds., *The Oxford History of Historical Writing, 4: 1800–1945* (Oxford: Oxford University Press, 2011), pp. 59–77.

the preferred mode of university History, but only gradually; of the original promoters of the subject, only the University of Manchester imitated the seminar and allied procedures of instruction the German universities had inaugurated and which played such a role in the consolidation and evolution of historicism: Oxford and Cambridge absorbed historicism within a system of lectures and tutorials, and the research doctorate was very late in establishing itself in England's ancient universities. American universities, especially new foundations such as Johns Hopkins University, adopted the university culture in which German historicism had originally thrived much more readily and much more deeply and thoroughly than did any of the British universities. In Britain, the cult of the amateur continued to affect the way in which history was written and thought about much longer than it was to do either in Germany or the United States.[4]

Historicism and Leopold von Ranke are now indissolubly connected, much as New Historicism and Stephen Greenblatt are, and the University of Berlin played its role in the formalisation of the one as surely and effectively as the University of California at Berkeley was to do in the other. So it is telling that the name of Ranke, and the nature of the enterprise in which he was engaged, was first broached for anything like a wide audience in Britain by T. B. Macaulay, historian, politician and imperial administrator; Macaulay, however, had had no academic attachments after abandoning his fellowship at Trinity College, Cambridge in his early 20s. What is more, Macaulay's essay on 'Ranke's History of the Popes' effectively side-stepped a feature of historicism which modern commentators avoid confronting at their peril: its indebtedness to, and imbrication in, religion.[5] Religion and historicism were inseparable in the opening decades of the nineteenth century, and in this respect, the influence on English thought of Niebuhr was as great as that of Ranke.[6]

[4] Peter R. H. Slee, *Learning and a Liberal Education: the study of modern history in the Universities of Oxford, Cambridge, and Manchester, 1880–1914* (Manchester: Manchester University Press, 1986); Michael Bentley, *Modernizing England's Past: English historiography in the age of Modernism 1870–1970* (Cambridge: Cambridge University Press, 2005); Philippa Levine, *The Amateur and the Professional: antiquarians, historians and archaeologists, 1838–1886* (Cambridge: Cambridge University Press, 1986); Peter Novick, *That Noble Dream: the "objectivity question" and the American historical profession* (Cambridge: Cambridge University Press, 1988); George G. Iggers and James Powell eds., *Leopold von Ranke and the Shaping of the Historical Profession* (Syracuse: Syracuse University Press, 1990).
[5] See Thomas Albert Howard, *Religion and the Rise of Historicism: W.M.L. de Wette, Jacob Burckhardt, and the theological origins of nineteenth-century historical consciousness* (Cambridge: Cambridge University Press, 2000).
[6] See Norman Vance, 'Niebuhr in England: history, faith, and order' in Benedickt Stuchtey and Peter Wende eds., *British and German Historiography 1750–1950: traditions, perceptions, and transfers* (Oxford: Oxford University Press, 2000), pp. 83–98.

As the late J. W. Burrow observed, Ranke had internalised, as an historian, what Hegel had externalised as a philosopher:

> States as Individualities in history were to Ranke thoughts in the mind of God, whose presence was continuously sensed ... 'the plans of the divine government' to which he refers (*History of the Popes*) are implicit, not spelled out in detail, and are glimpsed by the historian, not abstractly summarized as in Hegel's philosophy. Nevertheless, they are sometimes unignorable, as in the guiding idea of the existence of unique historical Individualities ... It was the historian, and he alone, who could discern the hand of God in unique historical configurations of events and forces. This is the core of what is sometimes called 'Historicism' (*Historismus*).[7]

Before investigating the impact of historicism in the nineteenth-century British historical imagination, it is important to absorb this pregnant moment in Burrow's *A History of Histories*, the work of the doyen of the modern understanding and appreciation of nineteenth-century historical writing. In doing so, it is important to hear (as it were) how deaf Macaulay was to this religious note in Ranke's *History of the Popes*. Macaulay, after all, was a legatee of the late Enlightenment, a pre-historicist writing in a historicist age (for so any historicist would surely have sought to define it).[8]

Macaulay approved of Ranke because he was a Lutheran, and Macaulay was nothing if not broadly Protestant (if not necessarily believing) in his historical prejudices.[9] But the detailed appraisal which Ranke made of the Roman Catholic Church in terms of theology and the nature of the dynamics of providence was of little interest to his English reviewer, who used the occasion to portray the Papacy as a temporal power built on the literally fascinating pomp of ritual and superstition, aided by the priestly militarism of Jesuit 'fanaticism', against which the meagre aesthetic resources of Protestantism had little to offer. It was not theology, still less the attentive, purely historicist reconstruction of it that Ranke gave, that mattered in Macaulay's analysis; what mattered was power, and in this respect Rome, he warned his readers, might yet supersede the Anglican union of Church and State of which Macaulay had been a prime celebrant, if of a mildly non-confessional, determinedly erastian kind.[10] The intellectual imperative which drove Ranke and his historicist

[7] J. W. Burrow, *A History of Histories: epics, chronicles, romances, and inquiries from Herodotus and Thucydides to the twentieth century* (London: Allen Lane, 2007), p. 460.

[8] P. R. Ghosh, 'Macaulay and the Heritage of Enlightenment', *English Historical Review* 112 (1997), 358–95.

[9] For an attempt to reverse these prejudices, see Robert E. Sullivan, *Macaulay: the tragedy of power* (Cambridge, MA: Harvard University Press, 2009).

[10] T. B. Macaulay, 'Ranke's History of the Popes' in *Lord Macaulay's Essays and Lays of Rome* (London: Macmillan and Co, 1885), pp. 541–62. More broadly, see Patrick Bahners, '"A Place Among the English Classics": Ranke's *History of the Popes* and its British readers' in Stuchtey and Wende, *British and German Historiography*, pp. 123–57.

perspective on the bond between politics and religion was of an altogether more sophisticated and refined quality than Macaulay's professedly 'Whig' interpretation of the European past. The intellectual ballast which maintained Macaulay's history would quickly prove unsatisfactory to professional English historians, but he was Ranke's direct contemporary; Ranke's followers in England belonged to a generation after that which established historicism in Germany. At the start of the nineteenth century, Macaulay's literary and political history set the tone in England; he took the 'philosophical history' of the Enlightenment in a rather different direction from his historicist contemporaries. Macaulay was a present-minded apostle of progress; about such matters historicists were more ambivalent.[11]

And here one comes to the central fact that has to inform any assessment of history (whether explicitly historicist or otherwise), when considered as a human science in nineteenth-century Britain: namely, that it is a development of approaches to thinking about the past that had their origin in the last third of the eighteenth century. These origins can be precisely located in two historical and historiographical moments: on the one hand, in the *sciences de l'homme* which originated in the immediate wake of the French Revolution, and which would strongly influence Auguste Comte and his followers; on the other, in the 'conjectural history' favoured by such Scottish Enlightenment historians as William Robertson, Adam Smith and Adam Ferguson.[12] It is with the British nineteenth-century history of a 'science of history' and its frequent collisions with historicism that this essay will primarily be concerned; historical prolepsis is a solecism especially associated with those historians who think that history *is* a human science, and it is, therefore, more than usually incumbent on

---

[11] Peter Gay, *Style in History* (New York, NY: W.W. Norton, 1974), pp. 97–138; J. W. Burrow, *A Liberal Descent: Victorian historians and the English past* (Cambridge: Cambridge University Press, 1981), pp. 9–93; John Clive, 'Macaulay's Historical Imagination' and 'Macaulay, History, and the Historians' in *Not By Fact Alone: essays on the writing and reading of history* (London: Harper Collins, 1989), pp. 66–73 and 220–7; Hugh Trevor-Roper, 'Lord Macaulay: *The History of England*' in John Robertson ed. *History and Enlightenment* (London and New Haven, CT: Yale University Press, 2010), pp. 192–222.

[12] J. W. Burrow, *Evolution and Society: a study in Victorian social theory* (Cambridge: Cambridge University Press, 1966); Herbert Butterfield, *Man on His Past: the study of the history of historical scholarship* (Cambridge: Cambridge University Press, 1955). On the complex genealogy of German historicism, see Friedrich Meinecke, *Die Entstehung des Historismus* (2 vols., Munich and Berlin: R. Oldenbourg, 1936); the English translation, by John Anderson – *Historicism: the rise of a new historical outlook* (London: Routledge Kegan Paul, 1972) – is not entirely satisfactory. The literature on historicism in Germany is exhaustive; for a recent survey, see Frederick C. Beiser, *The German Historicist Tradition* (Oxford: Oxford University Press, 2011).

any historian analysing such a claim not to be too readily implicated in making, let alone substantiating, this contention.

The first section of this chapter is devoted to the Comtist science of history, and the second to Thomas Henry Buckle's rival model and the evolutionary mode of historical explanation which originated in a fusion of conjectural history and Darwinism. Both Comtist and evolutionary approaches to a science of history are more representative of Victorian historical thought than was the work of Buckle, which was critically received both by Comtist and evolutionary historians.[13] Buckle was provocatively secular in orientation, a devoutly anticlerical author; this was somewhat less true of Comtist and evolutionary historians, and the religious background of much nineteenth-century historical reflection needs to be securely kept in mind, especially when considering the explicitly historicist work of Bishops (*sic*) Stubbs and Creighton and of Lord Acton, the self-proclaimed lay conscience of liberal Catholicism and a stern critic of rigidly scientific approaches to the past. It is with a consideration of the legacy of Stubbs, Creighton and Acton that this chapter will close.[14]

The story that will be told here is a history of the different receptions which particular philosophies of history experienced in nineteenth-century Britain. Nothing in that story made the triumph of historicism inevitable, and whilst it questions the claims made for the Europe-wide emergence of historicism at the close of the Enlightenment made by Michel Foucault, it does not do so on the basis of the sort of English 'exceptionalism' which Macaulay promoted. What it does suggest is that Foucault's account of the rise of historicism as a conceptual and organisational technique of newly bureaucratising states is too programmatic, and that it ignores religion far too much as a factor in thinking about History as a mode of human consciousness, preferring instead to emphasise the place of war in such historicised reflection. Characteristically, when religion appears in Foucault's appraisal of historicism it is in the context of European wars of religion.[15] Foucault offers an implicitly and formidably secularising account of the rise of historicism, but historicism

[13] Buckle was received as a Comtist in Germany, on which see Eckhardt Fuchs, 'English Positivism and German Historicism' in Stuchtey and Wende, *British and German Historiography*, pp. 229–50.

[14] See now J. M. R. Bennett, 'Doctrine, Progress and Religion: British religious debate 1845–1914', Oxford D.Phil. dissertation, 2015. James Kirby's important study, *Historians and the Church of England: religion and historical scholarship, 1870–1920* (Oxford: Oxford University Press, 2016), appeared after I had completed this chapter.

[15] Foucault, *The Order of Things*, pp. 217–21, 344–8, 367–73; Foucault, *'Society Must Be Defended': lectures at the Collège de France 1975–1976*, trans. David Macey (Basingstoke: Macmillan, 2003), pp. 43–238. For an account of Foucault's own 'problem' with

was, in its origins, fundamentally a religious way of thinking. It would
prove to be so in England until the opening decades of the twentieth
century, when the religious atmosphere in which it had flourished in the
late Victorian universities gave way to rather more secular-minded ways
of thinking. At Cambridge, Lord Acton was to be succeeded as Regius
Professor of Modern History by J. B. Bury, a consciously secularising
figure, and a promoter of history as a 'science'. Bury saw himself as a
historicist, but there is something of the nineteenth-century scientific
historian about him; Ranke would have recognised Acton as an intellectual heir, but he would have excommunicated Bury.

Positivism and History

With very few exceptions, nineteenth-century British historians were not
methodologically self-conscious, and even fewer set out a philosophy of
history as such. It is an indication of how influential Comtism, and a
more generalised Positivism, had been from the 1850s onwards in Britain
that it was a Comtean historian, Frederic Harrison, who issued a collection of ruminative essays and addresses – Comtism was nothing if not
public in its British manifestation – under the revealing title of *The
Meaning of History* in 1894.[16] Aside from a mild rebuke of Auguste
Comte for recommending the 'entirely uncritical' ecclesiastical history
of the Abbé Fleury as a complement to Gibbon's *Decline and Fall*,
Harrison's compilation of essays and addresses (many culled from *The
Fortnightly Review*) are consistently and resolutely Comtist.[17] Indeed,
they might be said to constitute a 'representative' work, to employ a
word and an ideal fundamental to Comtist reflections on history. It is
worth exploring them in depth as denoting the most considered deployment of Comtist thought in relation to historical thinking produced in
nineteenth-century Britain, when historicists of various stripes united
against Positivism as a mode of historical enquiry.[18] And not the least
interesting element informing Harrison's approach is that the first three
essays reproduced public lectures: the first two, 'The Use of History' and
'The Connection of History', were given in 1862 to a London audience;
the third, 'Some Great Books of History', in which the mild rebuke of

---

historicism as method, see *The Birth of Biopolitics: lectures at the Collège de France
1978–1979*, trans. Graham Burchell (Basingstoke: Macmillan, 2010), p. 3.
[16] See T. R. Wright, *The Religion of Humanity: the impact of Comtean Positivism in Victorian
Britain* (Cambridge: Cambridge University Press, 1986).
[17] Frederic Harrison, *The Meaning of History* (London: Macmillan and Co, 1894), p. 114.
[18] See Christopher Parker, 'English Historians and the Opposition to Positivism', *History
and Theory* 22 (1983), 120–45.

Comte was made, was delivered to summer vacation students at Oxford. Intriguingly, the fourth essay, 'The History Schools (An Oxford Dialogue)', was a semi-satirical riposte to what Harrison thought had gone wrong with the institutionalisation and professionalisation of history at his old university, where, as a young man, he had been a fellow of Wadham College, a hotbed of Comtism. All the essays in *The Meaning of History* were produced (and reproduced), as Harrison put it, 'to stimulate the systematic study of general history'.[19] A pithier characterisation of the Comtist incentive to study history could not have been made. But why should such a study have needed to be stimulated, and what purposes lay behind its inauguration?

It is now a commonplace in study of nineteenth-century Britain that 'public opinion' was pivotal to its self-image and to its accelerating rate of political, social and economic reforms; hence something of John Morley's interest in the 'history of opinion', a characterisation of the history of thought which he shared with such pioneers of British intellectual history as Mark Pattison and Leslie Stephen.[20] And Comtism invested in opinion in order to inform and shape, however subtly, opinion: as Harrison put it:

A man, provided he lives like an honest, thoughtful, truth-speaking citizen, is a power to the state. He is helping to form that which rules the state, which rules statesmen, and which is above kings, parliaments, or ministers. He is forming *public opinion*. It is on this, a public opinion, wise, thoughtful, and consistent, that the destinies of our country rest, and not on acts of parliament, or movements, or institutions.[21]

By directly addressing just such men (and more occasionally women), Harrison was seeking to ensure that the Comtist account of opinion formation would itself form opinion, thus guaranteeing that the doctrine of progress pivotal to that philosophy could take a continuing social and political shape, since 'Progress is but the result of our joint public opinion; and for progress that opinion must be enlightened.'[22] Comtism was a view of history that saw itself as descriptive, but which inevitably blurred into a prescriptive philosophy: indeed, properly understood, Comtism necessarily melded description and prescription, no less than Marxism, albeit its supporters thought it more genuinely disinterested as

---

[19] Harrison, *Meaning of History*, p. i.
[20] Stefan Collini, *Public Moralists: political thought and intellectual life in Britain 1850–1930* (Oxford: Oxford University Press, 1991); Jeffrey Paul von Arx, *Progress and Pessimism: religion, politics, and history in late nineteenth-century Britain* (Cambridge, MA: Harvard University Press, 1985); Stuart Jones, *Intellect and Character in Victorian England: Mark Pattison and the invention of the don* (Cambridge: Cambridge University Press, 2007).
[21] Harrison, *Meaning of History*, p. 20.   [22] Harrison, *Meaning of History*, p. 20.

a mode of social philosophising. But, to the Comtist, his (it was rarely her) philosophy was at least as scientific in its claims as was Marxism, and both philosophies were preoccupied by the French Revolution as the pivotal moment which provided the momentum, and the mechanism – once properly understood – of modernity. To achieve this objective was no small task, as Harrison observed: 'Nothing but a thorough knowledge of the social system, based upon a regular study of its growth can give us the power we require to affect it. For this end we need one thing above all – we need history.'[23] Harrison conceived of such history as constituting a fundamental contrast with historicism, and as forming an essentially extra-academic activity.

For the Comtist history was a story of progress and connection, a narrative with a directly organic impetus, in which mind and matter were interconnected in a philosophical–physiological manner:

The history of the human race is the history of a growth. It can no more be taken to pieces than the human frame can be taken to pieces. Who would think of making anything of the body without knowing whether it possessed a circulation, a nervous system, or a skeleton. History is a living whole. If one organ be removed, it is nothing but a lifeless mass. What we have to find in it is the relation and connection of the parts. We must learn first how age develops into age, how country reacts upon country, how thought inspires action, and action modifies thought.[24]

A telling parallel with the exact sciences was deployed, in which history looked even more precise:

Except for eclipses, some conjunctions of planets, and some minor changes, one year is as good as another to the astronomer; but it is not so to the political observer. He must watch successions, and a wide field, and compare a long series of events. Hence it is that in all political, all social, all human questions whatever, history is the main resource of the inquirer.[25]

Analogies were made with the systematisation of mathematics and geometry achieved by the ancient Greeks, and with the growth of the physical sciences in the seventeenth century: Comtism was to extend scientific understanding to society, thereby reforming both science and society. Where Euclid and Galileo had led in geometry and astronomy, so the great, representative men of the past, the likes of Caesar and Cromwell – considered by Harrison to be England's greatest leader (hence his admiration for Carlyle's edition of the *Letters and Speeches of Oliver Cromwell*, despite his more general disapprobation of Carlyle's historical practice

---

[23] Harrison, *Meaning of History*, p. 19.   [24] Harrison, *Meaning of History*, p. 22.
[25] Harrison, *Meaning of History*, pp. 14–15.

and influence) – were the master spirits of history.[26] Where Dante and Milton were not only poets but also epochal thinkers, so also was a major influence on the Comtist programme, Condorcet, whose *Historical Sketch of the Progress of the Human Mind* (1795) was apostrophised thus: 'The annals of literature have no more pathetic incident than the history of this little book – this still unfinished vision of a brain prematurely cut off.' Condorcet, in Harrison's estimation, had secured the status of a sociological martyr; awaiting execution, 'with death hanging round him, he calmly compiled the first true sketch of human evolution. Amidst the chaos and bloodshed he reviews the history of mankind.'[27]

Harrison knew what he did not want from history, and that was, above all, a non-scientific approach to the subject. Carlyle was plainly in his sights when he proclaimed that 'Brilliant and ingenious writing has been the bane of history; it has degraded its purpose, and perverted many of its uses.' Similarly, as a thinker, John Henry Newman, whose lectures on *The Idea of a University* had only just appeared when Harrison was delivering his lecture on 'The Use of History', was obviously in his mind when he declared that 'What some people call the pure love of truth often means only a pure love of intellectual fussiness.' The professionalisation of history, co-terminus with Harrison's lectures which were delivered as Modern History was being introduced as an undergraduate degree at Oxford, was a matter of which he was – surprisingly perhaps – suspicious, as in his insistence that 'It is possible to know something of history without a pedantic erudition.'[28] Pedantry was, he felt, the bane of academic history, and this was made manifest, some thirty years after he delivered his lectures, in his dialogue 'The History Schools', which appeared in the *Fortnightly Review* in 1893. This was the satire of regret, as Harrison inveighed, with heavy humour, against the minute Anglo-Saxon prejudices of E. A. Freeman – suitably defended in the dialogue by the absurdly named AEthelbald Wessex – but equally against the pronouncedly literary style of history associated with Freeman's successor in the Regius Chair of Modern History at Oxford, James Anthony Froude, whose cast of mind is represented in the dialogue by the no less preciously (and pointedly) named Philibert Raleigh (Froude was best known as a celebrant of the naval heroes of the reign of Elizabeth).

All that was wrong with the drily academic approach to study of the past as newly institutionalised – in Harrison's eyes – in the Oxford History School, with its prevailingly historicist assumptions, was

[26] Harrison, *Meaning of History*, pp. 11–13, 16–17, 23, 119–21.
[27] Harrison, *Meaning of History*, pp. 24–5, 214–15.
[28] Harrison, *Meaning of History*, pp. 8, 11, 20.

incarnated in AEthelbald Wessex, as when the clerical historian observed to his undergraduate charge, cramming for the History Schools, that 'we ask you to know – or, to be quite accurate, to satisfy the examiners'. Wessex stood solidly not only against Comtism – 'But you may write pages of stuff about what smatterers call the "philosophy of history," without a single sentence of solid knowledge. When every inscription and every manuscript remaining has been copied and accurately unravelled, then we may talk about the philosophy of history' – but also against the style of evolutionary history associated with the likes of Walter Bagehot:

You may chatter about 'evolution' as fast as you like, if you take up Physical Science and go to that beastly museum; but if you mention 'evolution' in the History School you will be gulfed – take my word for it! … All that you have to do, dear boy, is to choose your period (I hope it will be Old-English somewhere) – mark out your 'claim,' as Californian miners do, and then wash your lumps, sift, crush quartz, till you find ore, and don't cry 'Gold!' till you have had it tested.[29]

For Wessex, science in history was purely metaphorical: for him, all that glittered was *not* gold. When the young Raleigh protested, invoking his instruction at Eton by Oscar Browning and his reading of John Morley – both of whom had stressed the centrality of the history leading up to 1789 in their work – Wessex was more than prepared with a magisterial rebuke that summed up everything about the new historical profession against which the Comtists persistently, if ultimately ineffectively, protested:

'Oscar's a radical and John is a terrorist,' replied the Venerable, quite annoyed at the lad's pertinacity and his shallow turn of mind. 'The French Revolution is the happy hunting-ground of all the phrase-mongers like Carlyle, the doctrinaires like Louis Blanc, the epigrammatists like Michelet and Taine, and the liars like Thiers and Lamartine. There is no history to be got out of it for a century or two, till all the manuscripts have been deciphered and all the rubbish that has been published is forgotten.'[30]

Wessex is an unwitting self-parodist, and in this he is the very type of professional historian repudiated by Harrison; his pedantry is beyond even the claims of the Dryasdust condemned by Sir Walter Scott and Carlyle: 'in history you cannot trust a fellow who tries to be interesting. If he pretends to be "philosophical" you may know him to be an impostor.' Into this dialogue of the deaf enters a London barrister and MP, a Comtist spokesman with the yet more telling *nom de guerre*

[29] Harrison, *Meaning of History*, pp. 126, 132, 133.
[30] Harrison, *Meaning of History*, p. 134.

of Jack Middleman, who defends literary history as personified by Tacitus and Gibbon, and who systematically ridicules the academic historians and their distortions of the past with an interesting scientific simile: 'History seems to be seen nowadays with some such apparatus as the naturalists describe the eye of a fly magnified to ten thousand diameters.'[31]

As so often in the dialogue form, it is the disinterested, if intrusive, third character, the Eleatic Stranger, who is given all the best – in this case, Comtist – lines, and they justify quoting *in extenso*, as they provide as economic a presentation of the Comtist philosophy of history as one could hope to find for present purposes:

Well, what I would advise a young man going into the historical line to bespeak is – first, indefatigable research into all the accessible materials; secondly, a sound philosophy of human evolution; thirdly, a genius for seizing on the typical movements and the great men; and lastly, the power of a true artist in grouping subjects and in describing typical men and events. All four are necessary; and you seem to think at Oxford that the first is enough without the rest. But, unless you have a real philosophy of history, you have nothing but your own likings and dislikings to direct your judgement of men and movements. Unless you have the insight to select and classify your facts, you and your readers will be lost in a sea of details. Not one fact in a hundred is worth preservation, just as biology could only exist as a science by judicious selection of typical forms. To do anything else is to assume that induction could take place in logic, as Aldrich says, *per enumerationem simplicem*. And lastly, unless you can impress on your readers' minds a vivid idea of some given world or some representative man, you will only send them to sleep. If the historical romance can do nothing but mislead, the historical ditch-water will only disgust.[32]

Middleman expounds the social-scientific prescriptions of Comtism with continuous reference to their favourite natural science, as he concludes that 'History is only one department of Sociology, just as Natural History is the descriptive part of Biology. And History will have to be brought most strictly under the guidance and inspiration of Social Philosophy.'[33]

Echoing Harrison's own recital of 'Some Great Books of History' delivered some thirty years before, his spokesman Middleman recommends, above all other histories, Gibbon's *Decline and Fall* as 'the last example of that rarest of combinations – profound scholarship with splendid art'. Historians of the future, Middleman inaccurately predicted, would continue 'that general plan of the biography of humanity', instancing as good contemporary works of history Mommsen's *Roman Provinces* and Stubbs' *Constitutional History*, this last a rare

---

[31] Harrison, *Meaning of History*, pp. 135, 138.
[32] Harrison, *Meaning of History*, pp. 142–3.   [33] Harrison, *Meaning of History*, pp. 144–5.

example of history written by an Oxford Regius Professor of Modern History of whom Harrison actually approved. Such historians would avoid the extremes of E. A. Freeman and James Anthony Froude: 'They will no longer chronicle small beer or paint melodramatic scenes. They will illustrate philosophy.'[34]

Here, in essence, is the Comtist philosophy of history in which religion, especially Judaism and Christianity, is central only for it eventually, and organically, to be superseded by the true Religion of Humanity. It is a history which celebrates the foundational, if theocratic, civilisation of Egypt; inquiring ancient Greeks; the commercial Phoenicians; and the powerful Romans, all in a manner which was to be echoed in the 1930s by the young Ernst Gombrich in his *A Little History of the World*.[35] But the unequivocally secular Gombrich would have been appalled by Harrison's treatment of the Renaissance, which is curiously foreshortened by him, both in terms of its nature and its immediate influence, in favour of his beloved thirteenth century. Harrison lauded the thirteenth century for its proto-Comtist union of organic society with intellectual growth, of which Dante is at once the representative man *and* the man ahead of his time, this latter a figure fundamental to the intellectual history practised by Comte and his followers. As Harrison observed in 'A Survey of the Thirteenth Century', which appeared in the *Fortnightly Review* in 1893:

As to Dante himself, it is not easy to place him in a survey of the thirteenth century. In actual date and in typical expression he belongs to it, and yet he does not belong to it. The century itself has a transitional, an ambiguous character. And Dante, like it, has a transitional and double office. He is the poet, the prophet, the painter of the Middle Ages. And yet, in so many things, he anticipates the modern mind and modern art.[36]

The Victorian preoccupation with the Middle Ages had its Comtist element, and it is striking how often Comtist historians such as Harrison chose to write about the High Middle Ages just as much as they did the French Revolution, perpetually considered as the grand climacteric out of which arose their own social scientific brand of philosophical history.

In a centenary essay entitled 'What the Revolution of 1789 Did' (published in his favoured public space, the *Fortnightly Review*, in June 1889), Harrison summarised the Comtist view of the age of reason as an age of science perfectly and precisely; it is, therefore, best once more to give it in his own words, otherwise one would be forced to paraphrase a paraphrase:

[34] Harrison, *Meaning of History*, p. 145.
[35] Harrison, 'The Connection of History' in *Meaning of History*, pp. 26–80.
[36] Harrison, *Meaning of History*, p. 178.

Into the world of ideas France flung herself with passion and with hope. The wonderful accumulation of scientific discoveries which followed the achievements of Newton reacted powerfully on religious thought, and even on practical policy. Mathematics, astronomy, physics, chemistry, biology, began to assume the outlined proportion of coherent sciences; and some vague sense of their connection and real unity filled the mind of all. Out of the physical sciences there emerged a dim conception of a crowning human science, which it was the grand achievement of the eighteenth century to found. History ceased to be a branch of literature; it began to have practical uses for to-day; and slowly it was recognised as the momentous life-story of man, the autobiography of the human race. Europe no longer absorbed the interest of cultivated thought. The unity of the planet, the community of all who dwell on it, gave a new colour to the whole range of thought; and as the old dogmas of the supernatural Church began to lose their hold on the mind, the new-born enthusiasm of humanity began to fill all hearts.[37]

The ages of religion and metaphysics had given way to a truly scientific age, and the religion of humanity had supplanted, whilst it absorbed the best of, Christianity. But as with Christianity, so with Comtism, sacrifices had had to be made in order to usher in a new age; and whilst Condorcet acted as their martyr, it was an opponent of the French Revolution (and of martyrs), Gibbon, who provided their model of a philosophic historian. Significantly, when John Morley, a busy public moralist and politician who would enjoy more success in politics than had Macaulay, cast about for an author of a popular study of Gibbon in his *English Men of Letters* series, he turned to his undergraduate contemporary at Lincoln College, Oxford, James Augustus Cotter Morison. And Morison was not only a doctrinaire Comtist who explored and anticipated what Charles Homer Haskins would later call the twelfth-century Renaissance as appreciatively as Harrison would later explore the thirteenth century, but also a journalist and an independently wealthy man of letters; he had neither inclination for, nor any need to secure, an academic post.[38]

---

[37] Harrison, *Meaning of History*, pp. 208–9.

[38] James Augustus Cotter Morison, *The Life and Times of Saint Bernard, Abbot of Clairvaux* (London: Macmillan and Co., 1863), which was dedicated to Carlyle, his historian hero, treats Peter Abelard with respect and St Bernard with admiring suspicion; alongside the marginal note 'Reawakenment of learning', Morison wrote that 'The beginnings of a great change were there; the human mind had begun to move. Slowly, almost imperceptibly, like the gentle rising of a vast continent from the ocean, the questioning intellect again rose up, approached problems, and tried to solve them' (p. 349). Bernard was treated as 'one of the great active minds of his age ... one of the statesmen of history' (p. 367). For a full statement of his Comtism, see *The Service of Man: an essay towards the religion of the future* (London: Macmillan and Co., 1887), which is built on the observation that Morison and his contemporaries ought 'honestly' to 'take our side, and admit that the *Civitas Dei* is a dream of the past, and that we should strive to realise that *Regnum Hominis* which Bacon foresaw and prescribed' (p. 10).

He was a gentleman amateur, and in this he reflected not only Gibbon, about whom he wrote in 1878, but also the second historian whom Morley commissioned him to write about in 1882: Macaulay, about whose intellectual shortcomings Morison was completely unforgiving, noting in particular that whilst Macaulay's contemporaries – such as Sir James Stephen – admired him uncritically, the next generation was decidedly less indulgent (citing here Leslie Stephen).[39]

Varieties of Scientific History

In his review of the first volume of Buckle's *History of Civilization in England*, published in 1858 in a Roman Catholic periodical, *The Rambler*, Acton intriguingly pointed his finger with great certainty at the major interpretative fault of Buckle's 'philosophy of history'. Basing his judgement on the authority of a single footnote, Acton erroneously assumed that Buckle was a follower of Comte, consequently stating, with presumed authority, that Buckle's 'view seldom extends beyond the bounds of the system of that philosopher', and that he had not 'sought enlightenment in the study of the great metaphysicians of other schools'.[40] Not that, with few exceptions, it would have gone much better in Acton's view had he consulted other metaphysicians, as he was deeply suspicious of any philosophy of history – for history was always prior, in his view, to philosophy as a mode of understanding; philosophy, no less than any other humanistic study, was best understood historically. 'Philosophy', as he characteristically stated the case, 'must be seen by the light of history that the laws of its progress may be understood; and history, which records the thoughts as well as the actions of men, cannot overlook the vicissitudes of philosophic schools. Thus the history of philosophy is a postulate of either science.' Where Comtists (and such assumed Comtists as Buckle) made much of the eighteenth-century emergence of a philosophy of history, of a science of society, Acton the historicist counselled caution, observing that 'it naturally happened that the philosophy of history and the history of philosophy, as they proceeded from the same causes, began to be cultivated about the same time. They are scarcely a century old.'[41] For Acton, it was necessary to disaggregate the two

[39] James Augustus Cotter Morison, *Gibbon* (London: Macmillan and Co., 1878); *Macaulay* (London: Macmillan and Co., 1882), pp. 9, 41, and *passim*.
[40] Lord Acton, 'Buckle's Philosophy of History' in J. Rufus Fears ed., *Selected Writings of Lord Acton* (3 vols., Indianapolis, IN: Liberty Fund Press, 1988), iii: *Essays in religion, politics, and morality*, 443–59, at p. 450.
[41] Acton, 'Buckle's Philosophy of History', p. 445.

mental activities, and chronology provided the basis for a distinction that Comtists (and Buckle) were allegedly mistaken in not making for themselves. The eighteenth century, far from being a great climacteric in philosophical and historical understanding, was but one period of human history – and one, moreover, which preceded, in his estimation, the truly epochal achievement that was nineteenth-century historicism, of which Acton was England's greatest exegete, practitioner and occasional hanging judge.

Acton was hugely dismissive of such activity as that promoted by Buckle, as can be appreciated through a strikingly mordant aside: 'Twenty years ago, the well-known novelist Gutzkow was in prison, and not having books at hand to help him in writing a novel, beguiled the time by writing and publishing a philosophy of history.'[42] Acton had early enunciated the case that was to be made – and continues to be made, most recently by Richard J. Evans, an eventual successor to Acton's Cambridge Regius Chair – by historicists against 'theorists' of whatever kind. And, as characteristically, it was rather more Buckle's facts than his philosophy to which Acton took exception. It was such an examination of his sources and his conclusions that allowed Acton to insist that Buckle, 'in a word', was 'an impostor'.[43] Not accidentally, perhaps, Acton sounds, throughout his review, a little like a more imaginative and Catholic version of AEthelbald Wessex, and what matters in this comparison is Acton's character as a Catholic layman. Indicting Buckle for 'learned ignorance', and incidentally dismissing Mill as an 'eminent positivist' along the way, Acton issued his malediction in a manner typical of that of the many Christian critics who wrote not only against Buckle, but also against Comtism: 'In his laborious endeavour to degrade the history of mankind, and of the dealings of God with man, to the level of one of the natural sciences, he has stripped it of its philosophical, of its divine, and even of its human character and interest.'[44] And here is starkly revealed a constant in Victorian historical reflection rather more typical of the era than the intellectual activity of those who tried, in whatever way, to characterise and practice it as a science: the assumption for so many nineteenth-century historians, from Henry Hart Milman and his fellow 'Liberal Anglican Historians' to Acton and Mandell Creighton, that Christianity was of fundamental and truthful importance in any

---

[42] Acton', 'Buckle's Philosophy of History', p. 447.

[43] Richard J. Evans, *In Defence of History* (London: Granta Books, 1997); Acton, 'Buckle's Philosophy of History', p. 448.

[44] Acton, 'Buckle's Philosophy of History', pp. 457, 458.

genuine understanding of 'the meaning of history'. In this, they were historicists of a stamp that Ranke would have recognised.[45]

Acton's triumphant conclusion to his review has to be appreciated for the truism so many of his like-minded colleagues thought it to be if sense is to be made not only of Buckle's attempted philosophy of history, but also of the reception it received, which ultimately proved to be rather different among secular thinkers than it was among Christians:

We may rejoice that the true character of an infidel philosophy has been brought to light by the monstrous and absurd results to which it has led this writer, who has succeeded in extending its principles to the history of civilization only at the sacrifice of every quality which makes a history great.[46]

Few modern scholars would dissent from Acton's appraisal of Buckle's work as being nothing like a great history, but is he otherwise fair? Tonally, this seems a redundant question, so total is his disseveration of all that Buckle stood for and all he attempted to achieve from true history, but Buckle had his secular critics, including Harrison and Morley, as well as his religious ones. Why was this?

Buckle very largely had only himself to blame: a comfortably placed autodidact, he had a degree of arrogance that guaranteed him few admirers and even fewer friends. He, above all others, insisted on the originality of his philosophy of history; for him Comte had done the most to develop a true science of history, but, *contra* Acton, not as much as he, Buckle, was personally undertaking in an enterprise that only his early death denied any final, supposedly irrefutable, completion. His much-vaunted originality and lack of any associational contact with like-minded thinkers (something which the likes of Harrison and Morison enjoyed through the Positivist Society) further marginalised him, even within the ranks of those committed to a view of history as a human science. He was also stridently anticlerical, something which even the pronouncedly secular-minded found too much and too often in his writings; Comtism was never so dismissive of religion, and other writers were more careful in marking their distance from Christianity. As Acton's review resolutely demonstrated, Buckle's work proved anathema to the many religiously committed historicists. His only vociferous advocate as the century progressed was J. M. Robertson, an outspoken Rationalist and the leading light of the South Place Ethical Association of which Leslie Stephen and

[45] Duncan Forbes, *The Liberal Anglican Theory of History* (Cambridge: Cambridge University Press, 1952); Forbes, 'Historismus in England', *Cambridge Journal* 4 (1951), 387–400.

[46] Acton, 'Buckle's Philosophy of History', p. 459.

others were stalwart supporters, but Stephen had a good deal less patience with Buckle than had Robertson.[47]

Yet more importantly, in terms of his immediate reputation, Buckle's contention that he was more original than any of his contemporaries could be, and was, questioned. And this is the larger explanation for his brief moment in the sun. The key to history for Buckle was a combination of general and particular statistical inquiry with a belief in natural materialism as the basis of all human history – hence his interest in demography and geography, and thence of subsistence and patterns of settlement, and also in medicine and the history of disease and its palliation. Unfinished though this ambitious history was fated to be, it is again striking just how indebted what survives of it is to the eighteenth century, both as an age of reason in and of itself, and also as the intellectual progenitor and apologetic agent of all future reasoning concerning the human sciences. Eighteenth-century France is central to this historical project, and yet more so is the Scottish Enlightenment, a movement of ideas in which chemistry and medicine were as important as history, political economy, sociology and philosophy for Buckle's mode of historical enquiry.[48] Any reading of Buckle reveals immediately how great a contrast it offers with all other history, *qua* history, written in mid-nineteenth-century England, and this is true of Comtist historians as it is, more pronouncedly, of historicists. But this does not mean that his work was without connections with such approaches, only that they were less consistent with the approach made by the generality of contributors to those particular schools of historical research. His systematic appeal to, and use of, history is more reminiscent of Mill's ethology in the *Logic* than it is of more general enquiry; in historical terms, he is closer to Montesquieu than to Hume, to Adam Ferguson than to William Robertson.

Briefly notorious and fashionable though he was, Buckle was quickly eclipsed as an historian by others more obviously committed to the evolutionary mode of understanding. It is telling that Giles St Aubyn's 1958 study of Buckle treated him as a lost eminence, and, equally, that the most substantial recent study of his work and its context has been made by a German scholar, Eckhardt Fuchs, in a University of Leipzig dissertation published in 1994: ultimately, it has taken a modern

---

[47] J. M. Robertson, *Buckle and His Critics: a study of sociology* (London: Sonnenschien, 1895). For a sensitive treatment of which, see Joshua Bennett, 'A History of "Rationalism" in Victorian Britain', *Modern Intellectual History* (forthcoming).
[48] Henry Thomas Buckle, *The History of Civilisation in England* (2 vols., London: John Henry Parker, 1857–61).

historicist to do belated justice to a nineteenth-century historian who had attempted to replace historicism with a vision of history as a natural science rich with practical implications and applications.[49] Modern study of nineteenth-century historiography is littered with such paradoxes.

Buckle had looked back with something like equal favour both on the post-Revolutionary French generations *and* also on representatives of Scottish conjectural history: Acton, ever keen to detect heresy, was more inclined to notice his approving mention of Comte than he was Buckle's more extensively acknowledged approval of much eighteenth-century Scottish intellectual activity. As J. W. Burrow long ago demonstrated in his first book, *Evolution and Society* (1966), Victorian social scientists of an evolutionary cast of mind were much more strongly indebted to the Scottish style of conjectural history than they were to Positivism; indeed, the evolution of evolutionary social science is at least as much a development of conjectural history as it is of Darwinism, and nowhere is this clearer than in its impact on historical thinking. The most significant of such evolutionary historians was Sir Henry Maine, who also illustrates the fact, as Maitland did after him, that history and law were as intimately linked for many nineteenth-century students as they had been for their seventeenth-century common law ancestors, as J. G. A. Pocock demonstrated in his classic study, *The Ancient Constitution and the Feudal Law* (1957).[50] When Modern History was first mooted as a Final Honours School at Oxford it was to be in conjunction with study of Law. Consequently, even after the two subjects were quickly separated, constitutional history became a priority in the History School, flourishing from the age of Stubbs into the era of curriculum reform at Oxford in the 1980s. At Cambridge, the émigré scholar G. R. Elton similarly insisted on the central place of constitutional matters in the study of British history; and Elton, who ended his career as the Regius Professor of Modern History, was an unstinting admirer of F. W. Maitland, a firmminded, German-speaking and religiously agnostic historicist.[51]

Maine has been much studied, and it would be better, therefore, to consider a figure more akin to Harrison when treating the parallel career of history as a human science in an era in which historicism was slowly emerging as the orthodox academic mode of historical enquiry. In isolating the figure of Walter Bagehot, economist, journalist and

---

[49] Giles St Aubyn, *A Victorian Eminence: the life and works of Henry Thomas Buckle* (London: Barrie, 1958); Eckhardt Fuchs, *Henry Thomas Buckle: Geschichtsschreibung und Positivismus in England und Deutschland* (Leipizig: Leipziguniversitätsverlag, 1994).

[50] Burrow, *Evolution and Society*, pp. 137–78.

[51] G. R. Elton, *F. W. Maitland* (New Haven, CT: Yale University Press, 1985).

commentator, it is possible to see a writer who was, in his way, as least as much a public intellectual as he was a public moralist, a figure of cultural authority independent of the culture of the ancient universities in which historicism would flourish. As a Unitarian, Walter Bagehot had been obliged to study at University College London, and in his decidedly modern interests, from natural science to the human sciences and the mechanics of politics, he was an eminent instance of how such an education contrasted with that of the only slowly modernising, and long exclusively Anglican, universities of Oxford and Cambridge. And Bagehot was nothing if not modern. As a promoter of history as a human science, his work in the field provides a fascinating parallel with the work of Maine, which he cited approvingly on many occasions, but Bagehot's work also instances a telling contrast with the historicism that Acton was simultaneously promoting.

Bagehot produced a series of studies of Adam Smith and political economy to mark the centenary of the publication of *The Wealth of Nations* in 1876; he also collected a series of articles and essays as a book that year, entitled *Physics and Politics*.[52] The two sets of publications are intimately related intellectually: *Physics and Politics* is an exercise in what one might call conjectural pre-history, just as much of *The Wealth of Nations* is a study in conjectural history, and what Bagehot was offering was a deep history which simultaneously questioned and affirmed the lessons he had imbibed from Smith's work. It is, after all, in the opening chapter of *Physics and Politics*, 'The Preliminary Age', that Bagehot sets out a central organising principle, both of his own thinking about pre-history and concerning its implications for all students of politics, past and present:

Political economy is the most systematised and most accurate part of political philosophy; and yet, by the help of what has been laid down, I think we may travel back to a sort of 'pre-economic age,' when the very assumptions of political economy did not exist, when its precepts would have been ruinous, and when the very contrary principles were requisite and wise.[53]

Conjectural pre-history was both biological and psychological in orientation, and decidedly evolutionary in character. Bagehot cited T. H. Huxley

<hr/>

[52] Walter Bagehot, 'Adam Smith as a Person' and 'The Centenary of *The Wealth of Nations*' in Jacques Barzun ed., *The Collected Works of Walter Bagehot*, iii: *Historical Essays*, (London: The Economist, 1968), pp. 84–112, 113-19; Bagehot, *Physics and Politics: or thoughts on the application of the principles of natural selection and inheritance to political society* (London: Henry King, 1873). See John Burrow, 'Historicism and Evolution' in Stuchtey and Wende, *British and German Historiography*, pp. 251–64.

[53] Bagehot, *Physics and Politics*, p. 11.

on biology and physiology and Henry Maudsley on physiology and psychology, thereby drawing on Darwinism and the latest developments in the new science of psychology. Alongside these authorities, Bagehot quoted with approval from the recent pioneering work on pre-history and archaeology of Sir John Lubbock, whose association with the field was reinforced when, after political promotion to the House of Lords, he took as his title Baron Avebury, the site of a stone circle which he did much both to analyse and to preserve.[54] For Lubbock, as for Bagehot, pre-history remained potent in the present; there is a celebration of intellectual progress in Bagehot, but it is not as unqualified in its optimism as that earlier advanced by Buckle, of whom he was notably critical.

Fascinated by the relationship between the body and the mind, 'of the nervous organs as stores of will-made power' and thence of the problem of free will, Bagehot questioned the assumptions both of the 'Freewillist' and of the 'Necessarian'. The first he challenged in a notably selective, not to say elitist, mode, detailing social contrasts within the city of London, as he cuttingly noted that 'No Freewillist ever expects as much from St. Giles's as he expects from Belgravia: he admits an hereditary nervous system as a *datum* for the will, though he holds the will to be an extraordinary in-coming "something."'[55] Where the criticism of a metaphysical position was witheringly realist in its social exactness, his critique of Buckle's supposedly scientific history privileged the 'moral' over the physical, insisting that the relationship between body and mind entailed principles should not be confounded with 'Mr. Buckle's idea that material forces have been the main-springs of progress, and moral causes secondary, and, in comparison, not to be thought of'. Bagehot argued, determinedly, that:

On the contrary, moral causes are the first here. It is the action of the will that causes the unconscious habit; it is the continual effort of the beginning that creates the hoarded energy of the end; it is the silent toil of the first generation that becomes the transmitted aptitude of the next. Here physical causes do not create the moral, but moral the physical; here the beginning is by the higher energy, the conservation and propagation only by the lower.

But this did not undermine Buckle's claim that a science of history was possible; rather, it refined it, as Bagehot reversed Buckle's law of causation in order to strengthen their shared belief that a 'science of history' could be established to 'teach the laws of tendencies – created by the mind, and transmitted by the body – which act upon and incline the will

[54] John Lubbock, *Pre-Historic Times, as illustrated by ancient remains, and the manners and customs of modern savages* (London: Williams and Norgate, 1865).
[55] Bagehot, *Physics and Politics*, p. 10.

of man from age to age'.[56] Pre-history was, for Bagehot, quite literally an archaeology of all subsequent history; it is very tempting to see a parallel with Foucault. The ambitions for a history of human sciences that preoccupied Bagehot might not have been to Foucault's taste, but his own intellectual enterprise was not so very different as he attempted to show how indebted much modern thinking was to systems of thought that were often rather sinister in nature and origin. But where Bagehot pointed to a consistently resonant history, Foucault hinted at a liberation from the very same sorts of 'history'.

Bagehot's conjectural pre-history was a product of, and contribution to, a generalised social evolutionary theory, the sort of archaeology of the human sciences that so disturbed and fascinated Foucault. Bagehot's brand of evolutionary theory was profoundly antithetical to the Comtist school, as is made very clear in a damning paragraph in a chapter on 'The Use of Conflict' in which a fairly ruthless, menacingly combative form of evolutionary theory is deployed to undermine the very basis of Comtism – subtly characterised, but not quite traduced, as a complete misunderstanding of genuine historical forces and veridical principles of organisation. It is worth citing the paragraph in full, both to feel the sheer, appropriately almost physical force of Bagehot's appeal to the ancient and pervasively primitive strength of physical force – and hence of his sense of the way the pre-historic continues to inform the present – and also to appreciate how tendentiously abstract many of its critics considered Comtism as being, for all its supposed rootedness in genuine historical development:

Experience shows how incredibly difficult it is to get men to encourage the principle of originality. They will admit it in theory, but in practice the old error – the error which arrested a hundred civilisations – returns again. Men are too fond of their own life, too credulous of the completeness of their own ideas, too angry at the pain of new thoughts, to be able to bear easily with a changing existence; or else, *having* new ideas, they want to enforce them on mankind – to make them heard, and admitted, and obeyed before, in simple competition with other ideas, they would ever be so naturally. At this very moment there are the most rigid Comtists teaching that we ought to be governed by a hierarchy – a combination of *savans* orthodox in science. Yet who can doubt that Comte would have been hanged by his own hierarchy; that his *essor matériel*, which was in fact troubled by the 'theologians and metaphysicians' of the Polytechnic School, would have been impeded by the government he wanted to make? And then the secular Comtists, Mr. Harrison and Mr. Beesly, who want to 'Frenchify the English institutions' – that is, to introduce here an imitation of the Napoleonic system, a dictatorship founded on

[56] Bagehot, *Physics and Politics*, p. 11.

the proletariat – who can doubt that if both these clever writers had been real Frenchmen they would have been sent to Cayenne long ere now? The wish of these writers is very natural. They want to 'organise society,' to erect a despot who will do what they like, and work out their ideas; but any despot will do what he himself likes, and will root out new ideas ninety-nine times for once that he introduces them.[57]

Thus, a combination of 'experience' and Comtists' very own principles effectively undermined Comtism, just as it had their forebears, the thinkers of immediately post-revolutionary France – although intellectual progress, curiously perhaps, informed those earlier thinkers more than it did the Comtists in Bagehot's historicised appraisal of their achievements:

Later are the ages of freedom; first are the ages of servitude. In 1789, when the great men of the Constituent Assembly looked on the long past, they hardly saw anything in it which could be praised, admired, or imitated: all seemed a blunder – a complex error to be got rid of as soon as it might be. But the error had made themselves. On their very physical organisation the hereditary mark of old times was fixed; their brains were hardened and their nerves were steadied by the transmitted results of tedious usages. The ages of monotony had their use, for they trained men for ages when they need not be monotonous.[58]

The implied critique of the Comtists is clear: they imagined themselves an advance on the creators of putative *sciences de l'homme*, where they were in fact a wrong-headed deviation from the work initiated by their supposed intellectual progenitors. Furthermore, Bagehot himself, whilst an admirer of Smith, was more critical of many other thinkers of the Enlightenment, emphasising, for example, in his account of 'Nation-Making' that the 'conscious end of early societies was not at all, or scarcely at all, the protection of life and property, as it was assumed to be by the eighteenth-century theory of government'.[59]

Bagehot's references to religion were more studiedly ambiguous than those of the Comtists, or even of the likes of Hume, and infinitely more subtle than those of Buckle. 'Savage religion', as Bagehot defined it, was a series of superstitions associated with luck, but which later civilisations made into systems of ideas; consequently, he offers something like a résumé of a broadly Comtist natural history of religion, as he states in a manner that expected no serious objection from reasonable readers that:

Little popular and little deserving to be popular now-a-days as are priestly hierarchies, most probably the beginnings of science were made in such, and

---

[57] Bagehot, *Physics and Politics*, pp. 57–8.   [58] Bagehot, *Physics and Politics*, p. 30.
[59] Bagehot, *Physics and Politics*, pp. 137–38.

were for ages transmitted in such. An intellectual class was in that age only possible when it was protected by a notion that whatever hurt them would be punished by heaven.

But, in such traditional societies, reason was always either affirmed or challenged by force, and Bagehot equally characteristically developed his claim, with half an eye on India (where Maine had first thought through his history of law and civilisation):

Few nations mind killing their enemies' priests, and many priestly civilisations have perished without record before they well began. But such a civilisation will not perish if a warrior *caste* is tacked onto it and is bound to defend it. On the contrary, such a civilisation will be singularly likely to live. The head of the sage will help the arm of the soldier.[60]

Much can be inferred from Bagehot's firmly stated epigrams, but it is in an aside that he circumspectly reveals most about his distance from the more orthodox, more religious perspectives on such matters more conventionally held by many historicists. Noting, with the authority of Dr Johnson, that classical religion was tedious, and with his own that it was terrifying, he instances how much of this was conveyed by 'the great poem of Lucretius, the most of a nineteenth-century poem of any in antiquity'.[61] Bagehot was a man without religious certainty, and in this he considered himself typical of his age; the historicist generations then taking their positions in England's ancient universities were, on the whole, men of faith, and it is this striking aspect of their academic creed which most marks out their distance from Comtists, evolutionary historians and the combatively self-isolating figure of Buckle.

Religion and Historicism

Historicism has been treated as both a development from, and also a determined reaction against, the historical philosophy of the Enlightenment. In his classic study of *The Liberal Anglican Historians*, Duncan Forbes made much of this in sketching out the translation of German historicism into its peculiarly English variant; one of the most interesting features of this for Forbes was how firmly Christian, and Coleridgeian, this adoption of the new approach to the past was, from the 1820s onwards, in English historical culture. Thomas Arnold, in his brief

---

[60] Bagehot, *Physics and Politics*, p. 148.
[61] Bagehot, *Physics and Politics*, p. 56. Frank M. Turner, 'Ancient Materialism and Modern Science: Lucretius among the Victorians' in *Contesting Cultural Authority: essays in Victorian intellectual life* (Cambridge: Cambridge University Press, 1993), pp. 262–83, does not mention Bagehot.

tenure as the Regius Chair of Modern History at Oxford, pioneered the new historicism within the ancient universities, but most of his fellow practitioners, at that stage, were beneficed clergymen, at work on their historical labours in rectories and deaneries. Most of them had joined in the general 'revolt against the eighteenth century' of their generation, but their confrère Henry Hart Milman was not at one with them in this. As Forbes has noted, Milman was the only one of their number to admire Gibbon's *Decline and Fall*, even producing his own working edition of the text, along with translations of Guizot's notes.[62] And in this, Milman had something in common with Comtists; when rebuking Comte for championing the Abbé Fleuret's brand of ecclesiastical history, Harrison had proposed instead that Milman's *History of Latin Christianity* should act as the complement to Gibbon.[63] Milman, whose variety of Anglican minimalism is tellingly slighted in Robert L. Sullivan's recent condemnation of Macaulay and all his works, was an effective intermediary between the newly emerging English school of historicism and indigenous historical reflection in the style uniquely propagated in the *Decline and Fall*. Newman, predictably, disliked Milman and all his works almost as much as Sullivan does; Macaulay, on the contrary, was a friend and admirer.[64]

Where Milman's *History of Latin Christianity* was widely respected, his *History of the Jews*, which naturalised the accounts given by the Hebrew Bible, caused some consternation, especially among Christian readers.[65] Scepticism, albeit not of a purely Gibbonian quality, was essential to Milman's brand of transplanted historicism, but it was never irreligious either in tendency or intention; he did not offer ecclesiastical or religious history as apologetic, but nor did he write it in order to undermine the Church he served. Devout as he undoubtedly was, Milman was a critical historian, and it was his misfortune to be a pioneer of an approach to the past which his clerical successors used in a completely unproblematic manner in their own histories. As the Comtists might have said, he was a 'transitional' figure, recognisably of, but also (slightly) ahead of, his time. As his son wrote in justification of his compilation of the *Life and Letters of Henry Hart Milman* in 1900, it offered illustrations 'of the marked change which within my father's lifetime [i.e., 1791–1868] came over opinion, especially upon views of the proper method of dealing with religious history'.[66] And here is the key to understanding much of the career of

---

[62] Forbes, *Liberal Anglican Idea*, p. 2.   [63] Harrison, *Meaning of History*, pp. 112–14.
[64] Sullivan, *Macaulay*, pp. 58–9, 194–5, 353–5, 365, 472, 473, 480.
[65] Forbes, *Liberal Anglican Idea*, pp. 2, 34–5, 64, 76–82, 120–1, 143.
[66] Arthur Milman, *Life and Letters of Henry Hart Milman* (London: John Murray, 1900), p. 2.

historicism as the historical orthodoxy not only of the ancient universities, but also of their resident (and non-resident) Churchmen.

Historicism could not only accommodate religion, it could even be
seen as a considerable addition to its apologetic arsenal; Ranke's personal
piety demonstrated this almost from the academic inception of the
movement, and its subsequent career in England would only confirm
this tendency. In the generation immediately following Milman, the star
of historicism in England was William Stubbs, who, before his translation
first to the see of Chester and second to that of Oxford, had served as
Regius Professor of Modern History precisely when it was introduced as
an undergraduate degree. One could instance many moments in his
writings when Stubbs the Churchman intrudes into the work of Stubbs
the historian, although he himself would not have made such a demarcation. But rather than offer a potentially tedious series of examples of
such intrusion or alliance, it is worth quoting the opening paragraph of
an edition of *The Letters of William Stubbs*, the work of W. H. Hutton, a
clerical fellow of St John's College, Oxford. Again, it needs to be quoted
in full, as so much is at work in these words, which appeared in print
in 1904:

When the history of the intellectual movements of the Victorian Age in England
comes to be written, one name will stand out in the science to which it belongs as
the name of Butler stands out in the religious philosophy of an earlier day. A great
school arose in the middle of the nineteenth century which embodied and
expressed the enthusiasm of the time for an ordered study of the past. Of the
workers in that school, the greatest was William Stubbs, and his fame, if it be
possible for the generation which knew him to predict it, should be beside that of
Gibbon as the greatest historian of his country and his age. But he was much
more than an historian. If in the field of history the most enduring part of his work
was done, the Church of England will not cease to remember him as a faithful
ruler and a servant of the servants of God. On all his life was set the mark of
steady, unselfish service. He was a strenuous worker from his earliest years, and
he worked to the end.[67]

This decidedly clerical encomium, however cloying to the modern ear,
was actually, for all its apparent irenicism, an intervention in a contentious debate. Historicism, that 'great school', has been expertly and
cunningly claimed for religious apologetic, and not just in the implied
comparison with Butler's work as a philosophical apologist for Christianity, but also in the subtle, if perhaps unexpected, deployment of Gibbon.
Why should the arch-sceptic be introduced in this way? Partly, of course,

---

[67] W. H. Hutton, *Letters of William Stubbs, Bishop of Oxford, 1825–1901* (London:
Constable, 1904), p. 3.

to make the grandest claim possible for Stubbs, but also to separate Gibbon's achievements from those secular historians, from Harrison onwards, who claimed him for their own purposes; in the great history of History as a discipline, Anglican incense fumigated Gibbon's history of all its sceptical associations. (Milman would have been intrigued by this piece of licensed, if imaginative, genealogy.) And consider how much work the word 'enduring' is doing in this paragraph; Stubbs' historical work is substantial and lasting, constituting the great purpose of (and for) his life, but this melds almost imperceptibly into his subsequent career as a bishop. The two are but different strands of the same purpose. Stubbs was 'more than an historian', but it was because he was an historian that he mattered, and would continue to matter. Historicism, for Hutton as for Stubbs, was a religious enterprise, and in this they continued the work inaugurated by Ranke and continued by Milman. And Stubbs' work, for Hutton, was of much more than insular value, as he claimed that 'The *Constitutional History of England* belongs to the literary history of Europe'; it was 'the most monumental work of English historical scholarship since Gibbon's *Decline and Fall*'.[68] Anglo-German historicism had displaced Enlightenment historiography in the forward momentum of European History.[69]

What Stubbs concluded in the purple, Acton had long personified as a securely cosmopolitan Roman Catholic layman and a moralising historicist educated – because of his religion – at universities in Germany.[70] Dedicated to a natural law understanding of human actions, the one thing Acton failed, and consciously failed, to historicise was morality, and this was because, for him, morality could not be historicised: it was eternal, and therefore true. Hence the unexpectedly entertaining encounter between Acton, the severe moralist, and Mandell Creighton, shortly to become the Dixie Professor of Ecclesiastical History at Cambridge before becoming, successively, bishop of Peterborough and of London. Acton, having reviewed a volume of Creighton's *History of the Papacy* with censorious admiration, corresponded with his victim, whom he accused of being far too indulgent of the vices of the Medicean papacy

---

[68] Hutton, *Letters of Stubbs*, p. 135. See now, J. E. Kirby, 'An Ecclesiastical Descent: religion and history in the works of William Stubbs', *Journal of Ecclesiastical History* 65 (2014), 84–110.

[69] Unfortunately, and simultaneously, it had also done so architecturally and aesthetically at the ancient universities; on the 'historicism' of the High Church architect of Keble College and the chapel of Balliol College, see Paul Thompson, *William Butterfield* (London: Routledge Kegan Paul, 1971).

[70] See Hugh Tulloch, 'Lord Acton and German Historiography' in Stuchtey and Wende, *British and German Historiography*, pp. 159–72.

and the age in which it luxuriated. Creighton replied using two voices: the one was that of the consummate historicist, who argued, politely but unswervingly, that it was absolutely *not* the duty of the historian anachronistically to judge the mores of earlier ages; the other was that of a clergyman, who left all such judgements to God.[71]

The celebrated Acton–Creighton correspondence on history and morality was perhaps a rather curious episode in English historicism, but it was exactly that: an encounter between two different exponents of historicism in the 1890s, the decade when historicism was at its orthodox height in England's universities. And the lesson of historicism was the same for Acton and Stubbs as it was for Creighton, who spoke for the great majority of his historicist contemporaries when he made a statement that adroitly sums up the Anglo-German historicist school:

> When I say that ecclesiastical history must be studied in the same way as secular history, I do not mean that the student must lay aside the belief in a Divine purpose accomplishing itself by human means. All history alike teaches that.[72]

Naturally, there is much more that might be said about historicism in a nineteenth-century English context, not least about its literary formulation, its account of racial and national theories, its relationship with other European forms of historicism and the like, but much of this story has been more than satisfactorily told in J. W. Burrow's *A Liberal Descent* (1981).[73] What is more, what has here been interpreted as a series of divergences and contentions has recently been interpreted by Ian Hesketh as a converging narrative, as it had also been by Fuchs in his study of Buckle.[74] And, likewise, to suggest a neat demarcation between secular conceptions of history as one of the 'human sciences', on the one hand, and a religious orientation in historicism, on the other, is, one would have to acknowledge, not without its problematic components: where, for example, does one place J. R. Seeley, whose religion is very hard to place – as is his conception of historicism – and who held the Regius Chair at Cambridge immediately before Acton?[75] As Mandell Creighton's widow noted of his time at Cambridge, he gleaned little from Seeley,

---

[71] Lucy Creighton, *Life and Letters of Mandell Creighton* (2 vols., London: Longmans, Green, 1904), i., pp. 368–78.

[72] Creighton, *Life and Letters*, i., p. 285.

[73] For an allied argument to that made here, see Michael Bentley, 'Victorian historians and the larger hope' in Bentley ed., *Public and Private Doctrine: essays in British history presented to Maurice Cowling* (Cambridge: Cambridge University Press, 1993), pp. 127–48.

[74] Ian Hesketh, *The Science of History in Victorian Britain* (London: Pickering and Chatto, 2011).

[75] On whom see Deborah Wormell, *Sir John Seeley and the Uses of History* (Cambridge: Cambridge University Press, 1980).

and looked to another faculty than History when expounding his own vision of the subject: 'The traditions of theological learning have been thoroughly leavened by the historic spirit … Theology has become historical, and does not demand that history should become theological.'[76] Despite their dispute over morality, Creighton was an historicist in the mode of Acton; he was some distance intellectually from Seeley.

Acton's own successor at Cambridge, J. B. Bury, was the actively anticlerical son of an Anglo-Irish Protestant clergyman. Bury advanced beyond the scepticism of another lost eminence of Anglo-Irish historical thinking, W. E. H. Lecky, whose *A History of the Rise and Influence of Rationalism in Europe* (1862) was an enabling text for non-Comtist students of history as progress, as was his *History of European Morals from Augustus to Charlemagne* (1869) – although just how far Bury had moved from Lecky can be seen in Lecky's acknowledgement, in his later study, of the importance of Stubbs to his study of morals in Late Antiquity and the Early Middle Ages.[77] As an advocate of a scientific version of historicism, Bury absorbed something from Lecky, but rather more from such thinkers as Harrison, whom he praised in his vigorously tendentious *A History of Freedom of Thought* (1914), a sort of historicist analogue of the secularising human science associated with Harrison and his fellow Comtists. A critic of Buckle, Bury sang the praises of the eighteenth century as an age of liberation no less fervently than did Buckle, Harrison and Morley, and he sought to reclaim Gibbon from the entombing clutches of the Reverend W. H. Hutton, insisting that 'Of all the numerous freethinking books that appeared in the eighteenth century', Gibbon's *Decline and Fall* 'is the only one which is still a widely read classic'.[78] Bury wanted to engage with an audience beyond the university, and his little book was a contribution to a series, 'The Home University of Modern Knowledge', of which Macmillan's 'English Men of Letters' series had been the progenitor. Historicism was coming out of the universities, and its purposes were akin to those of the very historical philosophies which its pious promoters had so devoutly opposed. But again, any secularising narrative is difficult to sustain, for a later holder of the Regius Chair at Cambridge, the late Owen Chadwick, was also a clergyman, and, what is more, one of the most celebrated Acton scholars

[76] Creighton, *Life and Letters*, i., pp. 278–9.
[77] Tellingly, the best recent study of Lecky is in German: Benedickt Stuchtey, *W.E.H. Lecky (1838–1903): Historisches Denken und politisches Urteilen eines anglo-irischen Gelehrten* (Göttingen: Vanderhoeck and Ruprecht, 1997).
[78] J. B. Bury, *A History of Freedom of Thought* (London: Williams and Norgate, 1914), p. 129.

of the twentieth century. And yet, in his celebrated study *The Secularisation of the European Mind in the Nineteenth Century*, it was the scientific study of history which Chadwick identified as the chief solvent of Christian intellectual hegemony in the century when Acton attempted to use history as a defence of religion.[79] History, necessarily, is multifarious, and its own history as a discipline is at once contradictory and orderly.

Did Bury's succession to Acton in the Cambridge Chair in any way herald a confirmation of historicism as the professional commitment as much as the substantive intellectual requirement of academic historians, and if so, did his own commitment to something like a science of human history in any way compromise the variety of historicism to which Acton had been so signally committed?[80] In short, there was evidently continual contention over the meaning of the 'human sciences' within the study of history as a self-conscious disciplinary activity in nineteenth-century Britain, and the historicism championed by Acton and his allies was, in many ways, suspicious of the whole idea of the 'human sciences'. For Acton, as for Stubbs and Creighton, historicism was a humanistic, even a variously dispassionately religious, enterprise, and this made the putative identity of history as a strictly human science difficult, if not even impossible, to substantiate, let alone consistently maintain. For an unbeliever such as Bury, historicism needed to be purged of its religious origins.

As the case of Bury demonstrates, historicism was not entirely a monopoly of believers: agnosticism also grew alongside historicism in England in the 1870s, and, inevitably, the one began to affect the other: it was a decade during which Leslie Stephen not only popularised the word 'agnostic', but also successfully promoted the study of intellectual history in England, very much inspired by German examples.[81] (It is significant, when considering the later fortunes of British intellectual history, that Stephen did so outside a university.) What is striking is that Stephen's interests were in the eighteenth century; where its secularism had failed, Stephen wished to learn how to make sure that nineteenth-century unbelief could succeed. By historicising ideas, and above all theological

[79] Owen Chadwick, *Acton and History* (Cambridge: Cambridge University Press, 1998) and *The Secularization of the European Mind in the Nineteenth Century* (Cambridge: Cambridge University Press, 1975), pp. 189–228.

[80] See Doris S. Goldstein, 'J.B. Bury's Philosophy of History: a reappraisal', *American Historical Review* 82 (1977), 896–919.

[81] Leslie Stephen, *An Agnostic's Apology, and other essays* (London: Smith, Elder, 1893); Stephen, *History of English Thought in the Eighteenth Century* (2 vols., London: Smith, Elder, 1876); F. W. Maitland, *The Life and Letters of Leslie Stephen* (London: Duckworth, 1906); B. W. Young, *The Victorian Eighteenth Century: an intellectual history* (Oxford: Oxford University Press, 2007), pp. 103–47.

and religious ideas, Stephen sought to contain and undermine their supposed authority. The forward momentum of Stephen was towards a secular future, and in this he was followed by his Cambridge admirer, F. W. Maitland. At Oxford, James Anthony Froude's very Protestant form of agnosticism informed an older, Carlylean, literary style of history which was already old-fashioned when he was made Regius Professor of Modern History in 1892 – a capricious appointment, but one which confirms that historicism was frequently contested internally even as it secured its berth in England's ancient universities.[82] In Cambridge, the eventual accession to the Regius Chair of G. M. Trevelyan, a great-nephew of Macaulay, also indicated an ambiguously historicist inheritance. An agnostic, and a man reared in Cambridge historicism, Trevelyan also championed a literary approach to the writing of history.[83] And literature was to prove an important element in British historical debates about the legacy of historicism, from Hugh Trevor-Roper's call for the opening up to a lay audience of the work of 'academic' historians, made in his inaugural lecture as Regius Professor of Modern History at Oxford as recently as 1957, to more recent post-modernist debates about History, of the sort which Richard J. Evans has attempted to close down.[84] And Evans, a student of twentieth-century German history, is consciously and proudly historicist.

At the close of the nineteenth century, Ranke had begun to be revered in Britain's ancient universities, but someone more intimately related to him than any of his academic followers had marked a reaction against his conception of history in a telling and entertaining style in the inter-war years, in which attitudes to German-inspired orthodoxies had understandably begun to grow more complicated.[85] The novelist Robert Graves was a great-great-nephew of the historian – his middle name was von Ranke – and in *I Claudius*, published in 1934, Graves utilised the work of prominent historians of Imperial Rome in a fictionalised autobiography supposedly penned by the eponymous emperor. But what

[82] Burrow, *A Liberal Descent*, pp. 229–85; Jane Garnett, 'Protestant Histories: James Anthony Froude, partisanship and national identity' in Peter Ghosh and Lawrence Goldman eds., *Politics and Culture in Victorian Britain* (Oxford: Oxford University Press, 2006), pp. 271–91; Ciaran Brady, *James Anthony Froude: an intellectual biography of a Victorian prophet* (Oxford: Oxford University Press, 2013).

[83] David Cannadine, *G.M. Trevalyan: a life in history* (London: Harper Collins, 1993).

[84] Hugh Trevor-Roper, 'History: professional and lay', in Hugh Lloyd-Jones, Valerie Pearl and Blair Worden eds., *History and Imagination: essays in honour of H.R. Trevor-Roper* (London: Duckworth, 1981), pp. 1–14.

[85] On which ties, see Oded Y. Steinberg, 'The Illusion of Finality: time and community in the writings of E.A. Freeman, J.B. Bury and the English-Teutonic circle of historians', Oxford D.Phil dissertation, 2015.

matters here is how playfully Claudius thinks about (and through) history, and above all when 'history' is considered as a literary activity. It took a novelist to have an emperor write: 'Nobody can write history for more than five or six hours a day, especially when there is little hope of anyone ever reading it.'[86] The whole of the ninth chapter comprises an amusing and learned series of exchanges between the historians Pollio and Livy in which the young Claudius is engaged; it is in this competitive and occasionally mildly ridiculous conversation that the young future emperor finds his vocation, and thereafter history, *his* history, is what keeps him alive during reigns of unparalleled tyranny, savagery and corruption. History has at once the dignity that Livy extols and the indifference to rhetoric that informs Pollio, Claudius' preferred model of history writing. And at the very close of the novel, before his deification in *Claudius the God,* the newly declared emperor, terrified and amused, holds on to a thought of which he is simultaneously proud and ashamed:

But I shall be frank and tell you what it was, though the confession is a shameful one. I was thinking, 'So, I'm Emperor, am I? What nonsense! But at least I'll be able to make people read my books now. Public recitals to large audiences. And good books, too, thirty-five years' hard work on them. It won't be unfair. Pollio used to get attentive audiences by giving expensive dinners. He was a very sound historian, and the last of the Romans. My *History of Carthage* is full of amusing anecdotes. I'm sure they'll enjoy it.'

That was what I was thinking. I was thinking, too, what opportunities I should have, as Emperor, for consulting the secret archives and finding out what just happened on this occasion or that. How many twisted stories still remained to be straightened out! What a miraculous fate for an historian! And as you will have seen, I took full advantage of my opportunities. Even the mature historian's privilege of setting forth conversations of which he knows only the gist is one that I have availed myself of hardly at all.[87]

Graves, as a novelist, had, of course, done exactly in the words of 'Claudius' what Claudius, in that final sentence, had claimed never to have done. Graves had read Literae Humaniores at St John's College, Oxford, and was therefore familiar with the historicised mode of teaching ancient history then prevalent at the university; his novelistic repudiation of a Rankean perspective on the past was, then, more than merely a family romance: it marked a generational revolt against the imaginatively constricting orthodoxy of the many late Victorian dons who had sought to contain the historical sensibility of their pupils through a deep

---

[86] Robert Graves, *I Claudius* (London: A. Barker, 1934), p. 107.
[87] Graves, *I Claudius*, pp. 102–13, 396.

immersion in historicism as the only orthodoxy in the study and writing of History. For Graves, the literary and variously ethical historical register of Roman historians was superior to Ranke's historicism, just as tolerant heathenism was to be preferred, in a Gibbonian manner, to the Lutheranism of his distinguished ancestor. Historicism has, since the 1930s, been a debatable legacy.

8   Political Economy

Fredrik Albritton Jonsson

Post-Carbon Utopia

In 1872, the political economist and art historian John Ruskin moved north from his house in Herne Hill, on the outskirts of London, to the banks of Coniston Water in the English Lake District. He was looking for solace after a series of personal disasters. His parents were dead, his marriage had been annulled, and his fading hopes of a romantic relationship with Rose de la Touche were all but gone. But there was more to Ruskin's move than the disastrous state of his private life. The northern countryside seemed to promise the possibility of a sanctuary from the tawdry desires and industrial blight of the Victorian city. At his house, Brantwood, overlooking Coniston Water and the Old Man of Coniston – the great hill to the west of the village – Ruskin launched a moral crusade against mass consumption and urban life, under the name *Fors Clavigera* (1871–1884), for the benefit of the "workmen and laborers of Great Britain." It was here also that Ruskin's local artist, artisan, and preservationist followers fostered a thriving cultural scene and handicraft industry between 1880 and 1920 – what Sarah Haslam has called the Lakeland arts revival.[1]

For Ruskin and his friends, this social experiment was a harbinger of the postindustrial future and a taste of the stationary state. In the twenty-ninth letter of the *Fors Clavigera*, from 1873, Ruskin urged his followers to look forward to a "sweet spring-time" for "our children's children ... when their coals are burnt out, and they begin to understand that coals are not the source of all power Divine and human." Ruskin's prediction echoed the forecast made by William Stanley Jevons in *The Coal Question* of 1865. The political economist calculated that British coal production

---

[1] Tim Hilton, *John Ruskin* (Yale University Press, 2002), pp. 494, 497, 505; Sarah Haslam, *John Ruskin and the Lakeland Arts Revival, 1880–1920* (Merton Priory Press, 2004). The argument about Ruskin in this essay includes a few passages drawn from *Green Victorians: The Simple Life in John Ruskin's Lake District* (Chicago: the University of Chicago Press, 2016), which I co-authored with Vicky Albritton.

would soon reach its highest level of extraction. In fact, output peaked right before the Great War at 287 million tons. Ruskin's arts-and-crafts community in the Lake District sought to anticipate the social condition that he believed would follow the exhaustion of the British coalmines. Economic contraction and resource scarcity – the end of modern growth – offered an extraordinary opportunity to reject the structures of industrial capitalism and revive the creative labor and communal bonds of a past age. Ruskin's political economy mined medieval history to imagine a social order founded on skilled labor and the pleasures of the simple life rather than profit and competition. By the standards of our own time, it was the first attempt to forge a post-carbon society.[2]

A Dual Inheritance

Ruskin's critique of industrial society opens a revealing window on the character of Victorian political economy. The hopes and fears bound up with the concept of the stationary state and the physical limits to economic growth gave nineteenth-century economic thought a distinct conceptual unity and historical orientation. A quick comparison with twenty-first-century economics reveals a sharply different set of theoretical and methodological priorities. The old fear of physical limits has all but vanished and given way to a new cornucopian certainty about inexorable long-run growth and innovation. Few economists worry about the moral perils of consumer society. Historical scholarship and moral philosophy have become marginal to economic analysis. Instead economists aspire to produce a general theory of human action, which favors mathematical model-building as the proper tool to interpret social reality.[3]

What were the forces behind the peculiar character of nineteenth-century political economy? Recent scholars have explored a number of crisscrossing patterns of economic thought in the period, ranging over

[2] Donald Winch, *Wealth and Life: Essays on the Intellectual History of Political Economy in Britain, 1848–1914* (Cambridge University Press, 2009), pp. 63–8; William Stanley Jevons, *The Coal Question: An Inquiry Concerning the Progress of the Nation, and the Probably Exhaustion of Our Coal-Mines*, 3rd ed. rev. (Augustus M. Kelley, 1965), pp. 15–18; John Ruskin, *Fors Clavigera*, "Letter 29," in E. T. Cook and Alexander Wedderburn, eds., *Works of John Ruskin*, Vol. 27 (George Allen, 1907), p. 527. For "post-carbon" society, see Richard Heinberg and Daniel Lerch, eds., *The Post Carbon Reader: Managing the 21st Century Sustainability Crises* (Watershed Media, 2010); Bill McKibben, *Eaarth: Making a Living on a Tough New Planet* (St. Martin's Griffin, 2011).

[3] On the tenor of twentieth-century economics, see Geoffrey M. Hodgson, *How Economics Forgot History: The Problem of Historical Specificity in Social Science* (Routledge, 2001). For growth as common sense, see Fredrik Albritton Jonsson, "Cornucopianism: A Preliminary Genealogy," *Critical Historical Studies*, Vol. 1, No. 1 (Spring 2014), 151–68.

stadial history, evangelical religion, romantic poetry, geological science, statistical representation, evolutionary theory, and the drive toward mathematization. The special character of Victorian economic thought was determined in no small part by a dual debt to historical scholarship and natural science. The legacy of the Scottish Enlightenment fostered an historical understanding of economic exchange among nineteenth-century economists. Adam Smith's seminal *The Wealth of Nations* (1776) explored the historical pathways of economic development – what he called the natural and retrograde progress of opulence. Such an historical outlook was tightly interwoven with a naturalist understanding of change and stability in society. Smith found in the natural world a mirror for the social order. The legacy of the Scottish Enlightenment thus inspired at the same time a deductive and developmental understanding of economic exchange.[4]

This double inheritance continued to shape the economic theories of Smith's successors and critics. Nineteenth-century political economists populated a continuum between inductive and deductive approaches, drawn from rival views of nature and history. Historical investigation lent legitimacy to inductive models; concepts drawn from natural science bolstered deductive models. Natural history, geology, psychophysiology, and energy physics produced a rich harvest of metaphors for economic analysis. Malthus saw his theory of human population pressure as a subset of a universal natural history, drawn from observations of island biogeography as well as thought experiments about planetary carrying capacity. Ricardo's concept of differential rent reduced the social institution of rent to a matter of soil fertility. On this count, rent was merely an effect of the movement from the most fertile to less fertile land. Another strain of political economy looked inward to the mind in search of economic laws. Richard Jennings sought to explicate the nature of value by means of the nervous sensations associated with acts of consumption. William Stanley Jevons sought a warrant for his understanding of mental operations – the laws of human enjoyment – in the mechanical intelligence propounded by Charles Babbage and Jevons' own Logical Machine.[5]

---

[4] Boyd Hilton, *The Age of Atonement: The Influence of Evangelicalism on Social and Economic Thought 1785–1865* (Oxford University Press, 1988); Winch, *Wealth and Life*; Philip Mirowski, *More Heat than Light: Economics as Social Physics, Physics as Nature's Economics* (Cambridge University Press, 1991); Jennifer Pitts, *A Turn to Empire: The Rise of Liberal Imperialism in Britain and France* (Princeton University Press, 2006), pp. 29–30; Margaret Schabas, *The Natural Origin of Economics* (University of Chicago Press, 2007), pp. 79–101; Istvan Hont, *The Jealousy of Trade: International Competition and the Nation State in Historical Perspective* (Belknap Press, 2005), pp. 354–88.

[5] For Malthus and islands, see Fredrik Albritton Jonsson, *Enlightenment's Frontier: The Scottish Highlands and the Origins of Environmentalism* (Yale University Press, 2013),

For all this devotion to deductivist science, nineteenth-century political economy was rarely devoid of historical arguments and social analysis. Malthus looked to past trends in demography to substantiate his thesis. Ricardo added a social context to his concept of differential rent by seeing rent as the taproot of a growing conflict between landowners and other classes. Jevons sought to repackage historical events as economic data by means of time-series graphs. He also framed his theory of coal depletion as a historical account of national progress and decline. Meanwhile, other political economists turned to historical sources to articulate their critique of deductivism. For example, Richard Jones opposed Ricardo's concept of differential rent by arguing that rent was in fact a social institution which appeared in five distinct historical forms. T. E. Cliffe Leslie launched the field of economic history in Britain by questioning the "deduction from unverified assumptions respecting 'natural values, natural wages, and natural profits.'" He rejected the idea of political economy as a universal science, insisting that it was merely "an assemblage of speculations and doctrines which are the result of a particular history."[6]

The case of the stationary state provides an especially useful illustration of the intimate relation between nature and history in Victorian political economy. In this concept, an environmental and physical model of the natural limits to growth came together with a historicist understanding of how economies prosper and decay. It was the final stage in a complex process that combined elements of natural and civil history. Mark Bevir defines historicism as a diachronic form of thought which eschews more "formal or structural" types of explanation. A social phenomenon, simply put, must always be understood in terms of its specific place and time. Jonathan H. Turner contrasts historicist and positivist styles of explanation. The former "examines sets and sequences of empirical events to explain particular historical outcomes" whereas the latter aspires to "isolate the fundamental properties of the social universe and develop abstract laws and models that explain the operative dynamics of these properties." Geoffrey Hodgson sees the issue of historical specificity as the central neglected problem in the methodology of the social sciences. The complexity of socio-economic systems demands

pp. 188–95, 227–31; for Jennings and Jevons, see Harro Maas, *William Stanley Jevons and the Making of Modern Economics* (Cambridge University Press, 2005).
[6] Maas, *William Stanley Jevons*, pp. 233–48; Salim Rashid, "Richard Jones and Baconian Historicism at Cambridge," *Journal of Economic Issues*, Vol. 13, No. 1 (March 1979), 159–73; Leslie quoted in Dimitris Milonakis and Ben Fine, *From Political Economy to Economics: Method, the Social and the Historical in the Evolution of Economic Theory* (Routledge, 2009), p. 143.

careful attention to the specific properties of each social system, bounded in space and time. This makes a general theory of social phenomena impossible. A one-sided emphasis on commonalities across time and space leads to empty postulates, vacuous generalizations, and "computational limitations." However, Hodgson also insists that there can be no descriptive account of particulars without "prior theories or concepts," whether "explicit or tacit." Historicism thus still requires theoretical generalization, but primarily at the level of specific social systems, not in the universal sense.[7]

Most nineteenth-century political economists held that societies developed according to a teleological and historical logic, guided by reason and progress. History unfolded in a series of stages, each of which had to be understood in its own terms. The final phase of this process was the stationary state. From Malthus and Mill to Jevons and Ruskin, conservative, romantic, and liberal political economists worried that economic development must sooner or later encounter a physical ceiling. This anxiety about environmental limits to growth proved extremely fertile, giving rise to a wide range of different social and historical imaginaries. On the liberal side, nature was seen through the mirror of the market mechanism. The best means of managing resources was to let the laws of the market govern access and use. But conservative and radical critics insisted instead that nature was too complex or fragile to be left unattended by government and expert authorities. The precise character of natural limits was also subject to wide-ranging debate: competing arguments attributed the stationary state to population pressure, declining soil fertility, falling profits on investment, the proliferation of vice, the failure to innovate in husbandry, lack of colonies, or the exhaustion of coal supplies. For some, the stationary state was reversible and cyclical; for others it was a permanent trap. The concept also moved up and down temporal and spatial scales. Many savants thought of China as a long-standing example of an economy that had reached the natural limits to growth. Closer to home, some observers believed that quick population increase and bad soils destined the Scottish Highlands to stagnation. In the hungry 1840s, Robert Torrens linked the stationary state of Britain with the imperative of overseas colonization: "Our powers of production have outgrown the field of employment," he warned. Only "unappropriated territories" could rescue the nation. But for some critics

---

[7] Mark Bevir, "Why Historical Distance Is Not a Problem," *History and Theory*, Vol. 50 (December 2012), 25; Jonathan H. Turner, "Explaining the Social World: Historicism versus Positivism," *The Sociological Quarterly*, Vol. 47, No. 3 (Summer 2006), 461; Hodgson, *How Economics Forgot History*, pp. 21, 39–40.

of modern commerce and industry, the stationary state was not necessarily a dismal, pinched condition. They embraced the end of growth as an opportunity to revive traditional forms of faith, virtue, and crafts. Adam Smith argued that the falling rate of interest characteristic of a mature economy might be beneficial inasmuch as it encouraged thrift, hard work, and prudence. Thomas Chalmers believed that popular Malthusianism might strengthen the bonds of community and religion among the poor in Scotland. John Ruskin welcomed the exhaustion of coal as the first step toward recovering the virtues of premodern economies.[8]

Only with Alfred Marshall's *Principles of Economics* from 1890 did the fear of the stationary state lose its sting within the field of liberal economic thought. Marshall demoted the concept to the status of a heuristic device and useful fiction rather than a genuine social risk. This change of mind reflected the abandonment of much of the analytical apparatus of earlier generations, including the preoccupation with the finite supply of land. In this way, the rise and fall of the concept of the stationary state offers a useful signpost for the chronology and the thematic unity of Victorian political economy.[9]

Anxieties of Growth

The figure of Adam Smith may seem an unlikely departure point for the history of the stationary state. In popular culture today, the Scottish political economist receives notice mostly as an uncompromising enemy of the state and defender of free-market growth. But this is at best a crude and simplistic representation. Certainly, few historians would deny that Smith was sanguine about the effects of liberal conditions of trade. He expected the growth of commerce in town and country to promote productivity and prosperity. Yet it is quite telling that he singled out the colonies in North America as the most dynamic part of the British economy. The combination of cheap land and expensive labor there led

[8] Albritton Jonsson, *Enlightenment's Frontier*, pp. 124–5, 189, 194, 255–7, 262–4; Salah El Sarafy, *Macroeconomics and the Environment: Essays on Green Accounting* (Edward Elgar, 2013), pp. 98–100; Murray Milgate and Shannon C. Stimson, *After Adam Smith: A Century of Transformation in Politics and Political Economy* (Princeton University Press, 2009), pp. 191–210, Torrens quoted on p. 203; for Chalmers, see Hilton, *Age of Atonement*, p. 67; Royall Brandis, "Time Concepts in the History of Economic Thought: The Case of the Stationary State," in Donald A. Walker, ed., *Perspectives on the History of Economic Thought* (Edward Elgar, 1987), pp. 71–80.
[9] Joseph A. Schumpeter, *History of Economic Analysis* (Routledge, 1977), p. 966; E. A. Wrigley, *Energy and the English Industrial Revolution* (Cambridge University Press, 2011), pp. 47–8.

to high wages and quick population growth. The colonies were "much more thriving" than Britain itself. Within a century, Smith surmised, the center of the British Empire might well move across the Atlantic. This rather impish forecast hints at the more restricted prospects for growth in the Old World. Where land was scarce, long settled, and the population large, a different future seemed likely. "In a country fully peopled in portion to what either its territory could maintain or its stock employ, the competition of employment would necessarily be so great as to reduce to the wages of labor to what was barely sufficient to keep up the number of laborers." This was the "stationary" condition of a nation "which had acquired that full complement of riches which the nature of its soil and climate ... and its situation with respect to other countries allowed it to acquire." Such a country could "advance no further" and "the wages of labor and the profits of stock would probably be very low." The stationary state was not just a theoretical possibility to Smith, but an historical fact. He pointed to Holland as a region which was "approaching near to this state." Falling interest rates indicated that Holland had reached the "full complement of riches," "where in every particular branch of business there was the greatest quantity of stock that could be employed in it." To Smith, this predicament was not without benefits. He observed that low interest rates forced the great majority of the population to work for a living. In a thinly veiled critique of the British elite, Smith observed that few men in Holland could afford to live on the interest of capital. A society that had reached the "full complement of riches" thus produced a culture hostile to idleness and rentiers.[10]

Smith's concept of the stationary state reflected the constraints on the economy placed by the environment before the Industrial Revolution. Though Smith was familiar with the invention of the steam engine, *The Wealth of Nations* did not recognize steam and coal as the foundation for a new "mineral energy economy" which would break the shackles of the old agrarian regime. Instead, his political economy centered on the transition from feudalism to commercial society. At the heart of Smith's historical account was a "liberal ecology" of capitalism. Agricultural improvement provided the main avenue to expanded productivity. Market integration, secure farm leases, and growing urban demand encouraged the introduction of commercial agriculture and "mixed husbandry." This method of farming increased output by boosting soil

---

[10] Adam Smith, *An Inquiry into the Nature and Causes of the Wealth of Nations*, eds. R. H. Campbell, A. S. Skinner, and W. B. Todd (Oxford University Press, 1976 [1776], 2 vols.), I: 88, 111, 113, cf. 332, II: 626; Wrigley, *Energy*, pp. 197–8; Brandis, "Time Concepts," pp. 72–3.

fertility with cattle manure and legumes. Urbanization, manufactures, and trade stimulated agricultural production but were also fundamentally constrained by the productivity of the land. Demand for food, shelter, fuel, and clothing all relied on biomass production. In this "organic economy," soil fertility and photosynthesis determined the possibilities of growth.[11]

The tenor of political economy darkened at the end of the eighteenth century. The advent of a revolutionary regime in France transformed the political climate in Britain. Protracted warfare and ideological polarization bolstered authoritarian and conservative forces at home. This political crisis was compounded by social and ecological strain. Britain was afflicted by a series of bad harvests during the French Revolutionary and Napoleonic Wars. Administrators and improvers worried about shortages in fuel, naval timber, and other essential resources. Signs of exhaustion appeared common across the natural world in the late eighteenth century. John Sinclair's *Statistical Account of Scotland* contained numerous observations about shrinking peat moss supplies. The *British Merchant for 1787* offered a pessimistic view of national growth. In contrast with France, Britain was "a country, whose resources [have] already [been] brought into full exertion." John Sinclair calculated the total acres of arable land left in Britain as part of a campaign for wasteland reclamation and internal colonization. In his survey for the Admiralty from 1792, Charles Middleton declared that British supplies for the navy were dangerously depleted. The Welsh mining engineer John Williams warned in 1789 that the immense increase in coal consumption would soon finish off available reserves.[12]

The most famous prediction of resource strain to come out of the troubled 1790s was the population principle of Reverend T. R. Malthus. For Malthus, "geometric" population growth threatened to outpace the gains of agricultural improvement. The first edition of the *Essay on the Principle of Population* in 1798 employed a "quasi-mathematical" thought

---

[11] Hiram Caton, "The Preindustrial Economics of Adam Smith," *The Journal of Economic History*, Vol. 45, No. 4 (December 1985), 833–53; E. A. Wrigley, *Continuity, Chance and Change: The Character of the Industrial Revolution in England* (Cambridge University Press, 1988), pp. 17–19, Albritton Jonsson, *Enlightenment's Frontier*, pp. 129–34.

[12] Albritton Jonsson, *Enlightenment's Frontier*, pp. 157, 176–77; John Williams, *The Natural History of the Mineral Kingdom* (Edinburgh: Thomas Ruddiman, 1789, 2 vols.), I, pp. 171–2; Anon, *The British Merchant for 1787* (London, 1787), p. 54; Commissioners of His Majesty's Woods, Forests, and Land Revenues, *The eleventh report of the commissioners appointed to enquire into the state and condition of the woods, forests, and land revenues of the Crown, ...* (London, 1792), p. 19; compare Robert Greenhalgh Albion, *Forests and Sea Power; The Timber Problem of the Royal Navy, 1652–1862* (Naval Institute Press, 2000 [1926]), p. 136.

experiment to demonstrate the danger of unrestrained reproduction. While new scientific methods in agriculture might be expected to double production in Britain every quarter century, population growth would proceed at an exponential rate. In this simple model, population overshot food production within a generation, some time between 1820 and 1850. In social terms, Malthus imagined working-class sexuality as a realm of unreason and instinct, beyond effective state intervention. The failure of the poor to provide for offspring was an evil only to be remedied through the moral restraint and rationality of the individual. In the second edition of the *Essay*, Malthus added a wealth of empirical data to bolster and vindicate the outlines of the original thought experiment. On this score, Malthus was a follower of David Hume. Historical laws could be inferred from the principles of human nature in connection with regularly occurring historical patterns. Notoriously, in the first edition of the *Essay* Malthus saw little use for government intervention to ameliorate crises of subsistence. Generous poor relief would only exacerbate the problem by encouraging larger families and more reliance on the state. Positive checks such as famine and disease were the providential and natural means of reducing surplus population whenever the individual's power of "moral restraint" faltered. In later editions, Malthus softened his approach, suggesting a legitimate role for government. In particular, he endorsed the Corn Laws, that is, a policy of tariffs and restrictions designed to bolster the domestic food supply.[13]

We cannot understand the contemporary appeal of Malthus' political economy without recognizing the role of natural history in the argument. Malthus explicitly compared human sexuality to the vital force of reproduction in animals and plants. "The perpetual tendency in the race of man to increase beyond the means of subsistence" was but an instance of the "general laws of animated nature." It was an "obstacle" that humans could "never hope to overcome." This iron law of nature applied at every scale. The second edition of the *Essay* from 1803 began with a reverie about planetary population explosion borrowed from Benjamin Franklin. "Were the face of the earth ... vacant of other plants, it might be gradually sowed and overspread with one kind only." Indeed, the same species "would fill millions of worlds in the course of a few thousand years." Later in the same chapter, Malthus predicted that human population growth could overshoot the carrying capacity of the planet within a

[13] Thomas Robert Malthus, *An Essay on the Principle of Population* (London: J. Johnson, 1798), p. 23; Hilton, *Age of Atonement*, pp. 21–2, 376–7; Milgate and Stimson, *After Adam Smith*, p. 129; Donald Winch, *Riches and Poverty: An Intellectual History of Political Economy in Britain, 1750–1834* (Cambridge University Press, 1996), pp. 332–6.

few generations. "In two centuries the population would be to the means of subsistence as 265 to 9." The forecast for Britain thus offered a lesson for the species, "taking the whole earth instead of this island."[14]

The dismal news of Malthus' arithmetic penetrated far beyond the circles of economic writers. As the *Essay* went through six editions between 1798 and 1826, Malthusian political economy turned into a popular ideology, embraced by politicians and moralists. Boyd Hilton has shown how a synthesis of Malthusianism and evangelical faith shaped middle-class attitudes. The leading Scottish churchman Thomas Chalmers played a central role in forging this hybrid theology. Depraved by nature, humans had to seek atonement for their sins from a merciful God. This spiritual condition paralleled the problem of material scarcity. Chalmers imagined a benign version of the stationary state, in which material scarcity was met by good husbandry, conscience, and abstinence among the poor. In this situation, the finite supply of land would not press down wages, as long as working men learned to exercise moral restraint. In practical terms, Chalmers hoped to revive the spiritual community of rural parishes and extend them into the new industrial cities by mobilizing the evangelical wing of the Church of Scotland. His social ideal was the "godly commonwealth" of sixteenth- and seventeenth-century Calvinism rather than the Moderate Kirk of the Scottish Enlightenment.[15]

Malthus' insistence on the inefficacy of state intervention no doubt made his message especially palatable to those who favored government on the cheap. The amendment of the Elizabethan Poor Laws in 1834 stigmatized the "idle" poor and subjected them to a brutal workhouse regime. Prolonged depression, harvest failure, and social unrest in the 1840s reinforced Malthusian anxieties. Martin Daunton suggests that the specter of overpopulation and stagnation haunted the British public until at least the Crystal Palace Exhibition of 1851. E. A. Wrigley notes that a confident understanding of the Industrial Revolution emerged only belatedly at the end of the century. Many Victorian thinkers inherited from Malthus the fundamental suspicion that economic growth moved society inexorably toward an environmental and demographic trap. Despite the great dynamism of industrial capitalism, or rather *because of* the quick growth of the factory system, they held that material progress was

---

[14] T. R. Malthus, *An Essay on the Principle of Population* (J. Johnson, 1798), p. 346; T. R. Malthus, *An Essay on the Principle of Population*, 2nd ed. (J. Johnson, 1803), pp. 12–13.

[15] Thomas Chalmers, *On Political Economy...* (Glasgow, 1832), p. 447; Hilton, *Age of Atonement*; Stewart J. Brown, *Thomas Chalmers and the Godly Commonwealth in Scotland* (Oxford University Press, 1982), pp. xv, 89.

destined to plateau in a state of stationary population and capital when natural resources were fully exploited and the relation between land and labor had become fixed.[16]

This is not to suggest that the concept of the stationary state itself remained stationary. Malthus' main rival, the London financier David Ricardo, articulated a quite distinct version of the concept in the 1817 *Principles of Political Economy and Taxation*. Whereas Malthus moved from a simple deductive model in the first essay toward increasing empirical nuance and political pragmatism in the later editions, Ricardo never deviated from his goal of making political economy a proper science. He set out to discover a deductive method derived from a few general axioms, including the labor theory of value and the concept of marginal rent. In political terms, his treatise launched a liberal broadside against the power and wealth of landowning class. He argued that they had benefited disproportionately from the protectionist Corn Laws, which drove up rents and encouraged the exploitation of wastelands, while leaving the poor with high prices of provisions. Although Ricardo's approach jettisoned the historical complexity of Smith's political economy in favor of a more abstract model of exchange, he was no methodological individualist, but regarded the social order as the product of group interests: "[t]he produce of the whole earth ... is divided among three classes" – proprietors of land, owners of capital, and laborers. At "different stages of society," these groups commanded different portions of "rent, profit and wages." It was the task of political economy to "determine the laws which regulate this distribution." The foundation of this science was the labor theory of value: wages reflected the natural price of labor, that is, they reflected the amount of labor the worker needed to perform in order to produce "the food, necessaries and conveniences ... essential to him from habit."[17]

Ricardo's concept of rent has often been interpreted as a fundamentally pessimistic view of agriculture and soil fertility. Rent was the product of the expansion of cultivation from richer to less fertile land. When inferior soils were taken into cultivation, it became possible to charge rent on superior lands. In Ricardo's formal model, rent was the "difference between the produce obtained by the employment of two equal quantities of capital and labor." It was the payment to the landlord

---

[16] Martin Daunton, "Society and Economic Life," in Colin Matthew, ed., *The Nineteenth Century: The British Isles 1815–1901* (Oxford University Press, 2000), pp. 42–3, 52; Wrigley, *Energy and the English Industrial Revolution*, pp. 47–8.
[17] David Ricardo, *The Principles of Political Economy and Taxation* (London: J. Murray, 1817), pp. iii–iv, quoted in Milgate and Stimson, p. 51.

for "the use of the original and indestructible powers of the soil." Growing demand from an increasing population encouraged landowners to expand production. This notion of diminishing returns was central to Ricardo's reasoning, but it was in fact merely a means to an optimistic end, since Ricardo remained quite sanguine about the prospects of long-term growth. Liberalization of trade and improvement in technology could stave off physical limits to growth for a very long time: "[b]y the extension of foreign trade, or by improvements in machinery, the food and necessaries of the laborer can be brought to market at a reduced price." As long as commerce became steadily more liberal, the stationary state would remain "yet far distant."[18]

Ricardo's political economy must be placed in the longer philosophical and institutional history of free trade. Frank Trentmann distinguishes three phases of this process until 1900. The first saw the emergence of a moral vision of free trade, articulated by Francis Hutcheson, Adam Smith, and other Enlightenment thinkers. Commerce was for them a civilizing process, which broke the power of the feudal elite and fostered new more peaceful relations between nations. After the end of the Napoleonic Wars in 1815, the liberalization of commerce gained increasing support in British politics and civil society. This movement culminated in the repeal of the Corn Laws in 1846 and the Cobden–Chevalier treaty of 1860. But in the wake of a deep depression, the liberal forces on the continent lost ground. By the end of the century, British free-trade policy had become exceptional, cherished self-consciously and unilaterally as a mark of moral superiority and civilization. According to Trentmann, this marked the moment when free trade became a genuinely popular movement, espoused by suffragettes, working-class radicals, and adherents of the cooperative movement. Ricardo's political economy was the linchpin of the earlier popular turn, which united bourgeois interests in favor of industry, economic growth, and international trade. A number of figures helped diffuse this message to the middle-class public, including Ricardo's student John Ramsay McCulloch, the Anti-Corn Law agitator James Wilson, and the Unitarian liberal Harriet Martineau, whose *Illustrations of Political Economy* (1832–4) transformed the axioms of classical political economy into a series of widely read moral tales.[19]

---

[18] Ricardo, *The Principles*, pp. 7–8, 71, 115, 154, 464, 557–8; Winch, *Riches and Poverty*, p. 368.
[19] Frank Trentmann, *Free Trade Nation* (Oxford University Press, 2008), pp. 5–6, 8; Christopher Otter, "Liberty and Ecology: Resources, Markets, and the British Contribution to the Global Environmental Crisis," in Simon Gunn and James Vernon, eds., *The Peculiarities of Liberal Modernity in Imperial Britain* (University of California

Among radical philosophers, a different kind of deductive approach flourished. The amiable utilitarian Jeremy Bentham dreamt of reducing psychology to a simple calculus, which would take the quantity of pleasure and pain as the objective guide to value. The inventor Charles Babbage followed a parallel path, attempting to design artificial intelligence by constructing a series of calculating engines. The Scots chemist Andrew Ure explored the logic of factory production in his *Philosophy of Manufactures* (1835). He defined the machinery in the new cotton mills as a new form of material intelligence. Within these factories, "the elemental powers have been made to animate millions of complex organs, infusing into forms of wood, iron and brass an intelligent agency." Such machine-dreams about the "perfection of automatic industry" suggested that it was possible to give a materialist account of both human psychology and physical labor. The working body could be treated as an automaton within a larger system of automated manufactures. A generation later, Thomas Huxley declared in 1870 that natural philosophy would "sooner or later" arrive at a "mechanical equivalent" of consciousness. Inspired by Babbage and Ure, William Stanley Jevons set out at the same moment in time to replace the labor theory of value with a new materialist theory of consumer psychology and human labor. In a modified form, they became central tenets in twentieth-century neoclassical economics.[20]

However, these machine-dreams did not go unopposed. The development of the manufacturing system provoked a great deal of social and political debate. As early as 1819, there were attempts to regulate the use of child labor in the textile industry. Over the next few decades, a rudimentary body of factory legislation emerged. Karl Polanyi suggested long ago that the exploitation of working-class labor set in motion a counter-movement, instigated by observers who recognized the inhumanity of treating human beings as mere commodities or machines. But there was no necessary ideological unity to this "double movement." We can distinguish conservative, liberal, and socialist responses to the "social question." Edwin Chadwick's report on sanitation (1842) set out to expose the economic and social folly of government-on-the-cheap in the industrial slums. Friedrich Engels in turn dissected the political economy and psychology of working-class Manchester. For the technocrat

Press, 2011), pp. 182–98; Hilton, *Age of Atonement*, pp. 69–70; Willie Henderson, "Harriet Martineau or When Political Economy Was Popular," *History of Education: Journal of the History of Education Society*, Vol. 21, No. 4 (1992), 383–403.
[20] Andrew Ure, *The Philosophy of Manufactures* (London: Charles Knight, 1835), p. 2; Simon Schaffer, "OK Computer," in Michael Hagner, ed., *Ecce Cortex: Beitraege zur Geschichte des modernen Gehirns* (Wallstein Verlag, 1999), pp. 254–85; Maas, *William Stanley Jevons*.

Chadwick, the social question warranted state intervention in matters of public health. For the socialist Engels, urban immiseration was the necessary crucible of revolution.[21]

The social question also left a deep mark on the thought of John Stuart Mill, the greatest liberal political economist of the nineteenth century. Mill's *Principles of Political Economy* (1848) transformed the priorities of classical political economy by linking it to the possibility of creative development and "character." This shift was a direct outcome of Mill's attempt to synthetize disparate currents of Victorian thought. Mill admired the deductive rigor of David Ricardo's political economy. It was, he thought, a great improvement on the flawed historical reasoning of Adam Smith. But Mill was also aware that Ricardo's analytical model had spurred a strong social critique from literary figures, such as Samuel Taylor Coleridge and Charles Dickens, who excoriated the inhumanity of laissez-faire in favor of a more communal vision of society and the economy. Mill's aim in *The Principles of Political Economy* was to combine Ricardo's method with the concerns of the public moralist. While he defended the power of markets and competition to produce goods for public consumption, he also recognized the need for state intervention and social legislation to alleviate poverty and curb exploitation. The aims of social reform were in turn closely aligned with questions of psychology and history in Mill's imagination. This Victorian work of synthesis in turn stimulated critical responses from all sides, including attacks by Henry Sidgwick, William Stanley Jevons, John Ruskin, and Karl Marx. In the 1870s and 1880s, the so-called marginalist school launched a methodological challenge to Mill's synthesis by redefining economic analysis by way of the concept of marginal utility. Meanwhile, Karl Marx and his followers articulated a social critique of capitalism, predicated on the labor theory of value and the history of class struggle.[22]

The Principles of Political Economy is justly read as the towering summa of Victorian classical political economy. Yet it is a curiously uneven reflection of the age. One looks in vain for detailed analysis in Mill's work of many major features of industrial society, including the factory

[21] Karl Polanyi, *The Great Transformation: The Political and Economic Origins of Our Time* (Beacon Press, 2001); Boyd Hilton, *A Mad, Bad & Dangerous People: England 1783–1846* (Oxford University Press, 2006), pp. 588–99; Friedrich Engels, *The Condition of the Working Class in England* (Oxford University Press, 2009).

[22] Winch, *Wealth and Life*; Margaret Schabas, *A World Ruled by Number: William Stanley Jevons and the Rise of Mathematical Economics* (Princeton, 1990); Moishe Postone, *Time, Labor and Social Domination: A Reinterpretation of Marx's Critical Theory* (Cambridge University Press, 1996); Mark Bevir, *The Making of British Socialism* (Princeton University Press, 2011).

system and the urban slums. Instead, a large portion of the first part of the book is occupied with a comparative history of land tenure. Though Mill shied away from more radical projects of land reform, he strongly supported the cause of peasant proprietors. Land ownership was for Mill a matter of moral character as much as social stability. It promised to instill habits of "forethought, frugality [and] self-restraint" in the rural poor. Mill situated the problem of reproduction and preventive checks in a wider social and psychological context, emphasizing the effects of ownership, education, and equality of the sexes. The impetus for this orientation toward land may have come from Mill's reading of William Wordsworth's poetry and his pilgrimage to Wordsworth's Lake District in 1831. There, he encountered the figure of the Lakeland "statesman" – a class of farmer-pastoralists who seemed to have preserved a vestige of the "noble yeoman" tradition of the English past. The isolation and relative poverty of the Lake District had preserved the people and the land from the ravages of agrarian capitalism. Wordsworth's peasants were not only respectable and self-reliant, but also rooted and at home in a landscape of great beauty. In this way, Mill tempered the natural history of "bare life" in Malthus with a romantic–historical perspective, illuminating the potential for moral virtue and love of nature among the rural poor.[23]

This same ambition to marry Malthusian political economy to a romantic conception of the self-shaped Mill's famous discussion of the stationary state. In a short but provocative chapter toward the end of *The Principles of Political Economy*, Mill warned that the "richest and most prosperous countries would very soon attain the stationary state" unless "improvements were made in the productive arts" and capital was poured into "the uncultivated or ill-cultivated regions of the earth." Like Malthus, he feared that the very speed and scale of modern growth was carrying the advanced economies toward not an open horizon of possibility but a permanent ceiling beyond which it could not pass: "all progress in wealth is but a postponement of this ... each step in advance is an approach to it." The prospect of stagnation was no longer distant but "near enough to be fully in view ... we are always on the verge of it." For Mill, this crisis also threatened the diversity and wilderness of the natural world. With "every rood of land brought into cultivation ... all quadrupeds or birds which are not domesticated for man's use exterminated as his rivals for food ... and scarcely a place left where a wild shrub

---

[23] John Stuart Mill, *Principles of Political Economy* (Augustus Kelley, 1987), pp. 62–3; Winch, *Wealth and Life*, pp. 61–7, Mill quoted on p. 80. In urban settings, Mill favored cooperative labor associations; see Mill, pp. 763, 773.

or flower could grow without being eradicated as a weed." A crowded, domesticated world without wild spaces would harm the human mind irreparably. "Solitude, in the sense of being often alone, is essential to any depth of meditation or of character." Taking a position closer to John Muir than to T. R. Malthus, Mill observed that "solitude in the presence of natural beauty and grandeur, is the cradle of thoughts and aspirations, which are not only good for the individual, but which society could ill do without."[24]

Yet, paradoxically, the moral lesson of the forecast also made possible an alternative ending to the history of capitalism. Humanity should embrace the possibility of the stationary state long before the physical limits on growth became pressing and severe. Such a choice would permit people to transcend the brutality and ugliness of modern society. It would prove that the industrial age was merely a passing phase – "a necessary stage in civilization," to be sure, but not the crowning glory of human society. This prematurely stationary society would be free to redirect its fundamental creative urges in new directions: "There would be as much scope as ever for all kinds of mental culture, and moral and social progress; as much room for improving the Art of Living, and much more likelihood of its being improved, when minds ceased to be engrossed by the art of getting on." Throughout the chapter, Mill spoke of the problem as a universal choice of the "species" rather than the path of a single class or a nation. He also framed the value of the premature stationary state in terms of stewardship and biodiversity on the planet. "It is not good for man to be kept perforce at all times in the presence of his species."[25]

The Coal Question

Nineteenth-century political economy was a product of the first industrial economy. Yet, as we have seen, political economists failed to grasp the historical significance of industrialization until quite late in the century. This anxiety about limits to growth extended also to the energy base of industrial society. The fear of the stationary state emerged side by side with a forecast of mineral energy collapse. John Williams, a Welsh mining engineer, declared that Britain was running out of coal in *The Natural History of the Mineral Kingdom* (1789), published almost a decade before

---

[24] Mill, *Principles of Political Economy*, pp. 746, 750.
[25] Mill, *Principles of Political Economy*, pp. 748, 750–1. Cf. Graham A. Macdonald, "The Politics of the Golden River: Ruskin on Environment and the Stationary State," *Environment and History*, Vol. 18 (2012), 125–50.

the first edition of Malthus' *Essay*. Williams' warning provoked a long debate over the limits of the British coal reserves. A host of rival quantitative estimates of the coalfields were proposed between 1793 and 1865, culminating in *The Coal Question*, penned by political economist William Stanley Jevons.[26] The genre of coal forecasts shared many of the features that characterized Malthusian analysis. It adopted the same concept of a human economy bounded by physical limits to growth, derived from postulates of natural history. This naturalism also generated a stadial account of economies, by showing how the exploitation of fuel stock made possible historical stages of growth, prosperity, and decline. The main difference between Malthus' population discourse and the forecasts regarding coal exhaustion was that the natural history of fossil fuel followed a different trajectory of development than soil fertility, longer in duration because of the immensity of coal reserves, yet more final in decline because of the non-renewable character of mineral energy.

John Williams spent much of his career in Scotland, overseeing mining works and serving on the government board of the Annexed Estates. Williams' patrons included enlightenment figures such as David Erskine and Henry Home, Lord Kames. His prediction of peak coal followed a long, futile odyssey in the Highlands prospecting for coal and other minerals. This bitter lesson in regional development opened his eyes to the central place of coal in the British economy. Without cheap coal, the "prosperity and glory of this flourishing and fortunate island" would come to "an end." Despite the widespread reliance on coal in eighteenth-century Britain, few contemporary political economists were so clear-eyed about the crucial place of coal in the manufacturing sector. For Williams, the exhaustion of coal would spell the end of modern life. "Our cities and great towns must then become ruinous heaps for want of fuel, and our mines and manufactories must fail from the same cause, and then consequently our commerce must vanish." Unsurprisingly for a man who spent much time in the circles of the Scottish Enlightenment, Williams imagined this collapse as the reversal of stadial history. "[T]he commerce, wealth, importance, glory, and happiness of Great Britain will decay and gradually dwindle to nothing, in proportion as our coal and other mines fail; and the future inhabitants of this island must live, like its first inhabitants, by fishing and hunting."[27]

---

[26] Albritton Jonsson, *Enlightenment's Frontier*, pp. 181–7; Rolf Peter Sieferle, *The Subterranean Forest: Energy Systems and the Industrial Revolution* (The White Horse Press, 2001), p. 186.

[27] Williams, *The Natural History of the Mineral Kingdom*, I: 168, 172–73; Albritton Jonsson, *Enlightenment's Frontier*, pp. 168–75.

The great question was how much coal was still in the ground. Henry Grey Macnab – a mining entrepreneur from Northumberland, steeped in the same culture of improvement as Williams – made the first attempt to quantify the supply, focusing on the fields in the northeast and northwest of England. His findings were reassuring. Reserves would last "upwards of twelve hundred years" even if consumption grew significantly. Macnab's data opened the door to a host of rival conjectures regarding the future of coal. In 1797, John Bailey presented his own calculation in *The General View of the a Agriculture of the County of Northumberland*, a survey co-authored with George Culley and published at the behest of Sinclair's Board of Agriculture. His estimate suggested a duration of 200 to 400 years depending on the thickness of seams. In the next few decades, Thomas Thomson and Robert Bakewell carried on the quarrel over national exhaustion. Thomson revisited the output of the Newcastle seam in an 1814 essay to propose that the field would last 1,000 years, a slight downward revision from Macnab's original figure of 1,200. Bakewell revived Bailey's pessimistic estimate in his *Introduction to Geology* (third edition 1828). Though he expected that new sources of supply, especially from South Wales, would compensate for the eventual collapse of the Newcastle collieries, the greatly increased rate of consumption worried him.[28]

The problem surfaced again with renewed urgency in 1830 when a parliamentary committee examined the obstacles to the market for coal and the possible abolition of duties on coal shipping. In the hearings, the natural historians William Buckland and Adam Sedgwick challenged optimistic estimates about the total extent of coal deposits and the efficiency of extraction. In particular, they rejected the assessment of Mr. Taylor, the agent of the Duke of Northumberland, to the effect that the Newcastle fields contained the equivalent of 1,700 years of coal. Buckland saw in the British coal reserves a providential storehouse that had be carefully husbanded. God had laid up rich stores of fuel in the depths of the earth many "ages ago" for the "future uses of Man." To waste this coal without thought – as the mine owners did in the north

---

[28] Henry Gray Macnab, *Letters addressed to the Right Honourable William Pitt, Chancellor of the Exchequer of Great Britain; pointing out the inequality, oppression, and impolicy of the taxes on coal: and A Substitute for These Taxes on all Coals Consumed in England and Scotland* (London: J. Johnson, 1793), pp. 126–7; John Bailey and George Culley, *General view of the agriculture of the county of Northumberland, with observations on the means of its improvement; drawn up for the consideration of the Board of Agriculture and Internal Improvement* (Newcastle: Robinson and Nicol, 1797), pp. 11, 18–19; Thomas Thomson, "A Geognostical Sketch of the Counties of Northumberland, Durham, and Part of Cumberland," *Annals of Philosophy*, ed. Thomas Thomson, Vol. IV (July to December 1814), pp. 81–3, 410–12; Robert Bakewell, *An Introduction to Geology...*, 3rd ed. (London: Longman, Rees, Orme, Brown, Green, 1828), pp. 178–181.

when they burned the inferior type of coal in huge heaps on the side of the pitheads – was tantamount to sacrilege. Buckland's *Bridgewater Treatise* drove home the arithmetic of exhaustion in lavish illustrations of the coal-bearing strata. The public could now see clearly not just the abundance of the coal, but also the definite limits of the supply. By making deep time visible in depictions of geological strata, Buckland demonstrated just how quickly British manufacturing demand was exhausting layers of fuel built up by providence over eons of time. Buckland provided the political economy of coal with a providential–geological horizon.[29]

The debate about the coal supply continued in the next generation. Controversy about the duration of the coal seams became especially heated in the aftermath of the Cobden–Chevalier free-trade treaty with France in 1860. William Stanley Jevons revived the case for a pessimistic forecast by taking a Malthusian approach to the trend of consumption in *The Coal Question* (1865). He began with the assumption that "a nation tends to develop itself by multiplication rather than addition – in a geometrical rather than an arithmetical series." He postulated an "average annual rate of growth of our coal consumption [at] 3 ½ per cent." On his count, coal consumption had risen from 1 million [10,000,000] tons in 1801 to 39,000,000 in 1840. It stood at 83.6 million tons in 1861. Jevons then projected the average growth for the next century. By 1891 it would reach 234.7 million tons, in 1941 1,310.5 million, and in 1961 an incredible 2,607.5 million. Next, Jevons turned to the estimates of coal deposits made by Edward Hull for the Geological Survey of Britain between 1860 and 1864. The latter had assessed the total quantity of coal left in remaining fields at 83,544 million tons. Hull assumed that consumption would double every twenty years. This meant that all fields would be exhausted before the year 2034. Jevons disagreed, predicting that the mines would be exhausted in little more than a century. A year after Jevons published his calculations, a Royal Commission was convened to consider the state of the coal reserves. The Commission contemplated a series of alternative scenarios, predicated on diverging trends of consumption, population growth, and extraction depth. It pitted the pronouncements of the railway engineer R. Price Williams against Jevons' political economy. Williams' forecasts varied from three to twelve

---

[29] *Report of the Select Committee on the State of the Coal Trade* (London, 1830), pp. 231–47 (especially 238 and 240); Jevons, *The Coal Question*, pp. 16–19. For more on the background to the 1830s coal trade debate, see Sieferle, *The Subterranean Forest*, pp. 187–91; William Buckland, *Geology and Mineralogy Considered with Reference to Natural Theology* (London: William Pickering, 1836, 2 vols.), I, p. 538; Buckland, *Geology and Mineralogy* (London: Bell and Daldy, 1870), II, pp. 181–82.

centuries. When the committee added the possibility of extracting deep coal below Jevons' lower limit of 4,000 feet, the range widened to 1,695 years. Apparently, the strategy here was not to endorse a reassuringly distant date but rather to suggest that the whole matter lay beyond the power of forecasts. For the commissioners, the mass of contradictory calculations simply demonstrated that the future was hopelessly opaque. "Whatever view may be taken of the question of duration of coal, the results will be subject to contingencies, which cannot in any degree be foreseen." From the perspective of Jevons and his supporters, this insistence on uncertainty was a political tactic rather than a scientific rebuttal.[30]

William Stanley Jevons occupies something of a liminal position in the history of the stationary state. His pessimism in the first edition of *The Coal Question* was as profound as that of Malthus in the first edition of the *Essay on the Principle of Population*. Because Jevons saw no clear alternative to coal fuel and no benefit to more efficient technologies, there was a tragic tilt to his nationalism. Famously, Jevons posited a rebound effect for more efficient energy use. "It is wholly a confusion of ideas to suppose that the economical use of fuel is equivalent to a diminished consumption. The very contrary is the truth." While latter-day critics of Jevons insist that only taxes and caps on consumption enforced by the state can prevent the rebound effect, Jevons was similarly pessimistic about the prospects of such regulation. He wrote in the conclusion to *The Coal Question* that taxation of British coal would only serve to stifle the "talents and virtues" of the nation. It was the "lavish expenditure of our material energy" that had made possible Watt's steam engine, Adam Smith's political economy, and the rise of the middle class. For Jevons, this brief spurt of brilliant creativity justified the complete exhaustion of the British coal mines in the near future. "We have to make the momentous choice between brief but true greatness and longer continued mediocrity." "When our main-spring is here run down, our fires burnt out, may we not look for an increasing flame of civilization elsewhere?" As Britain contracted to "her former littleness," other countries with coal deposits would take its place, at least as long as their coal lasted... The pleasures

---

[30] Jevons, *The Coal Question*, pp. 261, 268–73; Peter Thorsheim, *Inventing Pollution: Coal, Smoke and Culture in Britain since 1800* (Ohio University Press, 2006), pp. 45–7; Nunu Luis Madureira, "The Anxiety of Abundance: Stanley Jevons and Coal Scarcity in the Nineteenth Century," *Environment and History*, Vol. 18 (2012), 395–421; House of Commons, *Report of the commissioners appointed to inquire into the several matters relating to coal in the United Kingdom. Vol. I. General report and twenty-two sub-reports* (London, 1871), pp. xiv, xvii–iii; Roy Church, *History of the British Coal Industry* (Oxford University Press, 1986, 3 vols.), III, p. 86.

of decline would be simple but authentic. Britain must return to the "homely ... hardy virtues" and "regard for law" that the nation had cultivated before the age of manufactures. Jevons thus took the edge off his own critique by embracing the peculiar utopia of mid-Victorian intellectuals like J. S. Mill and John Ruskin. At the end of the age of manufactures was Jevons' version of the stationary state – characterized by memories of grandeur, moral purity, creative expression, and liberal freedom. In T. B. Macaulay's image, made famous by Gustave Dore's 1870 print, visitors would one day survey the ruins of Victorian London: "Some traveler from New Zealand shall, in the midst of a vast solitude, take his stand on a broken arch of London bridge to sketch the ruins of St. Paul's."[31]

Yet for all this elegiac resignation, Jevons was also a leading figure in the great revolt against classical political economy that we now call the marginalist revolution. From this perspective, Jevons' work takes on a completely different meaning. *The Theory of Political Economy* issued a clarion call for economists to cast themselves "free from the Wage-Fund Theory, The Cost of Production doctrine of Value, the Natural Rate of Wages, and other misleading or false Ricardian doctrines." In Jevons' great spring-cleaning, the analytical category of land – central to the classical economists – would be abolished and subsumed into the category of capital. "We must regard labor, land, knowledge, and capital as conjoint conditions of the whole produce," Jevons admonished, "not as causes each of a certain portion of the produce." Hardly by coincidence, he also expelled the category of population, since it formed "no part of the direct problem of Economics." The aim of *The Theory of Political Economy* was to purge economic analysis from the confusing clutter bequeathed by the classical economists, including the concern with the finite supply of land and historical stages so typical of economic reasoning from Smith to Mill. In their stead, Jevons hoped for a science of "general principles" centered on "self interest and utility" akin to the place of "mechanics" in the natural sciences. A few years later, Jevons' fellow revolutionary, Alfred Marshall, completed the task when he made the Ricardian concept of diminishing returns subservient to the universal principle of substitution under conditions of scarcity. Now every kind of economic transaction involved the calculation of marginal utility. Businessmen and housewives alike had to constantly ask themselves whether

---

[31] Jevons, *The Coal Question*, pp. 140, 457, 459–60; Joseph Tainter, "Foreword," in John M. Polimeni, et al, eds., *The Myth of Resource Efficiency: The Jevons Paradox* (Earthscan, 2008), p. xv; Macaulay quoted in David Skilton, "Tourists at the Ruins of London: The Metropolis and the Struggle for Empire," *Cercles*, Vol. 17 (2007), 116.

they suffered a "diminishing rate of return from any excessive application of resources or of energies in any given direction." Marshall left a door open to historical scholarship in his 1885 lecture on the present state of economics: "if the subject-matter of a science passes through different stages of development, the laws which apply to one stage will seldom apply without modification to others." Yet he never explained how to reconcile this position with his general theory. Historical approaches to economic development in Britain survived outside economics proper in the new field of economic history. In Marshall's abstract model, soil fertility, coal exhaustion, and other problems of resource management lost their privileged status as a foundational problem of economic analysis. Precisely why this happened in the late nineteenth century and not earlier or later is a question for further research. Martin Daunton believes that the technological spectacle of the Great Exhibition of 1851 marked the moment at which the British public began to exorcise the ghost of Malthus. E. A. Wrigley proposes a slightly later date, somewhere between the first volume of Marx's *Capital* (1867) and Arnold Toynbee's coinage of the term "The Industrial Revolution" in his 1884 lectures. By subsuming the category of land into capital, the marginalist economists signaled that every problem of food production and natural resources could be solved with the methods and techniques of industrial production. The combined power of human ingenuity and capital could banish every kind of physical constraint. In this new world, the stationary state could be safely demoted to a mere thought experiment. For Alfred Marshall, the stationary state was explicitly a "fiction," a simplified model with which to start the work of analysis.[32]

The Politics of Limits

An historicist strain runs through much of nineteenth-century political economy from Malthus to Ruskin. Just about every political economist in the period made use of the language of historical stages to frame economic analysis. But as we have seen, this impulse was rife with contradictions. Civil history was frequently deeply entangled with natural

[32] Alfred Marshall, *Principle of Economics* (Palgrave Macmillan, 2013 [1890]), p. 305; Hodgson, *How Economics Forgot History*, pp. 99–100; Gerard Koot, *English Historical Economics, 1870–1926* (Cambridge University Press, 1987); Sandra Peart, "Theory, Application and the Canon: The Case of Mill and Jevons," in Evelyn Forget and Sandra Peart, eds., *Reflections on the Classical Canon in Economics: Essays in Honor of Samuel Hollander* (Routledge, 2001), p. 371 ; Daunton, "Society and Economic Life," p. 51; E. A. Wrigley, *Energy and the English Industrial Revolution* (Cambridge University Press, 2010), pp. 48, 51; Brandis, "Time Concepts," p. 77.

history. Some of the most concerted efforts to articulate the historical specificity of the age emerged as a by-product of deductive reasoning. Attempts to locate a natural foundation for political economy in accounts of rent, population, and coal stimulated a variety of dystopian, utopian, and romantic visions of the end of industrial capitalism. The drift of economic thought after Jevons and Marshall appears to confirm this interpretation. When land was banished as a major analytical category, the interest in the stages of capitalist development also faded.

The story of nineteenth-century political economy has acquired new significance in recent years. No longer is the achievement of the marginalists simply fêted as the moment when economics became a proper science. Instead, some scholars see the late nineteenth century as the turning point at which economics was first consumed by physics envy and forgot about history, to its great detriment. There is also increasing disquiet among some environmental scientists and social theorists about the cornucopian assumptions of mainstream economics. The idea of low-growth or zero-growth economics is enjoying a revival in certain quarters. Indeed, the Malthusian notion of physical limits to growth has found a second lease of life in environmental forecasts of overpopulation, planetary boundaries, ecological overshoot, and the Anthropocene – the new epoch of anthropogenic climate change.[33]

The entanglements of civil and natural history in Victorian political economy are perhaps best understood in the manner of a cautionary tale. Technical questions about the extent of coal reserves, the rate of population growth, and the sources of soil fertility provoked a politics of natural limits. Optimists (cornucopians) and pessimists (Malthusians) clashed over the capacity of technology and capital to overcome the limited supply of land and the tendency toward soil exhaustion. Yet more fundamental questions about social structure and political order were often buried in these technical controversies. Who defined the limits of nature and to what end? What remedies might be imagined for exhaustion and overpopulation? When political economists ventured into this

---

[33] Mirowski, *More Heat than Light*; Milonakis and Fine, *From Political Economy to Economics*; Hodgson, *How Economics Forgot History*; Libby Robin, Sverker Sorlin, and Paul Warde, *The Future of Nature* (Yale University Press, 2014); Johan Rockström et al., "Planetary Boundaries: Exploring the Safe Operating Space for Humanity," *Ecology and Society*, Vol. 14, No. 2 (2009), http://www.ecologyandsociety.org/vol14/iss2/art32/; Mathis Wackernagel, "Shrink and Share: Humanity's Present and Future Ecological Footprint," *Philosophical Transactions: Biological Sciences*, Vol. 363, No. 1491, Sustainable Agriculture I (February 12, 2008), 467–75; Will Steffen, Paul Crutzen, and John McNeill, "The Anthropocene: Are Humans Now Overwhelming the Great Forces of Nature," *AMBIO: A Journal of the Human Environment*, Vol. 36, No. 8 (2007), 849–52; Vaclav Smil, *Harvesting the Biosphere: What We Have Taken from Nature* (MIT Press, 2012).

field, they frequently mined the past for answers, seeking in history different ways of imagining the stationary state. This impulse was at the same time subversive and conservative. It moved political economists to consider with fresh eyes the underlying political and social principles of economic life. What was the purpose of material growth? How did consumption serve the public good? But the recourse to the past also limited what types of politics and social order could be conceived.

John Ruskin's critique of classical political economy is an excellent case in point. During the 1870s, he became increasingly preoccupied with the environmental degradation caused by industrial capitalism. From his turreted study at Brantwood, Ruskin charted disturbing atmospheric phenomena in the skies above the Lakeland hills. The prevailing winds from the southwest brought smoke from the new coal-fired furnaces on the coast. This new cloudscape, filtered by Ruskin's uncommonly sensitive powers of perception and intellectual acumen, led him to prophesy a coming crisis of climate – the Storm Cloud of the Nineteenth Century. The whole fabric of the natural world seemed to be coming apart. He warned about the universal reach of atmospheric pollution in the first letter to *Fors Clavigera*: "You can vitiate the air by your manner of life, and of death, to any extent. You might easily vitiate it so as to bring such a pestilence on the globe as would end all of you." At the heart of this crisis lay humanity's unchecked urge to consume, which threatened to make the entire planet into a great quarry or factory. Ruskin wrote in his diary in 1877, "Monday, half sleepless night again – and entirely disgusting dream." "[M]en using flesh and bones, hands of children especially, for fuel – being out of wood and coals."[34]

At the beginning of the century, Malthus had imagined the problem of natural limits primarily as the pressure of human populations on scarce resources. There was no place for environmental pollution or degradation in his calculus. At mid-century, John Stuart Mill's political economy saw the fundamental environmental problem as one of preserving rural haunts from the encroachments of suburbia. But for Ruskin, the destructive power of industrial capitalism had reached a new, fundamentally different scale. It was now a planetary force capable of destroying the atmosphere and the climate. This fear was directed at two closely connected characteristics of industrial society: on the one hand, the

[34] Helen Gill Viljoen, *The Brantwood Diary of John Ruskin* (Yale University Press, 1971), pp. 58, 146; *Fors* Letter 1 in Cook and Wedderburn, 27; contrast with Michael Wheeler's interpretation of the Storm Cloud, which downplays political economy and environmental concern in favor of apocalyptic theology: see Michael Wheeler, "Environment and Apocalypse," in Michael Wheeler, ed., *Ruskin and Environment: The Storm Cloud of the Nineteenth Century* (Manchester University Press, 1995), p. 169.

world-making technical impulse of industrial society – what Thomas Hughes calls the second creation of technology – and on the other, the myopic disposition of boosters and consumers. Yet however far-sighted Ruskin was in grasping the environmental cost of affluence, his political response was constrained by a peculiar historical vision. The twenty-ninth letter of *Fors Clavigera* counseled a waiting game. Only after the British coal reserves had been exhausted was there a possibility of reviving preindustrial forms of labor and consumption. Ruskin remained profoundly suspicious of technological innovation. He and his followers crusaded against the expansion of railways and telegraph lines into the Lakes. They poured their energies into the revival of rural handicrafts and the reestablishment of guild economies. The future was medieval. Ruskin's Tory response to the threat of ecological disaster illustrates the peculiar relation of natural and civil history in nineteenth-century political economy. The long-standing concern with natural limits to growth stimulated a persistent conceit that the future of the nation was to be found in the forms of the past.[35]

---

[35] Timothy Mitchell, *Carbon Democracy: Political Power in the Age of Oil* (Verso, 2011); Nicholas Xenos, *Scarcity and Modernity* (Routledge, 1989), p. 35; Winch, *Wealth and Life*.

9 Empire

Duncan Bell

For a long time the greatness of the ancient world lay with an oppressive weight like an incubus upon the moderns.[1]

Introduction

The Victorians were obsessed with decoding historical experience, endlessly scouring the past for lessons about how best to comprehend and navigate their world. Debates over empire were inflected by two conflicting narratives of historical time, one cyclical, the other progressive.[2] According to the former, empires followed a predetermined trajectory: they rose, they declined and ultimately they fell. Such was the monitory teaching of the historical record. Counselling vigilance, Goldwin Smith warned in the late 1870s that the 'decay of Empires is the theme of history'.[3] According to the other conception, the nineteenth century was an age of progress, of constant human improvement, with the British imperial state in the vanguard. The 'movement of humanity is not, as the ancients fancied, in cycles', James Bryce averred, 'but shows a sustained, though often interrupted, progress'.[4] Imperial discourse was shaped by a constant negotiation between the two positions, each of which can be seen as different modulations of historicism. They both posited historical experience as central to understanding contemporary politics, but they differed in how they related past to present. The progressivist view of empire was broadly Whiggish, divining in the evolution of ideas and institutions the teleological unfolding of cherished principles (most often

---

[1] J. R. Seeley, *Introduction to Political Science*, ed. Henry Sidgwick (London: Macmillan, 1896), p. 161.
[2] This chapter extends the analysis of imperial temporality in Duncan Bell, *The Idea of Greater Britain: Empire and the Future of World Order, 1860–1900* (Princeton: Princeton University Press, 2007), ch. 8.
[3] Smith, 'The Policy of Aggrandizement', *Fortnightly Review*, 22 (1877), 307.
[4] Bryce, 'An Age of Discontent', *Contemporary Review*, 59 (1891), 29.

liberty) over time.[5] The cyclical view, however, was one of eternal return, signifying a pattern of repetition and recurrence in which the fate of the present could be discerned by understanding the past.

While belief in progress suffused Victorian political consciousness, the trope of proleptic decline supplied critics of empire with powerful ammunition. It contained the seeds of its own destruction. Smith, for example, argued that in light of historical experience, the British 'policy of aggrandizement' was ruinous.[6] However, it is important to distinguish between two different conceptions of imperial cyclicality, one universal, the other more institutionally specific. The universal vision, which could draw on Polybian archetypes or Christian providentialism, viewed all human institutions – indeed, all life – as subject to the same temporal dynamics. Empires were simply an instance of a general historical pattern. While unusual in Victorian Britain, this position found eloquent defenders among Liberal Anglican historians, including Thomas Arnold, though it was also articulated in other idioms, such as the classically-inflected republicanism of the historian J. A. Froude. The history of all living things, including commonwealths, Froude maintained, was defined by 'recurring stages of growth and transformation and decay'.[7] It was thus imperative to recognise the ephemeral quality of imperial governance. Yet, even the universal account allowed room for human agency: impossible to defeat, historical fate could at least be deferred. For Froude, '[t]he life of a nation, like the life of a man, may be prolonged in honour into the fullness of its time, or it may perish prematurely, for want of guidance, by violence or internal disorders'.[8] Knowledge of history could guide the wise statesman in battling time. The more popular cyclical vision, however, regarded empires as a special, distinctive case. Empires were predestined to collapse due to their inherent weaknesses. Since this dynamic only affected a particular class of institutions, this view was compatible with the widespread Victorian belief in the progressive development of humanity. Such arguments were commonly employed to point to the aberration of empire, its temporal incongruity.

Most imperialists, though, insisted that the British Empire was somehow exempt from historical precedent. Achieving progress guaranteed an

---

[5] It thus fits within what Mark Bevir calls 'developmental historicism': Bevir, 'Political Studies as Narrative and Science, 1880–2000', *Political Studies*, 54 (2006), 583–606.

[6] Smith, 'Policy'. For a similar critique of American Empire, see Smith, *Commonwealth or Empire?* (New York: Macmillan, 1902).

[7] Froude, *Caesar: A Sketch* (London: Longman's, 1879), p. 2. See also Duncan Bell, 'Republican Imperialism: J. A. Froude and the Virtue of Empire', *History of Political Thought*, 30 (2009), 166–91.

[8] Froude, *Caesar*, pp. 3–4.

escape velocity, forestalling the cycle of imperial temporality. In what follows, I explore two broad variations on this theme. In the first, the empire was figured as uniquely progressive, as capable – either in actuality or *in potentia* – of avoiding the social, economic and political dynamics that had annihilated all previous examples. This argument was most frequently employed in relation to India. The other strategy was to maintain that the empire (or a part of it) was not really an empire at all, an argument that was increasingly applied to Britain and its settler colonies in the last three decades of the century. Greater Britain could attain permanence, a kind of historical grace.

Imperial discourse was diffused across mediums and articulated in a variety of registers. It was expressed in treatises, pamphlets, articles and editorials; encrypted in literature and the visual arts; and encoded in the built environment and soundscapes. It was braided through the emerging human sciences. Yet it is important to remember that many of the most important commentators on empire had little, if any, connection with universities or with particular scholarly traditions. Among the most influential were the proconsuls: men such as Cromer, Curzon and Milner. Others were poets: Tennyson and Kipling above all. Others still made their living in the precincts of Westminster, including Cobden, Gladstone, Disraeli and Salisbury. Scholars played an important role, though it was only in the final two decades of the century that the human sciences emerged as a relatively coherent assemblage of scholarly disciplines, sustained by their own specialist journals, bolstered by a stream of academic appointments, and legitimated by their own distinct norms.[9] Many of the most influential scholars of empire – including Bryce and Maine – juggled various public roles, spending only part of their working lives in universities.[10] Others never held formal academic positions: John Stuart Mill, Thomas Babington Macaulay, Herbert Spencer, Karl Marx, James Fitzjames Stephens, J. A. Hobson and E. G. Wakefield, to name but a few. We can thus draw a distinction between discourses and disciplines. The academic disciplines that emerged towards the end of the century drew on, and often radically modified, pre-existing scholarly

[9] On the imperial history of universities, see Tamsin Pietsche, *Empire of Scholars: Universities, Networks and the British Academic World, 1850–1939* (Manchester: Manchester University Press, 2013).

[10] Thus Bryce was, amongst other things, Regius Professor of Civil Law at Oxford; a Liberal MP, cabinet minister and peer; Ambassador to the United States; journalist; and historian. Maine, meanwhile, was Regius Professor of Civil Law at Cambridge, an editor and journalist in London, Legal Member of the Governor-General's Council in India (Calcutta), Corpus Professor of Jurisprudence at Oxford and Master of Trinity Hall, Cambridge. Their milieu is evoked wonderfully in Stefan Collini, *Public Moralists: Political Thought and Intellectual Life in Britain, 1850–1930* (Oxford: Clarendon, 1991).

discourses. Indeed, as we shall see, the knowledge produced in them began to challenge some existing modes of scholarly imperial legitimation while establishing or reinforcing others. In terms of empire, the most significant of the discourses-cum-disciplines were anthropology, political economy, international law and history. Since an adequate survey of the impact of empire on the human sciences would fill a large volume, in what follows I concentrate on the relationship between competing conceptions of historical temporality that infused debate across, between and beyond the human sciences, and focus, though not exclusively, on the writings of historians.

The Time of Empire: Narratives of Decline of Fall

Understandings of the past played a formative role in the construction, elaboration and defence of political arguments in Victorian Britain, and it was widely assumed that a proper appreciation of the vicissitudes of history could impart wisdom and sound judgement. The 'English', J. R. Seeley observed in 1880, 'guide ourselves in the great political questions by great historical precedents'.[11] The ancient world provided a common frame of reference, and a repertoire of images and arguments, for a classically educated intellectual elite to navigate contemporary culture and politics, and it played a privileged role in thinking about the nature and consequences of imperial rule.[12] Yet the Victorians disagreed profoundly over which particular lessons to draw from which particular pasts, and the meaning of history became a topic of intense ideological contestation.

They inherited – and sought to recalibrate or transvalue – one of the most venerable Western accounts of historical temporality. The *topos* of imperial decline and fall had for centuries shaped understandings of empire and the principles underlying historical development. The *Imperium romanum*, Anthony Pagden reminds us, 'has always had a unique

---

[11] Seeley, 'Political Somnambulism', *Macmillan's Magazine*, 43 (1880), 32. See John Burrow, *A Liberal Descent: Victorian Historians and the English Past* (Cambridge: Cambridge University Press, 1981); Burrow, *Whigs and Liberals: Continuity and Change in English Political Thought* (Oxford: Oxford University Press, 1988).

[12] There is a huge literature on Victorian appropriations of the classics. For a recent account, see Simon Goldhill, *Victorian Culture and Classical Antiquity: Art, Opera, Fiction and the Proclamation of Modernity* (Princeton: Princeton University Press, 2012). See also Frank Turner, *The Greek Heritage in Victorian Britain* (London: Yale University Press, 1984); Richard Jenkyns, *The Victorians and Ancient Greece* (Oxford: Blackwell, 1980); Norman Vance, *The Victorians and Ancient Rome* (Oxford: Blackwell, 1997); Christopher Stray, *Classics Transformed: Schools, Universities, and Society in England, 1830–1960* (Oxford: Clarendon, 1998).

place in the political imagination of western Europe,' infusing visions of
self, society, and state, and it supplied 'the ideologies of the colonial
systems of Spain, Britain, and France with the language and political
models they requires.'[13] The Romans had bequeathed modern Europeans an evocative narrative of self-dissolution: the drive for expansion
corrupted the polity and inevitably led to disaster. Drawing on the history
of Rome as mediated by Sallust and Polybius, Machiavelli had argued in
his *Discourses on Livy* that states would inexorably seek to expand, but in
so doing would forfeit their liberty before collapsing under the moral and
constitutional strain of the quest for *grandezza*.[14] Subsequent critics of
imperialism, including Montesquieu, Hume, Kant, Robertson and Constant, likewise pointed to the moral and physical collapse of Rome to
warn of a comparable fate for those who pursued rapacious military
policies. Edward Gibbon's *History of the Decline and Fall of the Roman
Empire* imprinted the narrative deeply into British historical consciousness: the disintegration of Rome 'was the natural and inevitable effect of
immoderate greatness'.[15] According to Seeley, Regius Professor of
Modern History at Cambridge and the most significant imperial ideo-
logue of late Victorian Britain,

Every historical student knows that it was the incubus of the Empire which
destroyed liberty at Rome. Those old civic institutions, which had nursed
Roman greatness and to which Rome owed all the civilisation which she had to
transmit to the countries of the West, had to be given up as a condition of
transmitting it. She had to adopt an organisation of, comparatively, a low type.
Her civilisation, when she transmitted it, was already in decay.[16]

---

[13] Anthony Pagden, *Lords of All the World: Ideologies of Empire in Spain, Britain, and France,
c.1500–1800* (London: Yale University Press, 1998), p. 11.

[14] Machiavelli, *Discourses on Livy*, ed. Julia Conaway Bondanella and Peter Bondanella
(Oxford: Oxford University Press, 1997), Bk II. See also David Armitage, 'Empire and
Liberty: A Republican Dilemma' in Martin van Gelderen and Quentin Skinner, eds.,
Republicanism: A Shared European Heritage (Cambridge: Cambridge University Press,
2002), II, pp. 29–46; J. G. A. Pocock, *Barbarism and Religion*, Vol. 3 (Cambridge:
Cambridge University Press, 2003), esp. Parts III–V.

[15] Gibbon, *The History of the Decline and Fall of the Roman Empire*, ed. J. B. Bury (London:
Methuen, 1905), IV, p. 161. Gibbon, though, made little of the connection between the
British and Roman Empires. John Robertson argues that he was more interested in the
fate of universal monarchy. Robertson, 'Gibbon's Roman Empire as a Universal
Monarchy' in Rosamond McKitterick and Roland Quinault, eds., *Edward Gibbon and
Empire* (Cambridge: Cambridge University Press, 1997), pp. 247–71. On the popularity
of the trope, see Vance, *The Victorians and Ancient Rome*, pp. 234–5; Richard Hingley,
Roman Officers and English Gentlemen (London: Routledge, 2000), ch. 3; Jenkyns, *The
Victorians and Ancient Greece*, pp. 73–7.

[16] Seeley, *The Expansion of England: Two Courses of Lectures* (London: Macmillan, 1883),
p. 246.

The 'discourse of the inevitable rise and fall of empires is', Julia Hell argues, 'always already part of all acts of imperial mimesis, of their imaginaries and specific articulations of space and time'.[17] During the Victorian era, the long-standing intellectual dependence on Rome was constantly renegotiated and sometimes rejected entirely.

The combination of narrative simplicity and analytical ambiguity helps explain the powerful resonance of the Roman story. At least three distinct (though often overlapping) interpretations of decline and fall percolated through Victorian political culture. First, it was frequently argued that Rome had collapsed as a result of the corrupting power of luxury – moral debilitation translating into political cataclysm. This was the most widely accepted plotline for much of the century, dominating both scholarly interpretation and vernacular narratives.[18] It was favoured by radical critics of empire, who stressed the potential dangers of aristocratic nabobs returning from colonial service and threatening British political virtue. 'Is it not just possible', asked Richard Cobden in 1860, 'that we may become corrupted at home by the reaction of arbitrary political maxims in the East upon our domestic politics, just as Greece and Rome were demoralized by their contact with Asia?'[19] Goldwin Smith – one-time Regius Professor of Modern History at Oxford – worried about the political influence that wealthy Anglo-Indians, used to governing in a despotic polity, might wield on their return to Britain. The danger to the British national character was clear: 'No political character could be stronger or more confirmed than that of the Roman, yet by Empire it was radically changed.'[20] Marshalling the authority of Gibbon (while ignoring his conclusions), Herbert Spencer claimed that 'in a conspicuous manner Rome shows how ... a society which enslaves other societies enslaves itself'. Extirpating the freedom of conquered peoples invariably corroded the freedom of the conquerors. 'And now what is the lesson?' he demanded. 'Is it that in our own case Imperialism and Slavery, everywhere else and at all times united, are not to be united?' Unfortunately, he complained, 'Most will say Yes.'[21] But the trope could also be deployed for imperialist purposes. In 1885 Montagu Burrows, Professor

[17] Hell, 'The Twin Towers of Anselm Kiefer and the Trope of Imperial Decline', *Germanic Review*, 84/1 (2009), 86.
[18] Linda Dowling, 'Roman Decadence and Victorian Historiography', *Victorian Studies*, 28 (1985), 579–608.
[19] Cobden, cited in Klaus Knorr, *British Colonial Theories, 1570–1850* (London: Frank Cass, 1963 [1944]), p. 359.
[20] Smith, 'Policy', 308.
[21] Spencer, 'Imperialism and Slavery,' in Spencer, *Facts and Comments* (New York: Appleton, 1902), pp. 162, 165. He traces the consequences in 'Re-barbarization' (pp. 172–88).

of History at Oxford, warned that the 'danger of our not perceiving our real position is exactly the same as was experienced by the old Roman Empire. The decay of the centre gradually makes its way to the extremities; and these drop off, one by one, till the seat of the Empire itself, unprotected and forlorn, goes down in the general crash.'[22] It could likewise serve as a salutary warning that the problem was not empire itself but 'imperialism' – a militant, territorially rapacious creed. With Disraeli in mind, W. E. Gladstone warned that like Rome, 'England, which has grown so great, may easily become little; through the effeminate selfishness of luxurious living; through neglecting realities at home to amuse herself everywhere else in stalking phantoms'.[23] The trope was politically indeterminate, available to both critics of empire and its supporters.

A second account argued that imperial overstretch was to blame. Once again, though, the image could also be employed by imperialists to caution against ignoring the teachings of history. 'I am amused at the people who call themselves Imperialists', wrote William Harcourt, a leading Liberal politician, for 'I always remember the first pages in Gibbon on the "moderation of Augustus," in which he shows how for the first two centuries of the greatest and wisest Empire that ever existed the cardinal principle was the non-extension of Empire, and whenever it was departed from they came to grief.'[24] Although he noted the role played by the 'moral decay' generated by excess luxury in the fall of Rome, Seeley argued that the main problem was the lack of military manpower brought about by over-ambitious expansion.[25] Robert Lowe, a leading British liberal politician, suggested that the Roman precedent, and in particular the transition from the republic to the empire, taught important lessons. 'This signal and prerogative instance, to which it would be easy to add many others, seems to show that when a nation has attained a certain amount of freedom and self-government, no step can be more fatal than a career of successful conquests.'[26] Two decades

---

[22] Burrows, 'Imperial Federation', *National Review*, 4 (1884–5), 369. An undistinguished historian, Burrows was Chichele Professor of Modern History at Oxford from 1862 to 1900.

[23] Gladstone, 'England's Mission', *Nineteenth Century*, 4 (1878), 584.

[24] Harcourt, letter to Rosebery (27 September 1892) in A. G. Gardiner, *Life of Sir William Harcourt* (London: Constable, 1923), II, p. 197. Widely distrusted by imperialists, Harcourt was Chancellor of the Exchequer in 1886 and again in 1892–5

[25] Seeley, 'Roman Imperialism, II', *Macmillan's Magazine*, 20 (1869), 54, 47–8. However, he was not consistent on this point (cf. Seeley, *Natural Religion* (London: Macmillan, 1882), p. 237).

[26] Lowe, 'Imperialism', *Fortnightly Review*, 24 (1878), reprinted in P. J. Cain, ed., *Empire and Imperialism: The Debate of the 1870s* (Bristol: Thoemmes, 1999), p. 265. See also the warning in Frederic Seebohm, 'Imperialism and Socialism', *Nineteenth Century* (1880), in Cain, *Empire*, p. 309.

later, Herbert Samuel, 'new liberal' thinker and later a senior politician, reiterated the point. History demonstrated, he admitted, that every previous example had 'decayed and was dissolved', but the lesson he drew from this was not that imperial activity was necessarily doomed, but rather that consolidation was preferable to further territorial conquest: 'Expansion that is too rapid and too wide may open the door to all three of the causes which, singly or in combination, have brought the downfall of the empires that have preceded – attack from without, revolt from within, disunion and weakness at the centre.' Benjamin Franklin, he continued,

> in one of the darkest times of our history, offered to furnish Gibbon with materials for a new work, on the 'Decline and Fall of the British Empire.' Four generations have passed since then, and events have not given room for a book on that subject. But if in a later day some historian is called upon to take up this melancholy task, it may well be that he would have to write down an excess of ambition as the chief cause of decay, and to point out that the most fatal danger which had faced the British Empire had been an over-fervent imperialism among the British people.[27]

Finally, it was argued that the over-centralisation of Roman institutions, and the concentration of power in the hands of the few, led to eventual collapse. This had been a major theme in Montesquieu's pioneering *Considerations on the Causes of the Greatness of the Romans and their Decline* (1734). In *Imperium et Libertas* (1901), Bernard Holland likewise argued that Rome had been destroyed by the degeneration brought about through centralisation. 'The Roman Empire perished not from over-greatness but from over-centralization, and the destruction of the provinces in favour of the metropolis.' Yet he concluded on an optimistic note: the 'failure of the Roman experiment does not prove that an empire which avoided this peril might not beneficially endure for a much longer period'.[28]

The Greek model of colonisation presented an alternative conception of political termination. 'The ancient Greek city', explained Holland, 'when its population became too large for its rocky island or edge of mainland shore, sent out a colony as a beehive sends out a swarm. The colonists took possession of a new territory and there built a city,

---

[27] Samuel, *Liberalism: The Principles and Proposals of Contemporary Liberalism in England* (London: Richards, 1902), pp. 342–3.

[28] Holland, *Imperium et Libertas: A Study in History and Politics* (London: Arnold, 1901), pp. 13–14 (though cf. his extended comparison of Rome and Britain, pp. 265–9). Holland was a barrister. The book was reviewed positively in the *Political Science Quarterly* by the classicist John Finley and in the *American Historical Review* by the historian A. L. Lowell.

maintaining a pious regard, except when interests clashed, for the Mother City, but not a true political connection.' This system, noted Seeley, 'gives complete independence to the colony, but binds it in perpetual alliance'.[29] It allowed for successful expansion without the internally corrosive dynamics of empire. This prospect appealed to many early Victorians, and in particular those associated with the vocal 'colonial reform' movement, prominent from the 1820s until the 1840s. Indeed, in a survey written in 1856, Arthur Mills observed that the 'model of Colonial policy most frequently and prominently exhibited for the emulation of modern States is that of Greece'.[30] The Roman alternative was, James Mill had argued in 1823, 'so very defective', for in it the 'Few' dominated the 'Many' to such an extent that expansion was pursued only in the interests of the aristocratic class. Mill and assorted radical 'reformers' thus argued that the Greek style of colonisation, premised on peopling distant lands and establishing self-governing communities with strong affective ties to the 'mother country', offered a more suitable model to emulate – although they were generally loath to demand immediate independence for the colonies.[31] In the 1840s John Stuart Mill eulogised the Greek colonies, praising them for 'flourishing so rapidly and so wonderfully' and for guaranteeing freedom, order and progress, and he argued that they served as an excellent template for British colonisation.[32] The philosophic radical MP J. A. Roebuck sang a similar tune. 'Their colonies', he wrote, 'were very unlike those of the Roman', and had far more in common with modern British experience. In particular, the Greeks were bound by a 'gentle, kindly tie' between the 'mother city' and her colonial offspring, of the kind 'we also wish to exist, and we endeavour to create'.[33] The reformers drew inspiration from the classics even as they made arguments structured by post-Smithian political economy and Benthamite utilitarianism.

The popularity of the Greek model waned from the 1870s onwards as advocates of Greater Britain sought to forge a permanent political union

[29] Holland, *Imperium et Libertas*, p. 15; Seeley, *Expansion of England*, p. 69.
[30] Mills, *Colonial Constitutions* (London: Murray, 1856), pp. xix–xx.
[31] Mill, 'Colony', in *Essays from the Supplement to the Encyclopedia Britannica, Collected Works* (London: Thoemmes, 1995), pp. 4, 5–9.
[32] Mill, 'Wakefield's 'The New British Province of South Australia'' in *The Examiner*, 20 July 1843, reprinted in John Robson, ed., *The Collected Works of John Stuart Mill*, 33 vols. (Toronto: University of Toronto Press, 1963–1991), XXIII, p. 739. For his admiration of the 'Greek empire' see 'Grote's *History of Greece*', II, [1853], *Works*, XI, pp. 321–4. See also Duncan Bell, 'John Stuart Mill on Colonies', *Political Theory*, 38 (2010), 34–64.
[33] Roebuck, *The Colonies of England* (London: Parker, 1849), p. 138. The utilitarians' views on Greece were shaped heavily by George Grote's seminal *History of Greece* (1846–56).

between Britain and the settler colonies. For the pugnacious historian E. A. Freeman, this unionist vision clashed disastrously with a proper understanding of colonisation. He argued that although the British colonies had much in common with their esteemed Greek predecessors, there was one crucial difference: they were not *ab initio* independent. Under the Greek system, the 'metropolis claimed at most a certain filial respect, a kind of religious reverence, which was for the most part freely given', which meant that arguments propounding an indissoluble Greater Britain were conceptually flawed and historically naive. 'Let us at least remember that what is proposed is unlike anything that ever happened in the world before.'[34] Instead, he was happy to advocate the independence of the settler colonies. In an obituary note, Bryce observed that 'the analogy of the Greek colonies' helped motivate Freeman's scathing criticisms of the imperial unionists. 'He appeared to think that the precedent of those settlements showed the true and proper relation between a "metropolis" and her colonies to be not one of political interdependence, but of cordial friendship and a disposition to render help, nothing more.'[35] History could not be ignored.

Traditional accounts of decline and fall were supplemented by distinctively nineteenth-century concerns. One of the most influential was sketched by C. H. Pearson, an historian and radical Australian politician, in his best-selling *National Life and Character* (1894). The text drew less on ancient precedent than on widespread anxieties about geopolitical exhaustion, and above all the potential role-reversal of the global racial hierarchy.[36] Only the year before, Frederick Jackson Turner had warned that the closing of the American frontier would dissipate the creative energies of American democracy.[37] Pearson alerted his readers to a similar process writ global, as the Western empires, Britain foremost among them, would be undermined by their own success. They were programmed to fail. After spreading civilisation to the rest of the world, the imperial powers would be thrown back onto their own continent by ungrateful subjects, and as a result their vitality would be sapped. Torpor, luxury and decline would follow. This account both drew on

---

[34] Freeman, 'Imperial Federation', *Macmillan's Magazine*, 51 (1885), 436 and 437–8. See also Freeman, *History of Federal Government* (London: Macmillan, 1863), pp. 5–26.

[35] Bryce, 'Edward Augustus Freeman', *English Historical Review*, 7 (1892), 502.

[36] Pearson, *National Life and Character: A Forecast* (London: Macmillan, 1894). The book caused a sensation. Prior to his political career, Pearson was Professor of Modern History at King's College, London (1855–1865).

[37] Turner, 'The Significance of the Frontier in American History', in J. M. Faragher, ed., *Rereading Frederick Jackson Turner* (London: Yale University Press, 1998). Jackson's frontier thesis is cited in Lord Curzon of Kedleston, *Frontiers* (Oxford: Clarendon, 1907), p. 56.

and subverted progessivist justifications of empire. While Pearson regarded empire as an agent of progress, the combination of imperial blowback and the exhaustion of planetary space meant that the future looked grim. Implicit in this argument were two claims: first, that other, perhaps less enlightened, forms of empire may be capable of reaching escape velocity, and second, that if only new spaces could be found, the restless dynamism of empire could be effectively channelled in their direction. It was this kind of thought, perhaps, that found expression in Cecil Rhodes' famous proclamation that he would annex the planets if he could.[38] By the turn of the twentieth century, then, classical accounts of imperial corruption had been reinforced by anxieties about national and racial degeneration.

The Victorians absorbed two divergent lessons about empire from their reflections on ancient history. In one of them, inherited from centuries of Western political thought, history taught that imperial decline and fall was inevitable. Both the empire and the British state would be emasculated. The other lesson, more popular and widely disseminated, allowed for the possibility of imperial redemption. Decline was *possible* but not *inevitable*; the future was open. Human choice – political decision – was assigned a central role, one that imperialists emphasized repeatedly. Though haunted by the image of failure, they were rarely fatalists.

Harnessing the 'Time Spirit': On Imperial Progress

Meditating on his long life during the dark years of the First World War, the liberal historian and politician Viscount Morley remarked that the nineteenth century had seen belief in progress emerge as the 'basis of social thought', even supplanting religion as the 'inspiring, guiding, and testing power over social action'. Progress, he mused, could be seen as the 'Time Spirit' of the modern world.[39] Soon after he penned those words, the first English-language history of the idea appeared. Its author, J. B. Bury, a prodigiously gifted historian and classicist, defined progress in appropriately capacious terms as the view that 'civilization has moved, is moving, and will move, in a desirable direction', where the desire was identified as increased human happiness. A famous secularist, he too emphasised its theological tenor: 'The fate of an ultimate happy state on this planet, to be enjoyed for future generations, has replaced, as a social

[38] Rhodes, *The Last Will and Testament of Cecil J. Rhodes*, ed. W. T. Stead (London: Review of Reviews, 1902), p. 190.
[39] Morley, *Recollections* (London: Macmillan, 1917), II, pp. 27, 30.

power, the hope of felicity in another world.' Progress was, he declared, the 'animating and controlling idea of western civilization'.[40] Imperialists of different stripes adapted their visions to fit the *zeitgeist*, seeking to reconcile the possession of empire with the idea of constant human improvement. The most common way of doing so, of escaping the cycle of rise and decline, was to insist that the British imperial model was itself uniquely progressive, a global agent of human advance. Past experience meant nothing, except perhaps as a hortatory reminder about what not to do. Liberal empire was simultaneously a cause and a consequence of progress.

The uniqueness of the British model was a recurrent theme in imperial writings. Combining *imperium et libertas* (as Disraeli put it), the British had managed to merge stable rule, ordered freedom and beneficent civilisation into a single progressive ensemble.[41] The conjunction of altruistic civilising ambitions and a high degree of colonial self-government was routinely praised as an extraordinary, matchless achievement. It stood at the heart of the liberal imperial mission.[42] The British had cracked the temporal code. This 'civilised' and 'civilising' imperial formation could, if managed carefully, escape the fate of all previous empires. Or so it was claimed.

Karuna Mantena has recently questioned the durability of civilisational justifications of imperial rule. She argues that confidence in imperial progress was undercut by the Sepoy rebellion of 1857 and successive moments of resistance. On this account, crisis and progress were figured as irreconcilable, and a markedly different 'culturalist' narrative emerged, chiefly under the influence of the eminent comparativist Henry Maine. This picture emphasised the fragility of local communities, the sheer

---

[40] Bury, *The Idea of Progress: An Inquiry into Its Origin and Growth* (London: Macmillan, 1920), pp. 2, viii, vii.

[41] Disraeli coined the (ungrammatical) phrase in 1851: Jenkyns, *The Victorians and Ancient Greece*, p. 333. He claimed Roman pedigree when he reused it in 1879: Moneypenny and Buckle, *The Life of Benjamin Disraeli*, 6 vols. (London: John Murray, 1910–20), VI, p. 495. As Norman Vance notes, however, his attribution was mistaken. Cicero once wrote of *imperio ac liberte*, though he meant the power to uphold and enforce law, not territorial empire. Disraeli probably had Tacitus in mind, since he had famously been misquoted by Francis Bacon in *The Advancement of Learning* (1605), where *principatum ac libertatem* was rendered as *imperium et libertatem*, before being translated by Bolingbroke in *The Idea of a Patriot King* (1738) as 'Empire and Liberty'. Norman Vance, 'Anxieties of empire and the moral tradition: Rome and Britain,' International Journal of the Classical Tradition, 18/2 (2011), pp. 246–261. Disraeli's phrase was widely employed in British imperial debate: see, e.g., Freeman, 'Imperial Federation', 444; Spencer, 'Imperialism and Slavery', 117; Holland, *Imperium et Libertas*.

[42] See the discussion in Duncan Bell, 'Empire and Imperialism' in Gregory Claeys and Gareth Stedman Jones, eds., *The Cambridge History of Nineteenth Century Political Thought* (Cambridge: Cambridge University Press, 2012), pp. 864–91.

difficulty of transforming colonised spaces in the image of liberal modernity. Yet rather than necessitating retreat, it provided Maine and his followers with an 'alibi' for the prolongation of empire, because they argued that Western intervention had so weakened traditional communities that withdrawal would herald disaster. Valuable as it is in delineating Maine's position, this argument underestimates the continuities in British imperial discourse.[43] The civilising vision of empire remained a staple of British imperial ideology. In an address to the Imperial Institute in 1892, the historian W. E. H. Lecky sketched a typically Whiggish paean to the glories of imperial progress:

Remember what India had been for countless ages before the establishment of British rule. Think of its endless wars of race and creed, its savage oppressions, its fierce anarchies, its barbarous customs, and then consider what it is to have established for some many years over the vast space from the Himalayas to Cape Comorin a reign of perfect peace; to have conferred upon more than 250 millions of the human race perfect religious freedom, perfect security of life, liberty and property; to have planted in the midst of these teeming multitudes a strong central government, enlightened by the best knowledge of Western Europe, and steadily occupied in preventing famine, alleviating disease, extirpating savage customs, multiplying the agencies of civilization and progress.[44]

Samuel too was spouting a commonplace when, in 1902, he lavished praise on the civilising potential of imperialism. 'A barbarian race may prosper best if for a period, even for a long period, it surrenders the right of self-government in exchange for the teachings of civilization.'[45] It took the industrial slaughter of the First World War to create a significant transnational intellectual revolt that challenged the civilising mission, chiefly by questioning the link between technological development and moral progress.[46] But even that wasn't enough to derail the imperial desire to transform the world, which endured deep into the twentieth century (and beyond).

---

[43] See also P. J. Cain, 'Character, "Ordered Liberty", and the Mission to Civilise: British Moral Justification for Empire, 1870–1914', *Journal of Imperial and Commonwealth History*, 40/4 (2012), 557–78; Peter Mandler, 'Looking around the World' in Adelene Buckland and Sadiah Qureshi, eds., *Time Travelers* (Chicago: University of Chicago Press, forthcoming).

[44] Lecky, *The Empire: Its Value and Growth* (London: Longman's, 1893), pp. 44–5. One of the most influential historians of the age, Lecky never held a formal academic post, though he was offered (and declined) the Regius Professorship of Modern History at Oxford after Freeman's death in 1892. For an earlier version of the refrain, see James Fitzjames Stephen, 'Liberalism', *Cornhill Magazine*, 5 (1862), 32.

[45] Samuel, *Liberalism*, p. 330.

[46] Michael Adas, 'Contested Hegemony: The Great War and the Afro-Asian Assault on the Civilizing Mission Ideology', *Journal of World History*, 15/1 (2004), 31–63.

The claims of British exceptionalism traversed the political spectrum. Writing at the turn of the twentieth century, as controversy over the war in South Africa raged, Charles Beresford, Tory MP and Admiral in the Royal Navy, celebrated freedom as the unique gift of the British Empire. In standard Polybian vein, he catalogued the traditional causes of decline:

The great weakness of the nationalities which have been engulfed by the irresistible march of time has been the despotism which underlay their governments, the corruption which sapped their liberties, the luxury and indolence which ate into their vitality, and the remarkable fact that they became worn out and vicious, while the countries they had conquered, and the dependencies they had absorbed, at last broke away, imbued deeply with the vices and but few of the original virtues of the sovereign state.

Yet, Beresford maintained, such a fate was not inevitable – the 'irresistible march' could be halted. Through accident or design, the British had managed to create an empire that could avoid the fate that befell all others, ancient and modern. 'The Anglo-Saxon has so far, chiefly owing to the mixture of blood in his veins, kept alive side by side both the military and the commercial spirit; and it is this unique combination of talents which offers the best hopes for the survival of the Anglo-Saxon as the fittest of humanity to defy the decaying process of time.'[47] At the same time, the historian and classicist J. A. Cramb launched a spirited defence of the empire. A conservative militarist, Cramb glorified war and regarded violence as a purifying, righteous instrument.[48] Bathed in philosophical idealism, he conceived of empire as a metaphysical principle, the vehicle for reason in history. It was, above all, 'the highest expression of the soul of the State; it is the complete, the final consummation of the life of the State'. And the British Empire was insulated from troubling precedents. While the 'Roman ideal moulds every form of Imperialism in Europe, and even to a certain degree in the East, down to the eighteenth century', the British presented the world with a new model, 'not Roman, not Hellenic'. Its historical exceptionalism resided in the British emphasis on freedom and justice. 'From this thraldom to the past, to the ideal of Rome, Imperial Britain, first amongst modern empires, completely breaks.'[49] It was attuned to the time spirit.

[47] Beresford, 'The Future of the Anglo-Saxon Race', *North American Review*, 171/529 (1900), 803, 806.
[48] In Karma Nabulsi's terms, he can be seen as a 'martialist', one of the 'high priests of the temple of Janus' – a species quite common in German intellectual circles at the time, though rarer in Britain. Nabulsi, *Traditions of War: Occupation, Resistance and the Law* (Oxford: Oxford University Press, 1999), ch. 4.
[49] Cramb, *Reflections on the Origins and Destiny of Imperial Britain* (London: Macmillan, 1900), pp. 216, 18, 23. Cramb was Professor of History at Queen's College, London.

As Cramb was penning his encomium to imperial power, J. M. Robertson, a prominent radical liberal, scornfully dismissed the various imperialist attempts to escape the gravitational pull of Rome:

One of the most unpromising symptoms of our case is the uncomprehending way in which the British imperialist always scans the story of ancient Rome. Noting the decadence which is the upshot of the whole, he seems to suppose that somehow Christianity will avail to save later empires from the same fate, though Rome was Christianised during the decline; of happily the elimination of chattel slavery will avert decay, though Christian Spain was free from chattel slavery at home, or that industrialism will avail, though the Moors and the Florentines were tolerably industrial. Any theory will serve to burke the truth that the special cause of decay is just empire.[50]

Unmoved by special pleading on behalf of the British, Robertson insisted that empires always and everywhere ended in annihilation. Products of avarice and arrogance, they were destroyed by their own internal pathologies. 'For persistent empire in the end infallibly brings the imperator, be the process slow or speedy; and with the imperator comes in due time the decadence of empire, the humiliation and paralysis of the spirit that had aspired to humiliate its kind.'[51] He repeated the message in a scathing attack on the idealist philosopher D. G. Ritchie's defence of liberal civilising imperialism: 'It seems the more necessary to point out that the *pax Romana* was of old a plea for the kind of policy de-fended by our imperialists to-day; and that the pursuit of that policy meant the final conquest of Rome by its own brutality and moral barbarism as surely as the conquest of the surrounding world.'[52] Contra the reassuring fantasies of Cramb and Ritchie, this was the true destiny of imperial Britain.

Yet even for believers in imperial progress, the empire was always seen as fragile, beset by challengers and sceptics. They were haunted by intimations of imperial mortality. As Peter Cain has demonstrated, normative justifications of empire during the late nineteenth and early twentieth centuries depended on a complex dialectical dance of 'character'. It was frequently argued that British imperial greatness was largely the product of the superior character of its people, individual and collective, and that this greatness generated both the capacity (military and economic strength) and the moral obligation (to spread the benefits of

---

[50] Robertson, *Patriotism and Empire*, 3rd ed. (London: Grant Richards, 1900), p. 151.

[51] Robertson, *Patriotism and Empire*, p. 157.

[52] Robertson, 'The Moral Problems of War', *International Journal of Ethics*, 11/3 (1901), 283. Cf. Ritchie, 'War and Peace', *International Journal of Ethics*, 11/2 (1901), 137–58.

this character to others) undergirding the pursuit of empire.[53] Moreover, the practice of imperial governance fostered the very greatness on which empire depended. 'The creed of the ultra-imperialists could be simply expressed. "Character" ... had given Britain its empire and, without that empire, character would atrophy and die and Britain's moment of greatness would quickly pass.'[54] The dissolution of empire was not, as some radical critics argued, necessary to protect Britain from the corrosive dynamics of imperial rule – it would instead herald the ruination of Britain itself. John Ruskin's inaugural lecture as Slade Professor of the History of Art at Oxford in 1870 included a stirring call for further imperial conquest, as the only alternative was to 'perish'. 'She must found colonies as fast and as far as she is able.'[55] Expansion was the only way to avoid declension. 'If the empire should dissolve', Holland warned, 'England would doubtless decay and decline, exhausted by the effort of creating so many new states'.[56] A process of *imperial involution* beckoned, the dismantling of the periphery leading inexorably to the degeneration of the metropole.

The universities were central to sustaining the civilisational endeavour, with the classics and history assigned a pivotal role. Oxford, above all, was a site of imperial pedagogic zeal.[57] From the 1850s, Benjamin Jowett, classicist and Master of Balliol, had been instrumental in directing graduates to the Indian Civil Service (ICS), the entrance examinations for which placed great emphasis on knowledge of the classics.[58] The effects were palpable. Between 1874 and 1914, 27.1 per cent of Balliol graduates went to work in the ICS, while between 1888 and 1905 three successive viceroys of India were products of the College. The bequest of Cecil Rhodes, himself a proud Oxford product obsessed with the ancient world, only deepened the connections with the university.[59]

---

[53] For relevant philosophical discussion of the civilizational obligations incurred by liberal empires, see J. H. Muirhead, 'What Imperialism Means', *Fortnightly Review*, 68 (1900), 177–87; Ritchie, 'War and Peace'.

[54] Cain, *Empire*, p. 269.

[55] E. T. Cook and A. Wedderburn, eds., *The Works of John Ruskin*, 39 vols. (London: George Allen, 1903–12), XX, p. 41. See also the *Stones of Venice* (1851) on how moral decline led to imperial collapse (*Works*, IX, p. 17).

[56] Holland, *Imperium et Libertas*, p. 265.

[57] Richard Symonds, *Oxford and Empire: The Last Lost Cause?* (Oxford: Clarendon, 1991).

[58] Phiroze Vasunia, *The Classics and Colonial India* (Oxford: Oxford University Press, 2013), ch. 5. Oxford graduates dominated the system (though Trinity, Dublin, also produced a disproportionate number of entrants): Symonds, *Oxford and Empire*, pp. 180–91. Jowett's project was continued by his successor at Balliol, J. L. Strachan Davidson.

[59] Philip Ziegler, *Legacy: Cecil Rhodes, the Rhodes Trust and Rhodes Scholarships* (London: Yale University Press, 2008). Unable to read the original languages, Rhodes employed a

Milner's 'Kindergarden', that group of thrusting young imperialists who played such a pivotal role in both the Round Table movement and the formation of the South African state, were virtually all Oxford-educated.[60] Indeed, in the early twentieth century, Alfred Zimmern revivified the tradition of yoking classical learning to imperial legitim-ation, presenting a modernising interpretation of ancient Athens which provided the intellectual inspiration for the 'commonwealth' vision of the British Empire articulated by Lionel Curtis.[61] In Cambridge, Henry Sidgwick tried to replicate the Oxford example, though with only mod-erate success.[62] Seeley's *Expansion of England* (1883), arguably the single most influential text on empire published in the second half of the century, was originally delivered as undergraduate lectures, though See-ley too was disappointed in his quest to turn the Cambridge History Faculty into a 'school of statesmanship'.[63] The importance of the univer-sities was acknowledged in 1907 when Curzon, in his Romanes Lecture at Oxford, called forth the spirit of imperial patriotism and demanded that the elite arrayed before him hold the line against the forces menacing Western civilisation.

To our ancient universities, revivified and re-inspired, I look to play their part in this national service. Still from the cloistered alleys and hallowed groves of Oxford ... let there come forth the invincible spirit and the unexhausted moral fibre of our race. Let the advance guard of Empire march forth, strong in the faith of their ancestors, imbued with sober virtue, and above all, on fire with a definite purpose.[64]

team of classicists to translate all of the references found in Gibbon's *Decline and Fall*, as well as numerous other classical texts, an exercise in historical recovery that filled over two hundred volumes in his personal library. See Victoria Tietze Larson, 'Classics and the Acquisition and Validation of Power in Britain's 'Imperial Century' (1815–1914)', *International Journal of the Classical Tradition*, 6/2 (1999), 211.

[60] On the Kindergarten, see Symonds, *Oxford and Empire*; John Kendle, *The Round Table Movement and Imperial Union* (Toronto: University of Toronto Press, 1975).

[61] Zimmern, *The Greek Commonwealth: Politics and Economics in Fifth Century Athens* (Oxford: Clarendon, 1911). He was later appointed to the first chair of International Relations in the world, at the University of Wales, Aberystwyth, before returning to an IR chair at Oxford. See Jeanne Morefield, '"An Education To Greece": The Round Table, Political Theory, and the Uses of History', *History of Political Thought*, 28 (2007), 328–61; Tomohito Baji, 'Commonwealth: Alfred Zimmern and World Citizenship', PhD thesis, University of Cambridge (2015).

[62] John Burrow, Stefan Collini and Donald Winch, *That Noble Science of Politics: A Study in Nineteenth-Century Intellectual History* (Cambridge: Cambridge University Press, 1983), pp. 354–5.

[63] On Seeley's vision, see Duncan Bell, 'John Robert Seeley and the Political Theology of Empire' in Bell, *Reordering the World: Essays on Liberalism and Empire* (Princeton: Princeton University Press, 2016); Deborah Wormell, *Sir John Seeley and the Uses of History* (Cambridge: Cambridge University Press, 1980).

[64] Curzon, *Frontiers*, pp. 57–8.

Empire, then, was a bulwark against degeneration, that insidious fear stalking *fin de siècle* Victorian culture, while the elite universities were construed as institutions to foster the imperial virtues necessary to counter the threat.

But even as the universities produced a steady stream of recruits for the empire, they were also producing knowledge that ultimately, though often unintentionally, helped to undermine some traditional narratives of imperial legitimation. The closing decades of the nineteenth century witnessed a tectonic shift in the scholarship on Rome. For much of the Victorian era, the popular mythopoeic narrative of decline and fall – and above all the moralised account of corruption and decay – had been bolstered by scholarly authority. So too was the idea that the Roman world taught immediate and pertinent lessons for the present. Niebuhr's *Römische Geschicte* exerted a huge influence in the middle decades of the nineteenth century, helping to (re)establish for the nineteenth century the 'plot of Roman history as the recurrent story of the world'.[65] In Britain, a series of liberal Anglican writers, including Thomas Arnold and Charles Merivale, followed Niebuhr's example in seeking to collapse the historical distance between the ancient and modern worlds, divining lessons for the latter from the vicissitudes of the former. Their narratives of ancient Rome were infused with a moral vision of the cycles through which all polities moved.[66] But the credibility of this approach was challenged by the great German scholar Theodor Mommsen, whose work began to circulate in the 1850s. Providentialism was gradually superseded by a model of historical positivism, whose proponents celebrated its purported objectivity and scientific superiority over earlier, primitive accounts. In Britain, this ambition was realised above all in the writings of Bury, Acton's successor at Cambridge.[67] In addressing the purported connection between Rome and Britain, Bury insisted that 'luxury and immorality do not constitute, and need not be symptoms of, a disease that is fatal to the life of States'. He then condemned 'all reasoning founded on historical analogy' as 'futile'.[68]

[65] Dowling, 'Roman Decadence', 595. Dowling gives an excellent account of the shift in scholarly practices.
[66] Duncan Forbes, *The Liberal Anglican Idea of History* (Cambridge: Cambridge University Press, 1952). See also Brian Young's chapter in this volume.
[67] Dowling, 'Roman Decadence.'
[68] Bury, 'The British Empire and the Roman Empire', *Saturday Review*, 27 June (1896), 645. Bury later revolted against his earlier positivism, developing a theoretical understanding of history based on contingency and rejection of the ability to discern general patterns of cause and effect. *Selected Essays of J.B. Bury*, ed. Howard Temperley (Cambridge: Cambridge University Press, 1930), chs. 1–5. This shift is traced in R. G. Colingwood's review (*English Historical Review*, 43/186 (1931), 461–5).

The British exceptionalism thesis was reinforced by a burst of prominent writings comparing the Roman and British empires that appeared after 1900. The main examples were James Bryce's long essay on 'The Ancient Roman Empire and the British Empire in India'; *Ancient and Modern Imperialism*, a short tract written by Evelyn Baring, the Earl of Cromer, one-time British consul-general in Egypt who then served as President of the Classical Association; and C. P. Lucas's *Greater Rome and Greater Britain*, the product of an imperial administrator turned Oxford don.[69] All drew, to varying degrees, on the shift in scholarship. While Bryce, Baring and Lucas would have demurred from Bury's strident denial of the value of historical analogies, they were adamant that the Roman and British empires were divided by far more than they shared. This act of disavowal served an important ideological function, allowing them to celebrate the unique virtues and continuing vitality of the British empire. All suggested that the British Empire escaped the worst aspects of the Roman precedent – its despotism, its political centralisation, its crude militarism and absence of economic creativity. Lucas, for example, asserted that 'loss of freedom' cemented the unity of the Roman Empire, whereas the diffuse British Empire became ever more decentralised 'as freedom has grown'.[70] Meanwhile, Cromer, writing in a symposium on his work, stressed the radical difference between the ancient and modern worlds: 'The records of the ancient world may be searched in vain for any guidance to show whether modern democracy ... is capable of sustaining the burthens of Empire at all.'[71] These authors presented an empire committed to freedom and justice, driven (in the present at least) by largely humanitarian impulses and ruling in a civilising manner. This allowed them to stress British superiority over even the greatest of their predecessors. The only area where the Romans were more successful was their ability to 'assimilate' different conquered races.[72] Yet here too the point was framed to signal the ultimate greatness of the British, for Roman success was largely dismissed as the product of a smaller, less complex and more racially homogeneous world. The British faced difficulties because their ambition and reach were all the grander. The simple message conveyed by the

---

[69] Bryce, 'The Ancient Roman Empire and the British Empire in India' in Bryce, *Studies in History and Jurisprudence* (Oxford: Clarendon, 1901), pp. 1–71; Baring, *Ancient and Modern Imperialism* (London: John Murray, 1910); Lucas, *Greater Rome and Greater Britain* (Oxford: Clarendon, 1912).

[70] Lucas, *Greater Rome*, p. 141.

[71] Cromer, 'History and Politics', *Classical Review*, 24 (1910), 116.

[72] Lucas, *Greater Rome*, pp. 91–112; see also Bryce, 'The Ancient Roman Empire', 54–63; Baring, *Ancient and Modern*, pp. 72–95.

texts was that the British had, uniquely among empires, escaped the gravitational pull of history. Rome offered little but forewarning. All three authors were also clear about the appropriate object of analysis, insisting that only India was suitable for comparison. Governed by radically different principles, the British settler colonies 'differ wholly in kind'.[73] Ontologically distinctive, they presented yet another way in which Victorians sought to circumvent the fate of empire.

The Transfiguration of Empire

One strategy that Victorian imperialists utilised to shed the weight of history was to argue that the British Empire, or parts of it, constituted a new type of political institution. This was a prominent theme in the late Victorian debates over 'Greater Britain', the totality of Britain and its settler colonies in Canada, Australia and New Zealand. It was not simply the case that Britain had developed a progressive form of imperialism, supposedly enacted in India and elsewhere, but also that it now also governed a vast *post-imperial* political community. The discourse contained two basic claims about novelty. The first recognised that Greater Britain formed an integral part of the wider empire, but that it was nevertheless a new kind of political structure, able to escape the dynamics of declension. Its uniqueness, it was commonly asserted, resided in the degree of political freedom accorded to its (white) inhabitants. The other denied that Greater Britain was an empire at all. While it had originated as part of an imperial order, it was now assuming a completely new form, transfigured from empire to state (or commonwealth). On either account, Greater Britain was a unique phenomenon that could be inserted into a progressive narrative of historical development.

At mid-century, Arthur Mills had observed that all of recorded history showed the pattern of imperial 'dismemberment and decay' resulting in eventual 'dissolution'. 'Is there any known principle of political life', he enquired, 'which history permits us to hope will be exceptional and peculiar to that cluster of communities which now own the rule of England?' He answered in the affirmative. Political de-centralisation, and above all the granting of self-government to the colonies, allowed the process of decay to be circumvented.[74] Later imperial unionists sought to harness this freedom in an overarching political structure. Half a century after Mills had praised the potential of self-government,

[73] Lucas, *Greater Rome*, p. 142; see also Bryce, 'The Ancient Roman Empire', 4–6; Baring, *Ancient and Modern*, pp. 17–18.
[74] Mills, *Colonial Constitutions*, pp. xxxix–xl.

Holland argued that the British could escape the fate of Rome because
they had avoided destructive over-centralisation. Sacrificing 'imperium'
in favour of more extensive 'libertas', they had saved the empire from
the clutches of time. 'In the British empire, apart from India, we have
learned ... to concede to the Colonies the fullest liberty consistent with
the maintenance of a common tie.'[75] 'The British Empire of to-day, it
cannot be too often repeated', intoned Hugh Egerton, another prominent historian of empire, 'is without precedent in the past'. The novelty,
he maintained, lay in the constitutional structure of Greater Britain, the
fact that the colonies had been granted 'responsible government'. In light
of this magnificent achievement, Egerton cautioned his readers against
drawing false inferences from the past: '[i]t is at once the glory and the
responsibility of nations that in their case, no ceaseless law of change is
operating, to make dissolution and decay inevitable. To each generation,
in its turn, is given the privilege and power to shape its own destinies.'[76]

For Seeley, the former professor of Latin and editor of Livy, the
ancient world did not present any important lessons for the 'boundless
expanses' of the settler colonies. In particular, viewing Britain as an heir
to Rome was a serious error.[77] In *The Expansion of England* he argued that
'[o]ur colonies do not resemble the colonies which classical students
meet with in Greek and Roman history, and our Empire is not an Empire
at all in the ordinary sense of the word'. There were various reasons for
this difference, including the 'ethnological unity' of the Greater British
population and the development of new communications technologies
that 'annihilated' time and space, facilitating the creation of a common
identity and enabling effective governance across planetary distances.[78]
This did not mean, however, that the classical world failed to offer Seeley
any insights into the patterns of contemporary international politics, for
the Roman archetype, he argued, bore some resemblance to the British
mode of rule in India. While the analogy was far from exact, they did
share the status of 'superior races' intent on 'civilising' those under their
control. As the Roman Empire in the West was 'the empire of civilisation

[75] Holland, *Imperium et Libertas*, p. 14.
[76] Egerton, *A Short History of Colonial Policy* (London, 1897), pp. 455, 478. At the time of
publication, Egerton worked in the Emigrants' Information Office. On the back of its
considerable success, he was elected (in 1905) the first Beit Professor of Colonial History
at Oxford. He retired in 1920.
[77] Seeley, 'Introduction' to *Her Majesty's Colonies* (London, 1886), p. xviii. For the
misleading argument that Seeley saw the British as heirs to Rome, see Reba Soffer,
'History and Religion', in R. W. Davis and R. J. Helmstadter, eds., *Religion and Irreligion
in Victorian Society* (London: Routledge, 1992), pp. 142–3; Hingley, *Roman Officers*,
pp. 24–5.
[78] On this central theme, see Bell, *The Idea of Greater Britain*, ch. 3.

over barbarism', so the British Empire in India was 'the empire of the modern world over the medieval'. Nevertheless, such comparisons had nothing to do with the settlement colonies.

> The colonies and India are in opposite extremes. Whatever political maxims are most applicable to one, are most inapplicable to the other. In the colonies everything is brand-new. There you have the most progressive race put in the circumstances most favourable to progress. There you have no past and an unbounded future. Government and institutions are all ultra-English. All is liberty, industry, invention, innovation, and as yet tranquillity.

India, though, 'is all past and, I may almost say, has no future'.[79] The British, then, governed spaces defined by two contrasting temporal regimes. One was characterised by novelty, creativity, movement and flux. Its boundless energies were perfectly suited for progressive historical development. The other was stagnant, immobile, rigid, and thus incapable of progress without exogenous shock. It was as if past and future co-existed in the same historical moment.

Many advocates of Greater Britain deliberately eschewed centuries of imperial political thought and the historicising trends of the time by actively dismissing the relevance of ancient empires for thinking about the future. They often sought authority in the image of America – a country that had, through the creation of a continental federal system, managed to solve many of the political problems facing the British.[80] Above all, the Americans taught that it was possible to sustain individual freedom in a vast polity. William Greswell, formerly a professor of Classics in South Africa, accentuated the fundamental differences between the ancient empires and the modern British and emphasised, echoing an argument made famous by Constant, the superiority of modern freedom: 'The Britannica *civitas* is a far wider, and we may be allowed to believe a far more honoured, privilege. It is a *civitas* built upon freedom not despotism, upon tolerance rather than upon force, upon voluntary effort and individual enterprise rather than upon bureaucratic orders and state diplomacy.' Greswell demanded a 'confederacy of the British race', but added the qualifier that it was foolhardy to 'refer for guidance to ancient or modern confederacies'. Rather, it was instructive to look to the edifying example set by the United States.[81]

---

[79] Seeley, *Expansion of England*, pp. 51, 244, 176.

[80] See Bell, *The Idea of Greater Britain*, ch. 9, for more detail. Contra Mark Bradley, I do not deny that ancient precedents had little or no impact in shaping visions of the British empire in general, only that advocates of Greater Britain tended to eschew them as institutional models to emulate. Bradley, 'Introduction' in Bradley, ed., *Classics and Imperialism in the British Empire* (Oxford: Oxford University Press, 2010), pp. 16–17.

[81] Greswell, 'Imperial Federation' in *England and Her Colonies* (London: Sonnenschein, 1887), p. 7.

The purportedly federal (or quasi-federal) character of Greater Britain meant that it was something wholly new. This was yet another expression of British imperial exceptionalism. In the *Considerations on Representative Government*, Mill had referred to the colonial empire as an 'unequal federation',[82] while four decades later Leonard Hobhouse talked of the 'loose, informal, quasi-Federalism of the British Colonial Empire', which he compared with the 'strict' American variant.[83] Some went as far as proclaiming that it already comprised a state – or, alternatively, that it should be transformed into one. Considered 'as a state', argued Seeley, 'England has left Europe altogether behind it and become a world-state'.[84] But this was only the beginning, and he called for the creation of a 'great and solid World-State', a vast enduring transoceanic polity.[85] The transmutation of empire into state implied by schemes for imperial federation was recognised by A. V. Dicey, the leading constitutional theorist in the empire, who complained that they called for a 'new federated state'.[86] In the Edwardian years, it was increasingly accepted that burgeoning colonial demands for national recognition and autonomy meant that a new form of political order had to be devised. The settler colonies could not be treated as imperial appendages. And so a more pluralistic commonwealth vision, centred on ideas about a multinational polity, began to eclipse the Seeleyan global nation-state. State and nation were decoupled. In 1905 W. F. Monypenny, a leading journalist with the *Times*, conceived of the empire as a 'world state', a polity defined by cultural homogeneity and unity of interests. This was, he claimed, the embodiment of a 'new political conception' which 'transcends nationality' while simultaneously allowing the flourishing of separate nationalities within it.[87] Leo Amery, meanwhile, wrote of the colonial empire as a 'single united whole, a great world-State, composed of equal and independent yet indissolubly united States'. This was, he proclaimed, a 'new ideal', a 'great federation' that corresponded to the

---

[82] Mill, Considerations on Representative Government [1861] in Mill, Collected Works, ed. J. Robson (Toronto: University of Toronto Press, 1977), XVIII, p. 565

[83] Hobhouse, *Democracy and Reaction*, ed. Peter Clarke (Brighton: Harvester, 1972 [1904]), p. 154. See also J. R. Seeley, 'Georgian and Victorian Expansion', *Fortnightly Review*, 48 (1887), 136.

[84] Seeley, *Expansion of England*, p. 293. See also Seeley, 'Georgian and Victorian Expansion', 133.

[85] Seeley, *Expansion of England*, pp. 169 & 75.

[86] Dicey, *Introduction to the Study of the Law of the Constitution*, 8th ed. (London: Macmillan, 1915), p. lxxxiv. Dicey presented his own vision of an Anglo-Saxon future, focusing on an Anglo-American 'isopolity' (a space of common citizenship). Duncan Bell, 'Beyond the Sovereign State: Isopolitan Citizenship, Race, and Anglo-American Union', *Political Studies*, 62/3 (2014), 418–34.

[87] Monypenny, 'The Imperial Ideal' in C. S. Goldman, ed., *The Empire and the Century* (London: Murray, 1905), pp. 23, 27.

'wider outlook and broader humanity of advancing civilization'.[88] The idea of an Anglo-Saxon commonwealth was also central to the Round Table movement during the Edwardian era and beyond.[89]

Other arguments stressed the priority of the periphery to the metropole. According to this picture, Britain may well be subject to decline, but the settler colonies, creative offspring of an old and vulnerable world, could escape that fate. They were the pioneers of progress. While Lecky was a true believer in the progressive nature of British imperialism, he still acknowledged the power of historical precedent: 'Nations, as history but too plainly shows, have their periods of decay as well as their periods of growth.' But even if Britain succumbed to decay, the future of the British 'race' was guaranteed, as it had spread beyond the confines of the homeland to occupy dynamic, prosperous colonies throughout the world. '[W]hatever fate may be in store for these Islands, we may at least confidently predict that no revolution in human affairs can now destroy the future ascendency of the English language and of the Imperial race.'[90] The (colonial) empire assured the permanence of the British people. This mirrored arguments that figured the colonies – above all New Zealand – as a utopia, a 'better Britain'.[91] The temporal dynamics of this trope were captured powerfully by Macaulay, in his famous depiction of the 'New Zealander'. In a review of Ranke's *The Ecclesiastical and Political History of the Popes of Rome*, he had marvelled at the longevity of the Catholic Church, its centuries of uninterrupted existence. In comparison, he suggested, other institutions seemed ephemeral: 'She [the Catholic Church] may still exist in undimmed vigour when some traveller from New Zealand shall, in the midst of the vast solitude, take his stand on a broken arch of London Bridge to sketch the ruin of St. Pauls.'[92] This image was later the subject of a haunting engraving by Gustave Dore, and became 'lodged in the collective cultural consciousness' of the Victorians.[93] It was the most famous Victorian instance of

---

[88] Amery, 'Imperial Defence and National Policy' in Goldman, ed., *Empire*, pp. 181–2.

[89] See, for example, Lionel Curtis, *The Problem of Commonwealth* (London: Macmillan, 1916), p. 68.

[90] Lecky, *Empire*, p. 47.

[91] Lyman Tower Sargent, 'Utopianism and the Creation of New Zealand National Identity', *Utopian Studies*, 12/1 (2001), 1–18.

[92] Macaulay, 'History of the Popes' (1840) in Macaulay, *Critical and Historical Essays*, ed. A. J. Grieve (London: Everyman, 1907), II, p. 39.

[93] Robert Dingley, 'The Ruins of the Future: Macaulay's New Zealander and the Spirit of the Age' in Dingley and Alan Sandison, eds., *Histories of the Future: Studies in Fact, Fantasy and Science Fiction* (Basingstoke: Palgrave, 2000), p. 16. For the image, see Gustave Doré and Blanchard Jerrold, *London: A Pilgrimage* (London: Grant, 1872), p. 188, or the cover of Bell, *The Idea of Greater Britain*. See also Julia Hell and Andreas Schonle, eds., *Ruins of Modernity* (Durham: Duke University Press, 2010).

what Julia Hell labels the 'scopic scenario', an image that both 'depicts
the imperial subject contemplating the ruins of empire' and simultaneously renders the 'trope of decline and fall visible'.[94] After spending
time in New Zealand, and in particular after inspecting its admirable
sanitation facilities, Froude proffered a quotidian response to Macaulay's
grandiose imperial metaphysics, concluding that 'I have come to believe
in that New Zealander since I have seen the country'.[95] Goldwin Smith
used it to draw a clear distinction between Britain and the empire,
one a site of productive energy, the other destined to follow the course
of history: 'There is no reason why British virtue, energy, and industry
should not continue as they are, or increase with the lapse of time; and
therefore, there is no reason why the New Zealander should ever moralize over the ruins of the British nation; but the man of the future, whoever
he may be, is pretty sure one day to moralize over the ruins of the British
Empire.' The lesson was clear: 'In England the strength of England
lies.'[96] Joseph Chamberlain, radical and Secretary of State for the Colonies, dismissed the metropolitan pessimism invoked by the image,
insisting that Britain and its empire were firmly embarked on a progressive trajectory: 'I do not ask you to anticipate with Lord Macaulay the
time when the New Zealander will come here to gaze upon the ruins of a
great dead city. There are in our present condition no visible signs of
decrepitude and decay.'[97] In the contest over the meaning of an image of
the future, we can divine the conflicting accounts of time structuring
imperial discourse.

Once again, the universities came to play a vital role in propagating imperial visions. Even as the latest wave of Roman scholarship was
beginning to undermine traditional narratives of luxury, decadence and
decline, so a new field of knowledge was beginning to emerge and others
were being revitalised. We have already seen how Zimmern helped to
inaugurate a renewed burst of Greek influence on imperial ideology.
Meanwhile, and despite his institutional failures at Cambridge, Seeley's
project to inject imperial history into the core of the discipline began to
bear fruit. During the early years of the twentieth century a new academic
field emerged, driven by a specific ideological purpose: to delineate
Greater Britain as a singular political unit and to insist on its central

[94] Hell, 'Katechon: Carl Schmitt's Imperial Theology and the Ruins of the Future',
    Germanic Review, 84 (2009), 284.
[95] Froude, *Oceana, or England and Her Colonies*, new ed. (London: Longman, 1888),
    pp. 236–7.
[96] Smith, 'Policy', 308.
[97] Chamberlain, 'The True Conception of Empire' (1897) in C. W. Boyd, ed.,
    Mr Chamberlain's Speeches (London: Constable, 1914), II, p. 5.

importance for the future of Britain. This vision motivated the endowment of the chairs of imperial history in Oxford, Cambridge and the University of London, and its intellectual inheritance persisted deep into the twentieth century.[98]

Conclusions

Throughout the Victorian age, commentators on empire wrestled with the meaning of history. This resulted in a clash between a progressive vision, in which the future was open, and a cyclical vision, in which empires followed pre-determined trajectories. Negotiating these temporal narratives required intellectual dexterity. Most advocates of empire acknowledged the previous cycles of imperial history, but suggested that there was something radically different about the age in which they lived and the kind of empire they defended. Avatars of progress, the British had managed to create a new form of empire, one that was not only compatible with a progressive understanding of human development, but which played a pivotal role in it. Critics demurred from this Panglossian view, suggesting that the British Empire was bound to follow the course of all others, and that in doing so it threatened the very things – liberty above all – which made Britain great in the first place. The muse of history whispered to the Victorians in different voices.

[98] Amanda Behm, 'The Bisected Roots of Imperial History: Settler World Projects and the Making of a Field in Modern Britain, 1883–1912', *Recherches Britanniques*, 1/1 (2011), 54–77.

Jennifer Pitts *

> It is only with the progressive societies that we are concerned, and
> nothing is more remarkable than their extreme fewness. In spite of
> overwhelming evidence, it is most difficult for a citizen of western
> Europe to bring thoroughly home to himself the truth that the
> civilisation which surrounds him is a rare exception in the history of
> the world.   Henry Maine, *Ancient Law* (1861)

Although international law in Victorian Britain was riven by some apparently profound theoretical divisions, between historical and analytical
approaches to jurisprudence and between naturalist and positivist commitments, Victorian international lawyers shared a set of historicist presuppositions that distinguished them from their eighteenth-century forebears
and that profoundly marked modern international law. These included,
above all, the belief that international law, although historically particular to Europe, was prospectively authoritative for the globe because only
Europe could claim to have produced and experienced the progressive
civilization that was ostensibly humanity's vocation and destiny. Despite
imagining a developmental process by which other societies would gradually be admitted to legal standing in the system of civilized states, these
thinkers naturalized the differences they asserted between Europeans and
others. And despite regarding Europe's system of international law as both
an index and an engine of progress, they professed impotence in the face of
European imperial expansion and fear that Europe's material civilization in
the form of increasingly destructive technologies of war might overwhelm
the normative achievements of European civilization.

A New Discipline, Historical and Scientific

In 1855, at the height of the Crimean War, the young legal scholar
Henry Maine (1822–88) delivered one of his early academic papers, on

* I am grateful to Mark Bevir, Inder Marwah, and Lisa Wedeen for their comments on
earlier drafts of this chapter.

"The Conception of Sovereignty, and Its Importance in International Law." The paper was an opening salvo in what would prove Maine's highly influential, though certainly not single-handed, campaign to historicize the British understanding of law, including international law. He lamented that "the great majority of contemporary writers on International Law tacitly assume that the doctrines of their system, founded on principles of equity and common sense, were capable of being readily reasoned over in every stage of modern civilisation," when in fact "the true explanation of those ambiguous dicta ... is entirely historical."[1] The lecture was an ambitious attempt to assert "the great speculative and practical importance" of a properly historical understanding of key legal concepts such as sovereignty in the face of perilous contemporary conflicts, from the 1848 Revolution in Germany, to the looming battle between the American states, to the Crimean War's combat between the Russian Emperor and the Ottoman Sultan, which had drawn in much of the rest of Europe. By the end of his career, Maine would come to characterize the Ottoman Empire and its inevitable breakup as "the most hopeless of all the problems which the civilised world has to solve."[2] This portentous sense of responsibility was characteristic of international lawyers, who, by the late Victorian period, had come to see themselves and their discipline as indispensable to the maintenance of order and the progress of civilization within the European "family of nations," and to the management of European imperial and commercial expansion around the globe.[3]

---

[1] Maine, "The Conception of Sovereignty, and Its Importance in International Law," read 16 April 1855; in *Papers Read Before The Juridical Society: 1855–1858* (London: Stevens and Norton, 1858), pp. 26–45 at 40. Maine's was one of the first papers delivered before the new society, founded to redress the traditional indifference of law professors to the advancement of their field, in contrast to "the anxiety shown by those who are engaged in other departments of science," and despite the fact that their "pursuits and studies are so intimately connected with the progress and well-being of mankind," according to the group's president; see Sir Richard Bethell, "Inaugural Address," ibid., pp. 1–2.

[2] Maine, *International Law: A Series of Lectures Delivered before the University of Cambridge, 1887* (London: John Murray, 1888), p. 4.

[3] My argument in this paper has been informed and influenced by the efflorescence of recent scholarship on nineteenth-century international law, especially Martti Koskenniemi, *Gentle Civilizer of Nations: The Rise and Fall of International Law 1870–1960* (Cambridge: Cambridge University Press, 2001); Antony Anghie, *Imperialism, Sovereignty, and the Making of Modern International Law* (Cambridge: Cambridge University Press, 2005); Brett Bowden, "The Colonial Origins of International Law: European Expansion and the Classical Standard of Civilization," *Journal of the History of International Law* 7 (2005), pp. 1–23; Matthew Craven, "The Invention of a Tradition: Westlake, the Berlin Conference and the Historicisation of International Law," in M. Vec and L. Nuzzo, eds., *Constructing International Law: The Birth of a Discipline* (Frankfurt am Main: Klosterman, 2012), pp. 363–403; and Craven, "Introduction: International Law and Its Histories," in M. Craven, M. Vogiatzi, and M. Fitzmaurice, eds., *Time,*

The rapid succession of conflicts that beset the political landscape during this period shaped and reflected the key preoccupations of Victorian international lawyers.[4] The Crimean War (1853–6), seen as the result of Russian belligerence and Ottoman weakness, entrenched in British observers a belief that the community of civilized Western European nations bore responsibility for maintaining peace in the face of threats from an uncivilized European periphery. The conflict concluded with the Treaty of Paris, which was described as having formally inducted the Ottoman state into international society, though many jurists continued to question Turkey's capacity to participate as a full member of the European "family of nations."[5] The 1857 Sepoy Rebellion in India shone attention on the status under international law of the Indian states not formally subject to Britain, and more generally on questions regarding whether Europeans had any obligations under international law in their relations with Asian states.[6] The American Civil War generated heated controversies around the question of recognition of belligerents and the rights and duties of neutral states.[7] Within Europe, the unforeseen violence of the Franco–Prussian War of 1870–1 provoked in the community of international lawyers a sense of their profession's vocation to tame and civilize modern states with alarmingly destructive military arsenals, and prompted the founding in 1873 of the *Institut de droit international*.[8] And at the watershed imperial negotiations at the Congress

---

History and International Law (Boston: M. Nijhoff, 2007), pp. 1–25, as well as the older work by Gerrit W. Gong, *The Standard of "Civilization" in International Society* (Oxford: Clarendon Press, 1984). On Britain, see Casper Sylvest, "'Our Passion for Legality': International Law and Imperialism in Late Nineteenth-Century Britain," *Review of International Studies* 34 (2008), pp. 403–23; Sylvest, "The Foundations of Victorian International Law," in Duncan Bell, ed., *Victorian Visions of Global Order* (Cambridge: Cambridge University Press, 2007), pp. 47–66; Sylvest, *British Liberal Internationalism, 1880–1930: Making Progress?* (Manchester: Manchester University Press, 2009); Michael Lobban, "English Approaches to International Law in the Nineteenth Century," in Craven et al., eds., *Time, History and International Law*, pp. 65–90.

[4] See, e.g., Maine's account of this history in *International Law*, pp. 3–6.
[5] Even moderate jurists such as Sir Travers Twiss questioned Muslim nations' capacity for reciprocity, and thus their eligibility for full legal personality. Still others, such as James Lorimer, insisted that the recognition of Turkey had always been a farce that was best abandoned for frank acceptance of Europe's duty to civilize the place by conquest.
[6] I discuss this point at greater length in "Boundaries of Victorian International Law," in Bell, ed., *Victorian Visions*, pp. 67–88.
[7] Georgios Varouxakis has argued convincingly that civil war greatly heightened John Stuart Mill's (and a broader English public's) interest in international law, through celebrated cases such as the *Trent* and the *Alabama*; see his *Liberty Abroad: John Stuart Mill on International Relations* (Cambridge: Cambridge University Press, 2013), chapter 2.
[8] Martti Koskenniemi's magisterial *Gentle Civilizer* offers the authoritative account of the self-understanding of the international lawyers he calls the "men of 1873," the founders of the *Institut*, who saw the legal profession as the "*conscience*

of Berlin in 1884–5, international lawyers served as energetic agents of the participating European states and associations.[9] Their understanding of all these events was framed by accounts of the evolution of societies toward civilization and of the historical trajectory and extension of the system of international law.

The Victorian era was a period of disciplinary consolidation for international law as it was for other social sciences such as anthropology and political science. The period saw the establishment of some of the first university chairs in the subject, the publication of unprecedented quantities of treatises, and the formation of professional societies and the first academic journals.[10] Even as the field became more highly technical and doctrinally complex, writers on international law saw it not as the exclusive province of professionals but as the instrument of an educated citizenry, largely enforceable only by public opinion. As the dean of late Victorian international law, John Westlake, wrote, "International law being the science of what a state and its subjects ought to do or may do with reference to other states and their subjects, everyone should reflect on its principles who, in however limited a sphere of influence, helps to determine the action of his country by swelling the volume of its opinion"; the "chief justification" for teaching it was "to prepare men for the duties of citizenship."[11] John Stuart Mill made the same case in his 1867 address to the University of St. Andrews on the purposes and appropriate subjects of a "complete scientific" university education. There he called for the teaching of international law as part of "direct

juridique du monde civilisé," as Article 1 of its founding statute put it (p. 47). Also see Vec and Nuzzo, eds., *Constructing International Law.*

[9] On the role of the lawyers at Congress of Berlin, see Craven, "Invention of a Tradition"; on Sir Travers Twiss's assiduous work on behalf of the claims over the Congo made by the Belgian King Leopold II and his private association, the International African Association, see Andrew Fitzmaurice, *Sovereignty, Property and Empire: 1500–2000* (Cambridge: Cambridge University Press, 2014), chapter 9.

[10] The Chichele Professorship of International Law and Diplomacy was established at Oxford in 1859; the Whewell Professorship of International Law at Cambridge was founded in 1869.

[11] Westlake, *Chapters on International Law*, p. v. Lassa Oppenheim, in an obituary of Westlake, wrote that "every writer on questions of international law must take into account the opinion of Westlake on the subject" and that "[i]n a sense it may even be said that every living jurist is his pupil"; reprinted in Westlake, *Collected Papers of John Westlake on Public International Law*, ed. Lassa Oppenheim (Cambridge: Cambridge University Press, 1914), pp. ix–x. Westlake, who had been briefly a Liberal MP as well as a co-founder of the Working Men's College and a champion of progressive causes such as women's emancipation, was Henry Maine's successor in the Whewell chair at Cambridge; Oppenheim succeeded Westlake. See Nathan Wells, "Westlake, John (1828–1913)," *Oxford Dictionary of National Biography* (Oxford: Oxford University Press, 2004); online edn., May 2008.

instruction in that which it is the chief of all the ends of intellectual education to qualify us for – the exercise of thought on the great interests of mankind as moral and social being."[12]

The nascent profession of international law in Victorian Britain was intimately linked to counterparts on the European continent, particularly through professional associations: the first periodical of international law, *La Revue de Droit International et de Législation Comparée*, was founded in 1869 by Westlake, the Belgian Gustave Rolin-Jaecquemyns, and the Dutch legal scholar Tobias Asser, who were all instrumental in the founding a few years later of the *Institut de droit international*. But the profession in Britain was also distinctively British and sometimes English in its concerns, thanks to factors including the country's insularity, its global dominance as the foremost imperial power, its relative lack of a civil law tradition, and the outsized influence of a new tradition of analytical jurisprudence associated with the utilitarian tradition and especially with Jeremy Bentham and John Austin.

Maine himself was to publish little on international law between his early paper on sovereignty and his posthumously published inaugural lectures, delivered in 1887, as Whewell Professor of International Law at Cambridge.[13] But his historicist program for the study of law, developed in *Ancient Law* (1861), *Village Communities in the East and West* (1871), and other works, not only profoundly influenced British jurisprudence generally but also significantly shaped the emerging discipline of international law. Maine's call to study law as a historical phenomenon, as a social construct responsive to and dependent upon other social institutions, faced the particular hurdle in British legal studies of the influence of the relatively ahistorical analytical tradition.[14] Maine's agenda no

---

[12] "To these studies I would add International Law; which I decidedly think should be taught in all universities, and should form part of all liberal education. The need of it is far from being limited to diplomatists and lawyers; it extends to every citizen." Mill, "Inaugural Address Delivered to the University of St. Andrews," in J. M. Robson and R. F. McRae, eds., *Collected Works of John Stuart Mill* (Toronto: University of Toronto Press, 1963–), 21:246 (hereafter *CW*).

[13] His early biographer wrote that "[b]efore he went to Calcutta [in 1862] he had written a book on International law, the manuscript of which disappeared in his absence"; Sir M.E. Grant Duff, *Sir Henry Maine: A Brief Memoir of His Life* (New York: Harper & Row, 1969) at pp. 69–73; quoted by Carl Landauer, "From Status to Treaty: Henry Sumner Maine's International Law," *Canadian Journal of Law and Jurisprudence* 15 (2002): 219–154 at 221.

[14] Bentham did not wholly neglect historical context in his treatment of law. His "Essay concerning place and time in matters of legislation" was one attempt to grapple with the question, though his method there involved beginning with a given code and thinking about what adaptations would be required to translate it to a different social context. The text was first published in John Bowring's 1843 edition of Bentham's works; also see "Place and Time," the new critical edition of the essay, in Jeremy Bentham,

doubt partly owed its great success, despite that hurdle, to its congruence with the general philosophical historicism that characterized social and political thought both in Britain and on the Continent, in the work of thinkers as diverse as Auguste Comte, the Saint-Simonians, J. S. Mill, and Marx.[15] For all their differences, these thinkers shared an aspiration to establish the study of society and politics on a scientific basis, and they did so by means of narratives of human progress that, although universal in scope, also posited the historical uniqueness of European civilization. Maine's work also followed the more specifically legal historicism pioneered in Germany by Friedrich Carl von Savigny, which was also advanced in Britain by Westlake and others.[16]

By the 1870s and 1880s, thanks both to general developments in social thought and to the particular influence of Maine, the major figures of Victorian international law – men such as Westlake, Sir Travers Twiss, James Lorimer, Thomas Erskine Holland, and William Edward Hall – were arguing that international law had to be understood as a historically particular system that had arisen under the distinctive circumstances of early modern Europe and was constantly adjusting to the "growing wants of a progressive civilisation."[17] They were, consequently, preoccupied in a way that earlier theorists of the law of nations had not been with delineating the scope of the international community, expounding the criteria for admission into that community, managing its gradual expansion to encompass some excluded states, and specifying the legal status of various societies which they deemed inadmissible. Victorian international jurists were anxious to establish the scientific credentials of their discipline; most shared with figures in other emerging social or human sciences of the period a conviction that the intellectual advances made over their eighteenth-century predecessors lay precisely in their

---

Selected Writings, Stephen Engelmann, ed. (New Haven: Yale University Press, 2011), pp. 152–219.

[15] On historicism in this broader sense, Friedrich Meinecke's *Historism: The Rise of a New Historical Outlook* (New York: Herder and Herder, 1972 [first published in German, 1936]) is the classic account. James Chandler, *England in 1819* (Chicago: University of Chicago Press, 1998) deftly charts scholarly disagreements around Romantic historicism.

[16] Koskenniemi notes that Westlake's 1858 treatise on private international law "had been systematically written to familiarize English jurists with continental scholarship, and Savigny in particular": *Gentle Civilizer*, pp. 45–6, citing A. V. Dicey, "His Book and His Character," in *Memories of John Westlake* (S.l.: Smith, Elder and Co., 1914), pp. 26–7.

[17] Travers Twiss, *The Law of Nations Considered as Independent Political Communities* (Oxford: Clarendon Press, 1884), "Preface to the Second Edition," p. v. This group, plus the Oxford professor Mountague Bernard, were the British members and associates of the Institute of International Law in its early years. See *Annuaire de l'Institut de Droit International* (Gand: Revue de droit international, 1877), pp. xiii–xv.

historical approach to their subject. International law could be scientific, and progressive, only by being historical.[18] The resulting constellation of beliefs – in the historical particularity of the European law of nations, the normative validity of the European legal system for the future of the world as a whole, and the possibility of rendering international law scientific – distinguished nineteenth-century international legal thought from the various eighteenth-century sources on which it drew and left a marked legacy for international law in the twentieth century.[19]

In what follows, I briefly chart the development of historicism in British international law from its early shape at the turn of the nineteenth century, through the challenge posed by Austin's analytical jurisprudence and Maine's response. I then offer an account of the distinctive preoccupations, narratives, and conceptual tensions that characterized the historicism of the mid- to late Victorian period as international lawyers were most zealously setting forth an intellectual and practical agenda for their new science. In the narrative they produced, of an international legal community with its historical origins in Europe but an emerging normative authority for the world as a whole, European civilization was understood as at once unique and exemplary and as a precious but possibly self-undermining achievement.

A Brief History of Historicism in British International Law

The idea that international law could be understood only as a historical phenomenon was perhaps first ventured, in English, in Robert Ward's

---

[18] See, e.g., T. E. Holland's claim that jurisprudence is "not a science of legal relations *à priori*, as they might have been, or should have been, but is abstracted *à posteriori* from such relations as have been clothed with a legal character in actual systems, that is to say from law which has actually been imposed, or positive law. It follows that Jurisprudence is a progressive science." T. E. Holland, *The Elements of Jurisprudence* (Oxford: Clarendon Press, 1880), p. 8. John Burrow attributed the influence of evolutionary social theory in Victorian Britain precisely to the "tension between English positivistic attitudes to science on the one hand and, on the other, a more profound reading of history, coming to a large extent from German romanticism, which made the older form of positivist social theory, philosophic radicalism, seem inadequate": Burrow, *Evolution and Society: A Study in Victorian Social Theory* (Cambridge: Cambridge University Press, 1966), p. xv.

[19] Anghie identifies repeated twentieth-century echoes of the "dynamic of difference" that governed Victorian international law, from the League of Nations mandate system through the techniques by which European used international law to perpetuate claims over natural resources in the decolonizing third world; see *Imperialism*. For the argument that twentieth-century international lawyers invented a caricature of their nineteenth-century predecessors, see David Kennedy, "International Law and the Nineteenth Century: History of an Illusion," *Quinnipiac Law Review* 17 (1997–8), pp. 99–136.

1795 *Enquiry into the Foundation and History of the Law of Nations in Europe from the time of the Greeks and Romans to the Age of Grotius*. Ward set out to refute what he saw as the misguided universalism of natural law accounts in the field's authoritative treatises (Grotius, Wolff, Vattel). Ward wrote of being struck by the conflict between the universalist language of the law of nature and the historical fact that "the system of the Law of Nations was neither more nor less than a particular, detailed, and ramified system of morals," that "what is commonly called the Law of Nations, falls very far short of *universality*; and that, therefore, the Law is not the Law of *all* nations."[20] He devised a theory, he wrote, according to which dense interactions among a set of states led to a law of nations for that set, so that there could be several laws of nations at any given time, and different laws of nations over the course of history; this was a theory to be "proved from history, if proved at all" (xi). Ward insisted that general terms such as "'the *Law of Nations*,' or '*the whole World*,'" should not be taken "in the extensive sense which is implied by those terms" but rather should be understood to mean "nothing more, than the law of the European Nations, or the European World" (158). Importantly, the particularism of the European law of nations meant, for Ward, that even as Europeans should understand themselves to be morally bound by its precepts, they had no "right to act toward all other people as if they had broken a law, to which they had never submitted, which they had never understood, or of which they had probably never heard" (x). If others followed precepts that threatened European "happiness and just rights," they might be treated as enemies, but never as if they were "punishable for *breaches* of those laws" (xi). Ward's historicizing of the law of nations was of a piece with a broader tendency at the end of the eighteenth century to specify the European law of nations or the *droit des gens de l'Europe* as the appropriate subject of study, and it was undoubtedly a precursor of Victorian historicism.[21] But there is a pluralism to Ward's account – a consciousness of the provincialism of European law – that sharply distinguishes his historical narrative

---

[20] As Ward wrote, "however desirable such an universality might be, the whole world were not susceptible of that intimacy and closeness of union, which many philosophers of high name are willing to suppose": Robert Ward, *An Enquiry into the Foundation and History of the Law of Nations in Europe from the Time of the Greeks and Romans to the Age of Grotius* (London: A. Strahan and W. Woodfall, 1795), pp. I.v and xiii–xiv.

[21] See G. F. von Martens, *Précis du droit des gens moderne de l'Europe fondé sur les traités et l'usage* (Gottingen: Dieterich, 1801), and Martti Koskenniemi, "Into Positivism: Georg Friedrich von Martens (1756–1821) and Modern International Law," *Constellations* 15 (2008), pp. 189–207.

from the developmental Victorian historicism based on an account of progressive civilization.[22] Ward also lacked the scientific aspirations of the Victorians.[23]

Ward's contemporary, the influential Admiralty court judge William Scott, Lord Stowell, shared Ward's sense of a "law of nations" as a social construct that developed out of a long history of dense commercial ties among a group of nations, such that Europe's law of nations was one of many such systems.[24] Both Ward and Scott believed that mutual recognition as legal entities was possible between European and non-European states such as the Ottoman Empire and the Barbary states, even though the latter were not participants in the European system. "Although their notions of justice, to be observed between nations, differ from those which we entertain," Scott wrote in one Admiralty court decision, "we do not, on that account, venture to call in question their public acts."[25] Neither Ward nor Scott, that is, held the view standard among the Victorian jurists, that the European law of nations was a global legal system in embryo, that other nations were lawless insofar as they failed to participate in the European system, and that one key task of European jurists was to construct a process by which those others might be granted admission to the European–global legal community.

Despite early efforts such as Ward's, during the first half of the nineteenth century historicism had less of a presence in Britain, thanks to the considerable influence of the analytical jurisprudence associated with Jeremy Bentham and his disciple John Austin, than it did on the Continent.[26] There legal historicism came to dominance under the

---

[22] Ward's pluralism was undercut by his belief in the unique truth of Christianity, which he saw as the basis of the European law of nations, but he nonetheless insisted on the valid legal nature of a plurality of legal systems around the globe.

[23] "In the course of this *Historical* part of the Enquiry, I have, I fear, pursued but little method" (xliv).

[24] Ward was a friend of Scott's brother John Scott, Lord Eldon, who held a series of important legal posts (attorney-general, lord chief justice, lord chancellor) under Pitt. It was William Scott (1745–1836), later the first Baron Stowell, who first proposed that Ward write the work: see Edmund Phipps, *Memoirs of the Political and Literary Life of Robert Plumer Ward, Esq.* (London: Murray, 1850), vol. 1, p. 15. All shared a hostility to the French Revolution that is arguably reflected in their criticism of abstract universal principles. The fullest treatment of Ward's thought, giving prominence to his counter-revolutionary views and context, is Diego Panizza, *Genesi di una ideologia. Il conservatorismo moderno in Robert Ward* (Padova: CEDAM, 1997).

[25] *The Helena, Heslop Master*, 4 Rob 5–6. I discuss Ward and Scott's thought further in "Empire and Legal Universalisms in the Eighteenth Century," *American Historical Review* 117(1) (February 2012), pp. 92–121.

[26] See Wilfrid E. Rumble, *Doing Austin Justice* (London: Continuum, 2004); and Rumble, "Nineteenth-Century Perceptions of John Austin: Utilitarianism and the Reviews of *The Province of Jurisprudence Determined*," *Utilitas* 3 (1991), pp. 199–216.

influence of Savigny and his critique of what he saw as Enlightenment abstraction and the artificiality and inflexibility of codification.[27] By mid-century, then, Maine's historicist agenda was timely – in keeping with major intellectual trends in Europe – but also required a distinctive sort of work in Britain.

From Maine's perspective, Austin's account of law was misguided precisely because it was analytical at the expense of any proper historical understanding. Austin's theory, in form, proposes a sweeping, *a priori* definition of law – as the command of sovereign – that seems to have little to say about historical change or the situatedness of law in a historical context. Maine held that the command theories of law developed by Bentham and then Austin "tally exactly with the facts of mature jurisprudence" – as he put it in his most influential work, *Ancient Law* – but are unhelpful as a picture of law in early stages of society, as well as of international law.[28] Maine's early paper on sovereignty had begun with a polite nod to the analytical power of Austin's approach. There he adopted most of Austin's definition of sovereignty, though he offered his own distinctively histor-ical account of the emergence of that conception of sovereignty under feudalism from the rival forms that had existed earlier (non-territorial "tribal sovereignty," and the idea of universal dominion).

In *Ancient Law* (1861), Maine more directly took on Austin along with other figures and lines of argument that he regarded as misguidedly *a priori*, especially Rousseau's state of nature and the natural rights claims that relied on such a device. Such "plausible and comprehensive" theor-ies of law's origins in natural law or social contracts had "obscured the truth" about the origins of law; indeed, it was their very plausibility and thus their power over the modern imagination that had enabled them to so mislead modern thinkers about the true origins of law, which, he argued, could be understood only through "sober research" into primi-tive history.[29]

---

[27] On Savigny (1779–1861), see Koskenniemi, *Gentle Civilizer*, 43ff.; Luigi Nuzzo, "History, Science and Christianity. International Law and Savigny's Paradigm," in Vec and Nuzzo, eds., *Constructing International Law*, pp. 25–50; Andrew Fitzmaurice, *Sovereignty, property and empire, 1500–2000* (Cambridge: Cambridge University Press, 2014), chapter 9.

[28] Maine, *Ancient Law: Its Connection with the Early History of Society, and Its Relation to Modern Ideas* (New York: Henry Holt, 1864), 3rd American ed., from 5th London ed., p. 7. On Maine's critique of Austin, see Rumble, *Doing Austin Justice*, chapter 7, and Collini, Winch, and Burrow, who write that Maine "made of historical jurisprudence the perfect stick with which to beat the Utilitarians for the widely sensed failure of their 'abstract' method": *That Noble Science of Politics: A Study in Nineteenth-Century Intellectual History* (Cambridge: Cambridge University Press, 1983), p. 211.

[29] See Maine, *Ancient Law*, p. 3. In *Ancient Law* Maine set out to deflate the universalist pretentions of the natural law tradition by identifying the historical origins of the modern

Finally, in his late lectures on international law, Maine applied his critiques of Austin and of natural law universalism to international law. He argued that only a properly historical study could salvage that powerful but precarious system:

If international law be not studied historically – if we fail to comprehend, first, the influence of the theories of the Roman jurisconsults on the mind of Hugo Grotius, and next, the influence of the great book of Grotius on International Jurisprudence, – we lose at once all chance of comprehending that body of rules which alone protects the European commonwealth from permanent anarchy, we blind ourselves to the principles by conforming to which it coheres, we can understand neither its strength nor its weakness, nor can we separate those arrangements which can safely be modified from those which cannot be touched without shaking the whole fabric to pieces.[30]

Maine used his historicist account of international law as a demystifying device, meant to strengthen the force of an ill-understood social construct by dispelling illusions, such as that international law is a reflection of an abstract and universal law of nature or a reflection of fundamental principles of human nature. Rather, and more humbly and idiosyncratically, international law's "rapid advance to acceptance by civilised nations was a stage, though a very late stage, in the diffusion of Roman Law over Europe," a fact that only historical research could reveal.[31]

As luck would have it for modern Europe, some of the misapprehensions at the heart of the older ahistorical tradition of the law of nations had proven salutary, Maine argued. Seventeenth-century jurists' view that natural law corresponded to a fundamentally pacific and sociable human nature was a false picture of a period that had in fact been "excessively inhuman" in war, as demonstrated by new research into "the actual childhood of the human race." But, though it was based on an "imaginary reconstruction" of early human history, the early modern law-of-nations system "more and more calmed the fury of angry belligerency, and supplied a framework to which more advanced principles of humanity and convenience easily adjusted themselves" (22–3). On the

law of nature in Roman law. He traced the transformation of the *ius gentium*, the rules that Romans applied to Italian tribes not subject to Roman civil law, into the broader *ius naturale*, which then acquired philosophical abstraction through the adoption of Stoic ideas of nature. See Karuna Mantena, *Alibis of Empire: Henry Maine and the Ends of Liberal Imperialism* (Princeton: Princeton University Press, 2010), pp. 122–4.

[30] Sir H. S. Maine, "Roman Law and Legal Education," in *Village-Communities in the East and West: Six Lectures Delivered at Oxford, to Which Are Added Other Lectures, Addresses, and Essays* (New York, 1889), at p. 352.

[31] Maine, *International Law*, p. 16. Identifying the law of nations with the law of nature was merely an old "habit" of European lawyers "for the purpose of giving it dignity." 20.

basis of poor historiography, then, Grotius and his successors erected a powerful system for the maintenance of peace by "creat[ing] a law-abiding sentiment" among European sovereigns (51). The task of scientific histories of law in Maine's day was to perpetuate that system by placing it on firmer ground. He believed the English were in particular need of a properly historical understanding of international law, because in taking seriously the Austinian question of how international law comes to have authority in particular countries (through legislative fiat, for instance), they placed themselves outside the consensus of "civilized nations" that international law is simply binding on nations as a condition of their membership in that privileged circle.

Austin's famously restrictive definition of laws as the commands of a sovereign posed a challenge – the question whether international law could justly be considered law at all – to which nearly all British theorists of international law felt obliged to respond. This was true both for historicists who rejected Austin's account of law as narrow and wrong-headed, and for analytical jurists who admired his rigor and yet wished to salvage international law.[32] And it was true even though Austin himself granted that international law could be understood as "analogous to jurisprudence" and "treated ... in a scientific or systematic manner."[33] A sense of the force of the Austinian view was arguably a distinguishing feature of British international law thinking in this period, in contrast to the Continental colleagues with whom British theorists worked closely in bodies such as the *Institut de droit international*, for whom Austin was largely irrelevant.[34] Austinians such as T. E. Holland tended to argue that international law was law by analogy: "a beneficent application of legal ideas to questions which, from the nature of the case, are incapable of a legal solution" and "the vanishing point of Jurisprudence; since it

---

[32] Maine himself may have coined the distinction between the analytical and historical schools: see C. Allen, *Legal Duties and Other Essays in Jurisprudence* (Oxford: Clarendon Press, 1931), p. 14 and R. C. J. Cocks, "Maine, Sir Henry James Sumner (1822–1888)," in *Oxford Dictionary of National Biography* (Oxford: Oxford University Press, 2004), www.oxforddnb.com/view/article/17808 (accessed October 26, 2016).

[33] Austin, *The Province of Jurisprudence Determined*, ed. W. E. Rumble (Cambridge: Cambridge University Press, 1995), p. 112. As Michael Lobban has noted, it was not so much Austin himself that the international jurists had to combat as it was "the spectre of the 'vulgar' Austin who seemed to many to dismiss international law as so much private opinion." Likewise, Lobban shows that Maine and others "took the edge out of Austin's language" while conceding that international law was "distinct and less precise than positive law": Lobban, "English Approaches," 80–4.

[34] As Maine noted, "Mr. John Austin's definition of Sovereignty is not that of International Law, though in almost all the very modern [British] treatises which have dealt with this subject some confusion between the two is observable" (*International Law*, p. 58).

lacks any arbiter of disputed questions, save public opinion, beyond and above the disputant parties themselves."[35]

Maineans who insisted on the historicity of law against what they saw as the static universalism of Austin nonetheless felt obliged to respond to Austin's implication that international law was not properly law at all.[36] Indeed, in the hands of Maine and his followers among theorists of international law, historicism is the method by which international law is vindicated against the Austinian challenge to its status as law. T. J. Lawrence, who taught international law at Cambridge, the University of Chicago, the Royal Naval College, and elsewhere, began his collection of *Essays on Some Disputed Questions in International Law* (1885) by responding to Austin with an essay titled, "Is There a True International Law?" As Lawrence put it,

> our notion of law is a development. This is a fact which once fairly grasped would save us from many historical and philosophical errors. The Austinian analysis of law into command, obligation and sanction applies with fair accuracy to the condition of some societies under strong and civilized governments; but it fails altogether if we attempt to bring under it the legal phenomena of earlier stages of human progress.[37]

Likewise, international laws "do actually regulate human conduct ... even when no definite punishment is annexed to the breach of them." Indeed, the efficacy of international law despite the absence of reliable sanction was precisely an indication of Europe's advanced civilization: "as man progresses, the notion of force as the most necessary element in the conception of law, tends to fall into the background," and just like maturing children, "so states in their development towards moral and intellectual manhood, need less and less the discipline of compulsion."[38] In this way a developmental narrative could subsume and transcend Austin, accepting his theory as a usefully scrupulous account of law within civilized societies while defusing its potentially destructive implications for the authority of international law.

---

[35] Holland, *Elements of Jurisprudence*, 11th ed., p. 386. Casper Sylvest has described Holland as "more Austinian than Austin": "The foundations of Victorian international law," p. 56. John Westlake also shared Austin's goals of parsimony and scientific rigor and wrote somewhat dismissively about historical approaches to law that collected ingenious discoveries about "remote state[s] of society" without first analytically establishing the meaning of law. But he quickly dispensed with Austin's command theory of law. Westlake, *Chapters on the Principles of International Law* (Cambridge: Cambridge University Press, 1894), p. viii.

[36] Lawrence, *Essays on Some Disputed Questions in International Law* (Cambridge: Deighton, Bell, 1885), p. 5.

[37] Lawrence, *Disputed Questions*, pp. 31–2.   [38] Lawrence, *Disputed Questions*, p. 25.

While Austin and Maine did offer radically different accounts of the place of historical reasoning in legal theory, even Austin's ostensibly ahistorical approach arguably invoked an implicit developmental narrative. In defining an independent political society as one whose members were "in a *habit* of obedience to a *certain* and *common* superior," for instance, Austin noted that it might not be possible to establish a determinate test. But he envisioned a spectrum, with "England, and ... every independent society somewhat advanced in civilisation" at one extreme of obviously political societies, and "the independent and savage societies which subsist by hunting or fishing in the woods or on the coasts of New Holland" at the other extreme of obviously natural or non-political societies.[39] More important, international legal theorists of both Austinian and Mainean bents generally sought some way to synthesize what they took to be the opposing analytical and historical approaches.[40] Whether they identified more with Austin or with Maine, Victorian theorists of international law shared the broad set of assumptions about the uniqueness and exemplarity of European progress and civilization that undergirded the period's distinctive brand of historicism.

The Narrative of Victorian International Law: European Past and Global Future

Victorian international law relied on a basic historical narrative beset by a distinctive tension. The human being, it was held, is an inherently historical animal, so that we cannot understand human nature without understanding how human society, and human individuals in their wants and needs, change over time. At the same time, Europe was seen to have a uniquely historical, and a uniquely progressive, nature. The key narrative was thus spatial as well as temporal: Progress meant the global spread of European norms and legal principles. The temporal and the geographic interacted, so that different places were understood as existing in different temporalities, in the senses both of where

---

[39] Austin, *Province of Jurisprudence Determined*, pp. 171–2. Also see 177ff, comparing contemporary savage societies to "the German nations whose manners are described by Tacitus."

[40] Natural law, though derided by some as a superannuated relic, was explicitly championed by several influential figures, notably Twiss, Phillimore, and the rather eccentric James Lorimer, Regius Professor of Public Law and the Law of Nature and Nations at the University of Edinburgh; see Fitzmaurice, *Sovereignty, property and Empire*. More important, moral universalism survived more generally even in thinkers explicitly critical of natural law in the form of progress narratives; see Pitts, "Boundaries," and Sylvest, "Foundations," both in D. Bell, ed., *Victorian Visions*.

a given society stood in the timeline of progress and of how quickly it was moving along that line.

Maine's account, if unusually thoroughly theorized, is characteristic. He saw the progress from "primitive" to "modern" society as of great general theoretical interest and as normative, while at the same time insisting that both progress and progressiveness were extremely rare, the achievement only of ancient Greece and Rome and their modern European heirs. As he famously put the point, "Except the blind forces of Nature, nothing moves in this world which is not Greek in its origin."[41] *Ancient Law*, in which Maine presented his argument that "the movement of the progressive societies has hitherto been a movement *from Status to Contract*," is centrally concerned with legal mechanisms of progress.[42] There he argued that legal systems adjust to social change through the devices of legal fiction, equity, and legislation – devices that, he proposed, emerge in that chronological order in the development of a society.

Maine regarded his historical practice as scientific and believed that the progress followed by European civilization could be given a scientific account, in terms of general laws. But he also noted, as quoted in this chapter's epigraph, that "[i]t is only with the progressive societies that we are concerned, and nothing is more remarkable than their extreme fewness."[43] Like others, Maine acknowledged the obvious sophistication of Chinese and Indian civilization while insisting that theories of progress did not apply to these societies ("there has been material civilisation, but

---

[41] "A ferment spreading from that source has vitalised all the great progressive races of mankind, penetrating from one to another, and producing results accordant with its hidden and latent genius, and results of course often far greater than any exhibited in Greece itself. It is this principle of progress which we Englishmen are communicating to India. We did not create it. We deserve no special credit for it. It came to us filtered through many different media. But we have received it, so we pass it on. There is no reason why, if it has time to work, it should not develop in India effects as wonderful as in any other of the societies of mankind" (Maine, *Village-Communities*, p. 238). Cf. J. S. Mill on the rarity of societies that have in them an "spring of unborrowed progress"; "Review of Grote's *History of Greece*," *CW* 11:313. For a more (but still ambiguously) biological argument, James Lorimer's aspiration to distinguish between progressive and non-progressive races and his view that there are "ethnical differences which for jural purposes we must regard as indelible"; Lorimer, *Institutes of the Law of Nations* (London: Blackwood, 1883), pp. 102 and 98.

[42] Maine, *Ancient Law*, p. 165; italics in original.

[43] Maine, *Ancient Law*, p. 21. As Maine later wrote, "the natural condition of mankind... is not the progressive condition": Maine, *Popular Government: Four Essays* (London: John Murray, 1886), p. 170. On the complexities of Maine's view of progress, see Krishan Kumar, "Maine and the Theory of Progress," and John W. Burrow, "Henry Maine and Mid-Victorian Ideas of Progress," both in A. Diamond, ed., *The Victorian Achievement of Sir Henry Maine: A Centennial Reappraisal* (Cambridge: Cambridge University Press, 1991).

instead of civilisation expanding the law, the law has limited the civilisation"). Maine's speculations about the reasons for failure of progress in "the East" included the tendency of legal codes in the east to bear religious rather than civil authority, the vast extent of Eastern societies, and the codification of their laws at a later and more "perverted" stage than those of Rome.[44] But in the end he simply restricted his "scientific" theory to the progressive societies, settling for the observation that the "difference between the stationary and progressive societies is ... one of the great secrets which inquiry has yet to penetrate ... the stationary condition of the human race is the rule, the progressive the exception."[45] European civilization was thus the only properly historical civilization as well as the only one amenable to scientific study.

This tension between European civilization's unique past and its universal future structured the dominant account of international law. Victorian jurists sometimes recognized European international law as simply one system among many possible interstate societies and their legal systems (as Ward and Stowell had earlier argued it was). On the other hand, grand claims were made for international law as comprising "all that can be said with some degree of generality about human action not internal to a political body."[46] W. E. Hall's account is typical in first positing European international law as simply one particular system in a world with multiple civilizations, but then recognizing only Europe's system as "law-governed," and thus granting Europeans gate-keeping authority over what turns out to be the world's only such system:

as international law is a product of the special civilisation of modern Europe, and forms a highly artificial system of which the principles cannot be supposed to be understood or recognized by countries differently civilised, such states can only be presumed to be subject to it as are inheritors of that civilisation. They have lived, and are living, under law, and a positive act of withdrawal would be required to free them from its restraints. But states outside European civilisation must formally enter into the circle of law-governed countries. They must do something with the acquiescence of the latter, or of some of them, which amounts to an acceptance of the law in its entirety beyond all possible misconstruction. It is not enough consequently that they shall enter into arrangements by treaty identical with arrangements made by law-governed powers, nor that they shall do acts, like sending and receiving permanent embassies, which are compatible with ignorance or rejection of law.[47]

---

[44] "Even now, Hindoo jurisprudence has a substratum of forethought and sound judgment, but irrational imitation has engrafted in it an immense apparatus of cruel absurdities"; Maine, *Ancient Law*, pp. 18–19.

[45] Maine, *Ancient Law*, pp. 22–3.

[46] John Westlake, "Introductory Lecture on International Law, 17 October 1888," in *Collected Papers*, p. 393.

[47] William Edward Hall, *A Treatise on International Law*, 2nd ed. (Oxford: Clarendon Press, 1884), p. 40.

Hall's account exemplifies the way in which the conception of civilization that governed these narratives operated in at least three registers at once: as an analytic or descriptive category, as a universal normative aspiration or telos, and – in the guise of the "standard of civilization" – as a mechanism of exclusion.[48]

As a descriptive category, civilization comprised individualism, contract relations, cognitive complexity, and intricate social interdependence. As a normative category it entailed the refinement of distinctively human faculties of moral judgment, artistic achievement, and scientific reasoning. As J. S. Mill noted in his influential 1836 essay on "Civilization," the term, "like many other terms of the philosophy of human nature, has a double meaning": it could mean, in a normatively charged sense, "farther advanced in the road to perfection: happier, nobler, wiser." But it also applied particularly to complex modern society, and in the latter sense it was a descriptive and normatively neutral term, such that one could speak of the "vices or the miseries of civilization."[49] As Travers Twiss used the idea of civilization, intertwining these various meanings, the "Law of Nations, as distinguished from the Law of Nature, is a rule of international conduct sanctioned by a practice, which has been found to conduce to the general welfare of the community of civilised States, which reason has moulded in conformity with the progress of civilisation, and the observance of which is obligatory upon every Nation that claims to participate in the common advantages of that civilisation."[50] T. J. Lawrence's *Principles of International Law* (1895) suggests the vagueness of the standard of civilization, even as it operated very precisely to exclude certain states from the bounds of the international community:

The area within which the law of nations operates is supposed to coincide with the area of civilization. To be received within it is to obtain a kind of international testimonial of good conduct and respectability; and when a state hitherto accounted barbarous desires admission, the leading powers settle the case upon its merits. In addition to the attainment of a certain, or rather an uncertain, amount of civilization, a state must have possession of a fixed territory before it can obtain the privilege of admission into the family of nations ... For there are many communities outside the sphere of International Law, though they are

---

[48] On the last, see Gerrit Gong's classic study, *The Standard of "Civilization."*
[49] Mill, *CW*, 18:117.
[50] Twiss, *The Law of Nations Considered as Independent Political Communities* (Oxford: Clarendon Press, 1884), p. xxxix; Twiss uses the term civilized ostensibly more descriptively when he writes that the law of nations "leaves untouched the maxim of Natural Law, that plighted faith is to be maintained even towards semi-civilised peoples, who are outside the pale of contemporary international law" (p. xxxviii). Likewise, in discussing the Suez Canal, he referred to the "friction that [the Canal] will create between the Christian States of Europe and the uncivilised tribes of Islam."

independent states. They neither grant to others, nor claim for themselves the strict observance of its rules. Justice and humanity should be scrupulously adhered to in all dealings with them, but they are not fit subjects for the application of legal technicalities. It would, for instance, be absurd to expect the king of Dahomey to establish a Prize Court, or to require the dwarfs of the central African forest to receive a permanent diplomatic mission.[51]

For all their aspirations that international law might serve as the "juridical conscience of the civilized world" and as an ever more potent mechanism for taming the power and violence of the modern state, jurists could also abdicate responsibility by declaring the impotence of law in the face of European colonial aspirations. As Westlake wrote regarding the limitations of international law in Africa,

But wherever the native inhabitants can furnish no government capable of fulfilling the purposes fulfilled by the Asiatic empires, which is the case of most of the populations with whom Europeans have come into contact in America and Africa, the first necessity is that a government should be furnished. The inflow of the white race cannot be stopped where there is land to cultivate, ore to be mined, commerce to be developed, sport to enjoy, curiosity to be satisfied. If any fanatical admirer of savage life argued that the whites ought to be kept out, he would only be driven to the same conclusion by another route, for a government on the spot would be necessary to keep them out. Accordingly international law has to treat such natives as uncivilised. It regulates, for the mutual benefit of civilised states, the claims which they make to sovereignty over the region, and leaves the treatment of the natives to the conscience of the state to which the sovereignty is awarded, rather than sanction their interest being made an excuse the more for war between civilised claimants, devastating the region and the cause of suffering to the natives themselves.[52]

In such accounts, the exclusion of Africans from the purview of international law appears over-determined: The passage implies, without interrogating, mutually reinforcing disparate grounds for limiting international law to the "mutual benefit of civilised states." Westlake's implicit developmental narrative suggests that a state apparatus to regulate commerce and land use is a telos of societal evolution (as well as a necessary condition for international recognition), but that as Africans cannot supply such government independently, their subjection to the sovereignty of a European power is inevitable. International law cannot prohibit economic exploitation and colonization by Europeans: To try would not only be futile but also would involve a bizarre fetishization of "savage" life. In insisting on the limited scope of application of

---

[51] T. J. Lawrence, *Principles of International Law* (London/New York: Macmillan, 1895), pp. 58–9.
[52] Westlake, *Collected Papers*, p. 145.

international law, Westlake renders it impervious to emendation or expansion to encompass either African claims or African interests. International law within Europe is both enforced and developed by means of public opinion: A "justly offended state" may be left "to fight its own battle, but it receives a moral support from the general recognition that its resort to arms was the exercise of a right," and the "offender is made to feel the loss of sympathy which his conduct has occasioned."[53]

Westlake's account is also characteristic in being racialized without advancing a theory of biological racial difference, as when he glosses international law as "the rules which are internationally recognised between white men" or notes the impossibility of halting the "inflow" of the white race.[54] Such naturalizing language reinforces the impression of the impotence of law in the face of fact and of possibly innate differences among peoples: "natives in the rudimentary condition supposed take no rights under international law," because, Westlake asserts by means of a tellingly naturalizing metaphor, "a stream cannot rise higher than its source."[55]

International law was based on the "common civilization" of Europe and America, by which he meant that

The same arts and sciences are taught and pursued, the same avocations and interests and protected by similar laws, civil and criminal, the administration of which is directed by a similar sense of justice. The same dangers are seen to threaten the fabric of society, similar measures are taken or discussed with the object of eluding them, and the same hopes are entertained that improvement will continue to be realised.[56]

Although countries such as Turkey, Persia, China, Japan, and Siam "must be recognised as being civilised, though with other civilisations than ours," international law was founded upon a "common and in that sense an equal civilisation" among European states. Turkey, geographically but not civilizationally a part of Europe, occupied an anomalous position. "She may benefit by European international law so far as it

---

[53] Westlake, *Collected Papers*, p. 7.
[54] Westlake, *Collected Papers*, p. 146. Lorimer, as noted above, was unusual in his explicitly racial argument. On race in Victorian discourse, see Patrick Brantlinger, *Taming Cannibals: Race and the Victorians* (Ithaca: Cornell University Press, 2011) and Nancy Stepan's classic *The Idea of Race in Science: Great Britain, 1800–1960* (London: Macmillan, 1982).
[55] Westlake, *Collected Papers*, p. 146. Westlake was denying the validity of treaties and other documents signed by Africans ceding sovereignty or territorial rights to European powers. For discussions of that practice, see Anghie, *Imperialism*, pp. 105ff; C. H. Alexandrowicz, *The European–African Confrontation: A Study in Treaty Making* (Leiden: Sijthoff, 1973).
[56] Westlake, "The Equality of States in Civilisation," in *Collected Papers*, p. 101.

can be extended to her without ignoring plain facts, but her admission to that benefit cannot react on the statement of the law, which is what it is because it is the law of the European peoples."[57] In other words, admission to the community under international law in principle did not put non-European states in a position to alter the content of that law. "This civilisation," Westlake wrote, had "grown up by degrees, and populations have become included in it among whom it did not originate" (104). European civilization, then, was at once developing and rigid: Although its membership was changing progressively to include new members, these apparently were not full and equal members entitled to contribute to its evolution.

A notable feature of the Victorian developmental narrative common in both legal writing and more general social and political theory is the tendency to individualize the narrative. Societal development was commonly conceptualized as, at root, the result of the improved faculties of individual members of a society: their capacity for abstract thought, their willpower, their ability to delay gratification, their ability to subjugate individual desires to the needs of the collective. Not only were nations analogized to individuals as having infancy, maturity, and senility or dotage, but also individual members of societies seen as being at an early stage of development were understood as having deficiencies of mind and character. This view of progress as a matter of individual cognitive development, as opposed to an irreducibly social phenomenon (as it was, for instance, in the work of Adam Smith), had direct implications for understandings of these societies' legal standing. Sometimes this tendency – the tendency, for instance, to speak of "the savage" or "the barbarian" in the singular – seems a mere quirk of language. In the course of his argument that western European progress is the exception to the rule of human stagnation, Maine wrote that "much the greatest part of mankind has never shown a particle of desire that its civil institutions should be improved since the moment when external completeness was first given to them by their embodiment in some permanent record," as though societal progress could be accounted for at the level of individual will or desire.[58] Likewise, as the Scottish jurist James Lorimer wrote, with characteristic asperity, "I would give up the farce of pretending that he ['the Turk'] was *sui juris* when, if not in his dotage, he was plainly in his minority."[59] Note the casualness of Lorimer's developmental claims – infancy and senility amount to the same thing, and there is

---

[57] Westlake, *Collected Papers*, p. 103.   [58] Maine, *Ancient Law*, pp. 22–23.
[59] James Lorimer, "Denationalisation of Constantinople," in *Studies National and International* (Edinburgh: W. Green and Sons, 1890), p. 129.

little need to specify the historical claim. Lorimer made this claim in the context of an argument that Constantinople should be, as he put it, "denationalised" – conquered and turned into a headquarters for international legislative, executive, and judiciary bodies (and a playground for global elites and their yachts). Only such a world government, incidentally, would make possible the "conversion of International Law from a positive system in the scientific sense, into a positive system in the practical sense."[60]

Developmental claims may have been under-theorized in the legal literature, but they drew upon a discourse more broadly pervasive in Victorian political and social thought. As J. S. Mill, in a typical instance, wrote, "The savage cannot bear to sacrifice, for any purpose, the satisfaction of his individual will. His social cannot even temporarily prevail over his selfish feelings, nor his impulses bend to his calculations."[61] After characterizing the failings of savages and slaves in their extreme forms, Mill extended the argument to peoples who "approach to the conditions of savages or of slaves" to explain, for instance, why civilized belligerents usually defeat their less civilized foes.[62] Mill argued that the reason for such patterns is that cooperation, like other attributes of civilization, "can be learnt only by practice," and he described this learning process as one undergone by individuals.[63] Like Maine and Lorimer, Mill held that such defects in powers of mind and will justified a suspension of international norms in European relations with non-European societies. In his 1859 essay on non-intervention, for instance, Mill used the categories of "barbarous" and "civilized" to argue for a strict distinction between the legal and political standards applied within Europe and those reserved for the treatment of others. Reciprocity, mutual respect for sovereignty, and the law of nations, he argued, should govern relations among civilized nations. Relations between civilized nations and "barbarians" cannot, properly speaking, be considered political relations at all. One of the reasons he offers, in a passage that recalls the account in "Civilization" of Indians' failure to ally against the British, is the incapacity of barbarians to abide by treaties and agreements: "barbarians will not reciprocate. They cannot be depended on for observing any rules. Their minds are not capable of so great an effort."[64] The essay is striking in its use of a philosophical

---

[60] Lorimer, "Denationalisation," 127.   [61] Mill, "Civilization," *CW*, 18:122.

[62] Because "discipline ... is an attribute of civilization," "none but civilized states have ever been capable of forming an alliance. The native states of India have been conquered by the English one by one." "Civilization," *CW*, 18:122–23.

[63] "Civilization," *CW*, 18:123.   [64] "A Few Words on Non-intervention," *CW*, 21:118.

anthropology, at best speculative, to justify the exercise of vast coercive political and military power:

> To characterize any conduct whatever towards a barbarous people as a violation of the law of nations, only shows that he who so speaks has never considered the subject. A violation of great principles of morality it may easily be; but barbarians have no rights as a *nation*, except a right to such treatment as may, at the earliest possible period, fit them for becoming one. The only moral laws for the relation between a civilized and a barbarous government, are the universal rules of morality between man and man.[65]

Mill withheld the application of law to relations with barbarians and justified civilizing despotism, not simply on the grounds that such rule was necessary to undermine the power of entrenched and oppressive political structures and social hierarchies; rather, his claim was that the rational capacities of *individuals* in such societies were so immature that they were incapable of being "guided to their improvement by conviction or persuasion," as he put it in *On Liberty*.[66]

Mill differed from the professional jurists in his judgment about the juridical nature of international law, for he accepted, as the lawyers did not, Austin's relegation of international law to the category of "positive international morality."[67] Mill did not share the lawyers' professional interest in defending international law *as law*, and his acceptance of Austin's view meant that Mill was more untroubled by the thought that the way to make international law progress and develop was precisely to break it. As he wrote (arguing for external intervention to "assist a people struggling for liberty" in the context of the 1848 revolution in France), "What is the law of nations? Something, which to call a law at all, is a misapplication of terms. The law of nations is simply the custom of nations. It is a set of international usages, which have grown up like other usages, partly from a sense of justice, partly from common interest or convenience, partly from mere opinion and prejudice." Given that no legislature existed in the international sphere to repeal bad or outdated

---

[65] "Non-intervention," *CW*, 21:119.

[66] *On Liberty*, *CW*, 18:224. Also see *Considerations on Representative Government*; *CW*, 19:567. Uday Mehta has argued that liberal universalism, notably in Locke and Mill, distinguishes "between anthropological capacities and the necessary conditions for their actualization": While the capacities are acknowledged to be universal, various peoples are politically disenfranchised as not being in a position to realize those capacities. Mehta, *Liberalism and Empire: A Study in Nineteenth-Century British Liberal Thought* (Chicago: University of Chicago Press, 1999), p. 47.

[67] Austin, *Province of Jurisprudence Determined*, p. 112. See Mill's "Austin on Jurisprudence" [1863], *CW*, 21:167–205, and, for an excellent discussion of Mill's acceptance of Austin's view of international law, Varouxakis, *Liberty Abroad*, pp. 19–25.

laws, "[t]he improvement of international morality can only take place by a series of violations of existing rules."[68] But even the international lawyers, who saw their own task as the codification of international law for the purpose of rendering it more distinct and authoritative, and who were solicitous of international legal precedent where Mill was extravagantly defiant of it, conceded the point that international law, unlike domestic law, was made by being broken. As Westlake more cautiously wrote, "an international rule can rarely be changed otherwise than by its ceasing to be followed and general approval being given to such change of practice, of which some state must set the example." The idea of a shared civilization tamed the threat of such an unstable process of evolution, since a state's defiance of a standing rule would be subjected to the collective judgment – the "moral support" or "loss of sympathy" – of the rest of the international society of civilized states.[69]

The Dangers of European Civilization and the Task of International Law

Victorian jurists saw international law as both an indication and a source of progress. Laws were becoming more precise and more authoritative with the progress of civilization in a teleological process, such that the existing framework of international law was the partial realization of a historical trajectory and the harbinger of the complete system that would someday emerge.[70] In this sense, the state of international law was a reflection of the state of human progress. International law could also drive that progress by securing the peace that would enable further material, cultural, and intellectual development, and also by codifying, entrenching, and therefore speeding the "progress of opinion."[71] International lawyers' accounts of the development of nations and of

[68] Mill, "Vindication of the French Revolution of February 1848," *CW*, 20:345–6. Westlake, *Collected Papers*, p. 80.

[69] Westlake, *Collected Papers*, p. 7.

[70] As Westlake put it, "in the gradual improvement of international relations the precision and observance of rules is constantly on the increase, and that therefore those international rules which may already be ranked as law are typical of the subject, in that they are the completest outcome of a tendency which pervades the whole": *Collected Papers*, p. 402.

[71] As Maine, Robert Phillimore, and Mountague Bernard wrote, as members of the 1876 Royal Commission on Fugitive Slaves, "International law ... is not stationary; it admits of progressive improvement, though the improvement is more difficult and slower than that of municipal law, and though the agencies by which change is effected are different. It varies with the progress of opinion and the growth of usage" ("Statement of Opinion on the Question of International Obligations, by Sir R. Phillimore, Mr. M. Bernard, and Sir H.S. Maine," *Report of the Commissioners, minutes of the evidence, and*

international practice were thus, as Martti Koskenniemi has so powerfully shown, also narratives in which they, as international lawyers,
figured prominently as those who could "articulate and ... represent"
Europe's evolving *conscience* – in the sense of both its moral conscience
and its consciousness of truth.[72]

Although Europe was understood to be the sole locus of progressive
civilization, however, it was understood that peace and order within
Europe were precarious, that international law needed to be codified
and extended precisely because the increasing sophistication of destructive weaponry and the increasing power at the disposal of states meant a
constant threat to peace within Europe. Peace and civilization thus stood
in a relationship of tension, and international law figured as a key means
by which the morally progressive features of civilization, including a
perceptible tendency toward peace (thanks, in one typical formulation,
to commerce, democracy, and Christianity), might be brought to triumph over its vices.[73] Maine's *International Law* exemplified concerns
that whatever tendencies to peace might be implicit in the development
of an increasingly integrated European system of states and civilization were simultaneously threatened by technological developments that
increased the destructiveness of war. The buoyant view, following the
long peace that had held from 1815 up to the outbreak of the Crimean
War, that "Captain Pen had vanquished Captain Sword" had been
defeated by the succession of subsequent conflicts that testified to the
"prodigious forces which seem now to make for war ... We know of no
limit to the power of destroying human life."[74] Indeed, Maine argued
that Europeans had lately abandoned a longstanding inclination to ban
the most horrific new weaponry, in part because technological innovation
was happening at such a fast pace that it was rarely possible to ban
particular weapons before others more or differently destructive were
invented. Maine held out hope that the "thrill of horror through the
civilised world" that would follow something like the torpedoing of
a neutral or friendly ship (though not horror at human suffering or
death as such) meant that it was still possible to use public opinion
and the international law that embodied it to tame state violence.[75]
But he expressed the late Victorian anxiety, the loss of mid-century
optimism exemplified by the Great Exhibition of 1851, that civilization

appendix... *Presented to both houses of Parliament by command of Her Majesty* (London:
Printed by G.E. Eyre and W. Spottiswoode, for H.M. Stationery off., 1876), p. xxv.
[72] Koskenniemi, *Gentle Civilizer*, p. 47.
[73] See T. J. Lawrence, "The Evolution of Peace," *Disputed Questions.*
[74] Maine, *International Law*, p. 3.   [75] Maine, *International Law*, pp. 147–8.

as a matter of material development posed a potentially lethal threat to civilization as a moral achievement.

Conclusion

In sum, Victorian international lawyers converged around a detailed and distinctive historical narrative, despite apparently deep divergences among thinkers around key theoretical questions, particularly those of natural law versus positivism and the relative merits of historical versus analytical approaches. Although Europe was sometimes recognized as a major source of violence in the world, both in major wars within Europe and in colonial expansion, as the vanguard of human progress it was also granted the benefit of the doubt as to its pacific "tendency" and also its right to continue to deploy violence through its "police authority over barbarous races."[76] Legal writers, like contemporary social and political theorists such as Mill who shared their progressive historical theory, routinely combined a series of narrative and argumentative moves: They registered anxiety about the state of European civilization while nonetheless affirming its progressive tendency. This tendency then underwrote Europe's right to adjudicate international legal status and to deploy violence in an administrative (rather than either political or legal) mode over those societies which Europeans deemed not yet candidates for legal inclusion.

---

[76] Lawrence, "Evolution of Peace," *Disputed Questions*, pp. 273, 276. Lawrence noted with some acerbity, but also a typical belittling of the effects of European violence on its victims, a different "tendency" of European commerce: "to cause little wars by forcing at the sword's point upon barbarous tribes the blessing of cheap calico and adulterated rum" (p. 234).

Index

Index263

Greek colonization model for, 218–20
in India, 131, 144, 213, 223, 231–2, 257
political economy of, 191–3
progress and growth in model of, 221–2,
236
Roman history as narrative for, 214–18,
224–5, 228–30
transfiguration of, to commonwealth,
230, 233–4
US as model for, 232–3
Browning, Oscar, 163–5
Browning, Robert, 139
Bryce, James, 211–13, 219–20, 229–30
Buckland, William, 203–4
Buckle, Thomas Henry, 154, 170, 173–4
Acton's review of, 167–70
character and reputation of, 158, 169–71
Comte compared with, 158, 169–70
Buckley, Arabella, 24
Buffon George Louis Leclerc, Comte de,
112, 124
Burrow, J. W., 156, 170–1, 180–1, 243
Burrows, Montagu, 216–17
Burton, Richard Francis, 65
Bury, J. B., 158–9, 181–2, 221–2, 228
Busk, George, 48–9
Butler, Samuel, 24
Buxton, Thomas, 55–6

Cain, Peter, 225–6
Calvinism, 195
Cambridge, 227–8, 235–6
Camper, Petrus, 59
capitalism, 186–7, 192, 201, 209–10
Carlyle, Thomas, 31–2, 41–2, 129–30,
163–6
on human character and morality,
135–7
Tyndall relationship with, 30, 33–6, 45–6
Carpenter, William, 29
Catholicism, 156, 234–5
Celts, 147–8
Chadwick, Owen, 181–2
Chalmers, Thomas, 190–1, 195
Chamberlain, Joseph, 234–5
character. *See* human character and nature
China, 190, 250–2
Christianity, 24, 46–7, 151, 212, 225
Christy, Henry, 56–7, 64–5
church. *See* religion and faith
citizenship, 141
Civil War, American, 239–40
civilization, 253, 257
definitions of, 251, 253–4
international law and, 237, 239, 253–9

Westlake on, 254–6
"civilizing" debate, 222–3, 225, 231–2
Clark, Rufus, 132–3
classification methods, 3–4, 21, 70–1
Cleasby, Richard, 100–1
Clodd, Edward, 24
coal production and consumption, 186–7,
201–2, 204–5
data and projections on, 203–5
government intervention on, 205–6
scarcity concern and debate on, 201–7
The Coal Question (Jevons), 186–7, 201–2,
204–6
Cobden, Richard, 213–14, 216–17
Coleridge, Herbert, 80
Coleridge, Samuel Taylor, 5, 7, 28–30
colonization models, 219–20, 231–2, 234–5
ancient Greek, 218–20, 235–6
"civilizing" argument for, 222–3
international law and, 243, 254–5
self-government and political freedom in,
230–1
Comte, Auguste, 7–8, 119–20, 159–65
Bagehot compared with, 174
Buckle compared with, 158, 169–70
Comtean-Spencerian thesis, 119–20
Comtism, 158, 160–1, 165–6. *See also*
Comte, Auguste
Harrison's approach to, 159–60, 163–5
human sciences influence on, 157–8,
161–2
on philosophy of history, 167–9
on public opinion, 160–1
Condorcet, 161–2
Cook, James, 15–16, 51–2, 87–8
Corn Laws, 194, 197
Cramb, J. A., 224–5
Cramp, William, 82–3
Crawfurd, John, 67–8
Creighton, Mandell, 158, 168–9, 180–3
Crimean War (1853–56), 237–40, 260–1
Crowley, Tony, 85–6
Curzon, Lord, 227–8
Cuvier, Georges, 63–4, 118–19, 124

Dante, 165
Darwin, Charles, 10–12, 21, 32–3, 46–7,
75. *See also Descent of Man, and
Selection in Relation to Sex*; natural
selection theory; *Origin of Species*
divine design theory and, 22
on human character and nature, 111
on human diversity, 49
Huxley on, 37–40, 66, 71
Lewes on, 123–4, 126–7

Greeks, ancient, 219, 250–2
  colonization of, 218–20, 235–6
  physical sciences and, 161–2
  race of, 73–4
Green, T. H., 140–1
Greswell, William, 232–3
Grimm, Jacob, 78–82, 102
Grote, George, 1, 219
growth. *See* progress and growth

Haeckel, Ernst, 39–40
Hall, W. E., 252–3
Harcourt, William, 217–18
Harrison, Frederic, 8, 160–2, 165–6
  Comtism approach of, 159–60, 163–5
  The Meaning of History by, 159–60, 163–6
Hayward, Abraham, 148–50
Henslow, George, 24
Herder, Johann Gottfried, 113–15
Hereditary Genius (Galton), 71–4
heritage preservation, 14, 103
historical novel form. *See* novel genre
historicist philosophy, 1–3, 103, 171–2.
      See also developmental philosophy and
      historicism; legal historicism
  in academia, 16, 154–5, 159–63, 171–2
  on British Empire, 211–13, 236
  Darwinism and, 43–5
  Enlightenment and, 4, 6–9, 109, 176–7
  fall of, 16–20
  history contrasted with, 1–2
  on human nature, 111–12, 118–19
  human sciences and, 43–5, 157–8,
      171–2, 181–3
  in international law, 242–5, 247–8
  in linguistics, 102–4
  literature as approach to, 183–5
  OED and, 80
  organicism and, 2–3, 9–10, 108–9
  policy guided by social sciences over,
      20
  political economy and, 207–8
  positivism and, 2–3, 171, 189–90
  prescriptivism and, 92–3, 103
  of race, 50, 75
  religion and faith relationship with, 8,
      155–9, 165–6, 169–70, 176–85
  rise and height of, 3–16
  scientific approach in, 161–2, 181
  secularism in, 158–9, 181–3
  themes in, 2–3
  Whiggism and, 5–6
history, 1–2, 167–9, 213–14. *See also* human
      history; pre-history; Roman history
  as human science, 171–2, 181–3

  national, 116–19
  Victorian treatment of, 2, 15–16, 214
History of Civilization in England (Buckle),
      154, 167–9
*History of the Decline and Fall of the Roman
      Empire* (Gibbon), 159–60, 163–5
  on imperial decline, 215, 217–18
  influence of, 164, 176–7, 179, 181,
      226–7
A History of the Popes (von Ranke), 156,
      234–5
Hobson, J. A., 150–1
Hodgkin, Thomas, 55–6, 64–5
Hodgson, Geoffrey, 189–90
Holland, Bernard, 215, 218–19, 226, 230–1
Holland, T. E., 243, 248–9
Hull, Edward, 204–5
human character and nature, 113–15, 118,
      130, 133–5. *See also Bildung*; moral
      character; progress and growth
  biology and, 125–7, 141–52
  Carlyle on, 135–7
  citizenship and, 141
  Darwin on, 111
  descriptivism on, 141–52
  developmental historicism of, 114
  economics and, 129, 132, 142, 151
  Eliot on, 111–12, 138–40
  embourgeoisement of, 133–4
  Enlightenment philosophy on, 112,
      132–3
  free will and, 173–4
  geopolitical factors in, 141–2
  historicist philosophy on, 111–12,
      118–19
  individual compared to species-wide,
      117–18
  instinct in, 113–14
  international law and, 250–4
  literature and poetry on, 12–13, 106–7,
      137–40, 151–3
  MacIntyre on, 128–9, 150
  Middlemarch on, 109–10, 125–7, 140
  population growth and, 194–5
  prescriptivism on, 130–41
  public opinion and, 160–1
  racial discourses on, 63, 131, 142–4, 153
  self-origin and improvement of, 129–30,
      132–3, 135, 138, 153, 256–7
  suffering in, 122–3
  Victorian view of, 129–31, 151–3
  World War I and view of, 18–19
human diversity, 50, 52–75
  Galton on, 71–4, 145
  Lawrence, W., on, 54–5